# MORE WILL SING THEIR
# WAY TO FREEDOM

# MORE WILL SING THEIR
# WAY TO FREEDOM

## INDIGENOUS RESISTANCE AND RESURGENCE

*edited by Elaine Coburn*

FERNWOOD PUBLISHING
HALIFAX & WINNIPEG

Editing: Nancy Sixsmith
Cover illustration: Robin Henry, gender queer/two spirited Anishnaabe artist
Cover design: ALL CAPS Design
Printed and bound in Canada

Published by Fernwood Publishing
32 Oceanvista Lane, Black Point, Nova Scotia, B0J 1B0
and 748 Broadway Avenue, Winnipeg, Manitoba, R3G 0X3

www.fernwoodpublishing.ca

Fernwood Publishing Company Limited gratefully acknowledges the financial support of the Government of Canada through the Canada Book Fund and the Canada Council for the Arts, the Nova Scotia Department of Communities, Culture and Heritage, the Manitoba Department of Culture, Heritage and Tourism under the Manitoba Publishers Marketing Assistance Program and the Province of Manitoba, through the Book Publishing Tax Credit, for our publishing program.

Library and Archives Canada Cataloguing in Publication

More will sing their way to freedom : indigenous resistance and resurgance / edited by Elaine Coburn.

Includes bibliographical references.
Issued in print and electronic formats.
ISBN 978-1-55266-780-4 (paperback).--ISBN 978-1-55266-781-1 (epub)

1. Native peoples--Canada--Social conditions. 2. Native peoples--Canada--Ethnic identity. 3. Native peoples--Canada--Government relations. 4. Nativistic movements--Canada. I. Coburn, Elaine, 1975- author, editor

E78.C2M6485 2015          305.897'071          C2015-905196-7
                          C2015-905197-5

# CONTENTS

Contributors ................................................................................................ix

Acknowledgments .........................................................................................xii

Preface *Elaine Coburn* ..................................................................................1

Foreword: "Resist No Longer"
Reflections on Resistance Writing and Teaching ......................................5
*Emma LaRocque*

Situating Myself: Personal and Political Contexts .......................................... 5
Developing the Native Studies Canon ............................................................. 7
Knowledge and Resistance Scholarship............................................................ 8
The Ethical Imperative of Native Studies......................................................... 9
Reworking and Establishing New Canons ..................................................... 12
Playing Defense, Playing Offense.................................................................... 13
Resistance Scholarship as Critical Inquiry .................................................... 17
We Cannot Be Owned.................................................................................... 18

Introduction: Indigenous Resistance and Resurgence ............................24
*Elaine Coburn*

"Knowledge About Hope and Courage": Situating this Book.................... 26
"Names Carry the Record of Our Relations":
Or What Does "Indigenous" Mean? .............................................................. 28
"Pathways to Freedom": Indigenous Resistance and Resurgence ............. 32
"We Know What We Know From Where We Stand" .................................... 40
"Relational Responsibility" and "Action That Effects Love"...................... 44

1    The Split Head Resistance: Using Imperial Law
     to Contradict Colonial Law for Aboriginal Justice............................50
     *James (Sa'ke'j) Youngblood Henderson*

The Difficult, Dark Agenda of Justice ............................................................ 50
The Birth of the Split-Head Generation......................................................... 52

Eurocentric Traditions and Law: The Good, the Bad and the Ugly .........................53
Indigenous Renaissance and the Just Society .........................55
Red Rage and Read Rage .........................57
Constitutional Struggles: Rights that "Might Have Been" .........................58
Traditions and Continuity .........................60
Aboriginal Rights Are Human Rights.........................62
The Split Head Dilemma.........................63

**2   Incarceration and Aboriginal Women in Canada:
Acts of Resilience and Resistance .........................67**
*Christine A. Walsh and Shirley A. Aarrestad*

An Invitation.........................67
Who We Are .........................68
A Call to Action.........................69
Hide and Seeking.........................69
The Opening.........................71
Other Colonial Contexts.........................73
Ways Forward .........................77
Acts of Resistance .........................80
A Closing .........................82

**3   Who Is Ready to Listen?: Aboriginal Persons with Disabilities.........................88**
*Douglas Durst and Elaine Coburn*

"Triple Jeopardy": Research on Aboriginal Peoples in Canada.........................89
Truth-Telling and the Risks of Stigmatization .........................91
The Complex Legal Definition of Aboriginal Peoples by Canada .........................93
Defining Disability .........................95
Aboriginal People with Disabilities.........................97
"The World Is Here for Us to Live": Fighting Back.........................102
"Giving Them That Chance": Strategies for Change .........................104

**4   Indigenous Resistance in Comparative Perspective:
An Overview with an Autobiographical Research Critique .........................111**
*Rima Wilkes*

The Indigenous Resistance "Dataset".........................114
Reflections on Research as a Scientific and Colonial Practice .........................119
Conclusion: Indigenous Struggle as an Ongoing Political Project.........................124

**5   Behaving Unexpectedly in Expected Places:
First Nations Artists and the Embodiment of Visual Sovereignty .........................129**
*Jennifer Adese*

Is it Worth Arguing Over "Tonto"? .........................130
The Legacies of Visual Imperialism.........................131
The Visual Sovereignty of the Indigenous Artist.........................133

On Colonialism and Sovereignty ........................................................134
Indigenous Resistance to Museum and Corporate Imperialism...........................137
Concluding Thoughts ...................................................................145

6   **Aboriginal Economic Development
    and Living Nuu-chah-nulth-aht** ........................................... **150**
    *Clifford (Kam'ayaam/Chachim'multhnii) Atleo*

Economic Life in Nuu-chah-nulth Territories.............................................151
Aboriginal Economic Development ........................................................155
Nuu-chah-nulth Life .....................................................................157
Critically Engaging Nuu-chah-nulth Traditions...........................................159
Contemporary Nuu-chah-nulth Economic Development........................................161
Living Nuu-chah-nulth-aht...............................................................162

7   **The Problem with "Indigenous Peoples":
    Re-considering International Indigenous Rights Activism** ............... **167**
    *Hayden King*

The Ongoing Inhumanity of Indigenous Peoples
in International Law and Society.........................................................169
The Doctrine of Discovery, UNDRIP, and the Politics of Recognition ......................172
Implications of the Elastic Conceptualization of Indigenous Identity ...................177
The Resurgence of Indigenous International Relations.....................................180

8   **Telling Stories: Idle
    No More, Indigenous Resurgence and Political Theory** .................... **184**
    *Kelly Aguirre*

Colonial Violence and Apologism ........................................................186
Heartbeat Drum Is on the Ground ........................................................188
How Do We Tell of the Drum? ............................................................191
We Have Never Been Idle ................................................................195
Feasting and Fasting, Always Dancing ...................................................197
What Are Our Roles as Storytellers? ....................................................199
Call to (En)action......................................................................201

9   **A Four Directions Model: Understanding the Rise and Resonance
    of an Indigenous Self-Determination Movement** .............................. **208**
    *Jeff Denis*

The Medicine Wheel: A Four Directions Model
of Indigenous Self-Determination Movements.............................................208
Indigenous Leadership: Taking a Stand..................................................218
Possible Objections....................................................................219
Responses and Responsibilities of Settler Canadians to Idle No More....................220
Indigenous Resurgence and Our "Last Best Hope".........................................223

**10  Rhythms of Change: Mobilizing Decolonial Consciousness, Indigenous Resurgence and the Idle No More Movement** ................. 229
*Jarrett Martineau*

Idle No More ........................................................................................231
The Round Dance Revolution ...........................................................232
Networked Resistance .........................................................................235
Mediatized Subjects and Spectacular Dissent .................................237
After the Storm ...................................................................................240
"Reactivism" and Sustaining Momentum ........................................241
Communicative Capitalism and Possible Politics ..........................243
The Indigenous Nationhood Movement and Reclaiming PKOLS ........247
Conclusion: New Beginnings .............................................................251

**Afterword: A Steadily Beating Heart: Persistence, Resistance and Resurgence** ............................................. 255
*Alex Wilson*

Relational Responsibility and Action that Effects Love ..................255
Undoing the Present Absence of Indigenous Peoples ......................257
Speaking Truth About Colonial Violence .........................................258
Persisting as an Ethical Human Being ...............................................259
The Language of Leadership ...............................................................261
*Awuskahwinuk*: Shaking It Up! Waking It Up! ..............................263

# CONTRIBUTORS

**Shirley Aarrestad** is a First Nations woman from Sturgeon Lake First Nation. She draws on her own history of personal struggles with homelessness and incarceration to become a strong advocate promoting social justice for Aboriginal women and other women facing similar circumstances. Shirley recently completed her Aboriginal Addictions Services Counselling Certificate at Bow Valley College in Calgary, Alberta and is currently enrolled in the diploma program.

**Jennifer Adese** is of the Oitpemisiwak/Métis, was born in British Columbia and raised in Ontario where she attended Lakehead University and McMaster University. She continues to live in Ontario and teaches in the Indigenous Studies minor and Canadian Studies graduate program in the school of Canadian Studies at Carleton University. Jennifer has published articles on representations of Indigeneity by Indigenous peoples and by settler-states, Métis identity and racialization, Métis literatures and creative city policies.

**Kelly Aguirre** is a PhD candidate in the Department of Political Science at the University of Victoria. Her work focuses on concepts of self-determination, decolonial knowledge practices and Indigenous scholarship. Kelly holds a Master of Arts in politics from the University Of Manitoba. This is her first publication.

**Clifford (Kam'ayaam/Chachim'multhnii) Atleo** is Tsimshian and Nuu-chah-nulth, descending from a long line of fishers and whalers. He is a PhD candidate in political science at the University of Alberta, and the fifth annual Henry Roe Cloud Fellow in American Indian and Indigenous Studies at Yale University. His research offers a critique of "Aboriginalized" capitalism and seeks out alternative economic practices rooted in Indigenous teachings and traditions.

**Elaine Coburn** is assistant professor at the American University of Paris and a researcher at the Centre d'analyse et d'intervention sociologiques, Ecole des Hautes Etudes en Sciences Sociales in Paris, France. She was formerly the editor of the interdisciplinary, peer-reviewed, open-access journal *Socialist Studies/ Etudes Socialistes.*

**Jeff Denis** is assistant professor of sociology at McMaster University, located on the traditional territories of the Anishinaabe and the Haudenosaunee in Hamilton, Ontario. His research investigates the barriers to overcoming racism and colonialism; and the strategies, alliances, policies and practices that can bring about more just and sustainable societies.

**Douglas Durst** is a professor of social work at the University of Regina, and teaches social research and social policy at the undergraduate and graduate levels. Underlying his research is an antioppressive approach by giving voice to marginalized peoples, including peoples with disabilities, the elderly, and immigrants and refugees. During his years in the Northwest Territories, he developed a love for the North and its peoples.

**James (Sa'ke'j) Youngblood Henderson** is an internationally and nationally recognized authority in Indigenous knowledge, heritage and legal traditions, as well as constitutional rights and human rights. He is a member of the Chickasaw Nation and is the research director of the Native Law Centre of Canada. He teaches Aboriginal law at the College of Law, University of Saskatchewan.

**Hayden King** is Anishinaabe from Beausoleil First Nation on Gchi'Nme Missing in Huronia, Ontario. He is the director of the Centre of Indigenous Governance and an assistant professor at Ryerson University in Toronto.

**Emma LaRocque** is a scholar, writer, poet and professor in the Department of Native Studies, University of Manitoba (since 1977). She specializes in colonization and its impact on Native/White relations, particularly in the areas of cultural productions and representation. Emma continues to research colonial interference and Aboriginal resistance strategies in the areas of literature, historiography, representation, identity, gender roles, industrial encroachment on Aboriginal (Indian and Métis) lands and resources, and governance. She is the author of *When the Other Is Me: Native Resistance Discourse 1850–1990* (2010), which won the Alexander Kennedy Isbister Award for Non-Fiction, and *Defeathering the Indian* (1975).

**Jarrett Martineau** is a Cree/Dene scholar, media producer, musician and community organizer from Frog Lake First Nation in Alberta. He is a PhD candidate in Indigenous Governance at the University of Victoria, and his research examines the role of art and creativity in advancing Indigenous nationhood and decolonization. He is the cofounder and creative producer of Revolutions Per Minute (RPM.fm), a new music platform to promote Indigenous music culture; an organizer with the Indigenous Nationhood Movement; and a founding director of the New Forms Festival, an annual festival focusing on contemporary art, culture and electronic music held in Vancouver.

**Christine A. Walsh** is a professor on the faculty of social work, University of Calgary. Her program of community-based research aims to promote social justice among vulnerable and marginalized populations, including Indigenous people, using participatory action and arts-based research. She is also a community activist, and her teaching interests are concerned with developing innovative, emancipatory and inclusive pedagogies.

**Rima Wilkes** studies Indigenous mobilization and resistance as well as how it is covered by the media. She is associate professor of sociology at the University of British Columbia and the current editor of the *Canadian Review of Sociology*. Rima is Canadian and is not Indigenous.

**Alex Wilson** (Opaskwayak Cree Nation) is an associate professor of education and director of the Aboriginal Education Research Centre at the University of Saskatchewan. Her academic and community work and passion focus on Indigenous land-based education and social ecological justice. As a community activist, Alex uses education and Cree philosophy to intervene in ongoing practices of colonialism, oppression, and the destruction of land and water.

# ACKNOWLEDGMENTS

Thank you to Taiaiake Alfred and Jeff Corntassel from the Indigenous Governance program at the University of Victoria for supporting a June 2012 seminar on Indigenous Resurgence. That seminar is one of the origins of this project.

Thank you to all the contributing authors for our conversations and for the varied perspectives you shared with me — and that this book now shares with others. In particular, thank you to Emma LaRocque for critiques at once forthright, kind and helpful; and for your typically incisive *Foreword*.

Thank you to Beth Cuthand for honouring this book by allowing us to use a line from one of your poems in the preface and title.

This book owes a great deal to the generosity of all who participated in making it, both directly and indirectly.

Thank you to colleagues for our exchanges. You are too numerous to be individually mentioned here but many of your names appear alongside your ideas in these pages.

Thank you to everyone at Fernwood Publishing for help readying the manuscript for publication.

Thank you to my parents, sister and brothers, and husband and children for support, patience and love. Thank you also to my extended family.

Finally, I hope that these words honour all those who have struggled and all those who continue to struggle for Indigenous freedoms and justice.

# PREFACE

*Elaine Coburn*

> And there are some who even after a hundred years continue to struggle
> for equality and justice for their people.
>
> —*Campbell 1973: 13*

This book is about Indigenous resistance and resurgence across lands and waters
claimed by Canada. By "resistance," I follow Alfred (n.d.) in meaning struggles
against an ongoing world colonial–capitalist political economy, including contemporary colonialism within the Canadian state. Resistance is necessary to Indigenous
survival against centuries of genocidal policies, and the ongoing dispossession
and destruction of Indigenous lands and water by the state, capital and many
non-Indigenous persons. Resurgence, however, is Indigenous self-determination:
renewing and re-creating diverse, specifically Indigenous ways of being, knowing
and doing (Alfred 2009: 36).

Of course, some might contest this distinction between resistance and resurgence. As Emma LaRocque (2010: 11) has argued, given the magnitude of the
dehumanization of Indigenous peoples, resistance has always meant both deconstruction and reconstruction. Deconstructing the idea of Indigenous peoples as
"savages," for example, is premised on the reconstruction of Indigenous peoples as
fully human. In this sense, there is no tension between resistance and resurgence.
Instead, both are part of the same overarching project: the full expression of self-
determining Indigenous peoples and of each Indigenous individual, who is at
once part of Anishinaabe, Métis, Dene, etc. peoplehoods and a unique member
of universal humanity (LaRocque 2010: 10–11).

In describing and analyzing — but also celebrating — Indigenous resistance
and resurgence, this book suggests "rough pathways to freedom," as Alfred (2009:

40) might put it, for diverse Indigenous peoples across lands and seas claimed by Canada. In her *Foreword*, Emma LaRocque reminds us of the multiple challenges but also accomplishments of Indigenous scholars. She writes of the political and ethical imperative of Indigenous research that at once resists legacies of centuries-old colonialism and critically innovates from diverse and changing Indigenous perspectives in the academy. My *Introduction* then draws upon a wide range of Indigenous scholars and actors to critically consider what is meant by the concepts "Indigenous," "Resistance" and "Resurgence," as well as the roles of both Indigenous and non-Indigenous academics in Indigenous struggles for justice.

In the first part of the book's main section, "Telling Stories of Resistance," contributors James (Sa'ke'j) Youngblood Henderson, Christine Walsh and Jennifer Aarrestad, and Douglas Durst and Elaine Coburn, respectively, consider resistance to colonial law by Indigenous lawyers; resilience by Indigenous women in conflict with the colonial justice system; and the challenges faced by, and activism of, Indigenous persons with disabilities. The last chapter in this section, by Rima Wilkes, describes Indigenous resistance in comparative perspective, across lands claimed by Canada since the 1980s, while offering an autobiographical critique of research about Indigenous peoples undertaken from mainstream sociological perspectives. In so doing, the authors describe and analyze Indigenous resilience and resistance, not least by those who are too often invisible in Indigenous struggles and scholarly appraisals of them. At the same time, there is reflexive consideration of the roles of both Indigenous and non-Indigenous researchers in seeking to accompany such resistance.

Chapters in the second part, "Telling Stories about Resurgence," written by Jennifer Adese, Clifford (Kam'ayaam/Chachim'multhnii) Atleo and Hayden King, are concerned with Indigenous resurgence in the realms of the visual arts, economics and international politics. Each suggests how diverse Indigenous actors are striving to reinvent Indigenous perspectives and practices in ways that are self-determining and transcending instead of reacting against colonial relationships, institutions and ideas. Such self-determination is expressed through works of visual art that are both intensely personal and political; by reinventing everyday economics to honour relationships with other Indigenous peoples and the natural world; and by reimagining international diplomacy in terms that centre Indigenous concepts, including the use of the drum to encourage empathy and compassion, and so bring about peace in a world of conflict.

Finally, in the third part, "Telling Stories of Idle No More," contributors Kelly Aguirre, Jeff Denis and Jarrett Martineau offer diverse understandings of the Idle No More movement, which began in December 2012 and swept across Indigenous nations in lands claimed by Canada. They consider the multiple dimensions of this struggle as a particular important instance of Indigenous resistance and resurgence, as well as the movement's transformations up to the present. In so doing, they not only offer insights into Idle No More but also shed light on many Indigenous struggles for justice. As Aguirre suggests, Indigenous resurgence includes joyful storytelling that is once continuous with ancestral knowledge and innovating from this knowledge. Denis explains how a "four directions" analytical model inspired by the Medicine Wheel informs new understandings of the physical, intellectual, emotional and spiritual elements of Indigenous resurgence. Martineau considers the tensions and ambivalent role played by mediatized activism, while arguing for a place-based Indigenous resurgence that brings into being "a new history of the *Indigenous* present." In the *Afterword*, Alex Wilson challenges Indigenous actors and allies to consider the possibilities of a transformative, even revolutionary Indigenous feminist politics that "enacts love" by developing responsible relationships with all living beings and the natural world.

Importantly, if these chapters together consider issues of state and political economy, culture and technology, activism and research, mobilization and repression, knowledge and being, they are never abstract matters. Instead, they are deeply personal, political and practical questions. Precisely because the political is personal, as well as the reverse (Bannerji 2000: 88), all the chapters emphasize Indigenous voices and perspectives on their own experiences, whether written by Indigenous or non-Indigenous scholars. This "makes real" the facts of colonialization in daily life, but also emphasizes Indigenous resistance and resurgence as practices rather than as abstract theory.

Finally, one underlying argument across this book is that colonial-capitalism is an historical fact, but not an inevitability. A possible world in which there is justice for Indigenous peoples is prefigured in today's acts of self-determination, small and large, well-known and anonymous. This is true even if these practices of self-determination are incomplete, sometimes contradictory and subject to sustained repression. We turn here to the words of Little Pine Cree Nation poet Beth Cuthand (2001: 136), who envisions resurgence in her own terms. Her words, like this book, do not speak prophecies but only possibilities:

> But
>> More will claim their warrior blood
>> More will pray their road to peace
>> More will dance under the thunderers' nest
>> More will sing their way to freedom.

## REFERENCES

Alfred, Taiaiake. n.d. "Colonialism and State Dependency: Prepared for the National Aboriginal Health Organization Project." <web.uvic.ca/igov/uploads/pdf/Colonialism%20and%20State%20Dependency%20NAHO%20(Alfred).pdf>.

____. 2009. *Wasáse: Indigenous Pathways of Action and Freedom*. Toronto: University of Toronto Press.

Bannerji, Himani. 2000. *Dark Side of the Nation: Essays on Multiculturalism, Nationalism and Gender*. Toronto: Canada Scholar's Press.

Campbell, Maria.1973. *Halfbreed*. Toronto: McLelland and Stuart.

Cuthand, Beth. 2001. "This Red Moon." In Jeannette C. Armstrong and Lally Grauer (eds.), *Native Poetry in Canada: A Contemporary Anthology*. Peterborough, ON: Broadview Press.

LaRocque, Emma. 2010. *When the Other Is Me: Native Resistance Discourse 1850–1990*. Winnipeg: University of Manitoba Press.

# "RESIST NO LONGER"
## REFLECTIONS ON RESISTANCE WRITING AND TEACHING

*Emma LaRocque*

The words "resist no longer" from the 1986 musical *Phantom of the Opera* run through my mind as I contemplate the changes of focus in research and writing in the discipline and field of study that I have been engaged in for more than three decades. The purpose of this essay is to provide a reflective overview of what I have come to call "resistance scholarship," an intellectual positionality I have practiced in my research, teaching and writing style. And because most of my academic years have been spent in Native Studies, I, of course, draw on this discipline as one model for resistance and for invention. My objective is not to detail the program of our department but to discuss what Peter Kulchyski (scholar, colleague and veteran of Native Studies) calls "the ethical impulse" (2000: 20). This ethical impulse directs the research and teaching we do and is embedded both in resistance and invention, or what I have elsewhere referred to as both deconstruction and reconstruction (LaRocque 2010).

### Situating Myself: Personal and Political Contexts

But first, consistent with my decolonizing approach, I begin by briefly situating (and linking) my personal and political location that forms the context to my thinking and pedagogy. I am Métis[1] and grew up in a land-based, Cree-speaking Métis culture in northeastern Alberta at a time when our socioeconomic conditions as a family and as a community were very bleak. Indeed, throughout the Depression era and into the 1960s, and really since the days of Red River (1869–70) and Northwest (1884–5) resistances against colonial incursions, the Métis were suffering extensively from land loss and displacement, poverty, and deadly diseases such as tuberculosis. In the aftermath of these resistances,[2] the Métis in Alberta (and throughout Western Canada) had become so marginalized that neither residential nor public schools were available to most.[3] Métis were often stranded between federal and provincial jurisdictions because neither governments wanted to recognize or acknowledge Métis as Indigenous peoples with land and resource rights.[4] And even though many Métis communities or families such as ours lived near or had access to urban centers, it was not until the 1950s that some small and socially segregated — and characteristically underfunded — public schools for Métis children became available.[5] Although not going to residential schools served to protect us from cultural and familial severance and the darker horrors of residential schools, we were not protected from psychological, cultural or corporeal abuse in public schools. Much like residential schools, public schools embraced colonial pedagogy, and most teachers engaged in racist practices and punitive treatment of Métis and other Aboriginal children. The vast majority of those of my generation quit school early (usually at around grades four to five) because public schools were so dehumanizing and alienating.

School was not available for my parent's generation (pre-1950s) in our area. Ironically — and thankfully — my parent's lack of formal schooling meant they were able to keep their children, speak their language and practice their land-based culture (which was combined with seasonal wage labour). It was my parents who, despite all odds, not only provided us with love, food and shelter but also shared the beauty and the vitality of their Cree-Métis/Michif cultural literacy. By so doing, they instilled and inspired in me a spirit of determination, independence and a love of knowledge. However, my love of learning was many times badly shaken as my school experiences — which were often pierced with bullying, classicism, racism and colonial denigration of Native histories — became fairly intolerable with each passing grade. But I was lucky: In grade seven, I could go to a new (public) school in which I had the great fortune of having the kindest and most perceptive teacher for grades seven to nine. This teacher helped me regain my confidence in learning and to go on to high school, and from there I finally made it to university. I finished my BA and my first MA in the United States and then came back to Canada to do graduate work in history at the University of Manitoba. While there, and again more by luck than my station in life, I was hired to teach a summer course for a newly established department of Native Studies (in the Faculty of Arts). I have been with the department ever since, rising eventually to the rank of professor.

## Developing the Native Studies Canon

Specifically, I have been teaching in the department of Native Studies almost from the very beginning of its inception (1975), and although I am not technically one of its founders in the formal or institutional sense, I developed or redesigned the majority of the core undergraduate courses taught in the early years (at the time, the department offered a BA program). This entailed developing historical, theoretical and conceptual frameworks relevant to Aboriginal (First Nation, Métis and Inuit) histories, cultures and contemporary experience. Of course, this is quite different from the task usually faced by novice professors who adapt their courses from pre-existing canons. In the 1970s, the Native Studies canon did not exist, but had to be invented, which required an enormous amount of intellectual and practical energies. We were an under-resourced and very small department. There were no role models, and it meant going against the grain in many instances; throughout the 1970s, 1980s and even into the 1990s, Native Studies was largely dismissed as a "cross-cultural" remedial program and not taken seriously as a scholarly unit. However, we were developing Indigenously based critical scholarship and creating courses that not only respected and foregrounded Aboriginal cultures and peoples but also questioned colonial history and knowledge. At the same time, we were aware that we had to make these courses meaningful to Aboriginal students and nonalienating for White Canadian students. These courses (and many more since then that colleagues and I have continued to develop because we now offer a doctoral program) have become critically central to our field and, in effect, have become part of a "Native Studies canon."

But what is a canon? In the context of academic disciplines, Joyce Green, Métis scholar in political science, describes a canon as "that core of material which is viewed as foundational to the discipline … and is considered essential reading for students, and is considered to be the base on which newer knowledge is based" (2001: 39). Green is quick to point out that the canon was "constructed primarily by Western European intellectuals, was imbued with and propagated the dominant philosophies, ideologies and analytical forms of the dominators" (39). In other words, the "canon" privileged European knowledge while it justified the colonial project. In contrast, the very basis of Native Studies depends on Indigenous knowledges and experiences that considerably expand upon, and in many crucial ways contradict or confront, traditional Western notions of what constitutes "knowledge" or "literature," and so radically transforms the idea of the "canon." In short, and among many other ways we can know outside of textbooks, we can create oral-based literatures and we can "read" in multiple, not singular (Western) ways. As decolonizing professors, we were engaged in an interpretative undertaking, bringing our worldviews, our colonial experience, our modes of understanding and research, and, of course, our personal styles into the curriculum and into our university classrooms. Some of us also brought our languages and our "lands," the epistemological bases to our cultures, into the classrooms. In my case, however, I was not doing any ordinary "cultural" or "cross-cultural" teaching; instead I was "combining cultural ethos with critical 'resistance' analysis" (LaRocque 2001a: 71) — that is, I was deconstructing colonial records and building Indigenous presence.[6] As Peter Kulchyski explains, "Native Studies can be seen as an interpretive practice, a mode and an ethics of reading that depends upon an exploded concept of text" (2000: 23). We "exploded" the concept of text in a wide variety of ways, and in so doing, we also challenged what it means to know and that what we "know" is culturally and politically informed.

## Knowledge and Resistance Scholarship

It is particularly important in Native Studies that students appreciate the environment in which scholarship develops. Most of us have been led to believe that scholarship is objective, impartial and apolitical (Said 1979: 9–10). But in fact, knowledge is culturally and politically produced, perhaps especially in the so-called Social Sciences. More specifically, we now understand that much of archival "knowledge" about Indigenous peoples was saturated with ideological content, to say nothing about distortion and just plain racism. Ethnohistorian Francis Jennings bluntly points out what Aboriginal scholars know so well: that the historical labeling and anthropological classifications of "the Indian," as Savage juxtaposed against the European as Civilized, "reflect words and concepts which have evolved from centuries of conquest and have been created for the purposes of conquest rather than the purposes of knowledge" (1976: 12).

In *The Colonizer's Model of the World*, J.M. Blaut argues that scholarly beliefs are "shaped by culture" (1993: 10) and "the ethnography of beliefs" or "belief licensing" (30–43, 59), and that Eurocentric scholars have shaped knowledge from a single theory (the "European Miracle"), in fact, a "super theory" from which other smaller theories have evolved that were and continue to be instrumental for colonialism. In brief, the "European Miracle" is the powerfully legitimating colonizer's belief that

> European civilization — "The West" — has had some unique historical advantage, some special quality of race or culture or environment or mind or spirit, which gives this human community a permanent superiority over all other communities, at all times in history and down to the present … Europeans are seen as the "makers of history." Europe eternally advances, progresses, modernizes. The rest of the world advances more sluggishly, or stagnates: it is "traditional society." (1)

This belief is at the same time "Eurocentric diffusionism," a related theory "about the way cultural processes tend to move over the surface of the world as a whole. They tend to flow out of the European sector and toward the non-European sector" (1). Colonialism then "must mean for the Africans, Asians and Americans, not spoilation and cultural destruction but, rather, the receipt by diffusion of European civilization: modernization" (2). Colonialism is refashioned as progress and enlightenment. Further, "the development of a body of Eurocentric beliefs, justifying and assisting Europe's colonial activities has been and still is, of very great importance. Eurocentrism is quite simply the colonizer's model of the world" (10). What's more, all other European ideas and philosophies have been advanced as universal truths, not as ideas bound to and limited by specifically European cultures and places. Such Eurocentric approaches and theories, embedded in Western scholarship, have been promoted as empirical and scientific, and until recently have enjoyed uncontested dominance.

The dominant Western narrative is knowledge that has been selected, assembled and arranged to facilitate and advance the heroification of the European in the Americas (and everywhere else), much to the expense of Indigenous peoples, including Canada's Aboriginal peoples (Duchemin 1990; LaRocque 2010). Clearly, and as so many scholars have long documented, there are ways to see the European/Indigenous encounter as other than the super theory of "civilization" conquering "savagery." Exploring these "other ways to see" is one of the critical tasks of Native Studies.

Native Studies, then, challenges dominant and hegemonic knowledge and theories. In Canada, the history, the diversity and the complexity of Aboriginal cultures has, until quite recently, been ignored or simply infantilized. The colonial project has been glossed over. And in terms of representation, Native peoples have been universally stereotyped and savagely dehumanized. On a more material level, there is virtually no end to the list of all the ways Indigenous peoples have lost entire populations, cultures, communities, lands and resources.

## The Ethical Imperative of Native Studies

In such a context, there is no way we can avoid taking ethical positions; as decolonizing scholars, and not just from Native Studies, we must interrogate false history that is on one hand, the glorification of Euro-resettlement of Canada, and on the other, the denigration of Aboriginal cultures. We must also respond to the ongoing injustices and other urgent needs as well as the resilience of Aboriginal communities. Therefore, central to Native Studies is the manifold task of challenging the resettler text and repositioning the place of Aboriginal peoples in Canadian (and international) history and society. For example, we hold that the construction of

Canada was a political act, and equally that the construction of Canadian historical and literary knowledge with respect to Aboriginal peoples was, and largely remains, a political act. In part, and as Joyce Green (2001) argues, "Native Studies exists because of relations of oppression. It exists because of the historical colonial relationship, in which the oppressor constructed knowledge as first, its own cultural and intellectual production; and second, as that which legitimated the colonial enterprise" (40).

And precisely because of such constructions, both in political life and in the production of knowledge, and in many ways as a corrective response, Native Studies places Aboriginal peoples at the centre of our inquiry and investigation, from which we challenge hegemonic canons and/or reassert Indigenous life, or totally create new theories and methodologies. It is in this sense that Native Studies appears as a form of "resistance scholarship." Of course, as scholars, we include a variety of meanings and interpretations; as scholars, we must constantly modify our data base, our understanding, our research methods and theories. In contrast with the European Miracle tunnel vision, or "tunnel history," that views non-European peoples as "rockbound" by supposedly "timeless, changeless tradition" (Blaut 1993: 5),[7] I have always understood our intellectual and scholarly lives as dynamic, dialogical and creative — much like how Native cultures have always approached life.

Green has also pointed out that Native Studies exists because other disciplines in universities have failed to treat adequately or fairly either Indigenous knowledge or the Native experience (2001: 42). Given this, a large part of our Native Studies efforts has necessarily involved the legitimation of Aboriginal cultures, knowledges and experience. However, more recently, focus has shifted from the more explanatory position of "legitimation" to the more proactive stance of cultural affirmation. Today's younger Aboriginal scholars are not so heavily burdened as my generation was to correct misinformation and to deconstruct racist portrayals and language; today's generation can and is moving on to more "positive" and (self) affirmative work.

But the differences in approach are actually slight because, as I have just noted, resistance work that perhaps characterizes previous generations has always been affirmative work. Doing a critique of archival or Hollywood stereotypes is asserting and affirming the integrity of Aboriginal cultures and the humanity of Aboriginal peoples. And really, in the context of this discourse, any validation of Aboriginal cultures is, in the final analysis, also a form of challenge to the mainstream canon. In any case, all this has been exciting because not only are we rebuilding our cultures by establishing new intellectual traditions for future generations but also because we are pushing the margins of Western academia as well as redefining it.

Not only do we seek to dismantle colonial paradigms and stereotypes but we also create new genres and languages. For instance, take the concept of "settler."

Within what I have called the "'civ/sav' dichotomy" (1983: 86; 2010), Europeans used the concept of "settlers/settlement" as a mark of civilization (assumed to be European) in direct opposition to the "nomadic" "Indians," nomadism being a sign of savagism.[8] So in archival literature, "Indians" are often described as "roaming" or "ranging rather than inhabiting" — an early colonialist mantra that rationalized and soon legalized dispossession of Native lands, resources and communities. The stereotype of the underpopulated, wandering and warring savage Indian on "empty lands" became the Cowboy/Indian genre in the comic book and movie industry. In courts in which the colonizers are at once party and judge, Native people have had to prove their "occupancy and use" of ancestral lands in order to win back portions of their stolen lands! The concept of "settlement/settler" became a moral argument eagerly advanced by European justifiers of colonization. Settlement, along with agriculture, became associated with "progress" and cultural evolution, with the nifty notion that farmers had prior land rights over hunters because they used and "settled" the land; hunters, or "savages," merely roamed over it (Pearce 1965: 70–71). This is one of many examples of how Aboriginal histories and cultures were/are falsified or grossly distorted.

In fact, there were a great variety of cultures, with many Indigenous groups engaging in forms of agriculture (Jennings 1976; Weatherford 1988, 1991; Wright 1993). But more importantly, those who were not farmers (in the European sense), such as the coastal, Plains and northern peoples, used and occupied and variously cultivated and harvested their resources, lands and waters. They had their own forms of territorial usage and settlements (Dickason 1992; Morrison and Wilson 1995). As we now know, pre-Columbian Indigenous peoples of the Americas were very heavily populated (Blaut 1993: 184; Jennings 1976: 30)[9] with extensive settlements and other modes and lifeways of rootedness to certain domains of lands. Those Native peoples, such as the Plains and some Northern peoples, who did migrate did so for resource management reasons and within bounded areas of lands; they were not aimlessly "wandering"[10] (which is Webster's original meaning for the word "nomadic"). Mobilization and rootedness within the context of land use by Indigenous peoples are not mutually exclusive — as European colonists very well knew, given they were often dependent on Native geographical expertise and/or produce.[11] The ultimate irony is that Europeans were just as mobile as anyone else, yet they claimed ownership of the concept of civilization/settlement for obvious political interests. There is no objective moral basis for the idea that those who built permanent settlements or practiced certain styles of farming had/have prior rights to those who have other relational uses, methods and attachments to lands. Frankly, I am not enamoured with the concepts or words "settler" or "settlement," given their colonial utility; but to make an obvious statement: Indigenous peoples were the original settlers of the Americas, whether they lived in city states or commuted between satellite camp sites. For this reason I cannot call Europeans "settlers" — to do so is to imply as well as to entrench the idea that Aboriginal peoples were not! In actuality, colonizers dispossessed and displaced Native (including Métis) settlers and settlements (as well as other relational attachments to lands) and resettled the lands. In the words of Jennings, "The so-called settlement of America was a *re*settlement" (30, his emphasis). This is why I refer to Euro-White North Americans as "resettlers."

There are many other colonial words and descriptions of Native life in areas of organization, governance, leadership, gender, spirituality and so forth, that serve to downgrade the cultures and dehumanize Native peoples (LaRocque 2010: 50).[12] Indeed, as Ronald Wright puts it, "An entire vocabulary is tainted with prejudice and condescension" (1993: xi). Such colonial texts invite "explosion," yet our challenge to such tendentious, sexist and racist use of words has been slow and uneven. One response has been to "reclaim" words (e.g., "squaw") that were meant to debase Native women and men. Another response is to use Native words and concepts, which in many contexts is a much needed cultural and political sign, and in literature is a thing of beauty. However, it is French and English words (within which we work in North America) as well as some ideological and/or discipline-bound phraseologies (i.e., tribal, traditional, hunters and gatherers, subsistence, chief, warrior) and concepts that, at the very least, require rethinking. Much work remains to be done in these areas of stereotyping, belittlement and disempowerment through language manipulation. We are now in the process of reworking and establishing new vocabularies, languages and canons in our fields. Of course, such struggles at the level of language and institutionalized canons are connected with material and legal struggles, given that the "subjectifying nature" (Coulthard 2007: 455) of colonial languages serves to undermine our humanity as well as our inherent rights to lands and governance, which are, of course, based on our settlement/s and continued occupation, use and relationship of lands since time immemorial.

## Reworking and Establishing New Canons

In Native Studies, "reworking and establishing new canons" is actually a very fluid process, one that requires respectful disagreements with colleagues because we are not uniform in this work and development. Because Native Studies is meta-disciplinary in nature, our faculties represent a wide variety of disciplines, research directions, methodologies and even ideologies. Our own department reflects such diversity. Some of our faculty emphasize community research; some tend to "traditional knowledge"; others focus on law and legislation or other urgent issues such as racism, poverty, violence against women, urbanization; while still others do archival, historical or literary work. But all of us concern ourselves with (as Peter

Kulchyski put it) "the righting of" and "the writing of…" (2000: 3) the names and places erased, lands and resources stolen, or beliefs, stories and visual arts distorted by both resettler colonial renderings and colonial governments.

Naturally, we each work in the areas we specialize in. While I have focused on the deconstruction of colonial misrepresentation in Canadian historiography, literature and popular culture, particularly the civ/sav paradigm, I have also advanced an Indigenous-based critical voice and theory (1990). For example, I have demonstrated that it is possible to appreciate the Aboriginal "voice," rooted in Indigenous and colonial experience, without compromising either that voice or scholarly protocols. This kind of critical positionality is an outgrowth of my "resistance" research in Native/White relations, an area of discourse and study that cannot be dealt with effectively only by standard Western models or by a unidisciplinary approach. Others may refer to such approaches as "engaged research." It depends somewhat on our respective disciplines, but again all of us in Native (or Indigenous) Studies do not accept without challenge the massive falsification of our histories, or all the insults to our cultures and intelligence extant in colonial records and literatures, and in the media and marketplace, for that matter.

It is the legacy of colonization that makes us resistance scholars. But this work is not unscholarly, parochial or blindly subjective; nor is it merely defensive (or offensive). It is not insular, simplistic or necessarily culturalist or nationalist in basis. Native Studies is an ambitious project. Our knowledge of the fields involved is wide-ranging, spanning five centuries of archival material, historical, anthropological and/or literary scholarship. We pursue our investigations and our arguments through the discourse of colonizer fur traders, explorers, missionaries, jurists, historians, anthropologists, playwrights, poets and novelists from the sixteenth to the twenty-first centuries; and through the counterdiscourse of Aboriginal intellectuals, including artists, writers and the growing numbers of Aboriginal scholars who have perforce challenged old imperialist schools of thought that continue even today to stereotype, ignore or discredit us. Needless to say, we are complex and diverse in our research, approaches and argumentations. Resistance scholarship entails and requires ethical and critical study, engaged research and intellectual freedom.

## Playing Defense, Playing Offense

However, not everyone agrees or is comfortable with the word "resistance," and some may find the phrase "resistance scholarship" an oxymoron. This may partly indicate the shift from having to play defense to being able to play offense. In the literary world, for instance, some Aboriginal novelists or poets and literary critics have turned to "writing home" (McLeod 2001) rather than "writing back" at the proverbial "Empire" (Ashcroft et al. 1989). Other scholars (both Aboriginal and non-Aboriginal, including some grad students) in various fields have turned their attention to the retrieval and foregrounding of cultural knowledge, both traditional and contemporary, with a focus on languages, literatures, land ways, epistemologies and philosophies, kinship and political systems, ideas of treaties, use of resources, or material art and so forth. In these contexts, if the meaning of the word "resistance" is taken literally (i.e., "striving against"), perhaps the notion of resistance research may be limiting. But it is also the case that many students and some scholars associate the word "resistance" as only oppositional and negative, whereas cultural matters or cultural portraiture is seen as inherently constructive, hence, positive. Some find that the word "resistance" is too "postcolonial" and as such, unbalanced and singular in its scope, and neglects centuries of Indigenous knowledge prior to colonial incursions. Aboriginal novelist and scholar Thomas King, in "Godzilla vs. Post-Colonial," finds the term "postcolonial" problematic for a number of reasons:

> And worst of all, the idea of post-colonial writing effectively cuts us off from *our* traditions, traditions that were in place before colonialism ever became a question, traditions which have come down to us through our cultures in spite of colonization, and it supposes that contemporary Native writing is largely a construct of oppression. (1997: 242–43)

Indigenous knowledge has indeed existed eons prior to European invasions, and Thomas King, of course, makes a very important observation. To what extent colonization has impacted on Indigenous knowledge, and whether this is even any longer important to consider, especially within postcolonial theory (or theories), remain issues of debate and perhaps some contention. More recently, Anishinaabe (Ojibway) scholar and colleague Niigonwedom James Sinclair has argued:

> Critical lenses of protest and resistance in Aboriginal literatures have now become so commonplace they are beginning to mirror the one-dimensional treatment Indigenous peoples receive in mainstream media … The issue is not that Indigenous peoples resist, for they must and do, but that these acts are fetishized, romanticized, and commodified into comfortable and consumable narratives. (2010: 26)

Sinclair goes on to advocate for an interpretive lens of "continuance" as a "methodology that considers Indigenous literatures not only as narratives of resistance but engages the other countless activities Native authors undertake as active and responsible members of communities and creation" (28). Such engagements and "lens" "opens up Indigenous literatures (and arguably Indigenous cultures) as expansive and adaptive, growing and innovative, instead of only staving off a colonial tidal wave" (28).

There has also been a thought that resistance work (associated with postcolonial criticism) necessarily recenters the colonizer. J. Edward Chamberlin, for example, has stated that postcolonial theories "reinforce the dominance it seeks to replace" (as quoted in Sinclair 2010: 26). In a very thoughtful essay, "Native Writing, Academic Theory, Post-colonialism across the Cultural Divide," Judith Leggat states that in an instance of unequal power relations between an Aboriginal writer and White academic, "The act of literary analysis can reinscribe colonialism" (Moss 2003: 120). In some ways and in certain contexts, all these cautionary arguments about the uses or abuses of postcolonial theories (under which resistance theory is often subsumed) have merit, of course. It may be true that for every theory and frame of interpretation Aboriginal artists, scholars and other intellectuals invent, there will be those who will not comprehend or who will oversimplify and form new stereotypes. And it may be true that in some cases our work will be used to "reinscribe" or recenter colonialism. Given the magnitude of Western arrogance and ignorance about Indigenous peoples and cultures, we should perhaps expect these sorts of obtuse and defensive manoeuvres. But surely such obstructive devices cannot block our work; nor should they in any way limit our scholarship and our right to theorize ourselves (or anyone else), our cultures and our experience, or to employ (always reflexively and critically, of course) or create whatever theories best assist in our work of deconstructing and reconstructing. Or simply because we love scholarship. It seems to me that there is a "European miracle" diffusionist assumption to all these obstructions, and the implications are unsettling. Is it that every time we Indigenous scholars and artists employ so-called Western tools or concepts, we are no longer who we are? Or that we recolonize or enslave ourselves just by using certain terms, languages or schools of thought? That we have none of our own thoughts? Obviously, this is a dead-end road to go on. This is to buy into the European diffusionist notion that everything originates or comes from Europe. That nothing belongs to us! That all we can ever do is borrow "the master's tools"! Intellectually speaking, there is no master here — unless we give it that power. "Borrowing" is a two-way street — if Indigenous peoples "borrowed" European tools, Europeans did so as well, more than amply at that (Axtell 2001; Jennings 1976; Weatherford 1988; Wright 1993). But there is another perhaps more important point here — we not only have dynamic cultural heritages but we also have a birthright to this contemporary world. And these two aspects, cultural heritage and contemporaneity is a matter of imbrication, not a matter of absolute ontological or fathomless chasm. We all have blended heritages, Europeans no less so, but it has obviously been to the advantage of colonizers to emphasize our differences, those real and those imagined or constructed.

I am not minimizing the challenges that confront us; the "master narrative" is powerful because it exercises what Said calls "flexible positional superiority" (1979: 7). That is, Eurocentric perspectives do have tendencies to absorb counterknowledges and reframe them within their own perspectives and for their own purposes. Or to shift terms of arguments or definitions both as "techniques of mastery" (Duchemin 55) and as a means of maintaining their super theory of civilization/savagery (LaRocque, 2010: 47–55). And it is still largely the case that the "globalization of knowledge and Western culture constantly reaffirms the West's view of itself as the centre of legitimate knowledge, the arbiter of what counts as knowledge and the source of "civilized knowledge" (Smith 1999: 63). However, we cannot keep giving power away by acquiescing to the popular but mistaken notion that all things belong to Europeans!! Or that "everything that belongs to the colonizer is not appropriate for the colonized," which Memmi deduces is "a confused and misleading conviction" (1967: 138). As far as I am concerned, Shakespeare is as much my heritage as a human being as is *Wehsakehcha*, the central Cree comic-psychologist, shape-shifting character in the numerous stories my mother entertained her children with. To believe otherwise or to in any way limit ourselves in our use of theory or terminology is to fall into the colonizer's model of the world, which is exactly where neo-imperialist thinkers would contain us. Moreover, we have our own tools. We have our languages, our literatures, our concepts, our theories, our ways of knowing and of discovering and arranging knowledge. And our knowledge cannot be defined by or confined to some old colonial stereotypes of "Native culture" or "traditional (now "Indigenous") knowledge." Our knowledges are transcolonial, expansive, unsedimented, and both ancient and contemporary. In many ways, Indigenous scholars can speak many languages; we too can exercise flexible positionality!

It is very true that Indigenous peoples' histories, languages, literatures, religions, worldviews, political systems, technologies, architectures, sciences and the arts did not begin with European arrivals! And amazingly, much has survived. To be sure, survival has not been universal or even in texture, but what has not survived in whole, we have and continue to reinvent. As I have long argued, pre-Columbian Indigenous peoples were dynamic and adaptive, and have continued to be, despite all the invasions and the massive depopulation and dispossession that go with it. Of course, we are not who we were, but neither is Europe: it is not as though the world that Shakespeare lived in hundreds of years ago —inhabited by monsters, witches and countless other religious beliefs and secular speculations that had no basis in observational truths (Dickason 1984) — is the world of contemporary Europeans. Both Indigenous and Western cultures, hence scholars, are confronted with the historical realities of continuance and discontinuance.

But it is European-based scholarship that has traditionally treated Indigenous cultures as stagnant, primitive clay pots into which progressive varnished European cultures infuse their "European miracle" through colonial diffusion. Such a view constantly measures Indigenous change and difference solely from Western cultural tenets that are assumed to be "the hub of the human wheel out of which emanate all things progressive in culture and intellect" (LaRocque 2010: 163). This sort of neocolonial thinking places Indigenous peoples yet again in an absolutely no-win situation. In fact, it translates to intellectual genocide because it demands that Indigenous peoples remain "traditional," that is, fixed and frozen in time; and when they change, they are charged with "assimilation" (even when assimilation is forced) — one way or another we are consigned to irrelevance, a modern version for the Vanishing Indian (Francis 1992; LaRocque 2010). Meanwhile, the Western world, which has more than liberally taken from the Indigenous (both materially and conceptually), acts as if it has neither been acculturated, indigenized, hybridized nor colonized by its own colonial globe-trotting.

## Resistance Scholarship as Critical Inquiry

Some may also assume that the very nature of "resistance" cannot be used in the same breath as "scholarship." Those who believe this are those who carry on old colonial ideas of scholarship as pure and uncontaminated by "the mud of politics" (Said 1979: 13). But as Said has argued, now echoed by numerous other decolonizing scholars since, scholars are products of their societies and as such are never free of their culturally formed perspectives and political locations. This is not to say that this renders scholarship useless or a joke. Arguably, no one was more passionate about scholarship than Edward Said. He practiced and advocated intellectual rigour, critical awareness and self-reflexivity in the pursuit of knowledge. What he understood is the intimate connection between "knowledge" and power. It is this connection that we seek to expose through our scholarship.

I for one believe strongly in critical scholarship; otherwise, I would not be in this vocation. There are protocols of research and study in the best of scholarly activity and dialogue that I believe have the capacity to enhance humanity. On a more personal note, my own resistance research approach has never been confined to Western knowledge, presuppositions or methodologies, or to Western definitions or theories. But again, I do not believe scholarship or science or technologies or any other cultural acquirements belong solely to the West. Innovation and learning have never been alien to Indigenous cultures; scholarship is as much my birthright as anything else, period.

I am in this work not only because I love knowledge and, obviously, all the complexities and nuances and questions of knowledge production but also because I am ethically committed to the vocation of humanization; that is, both to the ending of injustice and oppression, whether social or intellectual, and at the same time, to the reconstruction of Indigenous humanity. And ultimately, all humanity. I do not know how we can study colonization and all its manifestations through mass media stereotypes, or the ongoing destruction and invasion of Indigenous lands, or the daily indecencies of sexism and racism, without addressing the ethical, social and political ramifications of such study. To study any kind of human violation is *ipso facto* to be challenged in our ethics, and to be called into resistance! In this, Native Studies is decidedly and unavoidably political.

However, there is also much that we can and must celebrate. Decades — centuries really — of Indigenous resistance has produced many positive political, socioeconomic and cultural changes. In Canada, a number of our original languages are still in use; our philosophies, worldviews and narratives are increasingly studied and understood; spiritual beliefs and protocols are being practiced; we are reinventing many aspects of our arts, including song, storytelling, sculpture and many other forms of material and visual art; our written literatures are flourishing; our scholars are increasing, as is our largely excellent scholarship; some socioeconomic conditions have certainly improved, relatively speaking;[13] and our populations are rising. We are winning some significant battles over land and resource rights in courts, even as we face ongoing incursions in the form of industrial encroachments, legitimized by governments and "the national interest." Our presence in the culture and politics of Canada can no longer be dismissed or ignored. We are always resurfacing. And what may be called "resurgence" today is actually a continuation of Indigenous resistance and resilience. Take the 1970s. How well I remember reading Harold Cardinal's book *The Unjust Society* (1969) as a university student. It had a revolutionary effect on me. As did the many protests held by various Native (both First Nation and Métis) communities in northern Alberta. In that era, I witnessed and was part of the political awakening of Aboriginal peoples across Canada. If there is resurgence today, it is because of previous generations who refused to give up, who believed in the value of who they were/are, and who took their aspirations to the streets, to the courts and to the cameras for all Canadians to see. Some of us took to schools and scholarship.

## We Cannot Be Owned

Today, as always, the topic of Native peoples is politically charged. This renders scholars in Native Studies vulnerable to multiple criticisms or attacks, not only from Westernist intellectuals or societal conflicts that wind their way into our classrooms but also from cultural and political interests that come from the Native communities.

Although we want to be supportive to the work of reconstruction that Aboriginal nations are undertaking, we must be careful; we cannot become mouthpieces for any particular political or ethnic group, nor propagandists for any movement. We cannot be owned or dictated by any organization or constituencies, be they communities or universities.

Said reminds us:

> Loyalty to the group's fight for survival cannot draw in the intellectual so far as to narcotize the critical sense, or reduce its imperatives, which are always to go beyond survival to questions of political liberation, to critiques of the leadership, to presenting alternatives that are too often marginalized or pushed aside as irrelevant to the main battle at hand. (1996: 41)

Many of us in Native Studies or other resistance-based studies have made a living deconstructing Western hegemonic canons and ideologies; but we must also have the right to exercise our analytical skills and training in the service of advancing Aboriginal humanity, and sometimes this means we must offer some critical reflections. There are no flawless cultures in the world, even those that have been oppressed. Naturally, our analyses or criticisms may not be welcomed or understood. Indeed, given the educational and socioeconomic gap between Aboriginal scholars and the wider community, our critiques may be experienced as hurtful. The university culture of criticism is a very particular if not esoteric culture that many nonuniversity people, Native and non-Native alike, may misunderstand as simply "too negative." Put another way, there is tension between our critical, analytical commitments and the need to support Native struggles for social justice. Nonetheless, we must maintain our freedoms to practice our scholarship, our mandates to review information and to evaluate it, and if necessary, to debate and to disagree.

As may be appreciated, intellectual freedom ranks as one of my most cherished treasures, and indeed, practicing this freedom is one reason I have been a lifelong scholar. But this is not only because of my profession; it is also because I believe our freedom to research and to reflect is requisite to advancing our humanity. However, I hasten to add, such freedoms are not without context or social responsibilities. As a decolonizing Indigenously situated feminist scholar, I believe in the social purpose of knowledge, and further that my knowledge gained from intellectual freedom is informed by my cultural and social responsibilities.

The effects of colonization on both White and Native scholars and scholarship in Canada are just beginning to be appreciated; and indeed, in the area of scholarship, much has improved since the 1970s! There are now works in North America (too numerous to reference) from almost all disciplines that reflect appreciation of our cultural heritages as well as sound understanding of our colonial experiences. But as long as all the racist and dehumanizing archival, historical and literary portrayals continue to circulate in our library and publication systems as they do, we are put in a situation of having to continually address this material, especially as each new generation of students enter our classrooms. In addition, it is clear that we do still face misunderstanding and some resistance in the way our knowledge base and cultural information, as well as our decolonized methodologies, are received. For all these reasons and more, we are not in a position to "resist no longer."

However, although we have a significant role to play in resisting oppression, in theorizing its origins and demonstrating its social consequences as well as assisting in reconstruction, we cannot be distracted from our vocation as critical thinkers. Our research must be rigorous, but it cannot be aloof. Our research must be thorough, thoughtful and thought-provoking; and our scholarship must exude the highest of standards, but also be "transgressive" and humanized with a compassionate voice. As an intellectual and a scholar, I often call for that "critical and relatively independent spirit of analysis and judgement," which Edward Said argues "ought to be the intellectual's contribution" (1996: 86). This is the primary contribution that we can all make; this is the spirit in which I carry out my scholarly studies within a Native Studies mandate and program that is as open, vibrant and international in scope as any critical human inquiry. For me, this is the meaning of "resistance" scholarship.

### NOTES

1. Métis are one of three Indigenous groups recognized as Aboriginal in the Canadian Constitution. Métis' dual (First Nation–European) ancestry emerged out of the First Nation, French and English fur trade during the seventeenth century. However, these first "half-breed" peoples evolved into a distinct Indigenous ethnic culture; by the early 1800s, the majority of Métis located in the Red River area and developed a sense of nationhood. Although there are a number of different Métis communities across Canada, the Red River Métis, now known as Métis Nation, the majority of whom live in Western Canada, remain the most prominent. For more on the development of Métis identity, see Peterson and Brown (1985); see also my essay, "Native Identity and the Métis" (2001b).

2. For a detailed study of the two resistances, see Doug Sprague (1988); see also Sawchuk et al. (1981).

3. Although some Métis — or those arbitrarily identified as Métis by colonial agents such as priests, police or treaty commissioners — did attend residential schools, most Métis could not because legally they were excluded from the *Indian Act*. Residential schools were established for "registered Indians," as defined by the *Indian Act*, a federal statute. For more on Métis and residential schools, see Chartrand, Logan, and Daniels (2006).

4. For a useful survey of the different Aboriginal groups in relation to legal distinctions and exclusions in Canada, see James Frideres and Rene Gadacz (2001). For a good

discussion on the complexities of Métis constitutional, Aboriginal and/or land rights, see the Royal Commission on Aboriginal Peoples (1996).

5.  The exception to this may be found in the Métis Settlements that were set aside through Alberta's Métis Population Betterment Act in 1938. Public schools were probably available by the late 1940s to children whose parents lived in such settlements. However, the province's definition of "métis" was somewhat loose, and the Settlements were restricted to those "métis" seen as particularly "destitute." For a number of reasons, the majority of Métis in northeastern Alberta did not go into the Métis Settlements. My family and community (with Red River roots) were among them. For more on the Settlements, see Pocklington (1991) and Sawchuk et al. (1981), especially Chapter Six.

6.  I have written about some of these earlier challenges of teaching in a number of previous works; see especially LaRocque (1990; 1996; 2001a; 2002).

7.  Today, I do not think European scholarship views all non-European peoples in this way; after all, some of the most brilliant postcolonial scholars are non-European. But the notion lingers on that Indigenous peoples are still "traditional" in the sense Blaut (1993) discusses: "Europe eternally advances, progresses ... The rest of the world advances more sluggishly, or stagnates: it is 'traditional society'"(1).

8.  And not romanticized as it now appears to be, even in some postcolonial thinking. For an absorbing discussion on the conceptual and political problematics of rootedness, migrancy and nomadism, see the chapter on "The Rhetoric of Mobility" in *Travelling Knowledges* by Renate Eigenbrod (2005: 21–38).

9.  For a fuller discussion on Indigenous populations prior to Columbus's arrival, see Blaut (1993, especially Chapter Four) and Jennings (1976, Chapter Two).

10. Of course, at different periods and in different ways, post-Columbian Indigenous peoples were literally vanishing by the millions (Blaut 1993; Jennings 1976), and of those who survived, many were left homeless, and in various ways forced to wander, particularly Native Americans. The Hollywood version of either "nomadic" or "Vanishing Indians" straggling behind one lone horse with travois is in fact a political picture — and one that tells a very different story than what Hollywood meant to portray. For more on the Vanishing Indian, see Berkhofer (1978); see also Francis (1992: Chapters Two and Three).

11. See for example, Jennings (1976: 80).

12. In *When the Other Is Me* (2010), I analyze in Chapters Two and Three the "lexical strategies of belittlement that especially serve to degrade and infantilize Native peoples" (38); the instrumental role of the "war of words" (72) in colonial writing, and its impact on Native peoples is quite immense. See also Howard Adams (1975); Duchemin (1990).

13. This is not to suggest all is glowing in the socioeconomic area. Aboriginal peoples in Canada do still lag behind other Canadians in areas of education, employment, housing, health and so forth. Further, Aboriginal peoples suffer the highest rates of youth suicide and homicide, as well as the highest rates of incarceration. Poverty, racism and sexism are still a daily reality for Aboriginal peoples. But compared with the 1950s–70s era, the era I grew up in, the socioeconomic picture was in certain respects much grimmer than it is now. See Frideres and Gadacz (2001, Chapters 3–6).

**REFERENCES**

Adams, Howard. 1975. *Prison of Grass*. Toronto: General Publishing.

Ashcroft, Bill, G. Griffiths, and H. Tiffen. 1989. *The Empire Writes Back: Theory and Practice in Post-Colonial Literature*. New York: Routledge.

Axtell, James. 2001. *Natives and Newcomers: The Cultural Origins of North America*. New York and Oxford: Oxford University Press.

Berkhofer, Robert F. 1978. *The White Man's Indian*. New York: Random House.

Blaut, J.M. 1993. *The Colonizer's Model of the World: Geographical Diffusionism and Eurocentric History*. New York and London: Gulford Press.

Cardinal, Harold. 1969. *The Unjust Society*. Edmonton, AB: Hurtig.

Chartrand, Lionel, T.E. Logan, and J.D. Daniels. 2006. *Métis History and Experience and Residential Schools in Canada*. Ottawa: Aboriginal Healing Foundation.

Coulthard, Glen S. 2007. "Subjects of Empire: Indigenous Peoples and the 'Politics of Recognition' in Canada." *Contemporary Political Theory* 6, 437–460.

Dickason, Olive P. 1992. *Canada's First Nations: A History of Founding Peoples from Earliest Times*. Toronto: McLelland and Stewart.

____. 1984. *The Myth of the Savage and the Beginnings of French Colonialism in the Americas*. Edmonton: University of Alberta Press.

Duchemin, Parker. 1990. "'A Parcel of Whelps': Alexander Mackenzie among the Indians." In W.H. New (ed.), *Native Writers and Canadian Writing*. Vancouver: University of British Columbia Press.

Eigenbrod, Renate. 2005. *Travelling Knowledges: Positioning the Im/migrant Reader of Aboriginal Literatures in Canada*. Winnipeg: University of Manitoba Press.

Francis, Daniel. 1992. *The Imaginary Indian: The Image of the Indian in Canadian Culture*. Vancouver: Aresenal Pulp Press.

Frideres, James S., and R. Gadacz. 2001. *Aboriginal Peoples in Canada: Contemporary Conflicts*. Toronto: Prentice Hall.

Green, Joyce. 2001. "Canon Fodder: Examining the Future of Native Studies." In Jill Oakes, R. Riewe, M. Bennet, and B. Chisholm (eds.), *Pushing the Margins: Native and Northern Studies*. Winnipeg, MB: Native Studies Press.

Jennings, Francis. 1976. *The Invasion of America: Indians, Colonialism, and the Cant of Conquest*. New York: W.W. Norton.

King, Thomas. 1997. "Godzilla vs. Post-Colonial." In Ajay Heble, D. Palmateer Pennee, and J.R. Struthers (eds.), *New Contexts of Canadian Criticism*. Peterborough, ON: Broadview Press.

Kulchyski, Peter. 2000. "What Is Native Studies?" In Ron F. Laliberte et al. (eds.), *Expressions in Canadian Native Studies*. Saskatoon, SK: University Extension Press.

LaRocque, Emma. 2010. *When the Other Is Me: Native Resistance Discourse 1850–1990*. Winnipeg: University of Manitoba Press.

____. 2002. "Teaching Aboriginal Literature: The Discourse of Margins and Mainstreams." In Renate Eigenbrod and J. Episkenew (eds.), *Creating Community: A Roundtable on Canadian Aboriginal Literature*. Penticton, BC and Brandon, MB: Theytus Books and Bearpaw.

____. 2001a. "From the Land to the Classroom: Broadening Epistemology." In Jill Oakes,

R. Riewe, M. Bennet, and B. Chisholm (eds.), *Pushing the Margins: Native and Northern Studies.* Winnipeg: University of Manitoba, Native Studies Press.

____. 2001b. "Native Identity and the Métis: *Otehpayimsuak* Peoples." In David Taras and B. Rasporich (eds.), *A Passion for Identity: Canadian Studies for the 21st Century.* Scarborough, ON: Nelson, Thomson Learning.

____. 1996. "The Colonization of a Native Woman Scholar." In Christine Miller and P. Chuchryk (eds.), *Women of the First Nations: Power, Wisdom and Strength.* Winnipeg: University of Manitoba Press.

____. 1990. "Preface — or — Here Are Our Voices, Who Will Hear?" In Jeanne Perreault and Sylvia Vance (eds.), *Writing the Circle: Native Women of Western Canada.* Edmonton, AB: NeWest Publishers.

____. 1983. "The Métis in English Canadian Literature." *The Canadian Journal of Native Studies* 3, 1.

Leggatt, Judith. 2003. "Native Writing, Academic Theory: Post-colonialism Across the Cultural Divide." In Laura Moss (ed.), *Is Canada Postcolonial? Unsettling Canadian Literature.* Waterloo, ON: Wilfrid Laurier University Press.

McLeod, Neal. 2001. "Coming Home Through Stories." In Armand Garnet Ruffo (ed.), *Addressing Our Words: Aboriginal Perspectives on Aboriginal Literatures.* Penticton, BC: Theytus Books.

Memmi, Albert. 1967. *The Colonizer and the Colonized.* Boston: Beacon Press.

Morrison, Bruce R., and R. Wilson. 1995. *Native Peoples: The Canadian Experience.* Toronto: McLelland and Stewart.

Pearce, Roy Harvey. 1965. *Savagism and Civilization.* Baltimore: Johns Hopkins University Press.

Peterson, Jacqueline, and J.S.H. Brown (eds.). 1985. *The New Peoples: Being and Becoming Métis in North America.* Winnipeg: University of Manitoba Press.

Pocklington, Thomas C. 1991. *The Government and Politics of the Alberta Métis Settlements.* Regina, SK: Canadian Plains Research, University of Regina.

Royal Commission on Aboriginal People (RCAP). 1996. *Métis Perspectives* Vol. 4, Chapter 5. Ottawa: Supply and Services.

Said, Edward. 1996. *Representations of the Intellectual.* New York: Vintage Books.

____. 1979. *Orientalism.* New York: Vintage Books.

Sawchuk, Joe, P. Sawchuk, T. Ferguson, and Métis Association of Alberta. 1981. *Métis Land Rights in Alberta: A Political History.* Edmonton: Métis Association of Alberta.

Sinclair, Niigonwedom J. 2010. "Resistance and Protest in Indigenous Literatures." *Canadian Dimension* 44.2: 25–28.

Smith, Linda Tuhiwai. 1999. *Decolonizing Methodologies.* London and New York: Zed Books.

Sprague, Doug N. 1988. *Canada and the Métis, 1869–1885.* Waterloo, ON: Wilfrid Laurier University Press.

Weatherford, Jack. 1991. *Native Roots: How The Indians Enriched America.* New York: Fawcett Books.

____. 1988. *Indian Givers: How the Indians of the Americas Transformed the World.* New York: Fawcett Columbine.

Wright, Ronald. 1993. *Stolen Continents: The "New World" Through Indian Eyes.* Toronto: Penguin Books.

# INDIGENOUS RESISTANCE AND RESURGENCE

*Elaine Coburn*

All of us have the same beginning. We began first with the relationship to the earth, and then the relationship to the sky world, and then a relationship to the plant world and then a relationship to the animal world and then the relationship to each other.

—*Lee Maracle (Indigenous Peoples Solidarity Movement 2012)*

In making this affirmation about the place of each and all human beings in the world, Stó:lō writer, orator and poet Lee Maracle recalls relationships that, at least in principle, may be in relative harmony. In interpreting Maracle's statement this way, I am not suggesting that Indigenous peoples are superhuman, living in near-perfect peace with each other and the natural and spirit worlds over centuries. I am only supposing that at various times and places, these relationships have been and may be relatively better than they are now, including among Indigenous nations and non-Indigenous peoples across lands and waters claimed by Canada. Given the state of the world today, characterized by what Dene activist François Paulette calls "low spiritual IQ" (quoted in Cole-Dai 2013), this contention is not very ambitious. Centuries-long colonial policies have sought to eliminate and assimilate Indigenous peoples, purposefully sundering relationships of diverse Indigenous nations with each other and with the natural world. Colonial racisms combine with the capitalist profit imperative as the driving force behind such forcible dispossessions, backed by the state military and police, as well as private armies. Murderous apartheids are a fact of life for many. There are more than a thousand missing and murdered Indigenous women (Ambler 2014), an expression of gendered colonial violence across lands that Cree-Métis scholar and poet Emma LaRocque (2001) has in the past characterized as "Northern Canada South Africa."

Against this context of contemporary colonial dispossession and brutality, Maracle offers her vision to remind each of us that we have responsibilities to other human beings and to the natural world. The current state of violently sundered relationships is a fact, but not a fatality. In other words, Maracle's affirmation is both a critique of what Kahnien'kehaka scholar Taiaiake Alfred (n.d.: 5) might call the "colonial-capitalist" present and a reminder of responsibilities to act toward a more healthy and just future.[1] Re-establishing these healthy relationships is the major aim of many Indigenous resistance and resurgence movements. Deciding how this is best accomplished, however, is an ongoing political act of self-determination by and for diverse Indigenous peoples, in all spheres of life, ranging from the politics to the arts to economics to research to international diplomacy to storytelling.

Inevitably, given the unequal, violent nature of relationships in the world right now, these Indigenous movements are *struggles*. They face determined, concerted opposition that arises from the colonial state and is backed by the police, military and intelligence services. Likewise, there is opposition from multibillion dollar corporations that dispossess Indigenous peoples and exploit the land, seas and human labour, which are understood as nothing more than profit-making "resources." Opposition arises, too, among many non-Indigenous peoples who reproduce centuries-old racisms that are, furthermore, ingrained in colonial institutions and cultures. In addition, as Nuu-chah-nulth scholar Clifford (Kam'ayaam/ Chachim'multhnii) Atleo describes in Chapter Six of this book, some Indigenous actors may be complicit in aspects of colonial-capitalism, seeking to personally accrue greater proportions of rents from resource extraction rather than rebuilding healthy relationships with the natural world and other living beings. Indigenous agency does not necessarily mean resistance and resurgence. There is no "teleology of emancipation," to borrow from African-American philosopher Eddie S. Glaude Jr. (2007: 150), but only the possibility of such emancipation.

Given a centuries-old, murderous colonial-capitalist context, survival is the most basic form of Indigenous resistance. In other cases, however, resistance may include dramatic physical confrontations with colonial and corporate actors, including the police and military. At their most powerful, however, Indigenous movements move beyond resistance to resurgence; that is, to joyful affirmations of individual and collective Indigenous self-determination. Critically, such Indigenous movements require neither oversight nor "recognition" from colonial institutions and non-Indigenous peoples (Coulthard 2007; Hayden King, Chapter Seven of this book). Nonetheless, they matter to all peoples. To draw a parallel: Although he was labelled a terrorist and jailed for decades, much of the world came to celebrate Nelson Mandela's struggles against South African apartheid as at once specifically concerned with Black liberation and as a matter of human justice of concern to all (Mbembe 2013: 245–8). Likewise, although Indigenous movements are led by and for diverse Indigenous peoples, they are vital for all those who strive toward a just peace, one that restores and honours healthy, respectful relationships with the earth, sky, plants, animals and with each other.

## "Knowledge About Hope and Courage": Situating this Book

This book seeks to contribute to Indigenous resistance and resurgence through the critical description and analysis of existing Indigenous movements of self-determination. This scholarly "storywork," as contributor Kelly Aguirre of Nahua and Nuu Savi Mixteca ancestry, describes it, is one way of participating in Indigenous struggles. That might seem like a wishful statement, as if resistance and resurgence were theoretical rather than practical matters that redress and ultimately revolutionize the powerfully unequal relations of colonial-capitalism. As the late Blood tribal member Everett Soop, an artist and Native disability activist, put it with respect to Indigenous disability concerns:

> The real beef of the native handicapped is that there are so many experts, professionals and concerned government people that are ready to compile documents of good words. Anyone can go to the government and find very well written programs for the disabled. Some of these fancy worded programs for the disabled will never reach the native handicapped because of the political football game. Since the native handicapped is at the bottom of the totem pole in society he is not even in the game, he is just kicked aside. (1988)

The concern is that this book, like other scholarship and policy documents purporting to support Indigenous resistance and resurgence, is nothing more than a compilation of "good words," or worse, merely "fancy word(s)" disconnected from transformative change. As Soop (1988) observes, these words mean little without practical, concrete change that alters the rules of a rigged political game, revolutionizing power relationships to give new voices to Indigenous peoples and persons, including the Indigenous disabled who are too often "kicked aside."

Even worse, it might be argued that the academy from which scholarly books are (in part) written is a particularly compromised place for Indigenous persons, with universities more often a site for colonial oppression than a space for Indigenous self-determining reflection and debate. As Maori scholar Linda Tuhiwai Smith (1999) has powerfully argued, supposedly "scientific" colonial scholarship has historically been a critical part of the colonial project of naming and claiming Indigenous peoples, lands and knowledges for the colonizers. Yet, the once–totalizing colonial vocation of universities has changed, not least through concerted efforts of Indigenous movements outside and inside the academy (as LaRocque describes in her Foreword to this book). Thus, the development of Indigenous Studies programs is the most visible "space" for Indigenous voices and scholarship within universities, although they remain constrained by colonial interests, dependent on colonial state funding and increasingly on corporate and "philanthropic" donations.[2]

To those so far excluded from the academy, however, the university may appear a privileged place for the expression of Indigenous scholarship and voices, at least some of the time. Specifically, in Chapter Two of this book, non-Indigenous scholar Christine Walsh and her Indigenous coauthor Shirley Aarrestad share the voices of Indigenous women captured by the colonial injustice system. One woman, who asked to be anonymous, expresses her reflections this way:

> The other day I was walking I thought of the Indian Nation, I think we've survived against all odds. I'm sure they all thought we'd be gone by now, or assimilated into the White society. But we've stuck to our guns. But how often do we ever get that opportunity to actually be that voice? You know, to take our stories and make them into knowledge about hope and courage? I thought about this for a while and decided to go to university; I want to be that voice for our people.

Speaking this way may sound naïve because it appears to overlook the institutionalized ways that Indigenous authority is undercut by many routine university practices that disregard and belittle Indigenous knowledge-making and knowledge-sharing practices. The university may not usually, or even often, operate as a space where it is possible to be a "voice for our people." But this woman helpfully reminds academics that hard-won spaces in the university, including Indigenous studies programs, should not be taken for granted. They are not the only places for Indigenous self-determining expression, but they are one possible space, sitting alongside other ways of sharing Indigenous knowledges, including personal, face-to-face relationships, and preparation and participation in traditional ceremonies. At the same time, this woman reminds us of the importance of "contrapuntal" Indigenous epistemologies. Such knowledges seek explicitly to bolster hope and courage against hopelessness and fear, including that experienced by many Indigenous women in the colonial injustice system.

The diverse Indigenous scholars and contributors I cite here are writing from universities as well as from Indigenous nations across territories claimed by Canada and worldwide. This attests to the ways that colonial academic spaces have been at least been partially opened by and for Indigenous voices. Among other issues, these Indigenous (and a few non-Indigenous) scholars contribute to a wide-ranging interdisciplinary, multilayered debate and discussion. Among other concerns, they describe and analyze Indigenous agency within the contemporary world colonial–capitalist political economy (Altamirano-Jimenez 2013; Coulthard 2014; King 2013); Indigenous resistance and resurgence (Alfred 2009a; Corntassel 2012; Hokowhitu et al. 2010; Simpson 2008; Simpson 2011); Indigenous women and feminisms (Anderson 2011; Green 2007; Suzack et al. 2010); Indigenous genders and sexualities (Driskill et al. 2011a; Driskill et al. 2011b); Indigenous masculinities (McKegney 2014); Indigenous literary criticism (LaRocque 2010); urban Indigenous experiences (Peters and Andersen 2013), and Indigenous methodologies (Kovach 2009; Walter and Andersen 2013); as well as contributing to a wide range of historical and contemporary Indigenous fiction and poetry (for two useful anthologies, see Armstrong and Grauer 2001; Moses, Goldie, and Ruffo 2013). Taken together, these books (but also many other articles, conference presentations and classroom teachings) testify to and participate in an increasingly robust Indigenous presence in the academy, itself an outcome of important Indigenous movements in the 1960s and 1970s. At the same time, such diverse Indigenous perspectives contribute to critical human inquiry in the broadest sense, in fields that Western disciplines have divided up into political science and literary criticism, economics and environmental sciences; sexuality and gender studies; antiracism and research methodologies.

Like these recent contributions, this book seeks to support and participate in Indigenous resistance and resurgence, insisting that academic spaces may be used, if not always easily (see, for example, Coburn et al. 2013), to ask and explore answers to questions that matter to diverse Indigenous peoples. At the same time, we recognize, with Soop, that compilations of "good words" are not enough. They must be articulated with informed action to be meaningful.

### "Names Carry the Record of Our Relations": Or What Does "Indigenous" Mean?

Although the subtitle of this book is "Indigenous Resistance and Resurgence," not all authors in this book use the term "Indigenous." This diversity respects each author's decisions around terminologies that are not neutral but politically charged and emerge from specific histories. As Kelly Aguirre observes in Chapter Eight of this book, "Names carry the record of our relations." Without doing a full genealogy of the term "Indigenous," university library searches suggest that the word was used only occasionally in the 1990s and then became more widespread in the 2000s, at least in the academic literature. The signing of the United Nations Declaration on the Rights of Indigenous Peoples (UNDRIP) in 2007 is further evidence of the extent to which the term now, perhaps temporarily, has international currency in policy circles. So if many Native Studies programs were established across lands claimed by Canada in the 1970s, similar programs today are often called "Indigenous Studies." In the future, other names may develop, reflecting new moments within Indigenous struggles.

What is obvious is that before colonization more than five hundred years ago, there were no "Indigenous" peoples and nations. Instead, as non-Indigenous scholar Rima Wilkes observes in Chapter Four of this book, there were Cree, Nuu-chah-nulth, Haida peoples and so on. Despite immense pressures by colonial governments, since colonization, Indigenous peoples have never ceased to call themselves by their own names. To the colonizers, however, diverse nations were together designated as a single undifferentiated people, as "Indians" but also as "savages" and as "primitives"; and for women, in dehumanizing sexualized language and imagery, as "squaws" (LaRocque 2010, Chapter Two). Later, colonial administrations across what is called Canada named diverse Indigenous peoples "Aboriginal," a term institutionalized in colonial political and bureaucratic agencies, such as the Ministry of Aboriginal Affairs and Northern Development, and widely used today in colonial state and policy debates alongside the legal term "Indian."

Many Indigenous peoples have rejected the blanket colonial terms "Indian" and "Aboriginal" (for example, Alfred and Corntassel 2005), not least Indigenous women who have challenged patriarchal, colonial-legal definitions of "Indian" status. As a result of Indigenous struggles, these administrative and government statistical categories have been changed. Currently, they are often subdivided into three groups: "First Nations," "Métis" and "Inuit." Emerging out of the highly contested, unequal political struggles around colonialism, such legal-lexical developments are far from unproblematic. For instance, professor Maggie Walter of the trawlwoolway people of northeastern Tasmania and Métis social scientist Chris Andersen (2013) observe that the generation of statistical descriptions from First Nations, Métis and Inuit aggregations of Indigenous nations obscure important variations across diverse, distinct Indigenous peoples. Indeed, at the time of contact, there were more than one hundred distinct Indigenous peoples across lands now claimed by Canada (LaRocque 2010: 10). Such distinct histories and persistent, contemporary differences across Indigenous nations are erased through statistical aggregation as First Nations, Métis and Inuit. Worse, Andersen argues that "Métis" has been used and interpreted as meaning "having some Indigenous heritage," both by the colonial state and by some Indigenous persons, thus obscuring the unique national histories of a distinct Métis people historically centered on the Red River region in Alberta (Andersen 2014: 6–7, 17–19; LaRocque 2010: 7).

This suggests the politically consequential nature of conceptualizing what it means to be "Indigenous," especially in policy-relevant research, although the underlying argument that may be inferred from Walter and Andersen (2013) is that any disagreements across Indigenous nations and persons self-determining their designations are preferable to those problems arising from designations imposed by colonial governments.

Indigenous peoples' and persons' own vocabularies for talking about their histories, contemporary politics and futures are not static, but changing and contested. The term "Red Power" (Shreve 2011) is often identified with the American Indian Movement of the 1960s and 1970s. The concept, which is also used across lands claimed by Canada, seeks to reverse and reclaim stigmatizing colonial rhetoric about Indigenous peoples as an essentialized "red" race of subhuman beings, while insisting that Indigenous peoples are powerful and capable political actors. At the same time, the term "Red Power" echoes the important Black Power movement, centered in the United States in the same period, implicating Red Power in a broad wave of liberation movements. Other names include the "Fourth World" (Manuel and Posluns 1974), "Native," and "original peoples," each bound up with particular political, analytical and policy commitments. For instance, the "Fourth World" emphasizes the disastrous living conditions and life chances of some Indigenous peoples in the so-called First World since colonialization. At the same time, this concept alludes to dependency theories of colonial empires (Gunder Frank 1966) that emphasize that existing poverty in the colonized Third and Fourth Worlds is an outcome of pillaging by the colonial First World. This counters colonial attributions of poverty to "primitive" and deficient Indigenous cultures (for a critique, see Walter and Andersen 2013: Chapter One). The terms "Native," "First Nations" and "original peoples" all emphasize prior habitation, implying specific rights and responsibilities to lands and seas on which diverse Native peoples have historically settled and purposefully circulated. These terms likewise recall the 1970s pan-Indigenous mobilizations "when Status and non-Status Indians and the Métis of the Prairies embraced the name 'Native Peoples' with the shared understanding of themselves as a cohesive indigenous body in a common struggle against colonization" (LaRocque 2010: 7). Finally, but not exhaustively, the United States and Canadian governments have differently shaped the colonial experiences for Indigenous peoples on either side of the colonial border.

In this contribution, I use the term "Indigenous" to point to some partly shared histories, including prior occupation. They include shared (if often distinct) experiences of colonization, but also shared (if diverse) histories of survival and resistance. With Andersen (2014: 20), however, I would underline that "prior presence" does not imply shared biological, much less racial roots. Instead, Indigenousness is arguably best understood in the explicitly political terms of historical, "peoplehood"-based relationships (Andersen 2014: 11). This includes "shared memories of the territory, leaders, events and culture" (Andersen 2014: 13) that together constitute nationhood as a positive construction against the negative definition of the shared experiences of colonization. So the term usefully recognizes Indigenous Diasporas, both outside of traditional territories and worldwide. The idea of shared memories and relationships, however, does not mean that Indigenous nations are monolithic, much less inevitably egalitarian blocs. There is diversity, meaning both differences and inequalities, across and within Indigenous peoples. Some result principally from colonization, others predate colonialism and others are from a complex mixture of both. Indeed, the Indigenous scholarly literature cited earlier is rich precisely because it explores questions of gender, disability, sexuality, urban and rural residency and more, among different Indigenous peoples and from a wide range of Indigenous perspectives. Hence, the concept of the Indigenous is rightly consistently problematized to reflect the complex contemporary realities and ideas of diverse Indigenous peoples and persons.

Alongside the term "Indigenous," I use the purely negative concept of "non-Indigenous." Doing so avoids the word "Settler" that, as LaRocque observes in her Foreword (this book), self-interestedly erases the fact of Indigenous settlement prior to the arrival of colonial peoples. In addition, the term "Settler" may obscure the ways that, both historically and today, many Indigenous and non-Indigenous persons do not "settle," but purposefully move and circulate, including across colonial borders. (This is not to imagine a borderless world: Indigenous, working-class and racialized persons are often formally limited in their movements by interventionist states, while Indigenous persons must carry colonial passports. For challenges to this last practice, see Corntassel 2008: 109). Like the term "Indigenous," the concept of the "non-Indigenous" is thus a conceptual approximation that must be consistently nuanced, not least to acknowledge sometimes-antagonistic relationships of class, race, gender and dis/ability among non-Indigenous peoples. Among both Indigenous and non-Indigenous peoples, the rule is (unequal) diversity and ongoing (unequal) political argument amid and sometimes against hegemonic "common-sense" understandings of the world established by the dominant actors, including capital and the colonial state. If imperfect, however, both the terms "Indigenous" and "non-Indigenous" remain analytically and descriptively useful concepts because they purposefully center an ongoing colonial relationship as a fact of contemporary political and social relations, including across lands and seas claimed by Canada. They helpfully counter colonial ideologies that imagine colonialism as a merely historical, not contemporary phenomenon.

Finally and importantly, these concepts do not define the horizon of Indigenous possibilities, but only situate them within the contemporary colonial context. By definition, Indigenous liberation means transcending what Maori scholar

Brendan Hokowhitu (2013) calls the "necropolitical" relationship of colonialism, a concept he borrows from Camerounais political philosopher Achille Mbembe (2006). This reminds us that if Indigenous liberation means anything, it means moving beyond colonial politics, a politics premised on death, to self-determining Indigenous futures. When colonialism is transcended, the terms "Indigenous" and "non-Indigenous" will lose all but their historical meanings. In the still-colonial present, meanwhile, they are useful if approximate designations, alongside diverse Indigenous names for their own peoples.

### "Pathways to Freedom": Indigenous Resistance and Resurgence

What are Indigenous resistance and Indigenous resurgence? Arguably, resistance includes any refusal to accept any given aspect of colonialization in its multiple, shape-shifting forms. Insofar as colonialism has been premised on the death of Indigenous peoples, Indigenous survival constitutes the baseline of resistance. In Chapter One of this book, James (Sa'ke'j) Youngblood Henderson of the Chickasaw nation writes of his own experience and that of his generation:

> I was born in 1944. My generation of Aboriginal peoples grew up with pervasive indignities of forced assimilation through education into Eurocentrism. We were born into a grim, hopeless, confused world, a generation resigned to extinction by state-enforced assimilation, educational policies or in despair because of deep neglect. We struggled with Aboriginal nihilism, living in a meaningless world. We lived in despair and in resignation, trapped under an all powerful Indian Agent who controlled our life. Many of us did not survive the infamous residential schools in Canada, where at least four thousand Aboriginal children died of starvation, neglect and beatings.

For many in the contemporary generation, the struggle for survival is still acute. Many of the poems by Indigenous women captured by the colonial injustice system in Chapter Two of this book, for instance, attest to this everyday struggle for survival when they write and speak of feeling hopeless, lost and alone — but nonetheless "fighting to stay," as a woman named Darla emphasizes. In such contexts, Indigenous survival is a form of resistance.

Clearly, however, bare survival is not adequate for meaningful existence. Indigenous resurgence is thus about more than resistance; it is about the reinvention of diverse, specifically Indigenous ways of being, knowing and doing. Put another way, if resistance signifies challenges to colonial practices and ideas, resurgence decentres colonialism by reimagining and re-creating diverse Indigenous worldviews and practices. Of course, any particular empirical practice may contain elements of both, so that the analytical distinction becomes a matter of interpretive emphasis. In terms of both scholarly and "lay" storytelling practices, for instance, Aguirre writes of "stories of resistance to and resilience through violence ... that also regenerate and refigure still existing, particular and substantive alternatives to colonial forms of relationality." In other words, if the reinvention of Indigenous stories, the creation of specifically Indigenous narratives rooted in Indigenous understandings of relationships, is an instance of resurgence, it is at the same time necessarily resistance to colonial narratives and relations of violence. Following Maracle, but also Corntassel (2008) and Alex Wilson (Afterword in this book) among others, I suggest that Indigenous resurgence, broadly understood, is not primarily — or even at all — about new legal rights and recognition for diverse Indigenous peoples by colonial political bodies (King, Chapter Seven of this book). Instead, it is about relational responsibilities toward all living things and the Earth. As such, Indigenous resurgence "at its core" is about "spiritual and relational responsibilities that are continuously renewed" (Corntassel 2008: 117).

## Colonialism: Dispossession and Dehumanization

If Indigenous resistance is about challenging colonialization, and if Indigenous resurgence is about transcending colonialism by renewing relational responsibilities to all living things and to nature, it begs this question: What are the central dynamics of historical and contemporary colonialism? The necessity of this question, which foregrounds colonial relationships, institutions and ideologies, is itself indicative of the ways that colonialism saturates nearly every aspect of the present — without, however, being totalizing. Colonialism becomes the "ground zero" against which Indigenous perspectives and practices are measured, as if diverse Indigenous world-views and ways of living are not sufficient starting points for analysis and action. As Anishinaabe scholar Hayden King from the Beausoleil First Nation writes in Chapter Seven of this book with some exasperation, "history inevitably, but disap-pointingly so, begins with Christopher Columbus." There is nothing benign then about beginning a theoretical analysis of Indigenous resistance — and especially Indigenous resurgence — by centering colonialism, its characteristics, tensions and transformations. Nonetheless, if Indigenous resistance (and to a lesser extent Indigenous resurgence) is to be understood, it means characterizing colonialism, but doing so from Indigenous perspectives.

As Aguirre describes, colonial-capitalism is about "dispossession and displace-ment, an ongoing and insatiable capitalist accumulation of land augmented with the imperatives of Settler nation-building." This is a concrete, not abstract process because multinational corporations seek to profit from lands and waters understood as nothing more than potentially profitable resources while nation-states often mobilize at their behest, as well as in the colonial state interests of asserting national "sovereignty" through non-Indigenous settlements. In practice, as Nuu-chah-nulth scholar Clifford (Kam'ayaam/Chachim'multhnii) Atleo observes in Chapter Six of this book, colonial-capitalism is experienced as fundamental transformations, often over one or two generations. With respect to his own people, he observes:

> [It] was not long ago that every family was involved with fishing. Sadly, we can no longer accurately say that we are saltwater people. Today's reality, like that of many Indigenous communities in this country, is that we no longer have a direct relationship with our lands and waters for our sustenance, but instead participate in the wage economy and buy most of our food from grocery stores ... It is a tragic irony that in the space of one or two generations, so many Nuu-chah-nulth-aht have gone from fishers to farmers of fish.

Dispossession is experienced in such intergenerational movements from relationships with the land and waters into exploitative colonial-capitalist social relationships. This is a violent process, at its most acute in recent histories when "accomplished" through the murderous residential school system. But the process is no less violent, if differently achieved, in other configurations of forced assimilation. In the case of his people, as Atleo bluntly observes, "we have been starved into submission" because disconnection from the seas forces participation in the wage economy in order to survive.

At the same time, colonial-capitalist dispossession represents more than a loss of access to land and seas. Instead, this forcible loss of relationships with the seas, land and traditional ways of living puts tremendous strain on values that emerge from those intimate, everyday relationships with the natural world. In Atleo's view, Nuu-chah-nulth respect for the seas and an emphasis on the "oneness" of interrelated life is often subsumed in the contemporary generation in favour of "Aboriginal neoliberal" ideologies. Inspired by hegemonic, neoliberal, colonial-capitalist values, such ideologies emphasize the seas as a profitable resource and stress individual self-reliance and highly personalized forms of (economic) success. Consequently, many serious political conflicts within and across Indigenous nations centre on such transformations. To what extent are they necessary, even desirable "adaptations" to the broader colonial-capitalist context? To what extent do they fundamentally betray values and practices that make life meaningful and possible for diverse Indigenous peoples as Indigenous peoples? Another face of colonialism is that it creates these dilemmas for diverse Indigenous peoples. Importantly, this is not to suggest that political debate among Indigenous peoples is problematic. On the contrary, such debates express the vitality of Indigenous self-determining political practices. Rather, it is only to observe that colonialism profoundly shapes what appear to be "viable" political alternatives worth discussing and pursuing.

Colonialism is thus first and foremost, if not exclusively, dispossession and the associated pressures on traditional Indigenous ways of being, knowing and doing rooted in place-based practices. But this material loss is legitimated through elaborate, shape-shifting "zombie colonial" ideologies that, if they have been defeated a thousand times, nonetheless arise again and again.[3] One manifestation of zombie colonialism is the identification of history's point of origin with colonial conquest. This hegemonic tendency to conflate European history with world history is predicated on and reinforces the exclusion of Indigenous peoples from full humanity, making Indigenous peoples' ontologically imperfect and hence "suited" to colonial rule. As King observes in Chapter Seven of this book:

> This exclusion is represented symbolically in European cartography, as James (Sa'ke'j) Youngblood Henderson demonstrates in his deconstruction of the universally familiar geo-politic map. He notes "humanity is viewed as a set of political states, with Europe at the centre of the planet. The map does not reveal human or ecological diversity" (2008: 19). For Indigenous peoples who have never expressed political community as a geographic container with exclusive sovereignty historically or in contemporary times, the result is marginalization at best.

In other words, because Indigenous peoples have not historically organized through the European governing mechanisms of the sovereign, bounded state, they have been presumed incapable and unworthy of self-determining political diplomacy internationally. The colonial map "authoritatively" erases Indigenous political geographies, painting them over with colonial boundaries and colours. This reaffirms the idea of Euro-Canadian history as universal while denying Indigenous histories and presence. Ultimately, these assumptions are rooted in the premise that to be accepted as fully equal human beings means participation in Euro–Canadian relations and institutions.

The colonial erasure of Indigenous peoples takes place through high and popular colonial cultures, as well as through official colonial state representations of the world. Ironically, this erasure is accomplished through what LaRocque (2010) refers to as colonial hate literature that makes Indigenous peoples highly *visible* as dehumanized "savages," so justifying their marginalization and even elimination, historically through genocide and now through various forms of assimilation. In Chapter Five of this book, Jennifer Adese, of the Oitpemisiwak/Métis peoples, emphasizes that dehumanizing colonial ideologies are central, not secondary, to material processes of colonization, not least because they justify material dispossession:

If we are pictured as no more than grotesque caricatures like [film actor Johnny] Depp's "Tonto" (in the 2013 film *The Lone Ranger*) and like our earth, air, water, and animal relations as less deserving of respect and substantively equal treatment than peoples of European descent, we can be violated, discounted, ignored, commodified and consumed.

At the same time, such colonial misrepresentations depend on the material control of the means of producing images by colonial powers and non-Indigenous actors. Even when well-meaning — I assume that Gore Verbinski, the director of *The Lone Ranger*, did not set out with the specific intent of dehumanizing Indigenous peoples — non–Indigenous image-makers also often repeat damaging stereotypes. Although they may be intellectually analyzed and so placed as some distance, they perpetuate emotionally and spiritually harmful images. Crucially, these images are simultaneously productive and destructive: they construct the imaginary Indigenous person as a useful commodity to be consumed by the mass or discerning non–Indigenous paying public while denying the presence of real, diverse Indigenous peoples.

*Resisting Erasure, Making Visible, Reclaiming*
Resisting erasures, both literal and metaphorical, is a centuries-old practice for Indigenous peoples. Even since the 1980s, there have been literally hundreds of forms of Indigenous protest across lands and waters claimed by Canada, involving thousands of Indigenous persons, in actions ranging from road blockades to marches to boycotts to "fish-ins," as non-Indigenous scholar Rima Wilkes documents in Chapter Four of this book. Such resistance is often invisible, including to other, geographically distant Indigenous peoples. Sometimes resistance becomes spectacularly evident, however, even to typically inattentive non-Indigenous publics. In December 2012, the emergence of the Idle No More (INM) movement (whose name is misleading insofar as it obscures prior practices of resistance and resurgence) at least temporarily made Indigenous struggles self-evident for both Canadian and international audiences. Contributor Jarrett Martineau, a Cree/Dene scholar, producer and musician explains the significance of INM, sometimes also referred to as the "Round Dance Revolution":

(It) was both a representational gesture of Indigenous resistance and performance and a self-affirmation of Indigenous continuity, presence and struggle. It operated at both levels and frequencies simultaneously, making visible the disparity between settler colonial realities and the lived experiences of Indigenous peoples, dispossessed from our homelands and territories. The round dances were an evocative interimage of indigeneity that reterritorialized Indigenous presence beyond the normative borders in which it is often inscribed (reservation and rural communities), or otherwise erased.

Challenging erasure and the idea of the Indigenous person as "out of place" when off the reserve or outside of rural areas (see Adese, Chapter Five of this book), the evolving struggles of Idle No More (INM) reclaim places as Indigenous — including shopping centres — that are overwritten with state colonial, capitalist and consumer presence. At the same time as they resisted erasure, INM protests affirmed and reinvented Indigenous practices, including the Round Dance, which became an invitation for solidarity across Indigenous peoples and with non-Indigenous supporters.

INM was felt as a moment of urgency, not because Indigenous resistance and resurgence was particularly strong, but paradoxically because so many felt that Indigenous ways of being, knowing and doing were and are threatened in profound ways by the current moment of colonial-capitalism. In Chapter Nine of this book, non-Indigenous scholar Jeff Denis explains:

> Many Indigenous nations have a prophecy. The Anishinaabe call it the 8th Fire; other nations have other names for it. After seven generations of colonization and its devastating consequences, the people will begin to wake up and revive traditions. They will come to a fork in the road where they must choose between the current path of greed, competition, and destruction, where some individuals get very wealthy at the expense of widespread poverty and polluted air, water and soil, or an alternative path of working together to find new ways of living that will restore balance to both social relations and the ecosystems on which we depend.

Many argued that the "fork in the road" is right now; INM thus became invested with a strong spiritual charge, although two years later, it is clear that the struggle has not been resolved by INM but may only be beginning.

Here, I offer three deliberately contrasting, but complementary, examples from this book. Each describes prefigurative practices that have emerged, if not from INM, partly in conjunction with this recent moment of Indigenous uprising.

First, for King (Chapter Seven), Indigenous resistance and resurgence means speaking from particular, rather than nebulous "pan-Indigenous" places. Among other possible pathways, he calls for a revalorization of the Anishinaabe story of Grandfather Drum, bringing peace in a time of war through the generation of compassion and empathy. He suggests that beginning to interpret and understand this story may be a principled way of beginning to reimagine healthy relationships among Indigenous peoples — and perhaps, if they are willing to listen, with non-Indigenous peoples. Such an approach, he argues, might enable the creation of new

Indigenous relationships of responsibility outside of the narrow, colonial, international nation-state framework and its liberal, individual "rights" discourses. This does not simply reverse the charge by suggesting that Indigenous perspectives are better than liberal European statist assumptions. Instead, it re-centres Indigenous philosophies as a starting point for developing practices that encourage peaceful relationships in a violent world.

Second, as Adese describes in Chapter Five, resistance and resurgence can be manifest in joyful, even exuberant Indigenous expression. Many Indigenous artists are challenging colonial visual imperialism while offering both highly personal and politicized new Indigenous imaginaries. As Adese briefly describes, this artistic renaissance includes the work of contemporary artist Kent Monkman, of Cree ancestry. Through his alter ego, Miss Chief Eagle Testickle, Monkman challenges colonial stereotypes of Indigenous peoples while skewering colonial gender binaries and heternormative values: ·

> Miss Chief, in hot pink stilettos, mesh, fringe, and shiny regalia, is subject and object, painter and model. She flouts the ways in which Indigenous peoples have been represented in gendered and heterosexist European race-thinking ... Monkman also engages material culture, video and digital technologies, as in his presentation of the Boudoir de Berdashe, a full-size teepee installation — and the home of Miss Chief.

In so doing, Monkman challenges both colonial stereotypes and those Indigenous politics that marginalize gender and sexual minorities, in the name of tradition, religion or for any other reason. In this sense, Monkman's artwork contributes to efforts to create spaces for the self-determining participation of all Indigenous persons, within both Indigenous and non-Indigenous publics and politics.

Third, in Chapter Ten, Jarrett Martineau describes the "sacred act of reclamation and reoccupation on May 22, 2013 ... of PKOLS: the original SENĆOŦEN place name of a sacred site at the summit of a promontory in Saanich, British Columbia." Simultaneously a symbolic, communicative and embodied act of reoccupation, Martineau emphasizes the following:

> The reclamation of PKOLS ... signalled new possibilities for Indigenous–settler alliances, collective action and decolonizing praxis. The WSÁNEĆ did not seek permission from the State; they took action in alignment with their natural laws, customs, and inherent rights. In doing so, they were supported by a large community of local Indigenous nations, Indigenous visitors to their traditional territory and settler allies. Against the strictly delimited forms of "permissible" Indigenous activism, the reclamation of

PKOLS was empowering ... for ... local nations, but also for communities and supporters in solidarity across Turtle Island.

Taken together, these three examples of Indigenous resistance and resurgence suggest the breadth and range of Indigenous resistant and resurgent actions and struggles. They should not, however, be taken to suggest there is anything inevitable about such emancipatory developments. The creation of what Alfred calls "rough pathways to freedom" (2009b: 40) is never obvious.

Indeed, the current historical moment of colonial-capitalism may be particularly unpropitious for such developments. Enacting resistance and resurgence is often far from simple for those who participate in them. As Wilkes describes in Chapter Four of this book:

> While some might say that engaging in resistance is not a choice but is a natural response to an attack on land, family, home, and nation, this does not diminish the sacrifices activists make and the difficulties they confront. Activists do not always have the support of their communities, and endure racism and violence because, as Coulthard (2012) notes, "the Canadian state claims to hold a legitimate monopoly on use of violence."

### Resistance and Resurgence as Reinvention

If Indigenous resistance is about "decolonization," even in the face of violent state opposition, does this mean that Indigenous struggles refuse to embrace change as a matter of principle? The answer, if it is not already evident, is clearly "No." As Aguirre observes, "Tradition is understood to involve both continuity and motion; it doesn't imply invariance but adaptation." In other words, it is a colonial myth that Indigenous cultures exist outside of history, where "culture" is understood both as daily practices and as the meaning-making that emerges from them. Indigenous ways of living are not static, frozen in time, monolithic blocs, pristine in the year 1491 and corrupted ever after. On the contrary, many Indigenous scholars and writers emphasize the fluid nature of diverse Indigenous worldviews and practices, while at the same time warning against an excessive romanticization of all traditional beliefs and practices.

An emphasis on individual autonomy and moral responsibility within the context of broad respect for others, as Nishnaabeg writer Leanne Simpson (2011) suggests, for instance, may mean that many Indigenous peoples accepted a wide range of individual behaviours and values, not least with respect to gender, sexuality and in ideas relating to Indigenous governance. At the same time, LaRocque (2007: 59) warns against romanticizations that assume that, for instance, that Indigenous peoples were "free from patriarchal notions and practices" and other damaging relationships and values, whether these predate colonialism or emerged with colonialism. After all, Indigenous peoples are human and therefore imperfect. This means that if "contrapuntal" romanticization is necessary in the context of combatting colonial hate (LaRocque 2010: 11–16), it may be less helpful with respect to dealing frankly with scourges such as male violence that today affects both Indigenous and non-Indigenous societies (LaRoque 2007: 59–61). Indeed, it may be useful to separate the empirical question of what "was" or "is" traditional from what "ought" to be[4] because Indigenous resurgence is not about the mechanical reproduction of past traditions, in any case never static, but of Indigenous political self-determination.

If that argument is controversial, what is clear is that, as in all human cultures, Indigenous peoples transform over their histories, given inevitably changing circumstances and the human capacity for innovation and moral choice (LaRocque 2007: 61). As LaRocque simply states, "We reinvent ourselves, much as our ancestors from many roads have always done." Self-determination is "reinventing *ourselves*," as LaRocque observes, against the reproduction of colonial-capitalist subjectivities, whether these have been created by force or through the "soft" powers of colonial–capitalist jurisprudence and culture (2010: 160). The political issue for self-determining Indigenous peoples is deciding the inevitably varied directions of that self-invention while respecting the imperative of individual moral choice across diverse Indigenous human beings.

To return to Atleo's experiences: After initial skepticism, he surprised himself by finding that he agreed with the development of an experimental Ahousaht organic gardening project. For a sea-based people, organic gardening is clearly "nontraditional" and, moreover, land-based agriculture recalls the trauma of his people who, like other sea-based Indigenous peoples, were forced from the sea and into farm labour. But upon reflection, he considers that this gardening does fulfill the two key Nuu-chah-nulth principles of respect and oneness, even if they are not embodied here in salt–water based practices. Atleo writes:

> We could still honour iisaak and hishookish tsa'walk in new forms, even in an activity like organic gardening that is far from our original saltwater ways of living. In many ways this is necessary. Breathing life into our culture and fulfilling our sacred obligations requires creativity and flexibility.

### "We Know What We Know From Where We Stand"
In this book, there are both Indigenous and non-Indigenous contributors. If the participation of Indigenous scholars makes sense with respect to Indigenous self-determination, including within the academy, the involvement of non-Indigenous

academics is more suspect. What role does a non-Indigenous — White, female, able-bodied, straight — researcher like me have in relation to Indigenous movements? Some might argue there is no (useful) role at all. Alfred suggests, for instance, that when he was younger and quicker to anger, he used to respond to (hostile) non-Indigenous individuals who demanded, "What do you people want with us?" by answering, "I want you out of my face and off my land!" (Alfred 2009a: 187). Arguably, non-Indigenous scholars like me should heed this suggestion by getting "out of the faces" of Indigenous academics and "off" the (intellectual) territories developed by them. Certainly, spaces where diverse Indigenous peoples and scholars may develop and debate ideas without having to explain or justify themselves before non-Indigenous audiences, however well-meaning, are important. This is true because too often, as Andersen and Hokowhitu (2007: 43) observe, non-Indigenous participation may deteriorate into paternalistic displays of White "tolerance," as if Indigenous scholarship is not worthy of serious critique but only witless applause. Nonetheless, unequal coexistence is a fact of everyday life, including within the academy (Dei 2013: 30). This means that the question is not so much whether there should be collaboration across the colonial divide, but "collaboration on whose terms?" instead (see Dei 2013: 30).

At a minimum, beginning to decolonize as non-Indigenous academics requires us to abandon the pretense of an objective view from nowhere, as Geonpul feminist scholar Aileen Moreton-Robinson emphasizes (2000: Introduction). This means situating ourselves with respect to what feminists might call our "standpoints" (Harding 2004) within unequal relationships, including contemporary colonialism. Arguably, this is already largely common practice among Indigenous scholars. In *Indigenous Methodologies* (2009), Plains Cree and Saulteaux scholar Margaret Kovach states the importance of situating Indigenous scholarship, but indeed all scholarship, this way: "We know what we know from where we stand. We need to be honest about that" (7).

Importantly, situating a researcher's standpoint is not about establishing a rigid, fixed position, but acknowledging that standpoints are contextual and changing. Not least, different relationships may have greater or lesser significance in a given moment and before a given public. Hence, for the purposes of this book, LaRocque situates herself as a Cree-speaking Métis woman, as a professor, as a feminist, and as a unique member of universal humanity. The late Everett Soop (whose insights non-Indigenous researcher Douglas Durst and I lean on extensively in Chapter Three of this book), variously emphasized his identity as an artist, a one-time Blood Tribal council member and a "Native handicapped" man. Taken together, Soop thus draws attention to his relatively dominated position as a disabled Indigenous person while underscoring his agency as a Native handicapped politician, artist and activist. This personal positioning is at the same time a political statement, reminding his audience of the potential political agency of all Indigenous persons with disabilities.

In Chapter Two of this book, a formerly incarcerated woman, Chastity, calls herself a "3rd World Native." She is, however, ambivalent about this way of naming herself, fearing that it repeats stereotypes of the "so tragic" Indigenous person. Hence, she likewise affirms herself as someone with a "soul" that may come "alive" given the necessary support. In contrast, Atleo more confidently contextualizes his perspectives and responsibilities with this self-description:

> I am Tsimshian on my mother's side with relatives from Kitselas, Kitsumkalum and Lax Kw'alaams. On my father's side I am Nuu-chah-nulth-aht from Ahous. My Nuu-chah-nulth name is Chachim'multhnii or "One who does things properly" and I am from the house of Klaq-ish-piilth.

These various ways of situating the self are suggestive of the relational, changing and contextual nature of both shared and personal Indigenous identities. At the same time, they imply multiple diverse "standpoints" from which Indigenous persons know and share their knowledge.

In short, an Indigenous emphasis on relationality rejects the positivist assertion that the knower's social location is ideally irrelevant to research outcomes. If I situate myself, as non-Indigenous, White, female, able-bodied and straight, this reflexively positions my perspectives within multiple unequal relationships of colonialism, race, gender, disability and sexuality. At the same time, I live within a particular historical moment within unequal world relations that, following Alfred (n.d.), I characterize as colonial-capitalist. The world capitalist relations of this historical moment shape many aspects of my life, including the apparently "obvious" need to work for a salary to make a living, which has not existed for most human beings for most of history. But I likewise live in a moment when Indigenous struggles are particularly strong, if threatened, including in the academy, so that my own interest in Indigenous resistance and resurgence is "symptomatic" of this broader agency.

This may sound straightforward. In practice, however, it is not necessarily easy to be honest about where we stand within relations of inequality. It may be self-interested, as when non-Indigenous scholars do not see themselves as embedded within and benefitting from ongoing colonial relations. At the same time, however, as Wilkes observes in Chapter Four of this book, this is no mere "personal" failing of reflexivity. Instead, it reflects unequal relationships of power that naturalize and make us "take for granted" such inequalities, so that our blindness (to use a disability metaphor that may not be innocuous) is overdetermined. Besides Douglas Durst and me, for instance, who are writing specifically about Indigenous resistance and disability in this book, none of the contributing authors describes herself as "able-bodied" — or as "enabled," as one of my students puts it. For Indigenous authors, this may partly reflect Indigenous worldviews that have no comparable concept for what some, from non-Indigenous perspectives, call "defamiliar" (Davidson 2008) bodies. Today, however, many Indigenous persons do identify as "disabled." This means that this failure to situate ourselves with respect to disability arguably erases power inequalities around disabled and defamiliar Indigenous bodies and minds, including as they are manifest — most often by their marginalization — with respect to Indigenous resistance and resurgence. In turn, this reflects broader erasures, themselves suggestive of the relative domination and exclusion of persons with disabilities, including in social scientific literature that institutionally segregates and marginalizes contributions by both Indigenous and disabled persons.

Moreover, if reflexivity recognizes that ways that we are embedded in relationships, including those of contemporary colonialization, this does not resolve issues of power and how to negotiate them in research and teaching. On the contrary, awareness of such power inequalities may be experienced as "paralyzing" (Kovach 2013: 118), so that non-Indigenous scholars become so fearful of making a "mistake" or misinterpreting Indigenous scholarship in ways that cause further harm to Indigenous peoples, that they disengage entirely (Kovach 2013: 118). But Kovach argues that if this is understandable, it is not responsible because it perpetuates ignorance and the ongoing marginalization of diverse Indigenous perspectives. Instead, she suggests that non-Indigenous scholars need to be open to conversation, which means accepting the importance of "ongoing, accepting, caring dialogue" (2013: 120) with those who hold Indigenous knowledges.

Inevitably, this requires efforts on both sides of the colonial relationship. Non-Indigenous researchers must "suspend disbelief" in Indigenous worldviews that we have been taught to ignore or dismiss (Marlene Brandt-Castellano quoted in Kovach 2009: 106). Importantly, this is not the same as suspending all critical faculties, but rather engaging them seriously with an open mind. Meanwhile, Indigenous scholars must "suspend distrust" (106) despite the violence of colonial relationships. This is not simple. Indeed, Andersen and Hokowhitu's (2007) article, "Whiteness: Naivety, Void and Control," starkly suggests that White non-Indigenous actors and scholars are often, or even usually, naïve, vacuous and/or controlling in their interactions with Indigenous peoples and scholarship. Moreover, even if reasonable distrust is suspended, dialogue means accepting the (often time-consuming and tiring and therefore not necessarily welcome) role of "educator" to the non-Indigenous researcher. Ultimately, as LaRocque (2010: 13) suggests, the possibility of such encounters depends on the humanist conviction that if we cannot escape colonial relationships of inequality, neither are we the sum of these relations. Whether Indigenous readers find my own contribution to this book useful or not is for them to judge, but my participation, and those of other non-Indigenous contributors, depends in the final analysis upon this basic humanist conviction.

### "Relational Responsibility" and "Action That Effects Love"

Finally, I turn to the words that conclude this book. Among the ideas that Wilson shares in the Afterword of this book is the emphasis on relational responsibilities. This draws us back to Maracle's statement that opens this introduction: We, each and all of us, have responsibilities for healing relationships with all our relations in the human, natural and spirit worlds. This means that justice is not conceived in the mainstream, colonial language of autonomous liberal individual (or human) rights (see also Corntassel 2008; King, Chapter Seven of this book). Instead, justice appears as a matter of fulfilling responsibilities, in the familiar language, toward "all our relations." Wilson suggests that one of the ways of achieving these renewed, healthy relationships is through Indigenous resurgent "action that effects love."

From dominant academic perspectives, thinking through what love might mean politically — or even admitting that love might be an outcome of the right kind of political action — is unusual and may even look trivial.[5] That this is so is arguably symptomatic of just how twisted contemporary relationships are, including in the academy: as if love, which is necessary to healthy human relationships and actorhood, is not of interest — or only as a literary trope rather than as a political force and aim. In decades of work around international financial institutions, for instance, I do not recall a single reference to love in the academic literature, much less in policy documents. In the world of capitalist political economy, the driving dynamic is the profit motive, so that what might simply be called greed is extensively theorized. But consideration of other human emotions, including love, is excluded from serious analysis.

Even among those willing to consider the political implications of love, there may be skepticism. Human relationships are routinely violent within the world colonial–capitalist system. In such a context, love may appear (far) too much to ask. Afrofuturist jazz musician Sun Ra, for instance, declared himself an angel taking leave of a humanity he saw as irredeemably compromised by our brutal histories (Nelson 2014). Human beings may appear incapable of taking righteous political action, much less political action that "effects love." Furthermore, love may be a dangerous motivation. Christian missionaries inspired by divine love ripped apart Indigenous families and forcibly converted them. To the Church, this violence was forgivable given the vital stakes of saving "heathen" Indigenous souls for all eternity. Maybe we are better off not thinking about love, when love can so easily become a justification for any atrocity. Echoing Aretha Franklin's call for all Black women, I might settle for R-E-S-P-E-C-T (Collins 2009: 127), rooted in the shared humanity of each person on the earth that sustains us all, both as the normative ground zero of political action and its practical aim.

Nonetheless, it is striking that along with Wilson, the voices in this book that are most insistent that love matters both personally and politically are Indigenous women who have experienced incarceration (see Chapter Two of this book). These Indigenous women, among the most disempowered in contemporary colonial society, claim that love is essential against what Aarrestad describes as the "gut-wrenching pain" of becoming a "lost soul." Thus, a woman named Monica writes that if she could "turn back time," she would return to the moment when "I'd be loved, always trusted." Against a history of being "abused, beaten and left behind" that cannot be understood apart from centuries of colonial violence, Darla similarly insists — or more properly hopes — that "It's time to stand up and love me/ Inevitable." Love is asserted as a central, primary good, essential for well-being.

The powerful art exhibition Walking With Our Sisters (2014) may be understood in light of this observation. Hundreds of Indigenous women, including some contributors to this book, made "vamps" or moccasin uppers, left purposefully incomplete in order to "represent the unfinished lives of the (Indigenous) women," over a thousand of whom are missing or murdered across lands claimed by Canada. The exhibit's website insists that these Indigenous women "are sisters, mothers, aunties, daughters, cousins, grandmothers, wives and partners. They have been cared for, they have been loved, they are missing and they are not forgotten." These remembrances cannot bring these women back, but they do counter the colonial dehumanization of these Indigenous women by affirming that they are loved and remembered, that they do matter and that they deserve justice. Love is enacted here, at once artistically and politically, against murderous colonial hatreds.

To take another example described by Aguirre in this book: In Elsipogtog, the multibillion–dollar American company SouthWestern Energy sought to "open up" land for fracking, an ecological devastating process for securing natural gas. To gain access to Indigenous lands, they were supported by colonial legal decisions backed by the force of the Royal Canadian Mounted Police. In response, Indigenous women held up their drums — their beating hearts — against the guns of the colonizers, in defense of their lands, their peoples, their families. In so doing, these women affirmed their survival, their courage and determination to honour their relationships with their ancestors, each other and the natural world. This gesture, dramatically challenging the actions of the naked might of the colonial state acting at the behest of global capital, is another instance of politically enacting love.

To conclude on a personal note: when I read Alex Wilson's Afterword in this book, her call to politically enact love irresistibly reminded me of a passage I had recently read from Shakespeare. Shakespeare is, of course, a central figure in Western literatures, but his plays may be appropriated by any member of humanity who so chooses, as LaRocque (Foreword, this book) might insist. In an early scene of the eponymous play, Antony says to Cleopatra: "Rome in Tiber melt and the wide arch/Of the ranged empire fall. Here is my space" (Shakespeare 2007: 2163). Antony's passion for Cleopatra makes him neglect his empire, which is attacked from all quarters. His empire does not matter because his space is "here" in the love that he shares with Cleopatra.

Of course, today's colonial-capitalist empire will not fall through neglect, but only through sustained struggles and mass Indigenous resistance, supported by non-Indigenous allies. Moreover, as Aguirre specifies in Chapter Eight and as Martineau insists in Chapter Ten (this book), Indigenous worldviews and practices may be less about abstract "space" than about specific "place." So we can "indigenize" Shakespeare for our purposes and say that politically enacting love means making true the saying, "Here is our place." This is not a political principle for future actions, although it is also that. Instead, as this book suggests, this possibility is already being realized by many Indigenous peoples and their supporters, who are reclaiming responsibilities toward lands and seas, the Earth and the sky, the plants and the animals, and other human beings. They are doing so through the arts, in politics, classrooms, daily economics, international diplomacy and daily living, by treating these relationships as valued ends rather than instrumentally as means. Realists will object that there is little room in the colonial-capitalist world for Indigenous resurgence that is conceived in this way: as politically enacting love, so that each and all may truly say, "Here is our space." But that only suggests how necessary this vision is.

## NOTES

1. I understand colonialism as the forcible occupation and formal political rule of one people over another. Capitalism is rooted in the exploitative relationship between, on the one hand, capitalist owners of land, labour and resources and on the other, dispossessed workers alienated from the land, labour and resources who must sell their labour power to make a living.

2. Donations, often a tax break for the wealthy, offer targeted support to Indigenous scholarly programs. Insofar as this is a major source of academic funding, however, this leaves Indigenous voices in the academy dependent on the whims of philanthropists.

3. I adapt this term from John Quiggins's (2010) Zombie Economics: How Dead Ideas Still Walk Among Us.

4. I borrow the is/ought distinction from Western analytical philosophy.

5. But from Nishnaabeg teachings, see Simpson 2011: 74–81; from Black feminist perspectives, see Collins 2009: 185–186.

## REFERENCES

Alfred, Taiaiake. n.d. "Colonialism and State Dependency: Prepared for the National Aboriginal Health Organization Project." <web.uvic.ca/igov/uploads/pdf/Colonialism%20and%20State%20Dependency%20NAHO%20(Alfred).pdf>.

____. 2009a. *Wasáse: Indigenous Pathways of Action and Freedom.* Toronto: University of Toronto.

____. 2009b. "Colonialism and State Dependency." *Journal of Aboriginal Health* 5, 1 (November).

Alfred, Taiaiake, and Jeff Corntassel. 2005. "Being Indigenous: Resurgences Against Contemporary Colonialism." *Government and Opposition* 40, 4 (Autumn).

Altamirano-Jiminez, Isabel. 2013. *Indigenous Encounters with Neoliberalism: Place, Women and the Environment in Canada and Mexico.* Vancouver: University of British Columbia Press.

Ambler, Stella. 2013. *Invisible Women: A Call to Action. A Report on Missing and Murdered Indigenous Women in Canada.* Speaker of the House of Commons. <acatcanada.org/downloadXC2-411-2-1-1-eng.pdf>.

Andersen, Chris. 2014. *Métis: Race, Recognition and the Struggle for Indigenous Peoplehood.* Vancouver: University of British Columbia Press.

Andersen, Chris, and Brendan Hokowhitu. 2007. "Whiteness: Naivety, Void and Control." *Junctures* 8.

Anderson, Kim. 2011. *Life Stages and Native Women: Memory, Teachings and Story Medicine.* Winnipeg: University of Manitoba Press.

Armstrong, Jeannette, and Lally Grauer. 2001. *Native Poetry in Canada: A Contemporary Anthology.* Peterborough: Broadview Press.

Coburn, Elaine et al. 2013. "'Unspeakable Things': Indigenous Research and Social Science." *Socio* 2.

Cole-Dai, Phyllis. 2013. "Walking the Walk." LivingNonviolence (July 15). <livingnonviolence.com/2013/07/walking-walk.html>.

Collins, Patricia Hill. 2009. *Black Feminist Thought: Knowledge, Consciousness and the Politics of Empowerment.* 2nd ed. New York: Routledge.

Corntassel, Jeff. 2012. "Re-envisioning Resurgence: Indigenous Pathways to Decolonization and Sustainable Self-Determination." *Decolonization: Indigeneity, Education and Society* 1, 1.

____. 2008. "Toward Sustainable Self-Determination: Re-Thinking the Contemporary Indigenous Rights Discourse." *Alternatives* 33.

Coulthard, Glen. 2014. *Red Skin, White Masks: Rejecting the Colonial Politics of Recognition.* Minneapolis: University of Minnesota Press.

____. 2007. "Subjects of Empire: Indigenous Peoples and the 'Politics of Recognition' in Canada." *Contemporary Political Theory* 6.

Davidson, Michael. 2008. *Concerto for the Left Hand: Disability and the Disfamiliar Body.* Ann Arbor: University of Michigan Press.

Dei, George Sefa. 2013. "Critical Perspectives on Indigenous Research." *Socialist Studies* 9, 1.

Driskill, Qwo-Li, et al. (eds.). 2011a. *Queer Indigenous Studies: Critical Interventions in Theory, Politics and Literature.* Tucson: University of Arizona Press.

____. 2011b. *Sovereign Erotics: A Collection of Two-Spirit Literature.* Tucson: University of

Arizona Press.

Glaude, Eddie S. 2007. *In a Shade of Blue: Pragmatism and the Politics of Black America.* Chicago: University of Chicago Press.

Green, Joyce (ed.). 2007. *Making Space for Indigenous Feminism.* Black Point, NS: Fernwood Publishing.

Gunder Frank, André. 1966. "The Development of Underdevelopment." *Monthly Review Press.*

Harding, Sandra G. (ed.). 2004. *The Feminist Standpoint Theory Reader: Intellectual and Political Controversies.* New York: Routledge.

Hokowhitu, Brendan. 2013. "Producing Indigeneity." In Evelyn Peters and Chris Andersen (eds.), *Indigenous in the City: Contemporary Identities and Cultural Innovation.* Vancouver: University of British Columbia Press.

Hokowhitu, Brendan, et al. (eds.). 2010. *Indigenous Identity and Resurgence: Researching the Diversity of Knowledge.* Dunedin, NZ: Otago University Press.

Indigenous Peoples Solidarity Movement Ottawa. 2012. "Lee Maracle: The Connection Between Violence Against Women and Violence Against the Earth" (August 28). <youtube.com/watch?v=VdxJYhbTvYw>.

King, Thomas. 2013. *The Inconvenient Indian: A Curious Account of Native People in North America.* Toronto: Doubleday Canada.

Kovach, Margaret. 2013. "Treaties, Truths and Transgressive Pedagogies: Re-imagining Indigenous Presence in the Classroom." *Socialist Studies/Etudes Socialistes* 9, 1, 109–127.

____. 2009. *Indigenous Methodologies: Characteristics, Conversations and Contexts.* Toronto: University of Toronto Press.

LaRocque, Emma. 2010. *When the Other Is Me: Native Resistance Discourse 1850–1990.* Winnipeg: University of Manitoba Press.

____. 2007. "Métis and Feminist: Ethical Reflections on Feminism, Human Rights and Decolonization." In Joyce Green (ed.), *Making Space for Indigenous Feminism.* Black Point, NS: Fernwood Publishing.

____. 2001. "My Hometown Northern Canada South Africa." In Jeannette C. Armstrong and Lally Grauer (eds.), *Native Poetry in Canada: A Contemporary Anthology.* Peterborough, ON: Broadview Press.

Manuel, George, and Michael Posluns. 1974. *The Fourth World: An Indian Reality.* Fernie, BC: Free Press.

Maracle, Lee. 1996. *I Am Woman: A Native Perspective on Sociology and Feminism* second edition. Vancouver: Press Gang Publishers.

Mbembe, Achille. 2013. *Critique de la raison nègre.* Paris: Editions la découverte.

____. 2006. "Nécropolitique." *Raisons politiques: Etudes de pensée politique* 21.

McKegney, Sam. 2014. *Masculindians: Conversations About Indigenous Manhood.* Winnipeg: University of Manitoba Press.

Moreton-Robinson, Aileen. 2000. *Talkin' Up to the White Woman: Indigenous Women and Feminisms.* St. Lucia, AU: University of Queensland Press.

Moses, Daniel David, Terry Goldie and Armand Garnet Ruffo. 2013. *An Anthology of Canadian Native Literature* fourth edition. Don Mills, ON: Oxford University Press Canada.

Nelson, Jez. 2014. "Sun Ra: Jazz's Interstellar Voyager." *The Guardian,* June 15. <theguardian.

com/music/2014/jun/15/sun-ra-jazz-interstellar-voyager>.

Peters, Evelyn, and Chris Andersen. 2013. *Indigenous in the City: Contemporary Identities and Cultural Innovation*. Vancouver: University of British Columbia Press.

Quiggins, John. 2010. *Zombie Economics: How Dead Ideas Still Walk Among Us*. Princeton, NJ: Princeton University Press.

Shakespeare, William. 2007. "The Tragedy of Antony and Cleopatra." In Jonathan Bate and Eric Rasmussen (eds.), *The Royal Shakespeare Company: William Shakespeare's Complete Works*. Hampshire: MacMillan.

Shreve, Bradley Glenn. 2011. *Red Power Rising: The National Indian Youth Council and the Origins of Native Activism*. Norman: University of Oklahoma Press.

Simpson, Leanne. 2011. *Dancing on Our Turtle's Back: Stories of Nishnaabeg Re-Creation, Resurgence, and a New Emergence*. Winnipeg, MB: Arbeiter Ring Publishing.

____ (ed.). 2008. *Lighting the Eighth Fire: The Liberation, Resurgence and Protection of Indigenous Nations*. Winnipeg, MB: Arbeiter Ring Publishing.

Soop, Everett. 1988. "Being Indian and Handicapped." *Saskatchewan Indian* (April). <sicc.sk.ca/archive/saskindian/a88apr13.htm>.

Suzack, Cheryl, et al. (eds.). 2010. *Indigenous Women and Feminism: Politics, Activism, Culture*. Vancouver: University of British Columbia Press.

Tuhiwai Smith, Linda. 1999. *Decolonizing Methodologies: Research and Indigenous Peoples*. Winnipeg, MB: Zed Books.

Walking with Our Sisters. 2014. <walkingwithoursisters.ca>.

Walter, Maggie, and Chris Andersen. 2013. *Indigenous Statistics: A Quantitative Research Methodology*. Walnut Creek, CA: Left Coast Press.

Chapter One

# THE SPLIT HEAD RESISTANCE
## USING IMPERIAL LAW TO CONTRADICT
## COLONIAL LAW FOR ABORIGINAL JUSTICE

*James (Sa'ke'j) Youngblood Henderson*

Like all peoples, Aboriginal peoples are shaped by the contexts that we inhabit and know as the status quo. These contexts make us who we are, whether we want them to or not. We cannot pretend to float above them. We are marinated in the Eurocentric, colonial context. Yet the spell that the status quo cast on our experience is powerful, but never complete. It failed to exhaust us.

This chapter is about the struggle for justice among my generation of Aboriginal peoples, the sons and daughters of the World War II warriors. It is about living with a split head with two cognitive and language systems, and it is about the difficulties of using the legal tools and language of the oppressor to combat oppression. Living with a split head was the dilemma of my generation of Aboriginal peoples; it has changed the landscape of the struggles for current and futures ones.

### The Difficult, Dark Agenda of Justice
I was born in 1944. My generation of Aboriginal peoples grew up with pervasive indignities of forced assimilation through education into Eurocentrism. We were born into a grim, hopeless, confused world, a generation resigned to extinction by state-enforced assimilation, educational policies or in despair because of deep neglect. We struggled with Aboriginal nihilism, living in a meaningless world. We lived in despair and in resignation, trapped under an all–powerful Indian Agent

who controlled our life. Many of us did not survive the infamous residential schools in Canada, in which at least four thousand Aboriginal children died of starvation, neglect and beatings (Indian Country Today Media Network 2014). Some of us did survive the program of ruthless assimilation, but it became our cognitive prison house.

We were living in insidious, grinding poverty, which stemmed from state–sponsored forcible assimilation and hard-edged, colonial oppression and control of all our activities. Racial discrimination thrived everywhere. Little economic opportunity existed in our communities; employment was rare and confined to physical labour hard on the body, mind and spirit. The poverty of our communities was not our traditions; it was the violent tool of Canada to force us to assimilate. Our ancestors, living with nature, had created the fur-trading empire and treaty economy, and we had continued to live off the land. The poverty of my generation was based on lack of cash, but it was the dispossession of our lands and separation from nature that made us dependent on cash for survival. We were poor because we had no cash, but we needed cash because we had been dispossessed from land and nature.

The Department of Indian Affairs (DIA), as it was then known (it is now Aboriginal Affairs), exercised an unfathomable degree of authority over our lives on the reserves. Its mission was to make us vanish, make our heritage and memory disappear, and assimilate us to them. Typically, the DIA did a bad job. Despite our grinding poverty, we did not vanish, although many of us were murdered, including through overwork and starvation in residential schools. We survivors did hold onto our heritage and memories, even if this was enduringly complicated by the indoctrination of Eurocentric ideologies. We knew the facts of colonialism and racism because we lived them as suffering and as despair. But that knowledge was combined with a restless willingness to confront distorting and damaging accounts of our lives as Aboriginal peoples, to identify where they were coming from and whose interests they serve.

But the living conditions generated by the DIA were lower than Third World nations. The gifted leader of the National Indian Brotherhood, George Manuel — with his coauthor Michael Posluns (1974) — conceptualized our economic conditions as a "Fourth World" of Aboriginal Peoples within the first world. As students, we labeled the DIA "the Ministry of Misery." The Ministry created our forced bad education and conflicted identities. We could not escape its pathology of control and brainwashing, which the government determined was necessary to sustain the imaginary and artificial notion of Canada. But colonial ideas did not have a monopoly on our minds; they coexisted with our own sources of knowledge.

Struggling to transform an unjust colonial society was difficult for us, the Aboriginal peoples of my generation. We comprehended, in part, that we were entering into a difficult dark agenda. We were going to have to unravel and contest colonial assumptions. Our efforts would not be appreciated by the mainstream of Canadian society; we would be outcasts and we would be seen as threats. Our own people, who were living on the edge, would look at our efforts with deep concern and alarm. Unable to discern the reason for our existence in an unjust situation, many Aboriginal peoples are stuck in the colonial status quo and cannot conceive of a path for transformation of self, family or society to create a better future that does justice to our humanity. It was in these circumstances that we began our quest for a postcolonial society.

## The Birth of the Split-Head Generation

Despite the Fourth World living conditions and deep despair, the commitment to transforming social relations to achieve justice for Aboriginal peoples is profound and significant in our generation. But we usually lack the theoretical and conceptual foundations for this transformation. The most influential ideas about society deliberately mask colonial relationships of oppression. When we try and use dominant concepts and vocabularies to talk about colonial oppression, we are thwarted because they are designed to hide the colonial relationship. Colonialism is an elaborate ideology, but the colonial relationship itself is hidden and has few theoreticians. The doctrines of the status quo, the Eurocentric monologue, have spoken more loudly. This is true even in decolonized societies, in which colonial ways of thinking and vocabularies persist despite successful decolonialization struggles. Moreover, the task of translating the status quo into a future good is imperfect as we strive to achieve justice using imaginations and words born out of unjust colonial relations.

Of course, some of us are not able to resist, and we are assimilated and co-opted. But many others do resist, and we do so in many ways, including community building, pugnacious oratory, and writing inflammatory rhetoric and tracts. We express our resistance in racial, cultural and political animosity, in "red rage," and in armed as well as ideological rebellion. These pathways of resistance reflect the violent nature of colonialism and its version of power; too often, they trap Aboriginal resistance in the violence of colonial relations rather than subverting them.

In my generation, some of us chose another way to struggle: to enter legal education, deal with its premises, learn the semiotics and nuance of legal arguments, master the colonial and jurispathic legal system, and seek to transform the system. This was a cognitive and strategic resistance that engages the law, comprehends the array of institutions and influences exerted by the dominating power through law, and seeks to transforms them into tools for expressing and honouring deeply held Aboriginal knowledge of a sacred past. We had to master the colonial legal system without surrendering to it. It was the first hard step in a glacial journey toward generating justice out of unjust laws. It was the beginning of a generation of Aboriginal people as lawyers, more commonly known to the Elders as the split-head generation.

The split-head generation of Aboriginal lawyers and scholars were attempting to find resistance to our situation and to speak in the voice of an elusive future. As a first step, we attempted to acknowledge and restore our belief in ourselves and our knowledge systems. As young educators and lawyers, we turned to our ancestors and communities for sources for our collective and individual dignity. We searched for ways to eliminate the grinding poverty of our communities and generate comfort and prosperity. As vanguards, the less than 1 percent of our people who were lawyers, we were attempting to fulfil our destiny; to create and sustain a just society.

The split-head participants were the sons and daughter of the warriors of World War II. We were raised in our Aboriginal languages and worldviews. But the DIA took us away from our parents for residential education or adopted us out to non-Aboriginal parents. Either way, we were forced into a Eurocentric education in English, shaping our tender but not always innocent minds. From the ages of six to sixteen, we were legally required to attend assimilation schools. We were the traumatized students who were high-school educated and sometimes college-educated members in Eurocentric traditions. We didn't choose to be split headed, to live in diverse and divided cognitive realms and languages, but that was our legislative fate, the consequence of the endless but ultimately unsuccessful desire of the Canadian state to assimilate us into being them.

## Eurocentric Traditions and Law: The Good, the Bad and the Ugly

The Eurocentric traditions we were forcibly taught included the good, bad and ugly. They contained racism and colonialism, as well as ideas of human rights and democratic governments. Whether we found the ideas useful or not, we had to confront serious and inherent problems that exist within the English language, its dictionaries created at the height of colonialism. We called English the language of "anguish." It was difficult to learn, much less master. The English vocabulary is loaded with categorical biases, its words freighted with colonial assumptions. Many words we use to challenge the justice of the colonial system resonate with and are derived from the Eurocentric ways of knowing. Because legal words are derived from this system, they are difficult to use to transform the system. Moreover, the spirit of the law is often contradicted by the structure and process of the legal system.

Canadian law was not separate from the colonization process; the colonizers just pretended it was. Indeed, Canadian law was and remains the performance of an institutionalized form of colonization. It is the place in which detailed institutional arrangements of colonial society, created by the imperial Parliament, are made explicit and justified. The law does not "interpret" the empire; it fundamentally reflects the ideals and protects interests of empire. In this sense, the law produces empire. The dominate theme of the colonialists' legal discourse was that Aboriginal rights were extinguished through colonial settlement, the tide of history, and the colonial granting of land — to themselves. Through law, the imperial Parliament developed an innovative menu of how the extinguishment of Aboriginal rights occurred.

Under the theory of extinguishment, however, colonial legislation and the common law of colonization became a prison house for both the colonizer and the colonized. For the split heads, the struggle was to reclaim their knowledge systems, languages, legal system, and their treaties with the king and queen. For Canadians, it was the struggle to conceal how they had broken every treaty in the process of decolonizing their existence to become an independent nation controlling Aboriginal resources and wealth.

The way out of the colonial prison house for us, as Aboriginal lawyers of the split-head generation, was to restore our ancestors' aboriginal rights and imperial treaties with the king and queen of the United Kingdom rather than rely on the quest for equality with the colonists. More than three hundred treaties had conditionally allowed British settlements in their territories (Henderson 2007). These treaties had generated the concept of Canada, an idea appropriated from the Haudenosaunee language for their villages. The colonizers, however, used Canada to describe the fiction of the British and French as the two founding nations. They ignored the treaties, and colonized and oppressed Aboriginal confederacies, nations and peoples. The colonial and neocolonial society of constitutional aliens over Aboriginal peoples were generated by acts of the imperial Parliament. The imperial Parliament created the Dominion of Canada and gave to the newly created Canadian government the constitutional right to enact legislative power over "Indians and lands reserved for Indians" (United Kingdom 1867: s. 91(24)). The Dominion of Canada did not implement the treaties with their new power, although they were under the authority of the treaties; instead, they failed their imperial treaty obligations and made an oppressive and tricky federal Indian Act that bound the Indians in colonial chains and forced them to assimilate to British values.

The Indian Act created a DIA and its bureaucratic legacy that brought our families to the abyss. This bureaucratic consciousness was pervasive in all aspects of our life; the split heads captured this consciousness through the notion of the "bozone" the mental atmosphere around civil servants that stopped any good ideas from penetrating their consciousness. Their arrogant response to every attempt we made to change our fates was a discourse of impossibility. We were constantly told "that is impossible" or simply "no." Some were better than others at rejecting our ideals or suggestions, but whether they said "no" directly or meant "no" through innumerable codes, their steady purpose was to refuse our actions, our ideals, our purposes. We called them "ignoramus" for their stupidity, for acting like an ass. Others showed less dedication, so we merely called them the "old farts," but they opposed us just the same.

Ironically, with the introduction of an equal rights movement in the 1960s by Black people and women, life would get worse, not better, for Aboriginal peoples. The DIA was poised to launch its "equalization" plan for us, outlined in the 1969 White Paper, which would liquidate treaty rights, terminate Indian reserves and cut off the limited lifelines of federal welfare. This welfare was interpreted by the federal government as charity; it was barely enough to keep dispossessed Aboriginal communities alive, but even this meagre fulfilment of Aboriginal rights was interpreted as too much. In typical bozone reasoning, the DIA used the White Paper to assert that the Indians were disadvantaged because of their unique legal status under the constitution. They argued that this constitutional status of Indians and the policies that have flowed from it have kept the Indian people apart from and behind other Canadians (Government of Canada 1969). Aboriginal peoples recognized this plan immediately for what it was: the final solution or total assimilation.

## Indigenous Renaissance and the Just Society

Against these confident and rock-hard forces of assimilation, the Elders and the youth successfully fought this phase of the final solution. Critical to this struggle was the leadership of Harold Cardinal, a recent and brilliant college graduate. We had many gifted leaders, but none was better than Cardinal with his unique blend of Cree genius and Eurocentric strategy. His writing exposed the nature of the unjust society and gave the movement the goal of making Canada a just society (Cardinal 1969; Cardinal 1977; Indian Chiefs of Alberta 2011 [1970]). A few years earlier, in 1967, Chief Dan George had delivered his famous lament, "Oh Canada," which he pronounced during Canada's celebration of its centennial at the Empire Stadium in Vancouver (George and Hirnschall 2004: 12–13). This lament was at the same time a call to action, as he summoned us to "shatter the barriers of our isolation." Against the hard edge of contemporary colonialism, he told us to look forward and assert our sovereignty: "So shall the next hundred years be the greatest in the proud history of our tribes and nations." Together, Cardinal and George gave us our vision, a set of ideals, to which Aboriginal peoples could commit.

This inspired many different actions. We, the split heads, would use the law to make the just society that Cardinal and George helped us to dream. This vision directed our path to the society we wanted to live in: treaty promises fulfilled; freedom from being bossed around by Indian Act agents; the stabilization of Aboriginal society through law; the end of forced assimilation. We wanted choices of life and for all Aboriginal Peoples to live more fully and freely. We wanted to strengthen our knowledge systems, our languages and our heritages. We wanted to fulfill our gifts from the Creator, not be a copy of anyone else. After all, we were Aboriginals.

The split heads' various political and legal strategies against the final solution created doubts about the White Paper proposals in parts of Canadian society. They penetrated even the bozone layer of the Canadian government, and the policy was temporarily withdrawn. Toward the fall of 1973, Canada issued "a statement of policy" to "signify the Government's recognition and acceptance of its continuing constitutional responsibility to Indians and lands reserved for Indians" (Government of Canada 1973). Despite such statements, the vision of Aboriginal peoples that the White Paper outlined remained the enduring vision of the DIA (Weaver 1981).

Beginning in the late 1970s, the Aboriginal movement was led by split heads. We were educated in the colonizers' schools and we used this knowledge to challenge imperial rule. We seized the initiative through the National Indian Brotherhood, brought forth our grievances and proposed solutions, and more often than not accomplished the kind of progress and cultural restoration that they dared to dream of and seek. Their dreams, visions and action created the transformation. The transformation was not done by the state; it was forced on reluctant governments and ran counter to widely held assumptions and premises. Our parents saw this as a terrible and exceptional risk for us and for the ordinary and vulnerable. We knew this risk. Noel Starblanket, head of the National Indian Brotherhood, asserted in 1978: "It is clear that if Indians are ever going to acquire Indian control of Indian lands, we will have to assert those rights ourselves. And if it takes confrontation ... so be it." He also knew that "we must be collectively prepared to accept the consequences" (*Saskatchewan Indian* 1978: 4). Domination, humiliations and poverty press different peoples in fundamentally different ways. We knew most would have to endure turmoil to create and live this vision of Aboriginal justice.

Over the course of a generation, however, the split heads achieved a stunning transformation in the structure of law in Canada and the United Nations that is little understood or appreciated, even today. Reaching forward from a base in poverty and domination through the assertions and negations, the collusions and the transient confrontations, our practical problem solving led us to national and international sites of both "consistent resistance" and "constructive deconstruction." This would generate a struggle for abstract rights of human dignity and the constitutional recognition of aboriginal and treaty rights. Such struggles shaped the landscape of confrontation and the politics of accommodation. These situations and processes yielded to a right-based agenda as the style of our generation's

Indigenous renaissance, which focused on developing our Aboriginal knowledge systems and languages; sustaining our Aboriginal teachings and humanity; and asserting our dignity, goals and relationships.

## Red Rage and Read Rage

Despite important if partial political and legal victories in Canada, and in international bodies such as the United Nations, Aboriginal peoples continued then and still continue to live under colonial oppression. The consequences are great suffering. Our grim lives create a cycle of deep rage, often called "red rage." For the split-head generation, this was sometimes called "read" rage: We raged against the lies we read in the official colonial histories of our peoples and we raged against the colonial policies we read and were subject to, policies supposedly made for us but actually created to dominate us. This rage is manifested in bad health and bad choices. But more often than not, red rage brought Aboriginal people before the criminal justice system as "cases." Nihilism, red rage, poverty and a racist criminal justice system continue to cause the overpopulating of Aboriginal people in the prison system, at a world record pace. Currently, about 27% of people in provincial and territorial custody and 20% of those in federal prisons are Aboriginal, although Aboriginal peoples make up about 3% of the population in Canada (Statistics Canada 2013). Aboriginal women make up 40% of those in custody. These numbers tell us something about the scale of injustice, but they say nothing about the colonial circumstances and persistent racism faced by Aboriginal peoples, nor about the rage and suffering that are behind these numbers.

The Crown, that aloof monarch with whom we had entered into treaties, was never meant to apply her justice system to our peoples; in the treaties, our ancestors had never agreed to this idea. But confronted with the number of Aboriginal individuals before the criminal justice system, the split-head attorneys were faced with the practical necessity of trying to protect our people within this system. Tragedy-by-tragedy, we won many cases. We rebelled against the lack of justice as well as a lack of vision in the criminal justice system. We proved through many inquiries and in the Royal Commission on Aboriginal Peoples (Government of Canada 1996) that the criminal justice system was broken for First Nations and had failed Aboriginal people. Eventually, in the Gladue case (R. v. Gladue 1999: para. 58–64), even the Supreme Court formally acknowledged this failure. We knew we had to reform the criminal justice system or, better yet, re-create it consistent with our aboriginal and treaty rights. But instead of fixing the system, Aboriginal lawyers and their character got blamed for bringing attention to the broken, racist system. The character of Aboriginal peoples were blamed for the high numbers of our peoples being captured and criminalized.

We knew that the direct and indirect schemes of the DIA, its thick bozone, had created our intergenerational catastrophes. But the departmental failure to assimilate us had transformed into a hard-edge resentment, so that the department blamed us for our poverty and for our Fourth World living conditions. Through statistics, they created the idea of a deficient Indian culture. They emphasized a predatory chief and council system. And they communicated this message to Canadian politicians and citizens, rekindling the rawest nerves and explosive issue of race. At the same time, the DIA discourse ignored the fact that colonial governments had purposefully destroyed ancient governance traditions and created the chief and council system through legislation. The government camouflaged the legacy of White supremacy and colonialism and class injustices. This meant that despite the magnitude of the problem, which even its own statistics showed, and despite some victories we won for individual cases, we still wait for fundamental legal reform and action (Bilson, Dumont and Smith 1998: 383–430). In the meantime, Aboriginal people brought before colonial law are brutally confronted with the racism embedded in the so-called formal legal "justice" system.

## Constitutional Struggles: Rights that "Might Have Been"

Lacking any significant political influence or power, the split-head lawyers focused instead on the constitutional recognition of our Aboriginal and treaty rights. But the colonial response to our demands was incomprehensible and obstinate. In Canada, constitutional reform or patriation was a product of constitutional politics with the United Kingdom. Canadians were attempting to end formal ties with the United Kingdom while denying Aboriginal peoples treaty rights in the patriated constitution of Canada. Then-Prime Minister Trudeau cynically referred to Aboriginal rights as "might-have-been" (Trudeau 1969) in an act of erasure meant to deny that treaty rights had ever existed.

We in the split-head generation knew that we had to enshrine our rights in the constitution or forever be dominated by the political majority. Political solutions and policies were fragile in the Canadian parliamentary system because they depended on the capacity and willingness of the majority society to explore complex histories. They tended to address consequences, not causes. The existing process of democratic politics could not correct these accumulated effects of colonial law, both intended and actual, which represented frozen and entrenched prejudices of the colonial government and of the majority (Ministry of Indian Affairs and Northern Development 1997).

To displace the colonial structure of governmental powers that had been established and then nourished for more than a century was a monumental challenge. These institutions discriminated against Aboriginal people's knowledge and legal tradition as primitive (Henderson 2006: 8–16). They were rooted in the widespread belief in the collective inferiority of Aboriginal peoples and the idea that our Fourth World living conditions were the product of pathological cultures rather than the outcome of centuries of genocidal colonial policies and ongoing colonial oppression. In these circumstances, the idea of equal protection of the laws — legal generality — was ineffective and illusory. We needed to fight for specific protections of Aboriginal rights.

In 1978, Canada tabled another a statement, titled "A Time for Action," under the office of Prime Minister Trudeau. It aimed at constitutional reform to end Canada's colonial status in the United Kingdom and sought to finalize Canada's constitutional independence. For the first time, this statement recognized Aboriginal and treaty rights as one of the principles to guide the renewal of federation (Trudeau 1978). Its proposal on constitutional reform recognized the "original inhabitants" and provided a nonderogation clause for their rights of the Native peoples, mostly undeclared in colonial law (Pentney 1987: 1).

Yet in the unfolding constitutional process, Aboriginal peoples faced many obstacles. First, and most important, we were not organized for the fast-paced constitutional processes. Second, the federal and provincial governments dominated the debates with their quibbling concerns. Finally, when attention was focused on Aboriginal rights, Aboriginal peoples faced the task of articulating our concerns from the shadows of the hall and corners of the conferences; we were not allowed to participate in the First Ministers meeting. Our basic position was that until agreement could be reached on entrenchment of our Aboriginal and treaty rights, we opposed any patriation of Canadian independence by the United Kingdom. The imperial responsibilities of the United Kingdom arising from Aboriginal rights, treaties and imperial acts had never been transferred to colonial Canada, and any such transfer required the consent of the treaty nations.

We began a lobbying strategy and activities with the special joint parliamentary committee (Government of Canada 1980; 1981) and the United Kingdom (United Kingdom 1980; Sanders 1983), as well as the United Nations Human Rights Committee (Henderson 1980–81; Mi'kmaq Society 2005). Consistent with our shared position of Aboriginal peoples, in January 1981, the Government of Canada agreed to give positive recognition to Aboriginal and treaty rights in the proposed constitutional bill, the Canada Act:

(1) The aboriginal and treaty rights of the aboriginal peoples of Canada are hereby recognized and affirmed.

(2) In this Act, "aboriginal peoples of Canada" includes the Indian, Inuit and Métis peoples of Canada (Government of Canada, 1981).

These rights were shielded from the individual rights proposed in the Canadian Charter of Rights and Freedoms (1982: s. 25). Additionally, a future constitutional conference was established to identify and define these rights (Constitution Act 1982: s. 37(1)). We filed declarative actions in United Kingdom courts challenging the validity of enacting the proposed Canada Act, 1982 (Queen v. Secretary of State, 1981) without the consent of the treaty nations.

In 1982, the United Kingdom enacted the Canada Act, and these constitutional rights were affirmed in the patriation of the constitution of Canada. The Supreme Court in R. v. Sparrow (1990) understatedly admitted the governments' avoidance of aboriginal and treaty rights in the colonial era. The decision recognized the long and difficult struggle for the constitutional reconciliation of aboriginal rights. We finally had our rights constitutionally recognized.

## Traditions and Continuity

Implementing these constitutional rights became another tough battle. The Canadian government did not change any legislation to be consistent with the new constitution. The provincial governments, with the collusion of the federal government, turned to its courts to seek to show that they had extinguished our aboriginal rights prior to 1982. They argued that they had legal bases for eliminating our constitutional rights to life: our ability to fish, hunt and trap to feed our families. Fishing and hunting regulations became the source of judicial decisions concerning our constitutional rights. We spent millions of dollars, requiring important sacrifices in cash-strapped Aboriginal communities, to protect our right to eat for survival. The Crown rejected the premise because it feared the consequences: recognition of Aboriginal treaty rights enshrined in their own constitution.

In 1990, the Supreme Court decision in Sparrow (1990: 401) rejected all the extinguishment theories that had been proposed. It acknowledged that the monarch could extinguish Aboriginal rights, but the sovereign's intent must be clear and plain. It also noted that colonial actions and legislations were not the same as the sovereign's action. Of course, as Aboriginal peoples, we do not believe that our lands and our rights can be taken from us. These rights are inherent and Creator-given. Nonetheless, it is clear that even the Canadian Supreme court acknowledges that only the sovereign has the power to break treaties; this is not a power that the colonial legislatures hold.

Since 1997, however, the courts' analysis of existing aboriginal rights begins with the assumption, which Chief Justice Lamer articulated in Delgamuukw that "Let's face it, we are all here to stay" (1997: para. 186). This principle is used to justify the colonists' retention of lands that have been unlawfully taken from Aboriginal people. For instance, the court found that under the Royal Proclamation of 1763 and the Treaty of 1827, the original alienation of Aboriginal title to a land speculator and third parties were *void ab initio*. That is, that there was no evidence of extinguishment of Aboriginal title and no justification for the Crown activities on these lands (Chippewas of Sarnia 1999: para. 752). Yet these territories were not restored to the authority of Aboriginal peoples. Through such decisions, the courts taught us that the integrity of the law would not be given the highest possible importance; instead, what matters are protections for the colonists and their heirs. As Audre Lorde observes, "The Master's tools have not been designed to dismantle the Master's house" (1984: 110).

Instead of understanding Aboriginal rights within First Nations jurisprudence and legal traditions, the courts have been concerned with classifying the activities and practices of Aboriginal claimants within and against Eurocentric legal traditions (Henderson 2007: 178–227). Absurdly, Aboriginal claimants must prove their practices, traditions and customs based on evidence of precontact manifestations. They must travel to a distant, often silent past to reveal and demonstrate Aboriginal rights or title at the time when the British king asserted sovereignty over their territories. Specifically, before colonial courts, Aboriginal claimants are required to: (1) show to the perspective of Aboriginal peoples before contact; (2) identify precisely the specific nature of the claim being made; (3) ensure that the practice, custom or tradition is of central significance to the Aboriginal society in question; (4) ensure that the cultural claims are those which have continuity with those that existed prior to contact; (5) demonstrate that the right claim is not derived from European influence; (6) ensure that the right is of independent significance to the Aboriginal culture in which it exists; (7) take into account both the relationship of Aboriginal peoples to the land and the distinctive societies and cultures of Aboriginal peoples; (8) demonstrate how the common law rules of evidence have to be modified in adjudicating precontact evidence; and (9) demonstrate that Aboriginal right is cognizable to and conformable with the non-Aboriginal legal system of Canada. These requirements reveal a deep connection between judicial review and prejudice that entrench social hierarchies and colonial biases (Marshall/Bernard 2005: para. 48–50); only Aboriginal worldviews, customs, practices and proofs that conform to non-Aboriginal legal standards are accepted in colonial courts.

At the same time, common law assumes that every immigrant to Canada in possession of land is presumed to have a valid title (McNeil 1999). These settlers are not required to unearth centuries-old archival proof of title, to show the perspectives of Europeans prior to contact with Aboriginal peoples, to demonstrate that private property claims have existed in European communities prior to contact with Aboriginals, to prove the "independent significance" of private property rights to European culture and so on. They are certainly not required to show that their rights claims, including private property rights over the land, conform to Aboriginal ideas of justice. Colonial ideas are the unnamed, assumed standard for Aboriginal rights, but colonial rights do not have to be proved against any Aboriginal standards using Aboriginal notions of justice. This is the fundamental asymmetry of colonial relations as institutionalized in the legal system.

Some might argue that the legal struggles of the split-head generation were not useful, that they did not matter or that they showed only the intransigence and intolerance of colonial power. But we would argue that even with hindsight, these legal battles are not only about what happens in courts. They are our efforts to show, in the legal domain as in every sphere of life, that Aboriginal peoples are fully human. Of course, we know this. But we cannot allow our humanity to be attacked and undermined, including through colonial law. Nowhere is this struggle to make a statement about our humanity more evident than in the international arena.

## Aboriginal Rights Are Human Rights

The struggle for the split-head generation began during the constitutional struggle in Canada. This struggle was carried over into the thirty-year struggle to be recognized as a person with human rights in the United Nations (UN). We pursued this struggle in the various fora created by the UN, including the UN Working Group on Indigenous Populations, 1981, and the UN Working Group on the Draft Declaration (on the Rights of Indigenous Peoples), 1995. We went through two monumental struggles to create an international decade for the world's Indigenous peoples and to establish the UN Permanent Forum on Indigenous Issues, developing new forms of Indigenous diplomacy through these processes. Yet these struggles were not a legal intervention; they were about combatting Eurocentrism expressed in public international law. Colonial commitments masquerading as universal rights were quickly exposed in our struggles; our demands around self-determination ignored because our humanity was denied.

For many decades, these fora became the modern audience of deaf men, men who could not hear or understand our arguments. Our personhoood and our humanity were questioned in humiliating ways. Many representatives of colonial, decolonized and postcolonial nation-states called for the universalization of human rights, but interpreted them in ways that rejected our existence as distinct peoples. Others failed to understand the necessity of the equal application of existing human rights to Indigenous peoples (Cobo 1987; Barsh 1983; Anghie 1999). In particular, they rejected the right of Indigenous peoples to self-determination because it might lead to unacceptable limitations of their privileges and freedoms. The resistance of nation-states was based on their interpretation of state legitimacy and territorial integrity in colonial and UN law. They ignored the requirement that the law grants such immunity only to those states that conduct themselves in conformity with the principles of equality and self-determination of all peoples (Stavenhagen 1994; Battiste and Henderson 2000).

Very few academics or universities, either in law or the humanities, supported or helped the Aboriginal quest for equal human rights in these crucial discussions. Like their nation-states, Eurocentric scholars are struggling with our transformation from being a force of nature with no role in politics or production. They have known us when we were unable to act, barely able to survive, given the crushing legacy of genocidal politics and the horrors of the residential school system. But now we are becoming a force. We have always known our own humanity, but we are demanding that this be universally recognized. In the UN system, however, we learned — with difficulty — that civilization and its institutions, including the United Nations, sustain and develop colonial relations. In such systems, Aboriginal peoples are perceived only negatively, as outside of civilization, which is identified with the institutions of the European nation-state.

We did find some allies in the global assembly, with its complex structures and protocols. We learned European diplomatic skills to assert our human rights through peaceful dialogue (Henderson 2008). In the passage of the UN Declaration on the Rights of Indigenous People, signed in 2007, the UN General Assembly signaled a new global consensus that formally brought to an end the nation-states' history of oppression of Indigenous peoples. One hundred and forty-three countries affirmed the Human Rights Council's recommendation to extend human rights and fundamental freedoms to Indigenous peoples. Before this, we were not seen as humans in any global legal document. Canada voted against the declaration, but eventually had to endorse it (Government of Canada 2010). However, Canada refuses to implement it as it had other human rights covenants (Government of Canada 2001). Human rights are merely for external show.

## The Split Head Dilemma

Despite these legal changes in the constitution and human rights, the bozone still exists and controls many aspects of our lives. As Cherokee writer Thomas King (2012) commented, Canada loves dead Indians, ignores live Indians and hates legal Indians. The Canadian governments of the day do not recognize Aboriginal nation-states. They have ignored their own commissions and the decisions of their own courts. When they do recognize the decisions, they fail to fully implement them. They delay in the hopes of finding a legal loophole in their own laws. In short, they do not want to end their colonial fantasies and myths about their own nation or to expose the injustices that have informed the construction of state institutions and practices. They do not want to create an exemplary and just postcolonial state.

They do not want to sustain these constitutional efforts at institutional reform. They reject the idea of a compound sovereignty of the treaties that include Aboriginal peoples in the political and adjudicative realms. They want those Aboriginal peoples who have constitutional rights to vanish into separate institutions that mimic colonial ones and so confirm Eurocentric superiority. All these efforts are attempts to conceal the constitutive contradiction or unwanted side effects of the artificial settler state and its laws, which is premised on the idea that Aboriginals are not part of humanity and therefore do not have rights.

My generation, the split-head generation, was born in an unjust colonial society. We were educated in a system that conceals the unjust colonial nature of the society in which we live. This was the dilemma for both Aboriginal peoples and Canadians of my generation. The colonized have suffered from the dilemma, and the colonizers have profited from it, but neither has escaped the unequal relations of colonialism that govern our lives. Since the split-head generation, we have asserted ourselves and won some rights as Aboriginal peoples. In so doing, we have changed the landscapes of struggles for current and future generations of Aboriginal peoples. But colonialism and its multiple oppressions are still a reality; the dilemma of creating a just society out of an unjust present is the challenge that current and future generations have inherited.

## References

Anghie, Antony. 1999. "Finding the Peripheries: Sovereignty and Colonialism in Nineteenth Century International Law." *Harvard International Law Journal* 40, 1.

Barsh, Russel L. 1983. "Indigenous North America and Contemporary International Law." *Oregon Law Review* 62, 73.

Battiste, Marie, and James (Sa'ke'j) Youngblood Henderson. 2000. *Protecting Indigenous Knowledge and Heritage: A Global Challenge*. Saskatoon, SK: Purich Publishing.

Bilson, Elizabeth, Hélène Dumont, and Madam Justice Gene Anne Smith. 1998. *Justice to Order: Adjustment to Changing Demands and Co-ordination Issues in the Justice System in Canada*. Montréal: Les Éditions Thémis.

Cardinal, Harold. 1977. *The Rebirth of Canada's Indians*. Edmonton, AB: M.G. Hurtig.

____. 1969. *The Unjust Society: The Tragedy of Canada's Indians*. Edmonton, AB: M.G. Hurtig.

Chippewas of Sarnia Band v. Canada (Attorney General) 1999 O.J. No. 1406, affirmed (2000), 195 D.L.R. (4th) 135 (Ont. C.A.) application for leave to appeal dismissed without reasons, S.C.C. Bulletin, 2001 at 1998.

Cobo, Jose R. Martinez. 1987. *Study of the Problem of Discrimination against Indigenous Populations*. E/CN.4/ Sub.2/1986/7/Add.4. <undesadspd.org/IndigenousPeoples/ LibraryDocuments/Mart%C3%ADnezCoboStudy.aspx>.

Delgamuukw v. The Queen. 1997. 3 S.C.R. 1010.

George, Dan, and H. Hirnschall. 2004. *The Best of Chief Dan George*. Surrey, ON: Hancock House.

Government of Canada. 2010. *Canada's Statement of Support on the United Nations*

*Declaration on the Rights of Indigenous Peoples.*

____. 2001. *Report of the Standing Senate Committee on Human Rights: Promises To Keep: Implementing Canada's Human Rights Obligations.*

____. 1996. *Royal Commission on Aboriginal Peoples.* <collectionscanada.gc.ca/ webarchives/20071115053257/http://www.ainc-inac.gc.ca/ch/rcap/sg/sgmm_e. html>.

____. 1981. "Minutes of the Proceedings and Evidence of the Special Joint Parliamentary Committee of the Senate and House of Commons of Canada." January 30, Issue No. 49, at 9–10 at s. 34.

____. 1980–81. "Mi'kmaq Nationimouw and Human Rights: Communication to Human Rights Committee of the United Nations." Four-part series. *Ontario Indian* (December 1980 to April 1981).

____. 1980. "Minutes of the Proceeding and Evidence of the Special Joint Parliamentary Committee of the Senate and House of Commons on the Constitution of Canada." December 1. Issue No. 16 at 12–13; December 2, 1980, Issue No. 17 at 113–14; and December 16, 1980, Issue No. 27 at 87–88.

____. 1973. "Statement by the Honourable Jean Chrétien, Minister of Indian Affairs and Northern Development on Claims of Indian and Inuit People." (August 8.)

____. 1969. "Statement of the Government of Canada on Indian Policy." Ottawa: Author.

Henderson, James (Sa'ke'j) Youngblood. 2008. *Indigenous Diplomacy and Rights of Peoples: Achieving Recognition.* Saskatoon, SK: Purich Press.

____. 2007. *Treaty Rights in the Constitution of Canada.* Toronto: Carswell Publishing.

____. 2006. *First Nations Jurisprudence and Aboriginal Rights: Defining a Just Society.* Saskatoon, SK: Native Law Centre.

Indian Chiefs of Alberta. 2011. "Citizens Plus." *Aboriginal Policy Studies* 1, 2. <ejournals. library.ualberta.ca/index.php/aps/article/view/11690/8926>.

Indian Country Today Media Network. 2014. "More than 4000 Indigenous Children Died in Canada's Residential Schools: Commission." (January 7). <indiancountrytodaymedianetwork.com/2014/01/07/more-4000-Indigenous-children-died-canadas-residential-schools-commission-153011>.

King, Thomas. 2012. *The Inconvenient Indian: A Curious Account of Native People in North America.* Toronto: Doubleday Canada.

Lorde, Audre. 1984. *Sister Outsider: Essays and Speeches.* Freedom, CA: Crossing Press.

Manuel, George, and Michael Posluns, 1974. *The Fourth World: An Indian Reality.* New York: Free Press.

McNeil, Kent. 1999. "The Onus of Proof of Aboriginal Title." *Osgoode Hall Law Journal* 37, 775–803.

Ministry of Indian Affairs and Northern Development. 1997. *Gathering Strength: Canada's Aboriginal Action Plan.* <ahf.ca/downloads/gathering-strength.pdf>.

Pentney, W.F. 1987. *The Aboriginal Rights Provisions in the Constitution Act, 1982.* Saskatoon: University of Saskatchewan Press.

R. v. Gladue. 1999. 1 S.C.R. 688.

R. v. Marshall/ R. v. Bernard. 2005. 2 S.C.R. 220.

R. v. Sparrow. [1990]. 1 S.C.R. 1075.

Sanders, Douglas. 1983. "The Indian Lobby." In Keith Banting and Richard Simeon (eds.),

*And No One Cheered: Federalism, Democracy, and the Constitution Act.* Toronto: Methuen.

*Saskatchewan Indian.* 1978. "'We Should Assert Our Rights Now', Says Starblanket." (September). <sicc.sk.ca/archive/saskindian/a78sep04.htm>.

Statistics Canada. 2013. *Adult Correctional Statistics in Canada, 2010/2011.* <statcan.gc.ca/pub/85-002-x/2012001/article/11715-eng.htm#a7>.

Stavenhagen, Rodolfo. 1994. "Indigenous Rights: Some Conceptual Problems." In Willem Assies and André Hoekema (eds.), *Indigenous Peoples' Experience and Self-Government.* Copenhagen: IWGIA and the University of Amsterdam.

Trudeau, Pierre Elliott. 1978. "A Time for Action: Toward the Renewal of the Canadian Federation." Ottawa: Supply and Services Canada.

____. 1969. "Transcript of the Prime Minister's Remarks at the Vancouver Liberal Association Dinner, Seaforth Armories, Vancouver, British Columbia." (August 8).

United Kingdom. 1980. "Foreign and Commonwealth Affairs Committee of the British House of Commons." (The Kershaw Committee.) Report, 2, 2.

____. 1867. *British North America Act.* <solon.org/Constitutions/Canada/English/ca_1867.html>.

Weaver, Sally.1981. *Making Canadian Indian Policy: The Hidden Agenda, 1968–70.* Toronto: University of Toronto Press.

Chapter Two

# INCARCERATION AND ABORIGINAL WOMEN IN CANADA
## ACTS OF RESILIENCE AND RESISTANCE

*Christine A. Walsh and Shirley A. Aarrestad*

*Somewhere along the way I became hopeless.*
*I got lost in my soul.*
*Look, look closely.*
*Open your eyes to my soul. Do you dare?*
*I am right here, please don't look away.*
*I was one of the homeless people out there and you walked right by me.*
*Look, look I am here. Why did you walk by me and look right through me?*

*— Shirley*

## An Invitation

In this chapter, we respond to Shirley's call to attention. We invite your averted gaze to refocus on Aboriginal women who have been ensnared in the cycle of poverty, homelessness and incarceration in Canada. In doing so, we give primacy to Aboriginal women's lived experiences, women's voices, women's stories of resilience and women's acts of resistance. Too often in our everyday lives, in our activism but also in our scholarship, we "walk by" Aboriginal women like Shirley. In this chapter, we respond to Shirley's insistence that "I am right here." We "look closely" at what she and other Aboriginal women choose to share with us and we take seriously their experiences and their insights.

## Who We Are

I write as a White feminist settler. I write from my personal moral stance. I write from my social work professional discipline's imperative of social justice. I also write as an apology in an effort to redress "White expert" colonial dynamics. My profession is not benign in the oppression of Indigenous people. Undeniably, "early social work practices were complicit with government colonial actions" (Sinclair 2004: 50), contributing "to the practices of colonization and dispossession" (Healy 2000: 61). This process continues through Western social work practices and education, which have failed to incorporate Indigenous worldviews and epistemologies or account for the social, political, economic or worldview realities of First Peoples' daily lives (Dumbrill and Green 2008). I write as an ally of Aboriginal women, who according to Bishop (2002) are people who recognize the unearned privilege they receive from society's patterns of injustice and take responsibility for changing these patterns (Bishop 2002). I write in collaboration with my friend and colleague, Shirley.

*I am a First Nations woman born in Prince Albert, Saskatchewan. At six months of age, I was taken away from my birth family in Sturgeon Lake First Nations and placed into a foster home. My foster family, the Aarrestads, is White Norwegian of American descent. Consisting of my Mom and Dad, Mary and Ozzie, brother Joe, sister Rachel, and my best friend and sister Rosemary, my foster family legally adopted me at the age of two years old. I became a twin on August 26, 1970. My Mom still boasts about how she got twins that day. She was going into labour when the social worker came to either take me away or have the papers signed for my adoption. The adoption papers were signed and then Rosemary, my sister, was born: two daughters, with two very different beginnings and two very different lives as adults. I am short, stout, brown eyed, with black hair and yes, Aboriginal; Rosemary is tall, lean, blue eyed, with the blonde hair characteristic of her Norwegian heritage.*

*Why do I write? I have been questioning myself on so many levels. In my life now, I could be grieving for so much loss, for the pain I have endured. Instead, I have been given an opportunity to finally find me through writing about myself as an Aboriginal woman. Yes there have been many tears shed during this process. Yet I feel an excitement of letting go and finally feeling a sense of being able to find me within my own soul, that of being an Aboriginal woman. In writing, I am filling up that emptiness I have so faithfully carried around within me for so long.*

*— Shirley*

## A Call to Action

This chapter outlines the contextual factors drawn from the scholarly literature that place Aboriginal women at severe risk for being in conflict with the law. We highlight women's experience within the cycle of incarceration by sharing their own stories. By doing so, we hope to move beyond the usual rhetoric that casts women exclusively as stigmatized, victimized and oppressed subjects. Here we recast these women's experiences as stories that are also about agency, hope and renewal. This does not mean denying the hard truths of Aboriginal women's lives or denying the feelings of despair and hopelessness that many of them experience, often persistently over the course of their lives. Part of the story of Aboriginal women's resilience is precisely to recognize that survival in inhuman circumstances is itself an enormous, often valiant struggle. Importantly, this is not enough — bare survival is not the aim of Aboriginal women. They are seeking "a different life," one in which they are valued and loved as Aboriginal women. One in which they can be actors in their own lives and play key roles in their families, communities and in society.

## Hide and Seeking

*Growing up was painful, abused, beaten, and left behind*
*Starving, dirty, alone, not knowing which way to go.*
*Strangers, all around me with fake smiles at night,*
*Morning comes with pain*
*My doing hiding game*
*I thought and prayed, it ended, when I was little*
*Through my trials and tribulations, lost everything, even me*
*Some days I even changed my name*
*And feeling I'm the one to blame*
*My life is a mess the least to say*
*I tried to run away*
*How impossible that can be*
*So many times I cried 'poor me'*
*No families no ties, now which way to try*
*I lost me*
*I LOST ME*
*I begged and I prayed*
*I'm fighting to stay*
*I'm tired of hiding*
*I can see the light shining*
*Time is growing in a beautiful way*

*So one day I can play*
*Now no more wondering*
*If things will be the same*
*Just keeping the memories and changed old ways and remember*
*It's time to stand up and love me*
*Inevitable.*

— *Darla*

The women whose voices we attend to here are all in prison or have experienced incarceration. In attempting to answer the call to listen to and bring forth the voices of women who could best contribute to our understanding of this intricate problem, we include stories, poems, and excerpts of poems from Aboriginal women (Eastham et al. 2010; Walsh and Crough 2013; Walsh, Rutherford, Krieg, and Crough 2013; Rutherford, Walsh, Klemmensen, and Madden 2014). Like Darla, they often write of "starving" in both metaphorical and literal ways, of being "abused," of being "alone," of having "lost everything" — even themselves. Despite these profound offences and losses, women insist that they are "fighting to stay." They dream, as Darla articulates, that "one day I can play" rather than only struggle. Like Darla, they demand an "inevitable" against these histories of suffering and struggle: "It's time to stand up and love me."[1.] These women speak out of pain but — as we will see later — they also speak out of courage and hope.

In our research, which aimed to develop solutions for Aboriginal women caught in the cycle of homelessness and incarceration, women expressed their hopes and dreams and experiences of despair and disruption with poetry. All the women had endured repeated incarcerations; at the time of the research, some were incarcerated and others were prison survivors. Shirley shares her struggles here, including the "most painful times," the "gut-wrenching pain" and the exhaustion that comes of being "out there with no roots to ground" her. Similar to Darla, she speaks of hope amid her efforts to make sense of how she became "an incarcerated Aboriginal woman."

*I want to share with you my struggles as a Aboriginal woman who has been incarcerated on so many occasions that I forgot most or drank or drugged to forget those most painful times, simply because I didn't know what being a Aboriginal women meant and to cause such events of incarceration as for being Aboriginal. Truthfully I was tired of being a Aboriginal women out there with no roots to ground myself, so letting the tears flow, the gut-wrenching pain of this lost soul and in hopes to finding what has gone so terribly wrong for me to end up as a incarcerated Aboriginal woman.*

— *Shirley*

In sum, Shirley's story, like many others, speaks directly of loneliness, despair, hurt and feelings of being lost. But these women do not stop there — they demand we hear their voices and that we do not judge them. They speak of their own strivings to learn different, healthier ways of being where they can reclaim their identities as individuals who matter, against personal histories of pain and against the related, impersonal colonial histories that define Aboriginal women as less than human. They challenge historical systems and structures of oppression and current racism, stigma and inequities. They demand change.

## The Opening

The rate of women's incarceration in industrialized countries has, in recent decades, increased to astronomical proportions, leading many researchers to refer to the phenomenon as a women's incarceration boom (Kim 2002; Parsons and Warner-Robbins 2002; Sudbury 2005). The increasing rate of incarceration has been correlated to processes of globalization (Angel-Ajani 2005), including the criminalization of racialized migrant workers and refugees in Europe and North America in a world that may be globalized, but is far from borderless. Mass incarceration of women is also correlated with the transition to neoliberal social policies, including the demise of the welfare state, leading to an increase in what Neve and Pate (2005: 32) call "survival crimes" and the related increasing criminalization of poverty, the mentally ill, and those addicted to drugs and alcohol. More specifically, the patterns of female incarceration can be attributed to the gendered, racialized and classed systemic inequalities inherent in Western society. In this respect, the high rates of incarceration of young, racialized, Aboriginal and working-class women in Canada, as well as those with mental illness, mean that, "Prison is ... a continuation of the institutional and coercive control exercised by the state in the lives of these highly vulnerable women" (Neve and Pate 2005: 19).

The problems do not end for these women once released from prison. The systemic barriers, including economic, social and political; personal struggles including addictions, mental health and histories of abuse and trauma; as well as the societal barriers and stigmatization correlated with a criminal record compound and negatively affect incarcerated women's ability to find safe, affordable housing post-incarceration (Pollack 2004, 2009). Once women leave penal institutions, they frequently face the same conditions that lead to their incarceration: poverty, trauma, and chronic instability, leading to high rates of recidivism, often termed the "cycle of incarceration." Here Crystal addresses the terrible uncertainties women face when contemplating their release. Even those with "a clear mind" confront the dilemma of where they will be able to go when they get out — particularly, where they can go and be safe.

*Am I safer here than I am out there?*
*Will I ever overcome my addiction?*
*I say I won't ever use again*
*But is it cause of the situation I got myself into?*
*Now I have a clear mind*
*But still confused where will I go when I get out?*

— *Crystal*

The situation for Aboriginal people, including First Nations, Métis and Inuit in Canada, is more dire than the mainstream population across most economic, health and social indicators. According to the Office of the Correctional Investigator (2013), although Aboriginal people constitute approximately 4 percent of the Canadian population, almost one-third of the federal inmate population is Aboriginal. Of the approximately 3,400 Aboriginal offenders in federal penitentiaries, most were First Nation (71%), followed by Métis (24%) and Inuit (5%). The rate of incarceration for Aboriginal adults is about ten times higher than non-Aboriginal adults, and this rate is expected to increase.

Within the justice system, Aboriginal people are subjected to harsher treatment. According to the Office of the Correctional Investigator, compared with the non-Aboriginal prison population they are

released later in their sentence, ... over-represented in segregation and maximum security populations; disproportionately involved in use of force interventions and incidents of prison self-injury; and more likely to return to prison on revocation of parole, often for administrative reasons, not criminal violations [paragraph 1]. (2013)

Although this description is useful for summarizing the injustice suffered by incarcerated Aboriginal men and women, it does little to capture the physical pain of force interventions and self-injury, which join with the terrible emotional and spiritual pain of being imprisoned. Here, Shirley evokes images of "stinging," "searing pain" and "blood." In her words, they are more than a physical manifestation; they overwhelm her so that her thoughts also turn to "blood."

*As I awaken, the sound of steel hitting steel, there is a hard coldness against my*
*body. Why am I unable to move my arms? Shit, the stinging of pain around*
*my wrists, I squirm against the hard coldness. I fight with the inability to use*
*my arms, the pain searing through my body. Unable to stop the screaming of*
*searing pain rushing, rushing through my veins, I scramble on the floor, pain*
*shooting through my shoulders. Yes, as I thought, handcuffed sitting in the*
*middle of a holding cell. Looking down yes confirming my thoughts turning to*

*blood, yes blood, knowing the dryness, the smell of blood, the texture, and then*
*the sense of taste of blood, not only, but dried blood crusting my lips, ever so dry.*
— *Shirley*


## Other Colonial Contexts

The overrepresentation of Indigenous people in penal settings in Canada echoes the situation of Indigenous peoples in other colonial contexts. Although the emphasis here is on the Canadian case, it is worth observing that similar rates are common in other countries. For example, the incarceration rate of Native Americans is 38% higher than the national rate, which has been attributed to "differential treatment by the criminal justice system, lack of access to adequate counsel and racial profiling" (Bell 2010, paragraph 8). Similarly, in Australia, Aboriginal and Torres Strait Islander people represent approximately 3% of the population, yet more than 28% of Australia's incarcerated people are Aboriginal, with rates of incarceration increasing rapidly for Aboriginal people (Georgatos 2013). Also, the Māori in New Zealand, who make up about 15% of the population, comprise 58% of the prison population (Statistics New Zealand 2012), and are seven times more likely than non-Māori to be convicted and twelve times more likely to be sentenced to detention (Statistics New Zealand 2010).

The incarceration of Indigenous women worldwide is even greater than Indigenous men. In Canada, the situation for Aboriginal women has been described as "nothing short of a crisis" (Wesley 2012: 1). Despite representing less than 2% of the total female population, more than one-third of women incarcerated in Canadian federal penitentiaries are of Aboriginal origin (Office of the Criminal Investigator 2013). These rates have escalated dramatically and are not expected to decline, which portends a bleak "outlook for Aboriginal women, their families and communities" (Wesley 2012: 1).

Indigenous girls in Canada also have extremely high rates of justice system involvement. They are the fastest-growing population in youth custody today, accounting for 44% of all girls in youth custody in 2008–2009 (NWAC and Justice for Girls 2012). This injustice is not unique to Canada. Indigenous women in Australia, New Zealand and the United States are disproportionately targeted by the criminal justice system, even more so than their Indigenous male counterparts.

### Setting the Context

The overrepresentation of Aboriginal women in Canadian prisons has been attributed to a number of interrelated factors, including entrenched and systemic societal racism that has resulted in overpolicing and overcharging of Aboriginal peoples; uninformed and inadequate legal representation; and a history of social, economic, spiritual and political injustices inflicted on Aboriginal women. The criminal justice system, the RCMP and the police play a specific role in continuing the colonization of Aboriginal girls and women through the "failure to respond to the violence against Aboriginal girls and women, as well as over-policing, racial profiling and criminalization of Aboriginal girls and women" (NWAC and Justice for Girls 2012: 25).

Finally, as Taiaiake Alfred (2009a: 45) observes, the ongoing realities of "colonially-generated cultural disruption" endure, resulting in "social suffering, unresolved psychophysical harms of historical trauma and cultural dislocation ... crea(ting) a situation in which the opportunities for a self-sufficient, healthy and autonomous life for First Nations people on individual and collective bases are extremely limited" (42). Together, this makes Aboriginal women who have been released from prison extremely vulnerable to further harm and at high risk of re-incarceration.

The overrepresentation of Aboriginal women in the prison population arises as a consequence of the interplay between historical and contemporary factors that are inextricably bound up with persistent colonialism (Walsh et al. 2012). Historically, Aboriginal peoples have been subjected to varying attempts at colonization and assimilation, dislocation and dispossession, including the *Indian Act*, the residential school system, and the "sixties scoop." The legacy of the residential school movement, which explicitly sought to assimilate children by removing them from their communities and banning all forms of Aboriginal culture (Bennett, Blackstock, and De La Ronde 2005; Johnston 1988), has been profound and long-standing. New tragedies associated with the residential schools, such as the medical experiments performed on students, continue to emerge (Porter 2013). The "sixties scoop" refers to the period of time between the 1960s and 1970s during which high numbers of Aboriginal children were placed in foster care, typically with non-Aboriginal families (Kirmayer, Simpson, and Cargo 2003). Transgenerational effects of these colonial practices are apparent in the current functioning of many Aboriginal communities (Stangeland and Walsh 2013). The result of this persistent and extensive oppression of Aboriginal peoples has now been described as intergenerational trauma (Henderson, Chapter One of this book; McGill 2008; Yuen 2011). Hence, intergenerational trauma — and so the colonial context — must be considered when examining Aboriginal peoples' involvement with the criminal justice system. Indeed, as one woman reminds us here, if we want to understand how Aboriginal women end up in conflict with colonial law, we have to reach back before these women were even born.

*I guess if I was to look back at my life I would have to start before I was born. Both of my parents went to Residential School. Women went from being really important people in the community to being ashamed of our bodies and being women. At Residential School they didn't have those lessons and those ceremonies that teach young girls about the importance of being a woman and all of that power that that has, and as a result I had a really screwed up childhood.*

— Anonymous

Here, a direct connection is being made between colonial disruption of Indigenous knowledge and ceremonies that valued women and women's power and the subsequent "screwed-up childhood" experienced by many Aboriginal women. Colonial racism and patriarchy undermine Aboriginal women's agency, and the resulting family disruption and powerlessness is dangerous for Aboriginal women's well-being and self-worth. This is another factor pushing Aboriginal women into conflict with the law.

Poverty is another key contributor to escalating rates of Aboriginal women's incarceration. As Wesley articulates, "The story of how so many Aboriginal women came to be locked up within federal penitentiaries is a story filled with a long history of dislocation and isolation, racism, brutal violence as well as enduring a constant state of poverty beyond poor" (2012: 1). In fact, First Nations, Inuit and Métis women are among the poorest people in Canada (Wilson and McDonald 2010). The unemployment rate of Aboriginal women is twice that of non-Aboriginal women (Statistics Canada 2011). In 2005, the median income of Aboriginal women was just $15,654, about 77% of the average incomes of non-Aboriginal women.

Such deep poverty is inextricably linked with homelessness. Urban Aboriginal people in Canada are more than eight times likely to be or become homeless than non-Native urban individuals. "Historical dispossession of Aboriginal lands, colonial and neo-colonial practices of cultural oppression and erosion, intergenerational traumas, systemic racism, governmental policies, the current economy and housing markets" have all been cited as contributing to the staggering rates of homelessness and housing insufficiency for Aboriginal people in Canada (Patrick 2014: 10). Aboriginal women, specifically, are also disproportionally homeless: They account for 35% of the homeless Aboriginal population, whereas non-Aboriginal women account for 27% of non-Aboriginal homeless populations (NWAC 2007).

The legacy of colonial practices is foundational in and correlated with the high prevalence of substance abuse, family violence, suicide, and physical and mental health rates among Aboriginal peoples in Canada, both on the reserve and living in urban areas. Although this does not describe all Aboriginal homes, one woman shares the difficulty of growing up in a home environment characterized by alcoholism, hunger and child abuse. She emphasizes the need to reconnect with and be taught "a different life than that."

*Teach me something different than what I learned at home or you know, where everybody was drunk and passed out you know, kids are getting molested and you're hungry. Teach me that there's a different life than that. Teach me something that is, you know, something that's going to help me get over some hurts, you know.*

— *Anonymous*

Aboriginal women and girls in Canada face life-threatening, gender-based violence, and disproportionately experience violent crimes because of hatred and racism. According to the 2004 *General Social Survey* (Statistics Canada 2004), Aboriginal women experience much higher rates of violence, spousal violence, severe and potentially life-threatening forms of family violence and homicide compared with non-Aboriginal women. The level of violence experienced by Aboriginal women by official reports underestimates the true extent of the problem: "Six out of ten incidents of violent crime against Aboriginal people are thought to go unreported ... there are no standard policies covering whether and/or how police track violence experienced by Aboriginal peoples (NWAC n.d.: 5).

Recently released police-recorded incidents of Aboriginal female homicides and unresolved missing Aboriginal females total 1,181 (164 missing and 1,017 homicide victims), which far exceeds previous estimates (RCMP 2014). Despite the 2013 call by the United Nations Special Rapporteur on the Rights of Indigenous Peoples, James Anaya, for the Canadian government to "launch a comprehensive and nationwide inquiry into the case of missing and murdered aboriginal women," no inquiry has been launched to date, and his 2014 report highlighted that "indigenous women and girls remain vulnerable to abuse" (United Nations 2014: 1).

Explaining this as a subjective experience, Toni writes about being "alone and cold," "lost and blind" and "scarred from the inside out." She further castigates that if her cries for help fall too often on "deaf ears," we have a social and moral responsibility to listen. She is not, after all, "A childless mother/Also, the motherless child." She does have relations, whether they are blood relationships or other kinds of relationships, for as she fully acknowledges: "I AM your mother, your sister, your daughter."

> *Motherless Child*
> *I feel so alone and cold,*
> *I'm lost and blind.*
> *A childless mother,*
> *Also, the motherless child.*
> *I walk aimless around and around,*
> *What I am looking for, never finding.*

*I am scarred from the inside out.*
*Never to heal my wounds, lost, forgotten.*
*Who am I?*
*I am any and every woman you have judged on the street corner,*
*I have died alone in a shallow grave.*
*Never to be found,*
*And if found, never to be identified*
*I AM your mother, your sister, your daughter.*
*I am that voice crying for help that falls upon deaf ears.*

— *Toni*

## Ways Forward

The pervasive impacts of colonialism on Aboriginal people's involvement in the justice system has been recognized and various calls to redress have been made.

> When sentencing an Aboriginal offender, courts must take judicial notice of such matters as the history of colonialism, displacement, and residential schools and how that history continues to translate into lower educational attainment, lower incomes, higher unemployment, higher rates of substance abuse and suicide, and of course higher levels of incarceration for Aboriginal peoples. (Supreme Court of Canada 2012: 7)

The effects of colonialism on Canada's Aboriginal peoples was acknowledged, for example, by the Canadian government in 1996 with the introduction of Bill C-41, after long struggles by Aboriginal peoples to document the systemic racism of the colonial legal justice system and seek alternatives for Aboriginal peoples. Bill C-41 was promoted as a progressive reform to sentencing law, premised on curtailing the increasing rate of Aboriginal people being incarcerated. This law advised sentencing judges to give special consideration to Aboriginal offenders due to the legacy of colonialism. Judges were to consider the conditions of Aboriginal offenders' lives, including poverty, substance abuse, family breakdown and the effects of residential schools; and to "take into account all the possible alternatives to incarceration ... focusing on the least restrictive measure and community integration of offenders" (Balfour 2008: 101).

Bill C-41 was intended to marry the principles of retributive and restorative justice to slow down the rate of incarceration among Aboriginal peoples, but the rate of incarceration has doubled among Canadian Aboriginals since its induction. Among many other factors, the continued increase in incarceration rates can be attributed to uninformed legal representation available because many lawyers do not rely on Bill C-41 to avoid prison sentences for their clients or even use the legislation for appeals (Balfour 2011).

Activists and scholars have pointed to the creation of a victimization-criminal-ization continuum that is a result of the lack of understanding regarding the truths of Aboriginal women's lives, including the ways that they are shaped by persistent colonialism and associated dispossessions and racisms. For instance, Bill C-41, which was intended to reduce the rate of incarceration, clashed with an existing law that was intended to reduce incidences of gendered violence through mandatory charging. However, as Balfour points out, Aboriginal women have "fallen between the cracks of zero tolerance and restorative justice in that they are likely to be both severely victimized by gendered violence, and coercively punished" (2011: 102). Aboriginal women are now being punished more severely by a law intended to protect them, as women are increasingly being counter charged by police for using defensive violence against their abusers (Balfour 2011).

In the immediate term, promising practices for Aboriginal women within carceral settings have also been identified (Walsh et al. 2011). They must, how-ever, recognize the sociohistorical factors of colonialism and systemic racism, as previously discussed, which have contributed to criminality. Second, they must help to establish a sense of identity and connection with Aboriginal culture and spirituality. The intergenerational trauma of residential schools that (as Henderson observes in Chapter One of this book) "took our families to the abyss," did so by deliberately destroying family and community relations and by suppressing Indigenous worldviews and ways of doing. Hence, breaking this cycle means recon-necting with Indigenous practices and communities. Concrete opportunities to re-establish such relations must be available to incarcerated Indigenous women. Third, it addresses the particular needs of women, specifically the interpersonal violence that Aboriginal women have experienced throughout their lives and the importance of their relationships with children and family by using a restorative justice process to address transgressions within the community, for example.

In her poem, Monica writes of her desire to "turn back time" to "be somewhere else"; a time and place where she is "loved" and "trusted" and "strong" with family and friends to support her. Again, this suggests the need for holistic approaches to Aboriginal women who are incarcerated because these women need physically, emotionally, spiritually and intellectually healthy relationships to be embraced within.

> *Turn Back Time*
> *If I could turn back time,*
> *I'd be somewhere else,*
> *Somewhere besides here.*

*If I could turn back time,*
*I'd be loved, always trusted,*
*And always strong with family and friends.*

— *Monica*

Although recommendations for reform of the justice system were introduced more than twenty years ago by the Royal Commission on Aboriginal Peoples (RCAP)— and although the first generation of Indigenous lawyers have been fighting much longer to bend colonial justice laws in ways that will actually protect rather than persecute Indigenous persons (see Chapter One of this book) — recent findings suggest several additional opportunities for enhancement of Section 84 releases (Garnett, Walsh, and Badry 2013).[2] For example, enhancing Aboriginal community involvement in these releases has a role in influencing health outcomes for offenders by providing a continuum of care of connected, contextually appropriate resources to enhance their well-being (Mental Health Strategy for Corrections in Canada 2012).

In addition to increasing the effectiveness of Aboriginal community participation in releases of incarcerated women through Section 84, involvement through collaboration, education and resource allocation can strengthen and promote healthier, safer communities. Talking of the importance of "speaking my truth," Gloria insists that this requires community involvement — and that such collaboration makes a healthy return to community a possibility.

*It's helped me come in a positive way in speaking my truth. Because my community wants to know are you ready to come back? Eventually no matter what you're gonna' 'wanna go home. And if we work together we can do it.*
— *Gloria*

Other research has shown positive outcomes for enhancing collaborative community-prison programs for incarcerated women, and Aboriginal women specifically (see, for example, Granger-Brown et al. 2012). At a more fundamental level, however, the kind of language that has to be used pragmatically in the short term — such as "enhancing Aboriginal community involvement" — arguably skirts over the deep, seemingly intractable underlying issues and offers little opportunity for the level of change required. As Alfred maintains, this would require getting to "the root of the colonial problem in Canada" (2009a: 43) which necessitates "spiritual revitalization and cultural regeneration" (2009a: 45) through a return to land-based connections to culture, language and community.

While recognizing the importance of the broader context of Indigenous resurgence, we would argue that language of "collaboration" is necessary in the short term: Aboriginal women who are incarcerated can't wait for a postcolonial era.

Aboriginal women and girls need collaboration right now, however imperfect, and that means some cooperation with governmental agencies. This cooperation, however, should not undermine nor be seen as incompatible with longer-term struggles for Aboriginal self-determination, including specifically in the area of Aboriginal justice.

In short, we are developing ways to stem the flow of Aboriginal girls and women entering justice settings. This means attention to primary prevention strategies to address the sociohistorical causes of family disruption, poverty, addictions, violence and mental health problems that place Aboriginal women and girls at greater risk of being in conflict with the law. It requires that we create spaces for Aboriginal communities that will help incarcerated Aboriginal women right now, but we need to do this as part of broader support for Aboriginal communities in their struggles for self-determination that impact all areas of life. Real change, real equity, requires broader social action, including upholding treaty agreements; ensuring meaningful participation of Aboriginal people in program planning, implementation and governance; and strategies that redress the long-standing disenfranchisement of Aboriginal peoples in Canada. Insofar as Aboriginal women's incarcerations are ultimately rooted in colonial relations of inequality, improving the situation means transforming those relations.

## Acts of Resistance

Some Indigenous intellectuals and activists have argued that it is counterproductive to depend on government agencies to improve the situation of Indigenous peoples in Canada (e.g., Alfred 2009a). They do not believe that the justice system can be reformed in ways that will be responsive to Indigenous justice and the legacies and ongoing ravages of colonial inequalities. They argue that ways forward depend on autonomous Indigenous movements that do not ask the colonial state for permission to be, know and do in ways that are specifically Indigenous (e.g., Alfred and Corntassel 2005; see also Chapter Seven of this book).

Toward these ends, Aboriginal peoples across what is known as Canada have initiated several grassroots movements (see, for example, Chapter Four of this book). Most recently, these movements include the Indigenous Nationhood Movement, Idle No More, Environmental Justice, Justice for Missing and Murdered Women, and Police and Prison Abolition. Although they are important for addressing the numerous concerns for incarcerated Aboriginal women, none has specifically taken up their plight. And for many of the reasons already described here, Aboriginal women who are incarcerated or were formerly incarcerated have not yet formally organized on their own behalf. However, this absence of formal organization does not mean that they are not resisting (with varying success) individually, together, and with help from friends, family, community and other allies, as described here.

The role for allies in Indigenous social movements, including movements that seek to put the experiences and concerns of Aboriginal women in conflict with the justice system at their centre, is less clear. Alfred argues that "justice must become a *duty* of, not a *gift* from, the Settler" (2009b: 113). As Shirley insisted in her invitation, we cannot just "walk by" Aboriginal women like herself. However, non-Aboriginal people must join Aboriginal people as invited guests — as collaborators who support the vision, approach and work of Indigenous people. While referencing Aboriginal homeless research specifically, Patrick concluded that "the issues revealed in this review cannot be meaningfully changed without academics and key stakeholders declaring (and acting on) a clear position that also takes into account colonial and neo-colonial relationships between Aboriginal Peoples and governments/society" (2014: 62). This stance holds true for those interested in advancing social justice for Aboriginal girls and women in the justice system. Ultimately, non-Indigenous scholars must do more than acknowledge the colonial context, however; we must make space for Indigenous perspectives and voices on every matter that affects Indigenous peoples, including in our academic works and in our activism.

Oppressive forces do not give way easily; individual and collective acts of resistance are required. Women who have faced repeated incarceration and the social, economic and historic factors that lead to this cycle are both ill-equipped and best-positioned to resist. One woman explains it this way:

> *The other day I was walking I thought of the Indian Nation, I think we've survived against all odds. I'm sure they all thought we'd be gone by now, or assimilated into the White society. But we've stuck to our guns. But how often do we ever get that opportunity to actually be that voice? You know, to take our stories and make them into knowledge about hope and courage? I thought about this for a while and decided to go to university; I want to be that voice for our people.*
>
> — *Anonymous*

In other words, one way forward for Aboriginal women who are or were incarcerated is to assert their voices and their stories, re-creating them in ways that offer knowledge and provide insights into ways toward hope and courage. This is one way to relearn and re-enact diverse, vibrant Indigenous identities and enable these women to have a valued sense of self as Indigenous women. This is necessary to break the cycles of violence, substance dependency and the other multiple consequences of the generational trauma left by colonialism, behind Indigenous women's incarceration. Autonomous Indigenous justice systems are another way forward instead of trying to reform a colonial system some of these women see as irredeemably racist and corrupt.

Here, Chastity contrasts the "warmth of my families embrace," the feeling of being "on top of the world" that she experienced when she was young and living on her reserve. This writing is in marked contrast with the early description of abuse in the home related earlier. It is only later that she feels "loneliness and hardship" because she is now "marked with political status" as an Aboriginal woman by a mainstream society that assumes she is "ignorant" and lazy. She sets herself a task to defy the "despair" caused by such stereotypical hatreds, concluding with a vow to "strive for my soul to be alive."

> 3rd World Native
> When I was growing up on my reserve, I never felt cold or poor
> The warmth of my families embrace made me feel so rich
> I was on top of the world
> Until I grew up and began to realize the loneliness and hardship
> Sure we got free everything but yet we acted like savages
> So rabid to our advantage
> We were wolves starving for attention
> Turning on each other, hunting for greed
> But there was never no need
> I imagine 3rd world so tragic like I'm marked with political status
> That says 'ignorant', 'won't work'
> But how stereotypical of me
> One day I hope for the people to see me living
> Not in despair but in strive for my soul to be alive.
>
> — Chastity

## A Closing

In 2010, Canada supported the 2007 United Nations Declaration on the Rights of Indigenous Peoples:

> Article 3
>     Indigenous peoples have the right to self-determination. By virtue of that right they freely determine their political status and freely pursue their economic, social and cultural development.
>     Article 4
>     Indigenous peoples, in exercising their right to self-determination, have the right to autonomy or self-government in matters relating to their

internal and local affairs, as well as ways and means for financing their autonomous functions. (Aboriginal Affairs and Northern Development Canada 2010)

Yet these rights have not been fully realized; arguably, the current Canadian government has further undermined self-determination rights by opening up waters traditionally stewarded by Indigenous peoples to for-profit, corporate "development" and by unilaterally redefining Treaties and sovereignty in the omnibus Bill C-45.

Against such developments, the United Nations Special Rapporteur on the Rights of Indigenous Peoples, James Anaya, called on the Canadian government to follow the spirit of the declaration:

> Indigenous peoples' concerns merit higher priority at all levels and within all branches of government, and across all departments. Concerted measures, based on mutual understanding and real partnership with aboriginal peoples, through their own representative institutions, are vital to establishing long-term solutions. To that end, it is necessary for Canada to arrive at a common understanding with indigenous peoples of objectives and goals that are based on full respect for their constitutional, treaty and internationally recognized rights. (United Nations 2014: 2)

The noted failure of the Canadian governments to recognize Aboriginal peoples' inherent rights is not new. In absence of real change, real equity, we refer to Walker and Barcham's position, as they declare that "Aboriginal quality of life can be improved only on Aboriginal peoples' own terms and not prepackaged Eurocentric terms" (2010: 318).

Finally, we seek direction from Aboriginal women with lived experience of incarceration who call for further acts of recognition and resistance to see, listen and create change as women decree. Shirley insists that although she was treated as nothing more than "stupid, drunken Indian" and thrown "behind steel to try to break her," she has not been broken. On the contrary, she has learned to become "proud, thankful and hopeful as an Aboriginal woman" and with her sisters, she is "rising up":

> The cop called me a "stupid, drunken Indian." I then tried to tell them I had to go to work in the morning but the cops said, "Stupid, drunken Indians, don't work." As I write this today I do of course get sad, yet in the mist of the tears swelling in these eyes I know I have now proven to those cops wrong. Two grown men, with guns, a badge of authority, feeling so powerful to what? To handcuffing an Aboriginal women, kicking her down, calling her names, belittling her,

*throwing her behind steel to try to break her. Well here she is today writing this*
*and being proud, thankful and hopeful as an Aboriginal women. Aboriginal*
*women today in society are quietly rising up and our sisters that are trapped*
*within the correctional institutions across this Nation are slowly waking up.*
*— Shirley*

We conclude with words from another woman, who speaks out of her own experiences, but tells her story for "other women." She remarks that these stories may "help other people" and that you "gain more strength and power" in the telling that can be used to create change. She concludes, "Thanks for listening" — but this reminds us that we really *do* have to listen, to share stories so that we can become strong and powerful enough to bring about change "together."

*I used to cry to my Elders about all the time I spent wasting my life in jail.*
*They said, "no you didn't waste your life in jail that was your lesson that you*
*learned so that when you leave here you will be able to help people." And that's*
*why I think it's really important for all of us to tell our stories because other*
*women who are listening to your story will say, "I can really relate to that."*
*Your stories will help other people. And the more you tell your stories, the*
*stronger you get and the more strength and power we have together to create*
*change. Thanks for listening.*
*— Anonymous*

## NOTES

1. In offering interpretations of these women's poems, writings and words, we are not trying to suggest a definitive explanation of their meanings. Women's words, expressions and meanings are inevitably complex, multiple and are invariably subjected to each reader's interpretation. If so offering we do want to propose "an" interpretation of these stories as a means of explicitly articulating some of the analytical and political implications of what may appear at first to be purely subjective poetic expressions.

2. The Corrections and Conditional Release Act (S.C. 1992, c.20) section 84 reads as follows:

    If an inmate expresses an interest in being released into an aboriginal community, the Service shall, with the inmate's consent, give the aboriginal community

    *a*) adequate notice of the inmate's parole review or their statutory release date, as the case may be; and

    (*b*) an opportunity to propose a plan for the inmate's release and integration into that community.

## REFERENCES

Aboriginal Affairs and Northern Development Canada. 2010. *Canada's Statement of Support on the United Nations Declaration on the Rights of Indigenous Peoples.* <aadnc-aandc.gc.ca/eng/1309374239861/1309374546142>.

Alfred, Taiaiake. 2009a. "Colonialism and State Dependency." *Journal of Aboriginal Health* (November).

____. 2009b. *Wasase: Indigenous Pathways of Action and Freedom.* Toronto: University of Toronto Press.

Alfred, Taiaiake, and Jeff Corntassel. 2005. "Being Indigenous: Resurgences Against Colonial Capitalism." *Government and Opposition* 40, 4 (Autumn).

Angel-Ajani, Asale. 2005. "Domestic Enemies and Carceral Circles: African Women and Criminalization in Italy." In Julia Sudbury (ed.), *Global Lockdown: Race, Gender and the Prison-Industrial Complex.* New York: Routledge.

Balfour, Gillian. 2008. "Falling Between the Cracks of Retributive and Restorative Justice: The Victimization and Punishment of Aboriginal Women." *Feminist Criminology* 3, 2, 101–120.

Bell, Ryan J. 2010. "Mass Incarceration: A Destroyer of People of Color and Their Communities." *Huff Post Politics.* <huffingtonpost.com/jamaal-bell/mass-incarceration-a-dest_b_578854.html>.

Bennett, Marylyn, Cindy Blackstock, and Richard De La Ronde. 2005. *A Literature Review and Annotated Biography on Aspects of Aboriginal Child Welfare in Canada,* second edition. First Nations Research Site of the Centre of Excellence for Child Welfare and First Nations Child & Family Caring Society of Canada. <cecwcepb.ca/sites/default/files/publications/en/AboriginalCWLitReview_2ndEd.pdf>.

Bishop, Anne. 2002. *Becoming an Ally: Breaking the Cycle of Oppression in People,* second edition. Black Point, NS: Fernwood Publishing.

Dumbrill, Gary C., and Jacquie Green. 2008. "Indigenous Knowledge in the Social Work Academy." *Social Work Education* 27, 5, 489–503.

Eastham, Sarada, et al. 2010. "Out of the Lower Depths: The Power of the Arts for Social Justice Transformation." *Reflections: Narratives of Professional Helping, Special Issue on Social Justice* 16, 3, 52–61.

Garnett, K., Christine A. Walsh, and D. Badry. 2013. "Section 84 — Corrections and Conditional Release Act: Recommendations for Reform." *Pimatisiwin: A Journal of Aboriginal and Indigenous Community Health* 11, 2, 307–324.

Georgatos, Gerry. 2013. "Australia, the Mother of All Jailers of Aboriginal People." *The Stringer,* November 22.

Granger-Brown, Alison, et al. 2012. "Collaborative Community-Prison Programs for Incarcerated Women in BC." *British Columbia Medical Journal* 54, 10, 509–513.

Healy, Karen. 2000. *Social Work Practices: Contemporary Perspectives on Change.* Thousand Oaks, CA: Sage.

Johnston, Basil. 1988. *Indian School Days.* Toronto: Key Porter.

Kim, Seijeoung. 2002. "Incarcerated Women in Life Context." *Women's Studies International Forum* 26, 95–100.

Kirmayer, Laurence, Cory Simpson, and Margaret Cargo. 2003. "Healing Traditions:

Culture, Community and Mental Health Promotion with Canadian Aboriginal Peoples." *Australian Psychiatry* 11, 15–23. <dx.doi.org/10.1093/bmb/ldh006>.

McGill, Jena. 2008. "An Institutional Suicide Machine: Discrimination Against Federally Sentenced Aboriginal Women in Canada." *Race/Ethnicity* 2, 1, 89–119.

Mental Health Strategy for Corrections in Canada. 2012. "A Provincial-Territorial Partnership." <justice.gov.sk.ca/Default.aspx?DN=ca398c7d-99d1-41d6-bc18-425298f8388b>.

Neve, Lis,a and Kim Pate. 2005. "Challenging the Criminalization of Women Who Resist." In Julia Sudbury (ed.), *Global Lockdown: Race, Gender and the Prison-Industrial Complex.* New York: Routledge.

NWAC (Native Women's Association of Canada). 2007a. "Aboriginal Women and the Legal Justice System in Canada. An Issue Paper." <laa.gov.nl.ca/laa/naws/pdf/nwac-legal. pdf>.

____. 2007b. "Aboriginal Women and Homelessness. An Issue Paper." <nwac/hq.org/en/ documents/nwac.homelessness.jun2007.pdf>.

____. n.d. "Violence Against Aboriginal Women: Fact Sheet." <nwac.ca/files/download/ NWAC_3E_Toolkit_e_0.pdf>.

NWAC (Native Women's Association of Canada) and Justice for Girls. 2012. "Arrest the Legacy: From Residential Schools to Prisons." <nwac.ca/sites/default/files/imce/ Gender%20Matters%20English/1-Introduction_GM.pdf>.

Office of the Criminal Investigator. 2013. "Backgrounder: Aboriginal Offenders — A Critical Situation." <oci-bec.gc.ca/cnt/rpt/oth-aut/oth-aut20121022info-eng.aspx>.

Parsons, Mickey, and Carmen Warner-Robbins. 2002. "Factors that Support Women's Successful Transition to the Community Following Jail/Prison." *Health Care for Women Internationally* 23, 6–18.

Patrick, Caryl. 2014. *Aboriginal Homelessness in Canada: A Literature Review.* Toronto: Canadian Homelessness Research Network Press. <homelesshub.ca/sites/default/ files/AboriginalLiteratureReview.pdf>.

Pollack, Shoshana. 2009. "'Circuits of Exclusion': Criminalized Women's Negotiation of Community." *Canadian Journal of Community Mental Health* 2, 81, 83–95.

____. 2004. "Anti-Oppressive Social Work Practice with Women in Prison: Discursive Reconstructions and Alternative Practices." *British Journal of Social Work* 34, 1, 693–707.

Porter, Jody. 2013. "Ear Experiments Done on Kids at Kenora Residential School" CBC News (August 8). <cbc.ca>.

RCMP (Royal Canadian Mounted Police). 2014. "Missing and Murdered Aboriginal Women: A National Operational Overview." <rcmp-grc.gc.ca/pubs/mmaw-faapd-eng.pdf>.

Rutherford, Gayle, Christine A. Walsh, Meredith Klemmensen, and Sarah Madden. 2014. "The Individual Agency and Social Structure Dialectic: Exploring Women's Experiences of Remand Custody Through Arts and Community-Based Research." *International Journal of Criminology and Sociology* 3, 158–167.

Sinclair, Raven. 2004. "Aboriginal Social Work Education in Canada: Decolonizing Pedagogy for the Seventh Generation." *First Peoples Child & Family Review* 1, 1, 49–61.

Stangeland, Jade, and Christine A. Walsh. 2013. "Defining Permanency and Aboriginal Youth in Foster Care." *First Peoples Child & Family Review* 8, 2, 24–39.

Statistics Canada. 2011. *First Nations, Metis and Inuit Women Statistics.* Ottawa: Government of Canada. <statcan.gc.ca/pub/89-503-x/2010001/article/11442-eng.pdf>.

____. 2004. *General Social Survey (GSS)*. Ottawa: Government of Canada.

Statistics New Zealand. 2012. *New Zealand's Prison Population*. Wellington, NZ: Author. <stats.govt.nz/browse_for_stats/snapshots-of-nz/yearbook/society/crime/corrections.aspx>.

____. 2010. *Convictions Table Builder*. Wellington, NZ: Author. <stats.govt.nz/>.

Sudbury, Julia (ed.). 2005. *Global Lockdown: Race, Gender and the Prison-Industrial Complex*. New York: Routledge.

Supreme Court of Canada. 2012. "Justice LeBel for the Majority in R. v. Ipeelee." <lexisnexis.ca/documents/2012scc13.pdf>.

United Nations. 2014. "Report of the Special Rapporteur on the Rights of Indigenous Peoples, James Anaya: The Situation of Indigenous Peoples in Canada." <unsr.jamesanaya.org/docs/countries/2014-report-canada-a-hrc-27-52-add-2-en.pdf>.

____. 2007. *United Nations Declaration on the Rights of Indigenous Peoples*. <un.org/esa/socdev/unpfii/documents/DRIPS_en.pdf>.

Walker, Ryan C., and Manuhuia Barcham. 2010. "Indigenous-Inclusive Citizenship: The City and Social Housing in Canada, New Zealand, and Australia." *Environment and Planning* 42, 2, 314–331.

Walsh, Christine A., and Meredith Crough. 2013. "Mothering Through Adversity: Voices of Incarcerated Women." In G. Eljdupovic and R. Jaremko Bromwich (eds.), *Incarcerated Mothers: Oppression and Resistance*. Bradford, ON: Demeter Press.

Walsh, Christine A., Brigitte Krieg, Gayle E. Rutherford, and Meaghan Bell. 2014. "Aboriginal Women's Voices: Breaking the Cycle of Homelessness and Incarceration." *Pimatisiwin: A Journal of Aboriginal and Indigenous Community Health* 11, 3, 377–394.

Walsh, Christine. A., P. MacDonald, Gayle E. Rutherford, Kerrie Moore, and Brigitte Krieg. 2012. "Promising Practices for Reducing Homelessness and Incarceration Among Aboriginal Women: An Integrative Literature Review." *Pimatisiwin: A Journal of Aboriginal and Indigenous Community Health* 9, 2, 363–385.

Walsh, Christine A., Gayle E. Rutherford, Brigitte Krieg, and Meredith Crough. 2013. "Arts-Based Research: Creating Social Change for Women Who Have Experienced Incarceration." *Creative Approaches to Research* 6, 1, 119–139.

Wesley, Mandy. 2012. "Marginalized: The Aboriginal Women's Experience in Federal Corrections APC 33 CA." <publicsafety.gc.ca/cnt/rsrcs/pblctns/mrgnlzd/mrgnlzd-eng.pdf>.

Wilson, Daniel, and David McDonald. 2010. "The Income Gap Between Aboriginal Peoples and the Rest of Canada." <policyalternatives.ca/sites/default/files/uploads/publications/reports/docs/Aboriginal%20Income%20Gap.pdf>.

Yuen, Felice. 2011. "'I've Never Been So Free in All My Life': Healing Through Aboriginal Ceremonies in Prison." *Leisure, Space, and Social Change* 35, 2, 97–113.

Chapter Three

# WHO IS READY TO LISTEN?
## ABORIGINAL PERSONS WITH DISABILITIES

*Douglas Durst and Elaine Coburn*

Why I'm here today is because I'm bringing a message about a group of
people who I think, too often, are left out and who aren't heard ... I am
talking about people with disabilities. I'm a person with a disability myself
and ... I worked for many years advocating and trying to ... (put) the
issues that are important for people with disabilities (at) the forefront
and to not be forgotten and to not be left out. Many of us may not be here
today because many of us are in institutions, we might be in a hospital,
maybe we can't get out of our homes. There's many of us who live in First
Nations communities, isolated, alone. But it doesn't mean that we don't
have a voice. It doesn't mean that we shouldn't be heard.
— *Doreen Demas, Dakota woman and blind disability advocate*
*(Niiganii 2012)*

Whether on reserve or in the cities, Aboriginal persons with disabilities are virtually
unheard in much of Canada. Of course, this does not mean that Aboriginal persons
with disabilities do not have an impact on the lives of those around them; clearly,
Aboriginal persons with disabilities do matter to their friends, families and communities, although relationships may be neither straightforward nor easy. Indeed,
some may be characterized by neglect and hostility, whereas others are imbued
with love and support. Yet despite enormous challenges, Aboriginal persons with
disabilities are involved in individual as well as collective advocacy and activism

through their own efforts; with their families; and through Aboriginal disability organizations at local, national, regional and international levels. Nonetheless, much of the time — and despite their significant numbers — Aboriginal persons with disabilities are often an unheard, hidden and forgotten population.

### "Triple Jeopardy": Research on Aboriginal Peoples in Canada

Reflecting this broader invisibility and the relative scarcity of Aboriginal academics, especially Aboriginal academics who themselves have disabilities, few social researchers in Canada have taken an interest in these marginalized people. An exception is Doreen Demas (1993), who wrote an article, among others, titled "Triple Jeopardy: Native Women with Disabilities," and participated in numerous reports on disability in Aboriginal communities. A non-Indigenous researcher, Marcia Rioux from York University, is engaged in a research project called "Enlarging the Circle" that seeks to improve monitoring of disability and disability rights in collaboration with Aboriginal communities (Rioux 2014). Outside of Canada, there has been some research about Aboriginal peoples with disabilities, particularly in Australia (e.g., Gething 1995; Biddle et al. 2012). However, these are typically not from Indigenous perspectives. In the United States, there are a number of studies, including the works by Catherine Marshall and colleagues' work on urban and elderly Aboriginal persons (Marshall et al. 1996). Jeffrey Edward Davis has written a book called *Hand Talk* (2010) on the historical and ongoing use of sign language among Native Americans, including Native American deaf persons (importantly, many of those who identify as Deaf see themselves as belonging to a distinct community of difference rather than as having any physical impairment).

Outside of academia, the Assembly of First Nations has written occasional discussion papers, including policy perspective around children and health with relevance for disabilities. This approach, for instance, includes a complex model incorporating the medicine wheel and considering the broad social determinants of health and disability: Indigenous self-determination, ecological destruction, the role of Elders and so on (2008: 18). A decade ago in the United States, the National Council on Disability (2003) collaborated with Aboriginal nations to publish a 220-page report titled "Understanding Disabilities in American Indian and Alaska Native Communities." In Australia, the First Peoples Disability Network Australia (First Peoples Disability Network Australia 2014) conducts some of its own research from the perspectives of diverse First Peoples with disabilities. Internationally, the United Nations has published a number of reports and papers from its conferences on Indigenous persons with disabilities (e.g., United Nations Economic and Social Council 2013).

Douglas Durst's own research on this topic, now ongoing for close to twenty years, is one of the few sustained voices in this area of social research in Canada.

There was an abundance of research on disabilities and often oppressive research (research assuming that Aboriginal peoples are in a "deficit" against a supposedly desirable non-Aboriginal norm) relating to First Nations/Aboriginal peoples. There was a paucity of research that brought the two topics together in a way respecting Aboriginal perspectives, yet the issue is critical to the lives of thousands of Aboriginal people with disabilities. My work in Canada's north provided me with face-to-face contact with many of these individuals hidden and often unheard in their isolated communities.

This chapter draws on these past decades of research, including a project with the National Association of Friendship Centres (Durst 2006), a Canada-wide network of 119 off-reserve service providers for Aboriginal persons (nafc.ca). These centres are often the "front-line" service providers to Aboriginal persons with a range of disabilities. This study found that these people experience a triple jeopardy: they are Aboriginal, they have disabilities and they are often urban (off-reserve). Women are even further disadvantaged (Demas 1993; Durst and Bluechardt 2001). Aboriginal people with disabilities have experienced racism, oppression and discrimination from the larger society, and often in their home committees as well. As Doreen Demas observes, "The attitude of Aboriginal People toward those who live with any disability is not that much different from those of the rest of society. People live with fear of the unknown and ignorance of the facts" (Fierce 2011). Yet, like Doreen Demas, they survive and many fight back, demanding services and programs to enhance their quality of life inside and outside their communities and ameliorate disadvantages that are not inherent but emerge from unsupportive social conditions.

This chapter tells this story of survival and resilience within a policy approach; it includes some direct quotes from Aboriginal persons with disabilities about their own experiences. Not least, we draw on the words of the (late) Everett Soop, a former Blood tribal council member best known for his caustic cartoons lampooning both colonial and First Nations politicians, who was also a Native disability activist (Greer 2014). We conclude by drawing on organized advocacy by and for disabled Aboriginal persons to make specific, concrete suggestions that can make important differences to Aboriginal persons with disabilities right now. Arguably, major success in these areas will depend not on any single measure, but on broader movements of Aboriginal resurgence and strengthening the voices of Aboriginal persons with disabilities within these resurgence movements, so that the double stigmatization and profound social inequalities suffered by Aboriginal persons with disabilities are challenged. This will begin a process whereby preventable disabilities are lessened and where Aboriginal communities and disabled people can work from positions of strength, not poverty and discrimination, to support Aboriginal persons with disabilities as they seek to live full, meaningful lives.

## Truth-Telling and the Risks of Stigmatization

Given the long and unhappy relationship between non-Aboriginal researchers and Aboriginal communities (Durst 2010; Tuhiwai Smith 1999), it is important that we situate ourselves. Neither of us is an Aboriginal person. We do not have Aboriginal heritage nor a disability. However, Douglas's research has been conducted in close cooperation with Aboriginal communities and, more specifically, with the explicit aim of seeking to support Aboriginal persons with disabilities. Moreover, we have sought throughout this chapter to highlight Aboriginal persons with disabilities' perspectives, in their own words. This approach is not without its tensions. Aboriginal peoples are in an unequal, colonial relationship that has twisted settler-Aboriginal relationships. As educated White researchers, we are part of those unequal relations that colonialism has exacerbated. Despite our efforts and cautions, there are dangers of speaking "for" rather than "with" Aboriginal persons with disabilities.

Indeed, one consequence of colonialism is that Aboriginal persons with disabilities are often marginalized, both in mainstream society and often also by other Aboriginal persons and formal First Nations, Métis and Inuit leadership. Everett Soop, who liked to call himself "the pitbull of native journalism" (Galt Museum 2009) became a disability advocate when he became impaired because of muscular dystrophy. He described the marginalization he and other Aboriginal persons with disabilities experienced this way: "Without doubt, the Native disabled are the most discriminated by their own people, their own tribal leaders" (Crow 1987); but not only by their own leadership. To support Aboriginal persons with disabilities means truthfully describing the ways that this happens, as well as the ways they are marginalized by colonial federal and provincial governments, and by settler Canadians. In an article for *The Saskatchewan Indian*, Soop characterized what he saw as the very difficult political situation of Aboriginal persons with disabilities:

> To be handicapped and to be native means to be doubly pitted against the whole Canadian establishment. Compound this plight (of "struggling native populations") with a disability, physical or mental, and the result is awesome — human misery and hopelessness that takes more than a welfare cheque to alleviate. (1998)

The risk, however, in telling the truth is the stigmatization of Aboriginal communities by settlers, who are at the same time "experts," in a familiar scenario whose consequences are not usually borne by the researcher, but by the Aboriginal peoples. Moreover, such stigmatization is damaging to Aboriginal persons with disabilities, who face significant, institutionalized forms of racism and violence as a consequence of such pathologizing of Aboriginal peoples. To minimize if not eliminate these dangers while still accurately describing the challenges faced by Aboriginal persons with disabilities, we contextualize the realities presented here within the broader fact of the colonial relationship. Moreover, we make it clear that Aboriginal communities may be the sites for critical, positive interventions that must be extended and made more general so that Aboriginal persons with disabilities have their needs met and live full, self-determining lives. Certainly, Aboriginal persons with disabilities will continue to face deep inequalities as long as the communities they come from are mired in the poverty that is the deliberate consequence of centuries of colonization.

Nonetheless, we do make a case for a particular conception of self-determination and sovereignty by Aboriginal peoples. We are arguing that Aboriginal self-governance must include the voices of Aboriginal persons with disabilities, voices that are too often excluded. To quote Everett Soop, once again speaking more than two decades ago but in a way that is still too relevant today, "Along comes the Native Handicapped Groups with their proposals. Who is ready to listen? Not too many people" (1988). A precondition to hearing their voices in self-determining Aboriginal communities is ensuring that their needs are met; but meeting those needs means listening to how they are articulated by Aboriginal persons with disabilities who are experts about their own situations. As Soop explained, "I am not an expert on Indians ... I am an Indian and I have a right to speak my truth as I live and experience it" (Alia 2012: 160).

Given this, some might see our recommendations around Aboriginal persons with a disability as yet another instance of settlers imposing their views on Aboriginal communities, in addition to making recommendations for Canadian society and settler governments and agencies. Instead, we would suggest that our arguments support demands that emerge from Aboriginal persons with disabilities themselves. Again, this is an effort to speak "with" and not "for" Aboriginal persons with disabilities. But it means that we must frontally address the real everyday challenges faced by these people, both the ways that colonial society creates disability and the ways that Aboriginal people with disabilities have been failed by their own leadership. In this contribution, Everett Soop gives just one example of the ways that colonial relations combine perversely with impairments and difference to create intolerable situations:

> What about the disabled children who are forced (and I mean this literally as well as figuratively) to take up residences in strange homes leaving their parents, just so they can go to deaf or blind school. They go away, learn a sign language, only to come back to their families who cannot understand them. How many Canadian parents would protest strongly if they had to send their children hundreds of miles from home to live among strangers

with a different language and different customs. Let me say this: for every disability there are a multitude of problems to go along with it. (1988)

Like Everett Soop, however, we believe this situation is not a fatality, but a question of political will, which means taking Aboriginal persons with disabilities and their needs seriously and challenging a colonial context that creates "a multitude of problems."

## The Complex Legal Definition of Aboriginal Peoples by Canada

As Walter and Andersen (2013) argue, most of the statistical information we know about Aboriginal Peoples has been developed by the Canadian government, not by Aboriginal peoples themselves. This means that the statistical categories reflect Canadian state priorities and worldviews, not those of Aboriginal peoples. With that important caveat in mind, close to 4 percent of the total Canadian population report some Aboriginal origin (Statistics Canada 2006). The Aboriginal people in what is now Canada comprise numerous cultural and ethnic groups; all are diverse, with unique cultural systems and historical experiences. With the enactment of the federal Indian Act (1876) and the Constitution Act (1982), colonial categories were developed to classify Aboriginal people. The term "First Nations people" is used to describe persons who are status or registered Indians as defined by the Indian Act.

Many First Nations do not recognize the colonial government of Canada and maintain that they are sovereign peoples. Against such Aboriginal insistence on their own sovereignty against colonial "ownership," the Crown argues that federally recognized Aboriginal persons are under the fiduciary responsibility of the federal government. Status Indians are registered with the federal government and have special rights to income tax exclusion, healthcare, housing, and education in exchange for land surrendered to the federal government. This interpretation is contested by First Nations peoples, some of whom argue that they never "surrendered" lands because this idea of land as private property that can be owned and so surrendered is foreign to their worldviews (RCAP 1996a). For the purposes of the federal government, however, this interpretation is assumed, and special rights apply when they live on reserve; however, if they move off reserve, some of their treaty entitlements are restricted.

On the other hand, the phrase "Aboriginal people" is a broader term used to define all those people who identify with being of Aboriginal ancestry and may be of mixed background. The Indian Act does not apply to non-status Indians (Aboriginal persons) and they must receive benefits from the province, as do all other Canadian citizens (Brizinski 1989). "Métis people," to use Chris Andersen's (2014) definition, are a nation with shared history and culture historically centered on the Red River region. However, self-identification may mean that individuals of "mixed" Indigenous and non-Indigenous heritage are included in this category (Walter and Andersen 2013: 125). Like other Indigenous nations, many Métis argue that their sovereignty is self-determined and does not depend on colonial recognition. Pragmatically, of course, formal government recognition of the Métis as Aboriginal in 1982 has legal consequences, affecting Métis individuals, including those with disabilities. Finally, the "Inuit" are Aboriginal peoples of the Arctic and sub-Arctic regions of the North and are under a special agreement to receive federal benefits under the Indian Act. Importantly, in 1984, the federal Bill C-31 was passed to reinstate Aboriginal women, children and others who lost their status, notably as a result of legislated discrimination against women given off-reserve education, employment and marriage. The passing of this bill has led to the dramatic increase in the number of Indian people holding status in Canada.

Consequently, situations regarding Aboriginal/First Nations peoples are complex, including varying legal definitions by the colonial government, contested Aboriginal self-determination and with further diversity given urban and rural, on- and off-reserve populations, as well as diversity in language and culture. This complexity makes simple assumptions or generalizations misleading. In an immediate way, however, this complex legal environment around what it means to be "Aboriginal" matters in everyday life for Aboriginal persons with disabilities because it creates jurisdictional complexity and ambiguity. Demands that specific needs be met — for instance, for a motorized wheelchair to enable mobility or for special education support for a child with developmental disabilities — are sometimes resisted by Aboriginal authorities who say it is a provincial or federal responsibility. Such ongoing battles seek to make the federal government fulfill treaty rights where these exist, and so have broad political importance. However, they translate into immediate hardship for Aboriginal persons with disabilities. A similar justification is used by the colonial governments, which often argue that the needs of Aboriginal persons with disabilities should be paid through inadequate local Aboriginal budgets. As Soop describes it, both Canadian and tribal governments have been "kicking the football around as to who is responsible for Native disabled" (Crow 1987).

Moreover, the complex legal jurisdictional environment makes it difficult for Aboriginal persons with disabilities to know who they should approach for vital funding and service support, and it means that movement on- and off-reserve disrupts continuity of vital services to Aboriginal people with disabilities. Doreen Demas (1993: 54) explains one of her own experiences of this "ping-ponging" back and forth between different services this way:

> I was told by one worker at the Canadian Institute for the Blind [CNIB] in my response for my request for a closed circuit TV reader, which I needed

for my education, that as a Native person with status I was not eligible for VRDP [Vocational Rehabilitation of Disabled Persons] allocated equipment and that VRDP students had first priority to these devices. The worker told me that as a Native person I was not eligible for VRDP and as a status Indian I was the responsibility of Indian Affairs and it was to them that I should make the request. However, not more than two days prior to that, I had been told by someone from the education department of Indian Affairs that there was no money in their department for these devices and that I was registered with the CNIB and that I should make my request to [the] CNIB. This is just one example of a situation where the lack of clarity and the bureaucratic round-around prevents Natives with disabilities from getting adequate services.

## Defining Disability

The reader will note that terms like "the disabled" or "disabled person" are not used. Instead, the term "persons with disabilities" is applied because it attempts to recognize the person first and the disability second.[1] It attempts to reduce the objectification of this marginalized group. Adopting this term, however, does not resolve the questions around defining disability. Operationalizing the term "disability" is difficult considering the array of historically changing interpretations or meanings based on medical, administrative, and self-defined concepts of disability. Historically, these definitions have been used as a means of segregating individuals and limiting their access to goods and services.

In 1980, the World Health Organization (WHO) addressed the need for a more concise definition in the International Classification of Impairments, Disabilities, and Handicaps (ICIDH). ICIDH had as its principle aim to characterize three distinct dimensions of "disablement": impairment, disability, and handicap (WHO 1980: 27–29).

> Impairment: Any loss or abnormality of psychological, physiological or anatomical structure or function.
>
> Disability: Any restriction or lack (resulting from an impairment) of ability to perform an activity in the manner or within the range considered normal for a human being.
>
> Handicap: A disadvantage for a given individual, resulting from an impairment or disability, that limits or prevents the fulfilment of a role that is normal, depending on age, sex, social and cultural factors, for that individual. (WHO 1980: 27–29)

So a person might have limited vision that is an impairment, but corrective eyeglasses provides "normal" vision. The limited vision does not become a disability. A disability such as a leg injury may restrict walking and be a handicap in walking, but not for working on a computer. It is important to focus on the abilities of the person and not the limitations. However, these definitions are based on the assumptions of non-Aboriginal, able-bodied people about what is normal, and, as such, are situated within the experience of non-Aboriginal, able-bodied people.

Moreover, such definitions focus on the individual and take a medical or bio-physical orientation (Barnes 2012), which interprets "disability" as deficiency. Such an approach emphasizes finding a "cure" and "rehabilitation," because it assumes that the challenges encountered by peoples with disabilities are written into their bodies and minds. Therefore, this model can ignore the ways that disability is socially created and can also ignore the attendant violation of rights, societal exclusion and oppression that persons with disabilities experience. At worst, such models may reinforce or at least not contradict deeply damaging stereotypes. To quote Everett Soop once again, "When you say disabled people, some people will still think of us as freaks, Frankensteins, and stuff like that. I know it's ludicrous but nonetheless it's true" (Crow 1987).

Consequently, such medical definitions are now broadly contested, with persons with disabilities arguing that it is not the disability that is the problem, but how the society reacts to it. Among other insights, the social model of disability emphasizes that disability is the loss of a valued function, and what is valued is different in different cultures. Disability is a social and political construction. For instance, an Aboriginal person with disabilities who requests support for special needs education and is refused by both local Aboriginal and provincial governments on jurisdictional grounds (each holding the other authority responsible), is effectively "disabled" by this dispute. The problem is not her "impairment," but the social failure to provide her with the support she needs to be successful in school. Disability is thus a political and social issue, not an "individual" biomedical concern.

At the same time, disability is connected to culture (Stone 2005). Differences between Aboriginal cultures and the dominant culture, and even within Aboriginal cultures, lead to differences in what constitutes a disability, causes of disabilities, and appropriate interventions. Gething (1995: 78) notes that Aboriginal people may not see themselves as having a disability, whereas the "trained professional" might, an explanation for the fact that medical professionals "detect" higher rates of disability in Aboriginal communities than Aboriginal individuals report themselves. It may be that only obvious and noticeable conditions such as an amputation or severe physical impairment are thought of as a disability. Subtle forms of fetal alcohol syndrome or mental health issues are not identified as constituting disability by many Aboriginal persons, although medical professionals typically conceive these as related to disability. Although it is difficult to generalize, it may be that in many Aboriginal cultures "disability is rarely seen as a separate issue, but is perceived as part of problems which are widespread and accepted as part of the life cycle" (Gething 1995: 81).

In some Aboriginal languages, there are no words that can be directly translated from "disability" (Durst 2006; Steinstra 2012). Depending on the cultural beliefs and values, conditions that are classified as disabilities by dominant ideology may not be considered as such in a particular First Nation. In some contexts, some Aboriginal cultures do not accept biophysical causes for disabilities and understand them from a spiritual, Creator-given perspective (Thomas 1981). As such, the cultural definition of disability emerges out of social relationships, including spiritual understandings, not out of rigid medical or physiological criteria (Thomas 1981). For example, many Hopi believe that a person born with a condition that inhibits mobility, but can still contribute to the functioning of the community, is not disabled (Dapcic 1995). The Navajo culture emphasizes the cause of the disability and focuses less on the symptoms. In some contemporary Aboriginal cultures, some individuals may see disability as "bad medicine," a curse for which the person with a disability is blamed (Niganii 2011). There is also evidence that some disabilities are seen as special gifts from the Creator. Reflecting on a "disfiguring" disability, an elder states that "to be born imperfect was a sign of specialness" (Wiebe and Johnson 1998: 423). In such ways, some Aboriginal social constructions of disability may sometimes echo and sometimes differ radically from mainstream social constructions, which often understand disability as stigma or tragedy.

## Aboriginal People with Disabilities

Approximately 4.4 million or 14.3 percent of Canadians report having a physical disability for which they need some assistance in everyday activities (Statistics Canada 2006). Of course, the percentage of persons with disabilities increases with age. Only 4.7 percent of adults between 15–24 years of age have a disability, whereas 56.3 percent of adults 75 years of age or older have a disability. According to the WHO, six basic types of disability are identified: physical disabilities, developmental disabilities, psychiatric disabilities, learning disabilities, hearing disabilities, and visual disabilities.

The latest statistics on Aboriginal people with disabilities is more than twenty years old: the 1991 Aboriginal Peoples Survey. No serious data collection has been done since its publication. The survey found that 31.4 percent of the Aboriginal population reported some form of disability, which was more than twice the national average. There is no reason to believe that the numbers have decreased over the past two decades. Clearly, the rate of disability is high for this population, and it increases significantly with age. And because women normally live longer, they have higher rates than men. Approximately 66.5 percent of Aboriginal people who are 55 years or older live with a disability (Statistics Canada 1994).

Of those surveyed in the Aboriginal Peoples Survey, 72 percent classified their disability as mild, with 4 percent indicating a severe disability. Disabilities were most frequently caused by injuries, followed by aging and congenital factors (SK 1999). Although Aboriginal people have genetic disabilities at about the same rate as the rest of Canadians, they have a higher rate of disability due to environment and trauma-related disabilities. "The disparity between Aboriginal and non-Aboriginal rates of disability corresponds to disparities in rates of injury, accident, violence, self-destructive or suicidal behaviour and illness (such as diabetes) that can result in permanent impairment" (RCAP 1996a: 148). This is arguably where one of the clearest links lies between colonialism and Aboriginal rates of disability, as centuries-old efforts to destroy Aboriginal ways of being and knowing, including through the horrors of residential schools, have left their legacies in self-hatred and self-destruction.

What some call "lifestyle" diseases associated with socioeconomic conditions are quite prevalent among First Nations people (Frideres and Gadacz 2012). However, it might be more accurate to speak about the deliberately created poverty of Aboriginal peoples than individual "lifestyle" choices. Aboriginal peoples did not choose to be contained on reserves; did not choose to attend residential schools in which they were forcibly stripped of their languages and ways of knowing; and did not choose to subsequently live in poverty, cut off simultaneously from the natural world and from cash employment, as James (Sa'ke'j) Youngblood Henderson observes in Chapter One of this book. Unhealthy lifestyle choices take place within the historical circumstances of colonialism that were not chosen, but imposed by force and through law.

Likewise, the pollution of reserve lands has clearly led to disability in many Aboriginal communities; for instance, in the well-documented case of blindness and other impairments caused through mercury poisoning in the "Grassy Narrows" reserve near Kenora, Ontario, which now faces new threats from logging (Simpson 2014). In such ways, disability is bound into the reserve system of apartheid. The pollution of the natural environment on reserves is itself possible because Aboriginal persons' health is not important to racist colonial governments.

Finally, the moral turpitude of multinational enterprises that pollute, and the failure of colonial governments to hold them responsible, means that many Aboriginal communities face ongoing threats to their well-being and preventable disabilities, including blindness and other forms of disability. At this time, the conflict is being played out in the tar sands of Alberta and the Chipewyan people who live downstream from the development. Holistic Aboriginal worldviews, emphasizing the connectedness between the natural world, all living and human beings, arguably makes clear this connection between ecological destruction and disability.

In "policy" terms, Aboriginal people are positioned at the lowest end of the socioeconomic scale regarding education, employment, income, and health. Housing on many remote and rural reserves is inadequate and fails to meet basic housing standards for amenities and structure. The unemployment rate can be as high as 95 percent in some Aboriginal communities, although such statistics may likewise mask traditional forms of life-sustaining activities as well as unpaid caring work, often carried out by Aboriginal women. On average, Aboriginal people have lower education and often live in poverty with poorer health than mainstream Canadians. If Aboriginal persons with disabilities struggle to make their voices heard, including within their own communities, it is partly because of the magnitude of these pervasive dehumanizing conditions that make advocacy and organizing difficult.

Moreover, the situation is even worse for those with disabilities. Seventy percent of First Nations people with disabilities have low literacy levels (NAND 1994; RCAP 1996a). Ninety percent of all First Nations people with disabilities living on reserve have income levels well below the poverty line (NAND 1994). In summary, they suffer under poor economic, political and social living conditions (RCAP 1996a). Everett Soop summarized the situation this way: "the native handicapped is at the bottom of the totem pole in society" (1988).

Many First Nations people with disabilities move to urban areas to obtain treatment or to be closer to services. They find that accessible housing is scarce and education and training opportunities are inadequate, as are home care services, employment opportunities and transportation. In addition, many are isolated and have limited opportunities for social interaction (RCAP 1996a). Soop refers to "that hideous feeling of isolation," often experienced by "a native person with even a relatively minor handicap trying to make it by using the existing services in a nearby town or city" (1988). This is suggestive of the complex challenges facing Aboriginal persons with disabilities, including both the need for support services within Aboriginal communities and support that is also culturally appropriate specifically for Aboriginal persons with disabilities in urban settings.

### Aboriginal Persons with Disabilities: A Closer Look

Because the rate of disability among Aboriginal peoples is more than double the national average (31.4 percent), one can estimate that there are approximately 267,389 First Nations persons and approximately 439,815 Aboriginal persons with a disability in Canada (Statistics Canada 2011). Despite their numbers, these people have become a hidden population and are lost in the overall health and social service systems.

Based on census data, Table 1 presents a reasonably accurate reflection of types of disabilities among Aboriginal peoples. In the first two columns, percentages of six categories of disabilities have been reported from the total population of persons with disabilities comparing the Canadian and Aboriginal populations. The other columns present the percentage of First Nations with status who live on a reservation and those who do not, by Métis persons and Inuit persons. The census was self-reported; hence the figures represent the respondent's perception of his/her disability.

**Table 1 Percentages of Adult Aboriginal Persons**
**with Physical Disabilities Across Canada**

| Disability | Total Population | Total Aboriginal Population | First Nations On-reserve | First Nations Off-reserve | Métis | Inuit |
|---|---|---|---|---|---|---|
| Mobility | 45 | 45 | 47 | 45 | 44 | 36 |
| Hearing | 23 | 35 | 39 | 33 | 34 | 44 |
| Seeing | 9 | 24 | 32 | 21 | 22 | 24 |
| Agility | 44 | 35 | 34 | 36 | 38 | 26 |
| Speaking | 10 | 13 | 14 | 13 | 13 | 10 |
| Other | 37 | 36 | 37 | 37 | 35 | 36 |

*Source: Statistics Canada 1994, #11—001E*

Results indicate that mobility is a serious problem for all groups and is reported equally, except for the Inuit. The Inuit primarily live in small Arctic communities and close to family, so help is generally available, which may explain why mobility is perceived as less of a problem. The same explanation is offered for the lower rates of disability around agility, with Aboriginal persons reporting lower rates of disability than non-Aboriginal populations. Although some urban Aboriginal persons with disabilities may be isolated, many other Aboriginal people do not live alone so having somebody to assist with putting on a coat, or opening a tight-fitting jar is less of a problem for persons with disabilities than in more individualistic living arrangements. There is evidence to suggest that it is the perception of the disability that plays out in the reporting; and in other social and cultural contexts, they would be reporting a "disability."

Hearing disabilities are also a concern and their prevalence is much higher among Aboriginal persons; it is twice the national average among the Inuit. It is suspected that this disability is related to two environmental concerns. First, many children live in inadequate and cramped quarters and high rates of childhood ear infections have been consistently reported. These ear infections have resulted in permanent but preventable hearing loss. The lack of prompt action at the onset of the infant's infection can have permanent effects, demonstrating the need for education and prevention. The cramped quarters are a consequence of poverty, so the high rates are related to socioeconomic determinants of health, as well as the lack of funding for health and medical care, especially in on-reserve communities.

Second, the hunting culture sustained among the Inuit involves guns, snow-mobiles, and outboard motors. These loud and continuous noises are creating long-term hearing loss, particularly in the absence of protective gear. However, such protective equipment, which requires new habits, may furthermore be expensive and hence inaccessible. The issues then, are not the supposedly "deficient" cultures of Aboriginal peoples, but sociodeterminants of health, including poverty, inad-equate, underfunded healthcare especially in on-reserve communities and lack of access to equipment that prevents disability.

The higher rate of a visual disability (seeing), which is two to three times the national average, is alarming. The loss of vision has a high personal cost and can lead to isolation and loneliness, in addition to the high financial costs associated with healthcare and caring. Visual disabilities among Aboriginal persons are related to high rates of Type II diabetes. Type II diabetes is a condition that can be amelio-rated or perhaps prevented with lifestyle changes such as exercise and diet, thereby controlling glucose levels. But more holistic Aboriginal worldviews suggest that such changes are not enough. For instance, the Native Women's Association of Canada (2008) uses a medicine wheel that lays out environmental, physical, emo-tional and spiritual components that must be addressed when developing ways to combat diabetes among Aboriginal women. Some prevention is possible. Ironically, however, the "lifestyle changes" that have led to widespread diabetes are largely the result of colonization and the deliberate destruction of traditional Aboriginal ways of living. This suggests that healthier lifestyles depend on Aboriginal resurgence and reclaiming and reinventing traditions so that Aboriginal health is improved.

In the final categories of speaking and "other," the percentages of disability are similar among all groups. Speaking disabilities would be predominately related to strokes and heart disease, which has been increasing in recent decades.

The academic literature makes the link between health, socioeconomic, political and cultural conditions, and disability. The issues are complex and interrelated; however, the article by Durst, Manual and Bluechardt (2006) identifies and explores these themes. Aboriginal people with disabilities face the same difficulties as others with disabilities, but because of their Aboriginal ancestry, they encounter racism, oppression and discrimination. They experience these difficulties in living independently and accessing resources to maximize independence. The idea of independence is widely understood as the ability to be able to live a lifestyle that allows for individual choices and decision-making. Sadly, they feel discriminated based on their Aboriginal descent.

*Being disabled is one thing, but being disabled and Indian is a whole other problem. Indian people do not have a very good reputation and it makes it hard on us to get ahead. The Bands don't want to help us, once we leave the*

*reserve and the services in the city might not help you because they don't get*
*funding for you. Also, if you are applying for a job, some employees are racist,*
*so are some landlords.*

—Female, 51: Agility

Accessible and affordable transportation both on- and off-reserve is a constant hassle. Access to education and training continues to be a problem, and completing programs is difficult with related transportation and health issues. Finding adequate employment and income leaves many fully dependent on social assistance, making them feel like welfare clients. Their self-worth is greatly diminished. Although Aboriginal culture stresses family support, many families are struggling to survive and have little left to support family members with disabilities. Accessing reliable and confidential personal supports is difficult.

Personal supports, such as attendant care, equipment repair, service provision and counselling, were supposed to be available, but these services are difficult to access. The responsibility often falls on family members.

*There is not any compensation for the family and that's who you rely on or that's*
*who you have to rely on. The family system can burn-out really fast without*
*help, and that has a big effect on the disabled person.*

—Male, 36: Able-body

*About care giving, it's really lacking … I know [my husband] took a care-giving*
*course three years ago. They started having their meetings and after a while*
*everyone started saying they just didn't have the time because they had people*
*at home they had to look after and there were no supports in place to help out*
*during those times, when they had to be away from home.*

—Female, 35: Quadriplegic

## "The World Is Here for Us to Live": Fighting Back

Aboriginal persons with disabilities face enormous challenges, but they have fought back both through heroic individual actions and sometimes through collective agency. For instance, since the 1960s and until his death in 2001, Soop (best known for his biting, satirical cartoons and column in the *Kanai News*) was an advocate for Aboriginal persons with disabilities, driven by his own challenges as a Native individual with muscular dystrophy. He emphasized, however, "I think that the world is here for us to live and that is what I am going to do, live. I'm not sick, I'm disabled, there is a difference" (Chopra 2001). An official advisor to the Alberta government, he helped produce the 1993 report "Removing Barriers: An Action

Plan for Aboriginal Peoples with Disabilities," although like too many other reports, many good recommendations in it have never been implemented.

In 1989, Gary Tinker, a Métis disability advocate who has cerebral palsy, walked 650 km on his crutches from La Ronge to Regina (Gary Tinker Federation for the Disabled 2014). Through his foundation and numerous related activities, he has sought to organize and advocate for northern people with disabilities and was on the 2010 Métis National Council that is creating a national advisory group to improve the employment of Métis persons with disabilities. His foundation also has other gatherings, such as a "From Compassion to Action" meeting of Northern Aboriginal persons with disabilities in Saskatchewan.

Doreen Demas (International Disability Alliance Secretariat 2013), a blind activist already quoted, has spoken and written about disabled Aboriginal peoples over the past several decades, including as a voice at international conferences through the auspices of various United Nations bodies. There, she wryly observes, she sometimes has to explain to disabled persons from developing countries that although Canada is a wealthy nations, many disabled Aboriginal people still struggle for basic access to decent housing, education and other vital supports.

These individuals join many more anonymous activists who have created organizations such as the British Columbia Aboriginal Network on Disability Society (2014). Organizations such as the Native Women's Association of Canada have produced reports that are concerned with Aboriginal women with disabilities. In 2013, for instance, it published a report titled "Understanding Within," making the voices of Aboriginal women with neurological disorders heard and offering policy recommendations.

Collectively, these voices have often asked for straightforward improvements, including these: an immediate resolution of jurisdictional issues so that services are accessible for Aboriginal persons with disabilities; mainstream agencies for the disabled must hire and adapt services for Aboriginal persons with disabilities; First Nations leadership needs to take disabled Aboriginal persons seriously and begin a sustained dialogue; and coordination among Aboriginal persons with disabilities must be facilitated, through funding, services, technologies and more at the local, regional, national and international levels. The following quotes succinctly express this frustration, especially with respect to the failure of many First Nations' governments to take seriously the voices and needs of Aboriginal persons with disabilities:

> *Disabled people will altogether be forgotten about, because right now we are at the bottom of the pile, but with self-government we won't be in the pile at all. They aren't concerned with the disabled, they're more concerned with making money. Even though they are supposed to get additional funding for the disabled, we don't see any of that.*
>
> —*Female, 35: Quadriplegic*

*It is necessary for the Bands, more specifically, Chief and Council to become aware. Chief and Council are not very supportive because they are not aware or because disability issues are just not a priority to them. But that's where it starts because they could start creating services like counselling services and attendant services. They need to be willing to allocate money. Nowadays you hear about all those reserves getting land claim dollars back, you think they would have some dollars to help disabled Band members.*

—Female, 35: Quadriplegic

This coordination and support is necessary because Aboriginal persons with disabilities are a diverse group, with many different needs and varying demands about how these can be met. But it is up to them to determine their own needs, so their voices and agency must be supported.

This will not be simple. Even the idea of "inclusion" of Aboriginal persons with disabilities is contentious. Not least, the idea of "inclusion" may recall colonizing efforts to "integrate" Aboriginal persons into mainstream, colonial society. When applied to Aboriginal persons with disabilities, it may additionally imply efforts to "normalize" into able-bodied practices and values. The real question may not be "inclusion" so much as: "Inclusion on whose terms?" Such difficult questions cannot be resolved until there are regular forums supporting Aboriginal persons with disabilities, so that their voices are heard within and across their own communities as well as in formal political bodies and civil society. The disability slogan "Nothing About Us, Without Us" arguably needs to be "Indigenized" and reclaimed so that Aboriginal persons with disabilities are self-determining actors, to give new meaning to a word associated with Aboriginal struggles.

Many Aboriginal families with disabilities are not living an independent lifestyle, and the numerous barriers that inhibit independent living are deeply entrenched within society. Not all, but many parents have multiple problems and disabilities themselves. Although a strong and effective voice is required to initiate change and improve the conditions for persons with disabilities, this will not occur until Aboriginal persons participate in the decision-making processes that ultimately have an impact on their lives and the lives of their children.

## "Giving Them That Chance": Strategies for Change

Most of the previous studies have identified the barriers but offered few concrete solutions. This chapter offers four specific courses of action for resolving these issues. Listed in the following sections, these strategies for change can begin immediately and have to be done for real, long-lasting and significant change. These strategies are not based on a postcolonial situation. Indeed, although many Aboriginal persons with disabilities support self-government, as Doreen Demas explains, "there is a concern that their needs as persons with disabilities may not be included in the self-government processes" (1993: 53). Here, we take colonial structures such as provincial governments for granted because right now these are potential sites for positive change and because right now they do exercise powers that can make a difference, if properly channeled, to the lives of Aboriginal persons with disabilities.

Action #1: Establish Provincial Advocate Offices

Services and programs, which are readily available for many persons, are often inaccessible or denied to Aboriginal/First Nations persons and families with disabilities. An intergovernmental office should be established that could be based on Aboriginal people with disabilities and the provincial/federal and Aboriginal leadership. This intergovernmental effort should establish advocate offices for each province, with a director whose primary responsibility is to ensure that Aboriginal and First Nations persons with disabilities and their families receive the basic services and programs they are entitled to receive from whatever government is responsible. This "ombudsman" for Aboriginal persons with disabilities would facilitate the access to services and would be prepared to facilitate the client in achieving his/her rights. Achieving this may mean taking agencies, both government and nongovernment, to court; the position must have "teeth."

Action #2: Implement a National Jurisdictional Review Panel

There is an immediate need to resolve the jurisdictional problems outlined in the preceding pages. Repeatedly, studies have identified the jurisdictional difficulties and reported that these are a major barrier for this population. This intergovernmental team would complete a comprehensive review of the jurisdictional issues and propose a realistic system to adequately resolve it.

An intergovernmental review team should be established that could be based on the partners suggested for the ombudsman offices. It also must include Aboriginal persons with disabilities and the various levels of Aboriginal and non-Aboriginal governments. It must propose a system design or organizational structure to resolve this long-standing problem.

Action #3: Create a National Network of Aboriginal Health and Social Services Centres

As stated previously, there are overriding issues facing Aboriginal families in all major cities in Canada. They lose contact with their cultural and family supports. They face agencies and service providers who are intentionally and unintentionally unwelcoming. They face administrative bureaucracy and a cold impersonal system. Although the Friendship Centres attempt to address some of their needs, with funding dependent on multiple sources, the workers live with insecurity and instability. These Friendship Centres cannot do it alone.

There is a desperate need to take a hard and critical look at the provision of health and social services to off-reserve First Nations/Aboriginal individuals and families. The model of cooperation between the Vancouver Friendship Centre and Vancouver Native Health Society may be an example, but again, funding prohibits any long-term strategic planning. Each of the major cities should have a professionally staffed and self-governed Aboriginal Health and Social Services agency that delivers a variety of health and social programs such as outpatient addictions counselling, family supports, education, public health, and health prevention. Comprehensive services should be available, and management/administrative systems should be developed. Secure and dependable financial arrangements should be established in the same way provincial health and social services are organized.

Action #4: Expand the Research Knowledge Base

It is recommended that the federal government departments, including Human Resources Development Canada, in conjunction with relevant partners, initiate expanded and strategic research endeavours in the areas of need identified in this report. Effective and efficient policy development, both nationally and regionally, as well as programs for planning and service delivery, must be based on empirical research findings completed under the rigours of accepted systematic inquiry. Importantly, this should include research done from Aboriginal perspectives, including Aboriginal persons with disabilities. The relationship between social and policy research and sound practice has too frequently been ignored.

Four potential research areas are

- disabilities among Aboriginal children, with a focus on prevention;
- issues facing specific disabilities, including strategic interventions;
- issues regarding the family and its role; and
- aspirations of Aboriginal families regarding inclusion and integration.

Here, inclusion and integration does not mean assimilation into "mainstream" Canadian society and alienation from Aboriginal communities; rather, it means the inclusion and integration of Aboriginal persons with disabilities across all areas of life, especially their own communities. Although some literature does exist regarding the adult population of persons with disabilities, little information is available on the infants, children and adolescent Aboriginal population. Considering the increasing rate of a young Aboriginal population, an understanding of their circumstances and issues is crucial to providing proactive measures in the detection, prevention and intervention of disabilities. Also, it would be beneficial to examine the causes and implications of potentially disabling conditions such as chronic ear infections and fetal alcohol syndrome. As Alfred argues, this will require a serious look at the effects of colonization and the need for "holistic reconnection of people to each other and the land" (n.d. 33), so that such decolonization is ultimately an important foundation to meaningful policy and prevention strategies.

Further study is required to examine the role of the family in the care of family members with disabilities. The exploration of how Aboriginal families cope with family members who have disabilities, and how communities assist or alienate these families, needs further study. Considering the lack of support and services available to families with disabilities, it would be beneficial to examine what services and supports are available to family members both on- and off-reserve, and whether there is compensation.

There is also the need for an improved understanding of "inclusion" and "integration" from the families' perspectives. There are many assumptions of what citizenship and participation in Aboriginal nations and the broader Canadian society mean from different partners, and these assumptions may not coincide with the aspirations and goals of this population. Getting their voices heard is an important start to this process. Soop, while acknowledging enormous frustrations, put it this way:

> Most disabled Natives are highly motivated but nobody is giving them the chance. I think I have more or less been in the forefront because I have tried council, I have had access to the media and I have had so many other opportunities. These young people and other disabled have not had the opportunity and that's what we have to do is give them that chance. (Crow 1987)

The old man said, to have been born imperfect was a sign of specialness. As Canadians, where have we gone wrong? It is time to start to right the wrongs. It is hoped that this chapter will raise awareness and stimulate action in a collaborative, positive manner.

## Notes

1. Such terminology is not unanimously used within a diverse population of persons with disabilities. For instance, some advocates argue that "disabled person" is a political term. This term emphasizes that individuals — who may or may not consider themselves as having a physical or mental impairment — are disabled by social relations and infrastructures created for "standard" and normative bodies and minds. Hence, they prefer "disabled person" because it makes visible the political nature of disability. Disability does not result from anything inherent in their bodies or minds, but from social and political choices to not meet needs.

## REFERENCES

Alfred, Taiaiake. n.d. "Colonialism and State Dependency." Prepared for the National Aboriginal Health Organization Project. <web.uvic.ca/igov/uploads/pdf/Colonialism%20and%20State%20Dependency%20NAHO%20(Alfred).pdf>.

Alia, Valerie. 2012. *The New Media Nations: Indigenous Peoples and Global Communications.* New York: Berghahn Books.

Andersen, Chris. 2014. *Métis: Race, Recognition and the Struggle for Indigenous Peoplehood.* Vancouver: University of British Columbia Press.

Assembly of First Nations. 2008. *The Health of First Nations Children and the Environment.* Environmental Stewardship Unit. <afn.ca/uploads/files/rp-discussion_paper_re_childrens_health_and_the_environment.pdf>.

Barnes, C. 2012. "Understanding the Social Model of Disability: Past, Present and Future." In N. Watson, A. Roulstone, and C. Thomas, (eds.), *Routledge Handbook of Disability Studies.* Oxon, UK: Routledge, Taylor and Francis Group.

BCANDS (British Columbia Aboriginal Network on Disability Society). 2014. <bcands.bc.ca>.

Biddle, Nicholas et al. 2012. *Indigenous Australians and the National Disability Insurance Scheme: The Extent and Nature of Disability, Measurement Issues and Service Delivery Models.* Commonwealth of Australia. May be requested via <ag.gov.au/cca>.

Brizinski, P. 1993. *Knots in a String: An Introduction to Native Studies in Canada.* Saskatoon: Division of Extension and Community Relations, University of Saskatchewan.

Chopra, Gauri. 2001. "Everett Soop Footprints." Aboriginal Multi-Media Society (AMMS) (August 12.) <ammsa.com/content/everett-soop-footprints>.

Crow, Jackie Red. 1987. "The Two Sides of Everett Soop." *Windspeaker* 21, 5. <ammsa.com/node/16481>.

Dapcic, B. 1995. *Socio-Cultural Understanding of Disability: Perspectives from Members of the Hopi Tribe.* Flagstaff: Northern Arizona University.

Davis, Jeffrey Edward. 2010. *Hand Talk: Sign Language among American Indian Nations.* Cambridge, UK: Cambridge University Press.

Demas, Doreen. 1993. "Triple Jeopardy: Native Women with Disabilities." *Canadian Woman Studies* 13, 4.

Durst, Douglas. 2010. "Social Work Research with Aboriginal Students and Communities: Seeking Social Justice." In K. Brownlee, R. Neckoway, R. Delaney, and Douglas Durst (eds.), *Social Work and Aboriginal Peoples: Perspectives from Canada's Rural and Provincial Norths.* Thunder Bay, ON: Centre for Northern Studies, Lakehead University.

____. 2006. *Urban Aboriginal Families of Children with Disabilities: Social Inclusion or Exclusion?* Ottawa: National Association of Friendship Centres.

Durst, Douglas, and M. Bluechardt. 2001. "Urban Aboriginal Persons with Disabilities: Triple Jeopardy!" Regina, SK: Social Policy Research Unit, University of Regina. <uregina.ca/spru/spruweb/durst.html>.

Durst, Douglas, S. Manuel South, and M. Bluechardt. 2006. "Urban First Nations People with Disabilities Speak Out." *Journal of Aboriginal Health* 3, 1.

Fierce, Geoff. 2011. "Aboriginal Blindness." *Alliance for Equality of Blind Canadians.* <blindcanadians.ca/publications/cbm/23/aboriginal-blindness>.

First Peoples Disability Network Australia. 2014. <fpdn.org.au>.

Frideres, J., and R. Gadacz. 2012. *Aboriginal Peoples in Canada: Contemporary Conflicts*, ninth edition. Toronto: Pearson Canada.

Galt Museum. 2009. "Everett Soop Recognized in New Exhibit at the Galt." <galtmuseum.com/media/Everett%20Soop%20media%20kit.pdf>.

Gary Tinker Federation for the Disabled Inc. 2014. <garytinker.ca>.

Gething, L. 1995. "A Case Study of Australian Aboriginal People with Disabilities." *Australian Disabilities Review* 2, 1.

Greer, Sandy. 2014. "Everett Soop: A Story About Truth and Identity." <abilities.ca/everett-soop/>.

International Disability Advocacy Secretariat. 2013. "IDA and DRAF Side Event on Indigenous Women and Girls with Disabilities" (April 17). <internationaldisabiltyalliance.org>.

Marshall, C., M. Johnson, and S. Johnson. 1996. "Responding to the Needs of American Indians with Disabilities through Rehabilitation Counselor Education." *Rehabilitation Education* 10, 2 and 3.

NAND (National Aboriginal Network on Disability). 1994. *Little Mountain: A Mother's Story* and *If They Would Only Listen*. Ottawa: Status of Disabled Persons Secretariat, Human Resources and Labour Canada.

National Council on Disability. 2003. *Understanding Disabilities in American Indian and Alaska Native Communities: Toolkit Guide*. Washington: National Council on Disability. <ncd.gov/publications/2003/Aug12003>.

Niganii, Diane Scribe. 2012. "Idle No More Winnipeg: Doreen Demas at Odena." December 21. <youtube.com/watch?v=dT3cGyaasP0>.

____. 2011. "Disability: Curse or Gift?" October 7. <facesofankylosingspondylitis.com/diane-scribe-niiganii/>

NWAC (Native Women's Association of Canada). 2013. *Understanding Within: Research Findings and NWAC's Contributions to Canada's National Population Health Study on Neurological Conditions*. Ohsweken, ON: Author.

____. 2008. "Prevention of Type 2 Diabetes in Aboriginal Women." <nwac.ca/programs/nwac-diabetes-action-plan>.

RCAP (Royal Commission on Aboriginal Peoples). 1996a. *Aboriginal Peoples in Urban Centres: Report of the National Round Table on Aboriginal Urban Issues*. Ottawa: Ministry of Supply Services.

____. 1996b. *Gathering Strength*. Volume III. Ottawa: Ministry of Supply Services.

Rioux, Marcia. 2014. *Expanding the Circle*. Principal investigator for the Project and Co-Director of Disability Rights Promotion International, Faculty of Health, York University. <drpi.research.yorku.ca/NorthAmerica/ExpandingTheCircle>.

Simpson, Leanne. 2014. "Grassy Narrows First Nation 'Not Victims,' Says Advocate." July 31. <cbc.ca/news/aboriginal/grassy-narrows-first-nation-not-victims-says-advocate-1.2721974>.

SK (Saskatchewan's Women's Secretariat). 1999. *Profile of Aboriginal Women in Saskatchewan*. Regina: Author.

Soop, Everett. 1988. "Being Indian and Handicapped." *The Saskatchewan Indian* (April). <sicc.sk.ca/archive/saskindian/a88apr13.htm>.

Statistics Canada. 2011. "National Household Survey, 2011." Ottawa: Author. <statcan.

gc.ca/daily-quotidien/130508/dq130508a-eng.htm>.

____. 2006. "Persons with Disabilities." <statcan.gc.ca/tables-tableaux/sum-som/l01/cst01/health71a-eng.htm>.

____. 1994, 1991. *Aboriginal Peoples Survey: Disability and Housing.* Ottawa: Author.

Stienstra, D. 2012. *About Canada: Disability Rights.* Black Point, NS: Fernwood Publishing.

Stone, J. (ed.). 2005. *Culture and Disability: Providing Culturally Competent Services.* Thousand Oaks, CA: Sage.

Thomas, R. 1981. "Discussion." In F. Hoffman (ed.), *The American Indian Family: Strengths and Stresses.* Isleta, NM: American Indian Social Research.

Tuhiwai Smith, Linda. 1999. *Decolonizing Methodologies, Research and Aboriginal Peoples.* Dunedin, NZ: University of Otago Press.

United Nations Economic and Social Council. 2013. *Study on the Situation of Indigenous Persons with Disabilities with a Particular Focus on Challenges Faced with Regard to the Full Enjoyment of Human Rights and Inclusion in Development.* New York: United Nations. <un.org/disabilities/documents/ecosoc/e.c.19.2013.6.pdf>.

Walter, Maggie, and Chris Andersen. 2013. *Indigenous Statistics: A Quantitative Research Methodology.* Walnut Creek, CA: Left Coast Press.

Wiebe, R., and Y. Johnson. 1998. *Stolen Life: The Journey of a Cree Woman.* Toronto: A.A. Knopf Canada.

Withers, A. 2012. *Disability Politics and Theory.* Black Point, NS: Fernwood Publishing.

WHO (World Health Organization). 1980. *International Classification of Impairments, Disabilities and Handicaps.* Geneva: Author. <whqlibdoc.who.int/publications/1980/9241541261_eng.pdf>.

Chapter Four

# INDIGENOUS RESISTANCE IN COMPARATIVE PERSPECTIVE
## AN OVERVIEW WITH AN AUTOBIOGRAPHICAL RESEARCH CRITIQUE

*Rima Wilkes*

The following two photographs show Tsimshian Guardians demonstrating against the proposed Enbridge Northern Gateway pipeline. The pipeline would not only bring oil tankers into Tsimshian territory but would also cross the land of the many other First Nations whose territory spans the Pacific Ocean to the Alberta Tar Sands. And even though it is legally mandated in the Canadian Constitution that national energy projects and the provinces have a legal duty to consult Indigenous peoples, and even though the pipeline would cross unceded/stolen Aboriginal lands, from the outset the British Columbia and Alberta governments, as well as the representatives of Enbridge, have treated the pipeline as *un fait accompli*. They have been forced to backtrack in response to many Indigenous resistance events, such as the one pictured here. An ongoing multimillion dollar advertising campaign has tried to sell the project to First Nations as well as the non-Indigenous public.

Although the outcome of this advertising campaign is uncertain, what is certain is that there will continue to be opposition and resistance to this project. This example is just one of the many direct actions that the members of Indigenous nations have used to resist Canadian state colonialism. Colonial practices such as the imposition of the Northern Gateway pipeline assume that Indigenous lands and resources are *de facto* Canadian/provincial lands and resources, and treat

*February 2012, reproduced with permission from Charles Menzies*

consultation as a box to be checked off rather than a relationship with partners. Indigenous peoples have long brought attention and often successfully resisted these practices, although as Clifford (Kam'ayaam/Chachim'multhnii) Atleo observes in Chapter Six of this book, many have been cut off from the land and resources. Many Nuu-chah-nulth people, for example, now work for wage labour, although there are efforts to reinvent Nuu-chah-nulth economics.

Among the events written about by academics, both Indigenous and non-Indigenous, include campaigns by the Innu to resist low-level military flights over their territory (Alcantara 2007; Armitage and Kennedy 1989; Wadden 1996); resistance by Kettle and Stoney Pointers to the expropriation of their land for the Canadian Forces Base at Ipperwash (Edwards 2003; Miller 2005); the Siege at Kanehsatà:ke/Oka Crisis over the expansion of a golf course (Goodleaf 1995; Kalant 2004); the Gustafsen Lake standoff (Lambertus 2004); anti–2010 Olympic opposition (O'Bonsawin 2010); Lubicon Cree resistance (Goddard 1991); James Bay Cree activism (Niezen 2009); Tyendinaga Mohawk land reclamation (Pasternak et al. 2013); and the Six Nations land reclamation (Turtle Island Network News 2011). As a whole, not including the many Idle No More events, there have been more than five hundred resistance "events" since the 1980s.

These moments and movements of resistance have many different significations for their participants, and several chapters in this book explore these different meanings that, as Jeff Denis observes in Chapter Nine of this book, include intellectual, spiritual, emotional and physical aspects. In this chapter, I have two aims. First, I describe the contents of a database I have created that documents several hundred resistance events. As a non-Indigenous person, I have attempted to document aspects of Indigenous struggles against the Canadian state using the tools of mainstream sociology. This has advantages, but at the same time important limits. I continue to contend with these limits as a researcher and as someone who supports Indigenous self-determination and advocates Canadian divestment. My second aim in this chapter is therefore to reflect on the nature of these limits, which are not simply personal but also outcomes of being situated within a particular set of relationships inside and outside of the academy.

In considering both these aims, what is clear is that politics in Canada is business as usual. The Canadian state changes only when it is challenged to do so on political and/or legal grounds (Henderson, Chapter One of this book). And in the words of Irlbacher-Fox (2012), "successive generations of settler Canadians have normalized looking to government rather than themselves to resolve 'the Indian problem.'" If Canada and non-Indigenous Canadians are serious about divestment and decolonization, rather than simply *responding* to the many political and legal challenges made by Indigenous peoples and nations, they would reflect on and change their own practices of their own accord. If there is a problem, it is a "Non-Indian problem" — a failure of political will among non-Indigenous Canadians.

## The Indigenous Resistance "Dataset"

There are certain resistance "events" that have generated significant media and scholarly attention among non-Indigenous publics: the Siege at Kanehsatà:ke/Oka, the protection of Lyell Island and the standoff at Gustafsen Lake, to name a few from recent decades. My aim has been to document the occurrence not only of the more well-known events but also of the others that may have received less publicity in these venues. Although the people involved in these other events clearly know that these events occurred, and although many of these events have been discussed as comprising a larger program of resistance (Alfred and Lowe 2005; Smith 1999), they have not been systematically documented. What this means is that the scale and the extent of resistance has been unknown.

I define a resistance "event" as any event involving noninstitutional political tactics conducted by two or more individuals (Olzak 1992). I used sociological methods of gathering information from newspaper articles about resistance (see Earl et al. 2004 for a review). These methods included gathering data from Indigenous-focused media such as *Akwesasne Notes* and *Kahtou News*; and also from dominant, mainstream media such as *The Globe and Mail* and the *Vancouver Sun*. The resulting database includes events such as marches, demonstrations, road blockades, rail blockades, land occupations, building occupations, and "other" events such as hunger strikes and boycotts. Table 1 provides a snapshot of the structure of the database for the early 1980s.

**Table 1 Sample of Events Documented in Resistance Database**

| Group Name | Year | Month | Day | Duration (in days) | Number of participants | Tactic | Province |
|---|---|---|---|---|---|---|---|
| Sarcee | 1981 | 11 | 2 | 3 | n.a. | Building occupation | AB |
| Shawanaga | 1981 | 5 | 11 | n.a. | 75 | Road blockade | ON |
| Peguis | 1982 | 5 | 12 | n.a. | 600 | March/demonstration | Manitoba |
| Peguis | 1983 | 3 | n.a. | 6 | 220 | Boycott | Manitoba |
| Cross Lake | 1983 | 6 | 10 | 86 | 800 | Boycott | Manitoba |
| Nuxalk | 1984 | 8 | 14 | n.a. | n.a. | Other tactic | B.C. |
| Peguis | 1984 | 5 | 7 | 1 | 150 | Building occupation | Manitoba |
| Peguis | 1984 | 5 | 2 | n.a. | 500 | March/demonstration | Manitoba |
| Fountain | 1985 | 9 | 27 | 1 | 3 | Road blockade | B.C. |
| Giwangak | 1985 | 12 | 2 | 9 | 35 | Rail/boat block | B.C. |
| 36 Interior Bands | 1985 | 2 | 2 | 67 | 13 | Rail/boat block | B.C. |

| Group Name | Year | Month | Day | Duration (in days) | Number of participants | Tactic | Province |
|---|---|---|---|---|---|---|---|
| Nuu-chah-Nulth | 1985 | 1 | 26 | 11 | n.a. | Road blockade | B.C. |
| Haida | 1985 | 10 | 30 | 61 | 20 | Road blockade | B.C. |
| Tsawout | 1985 | 11 | 25 | 1 | 12 | Other tactic | B.C. |
| Ottawa Haida support | 1985 | 12 | 12 | 1 | 200 | March/demonstration | Ontario |
| Stein protest | 1985 | 10 | 13 | 1 | 500 | March/demonstration | B.C. |
| Gitksan-wet'suwet'en | 1986 | 7 | 2 | 46 | 100 | Fish/hunt/log-in | B.C. |
| Stoslo | 1986 | 8 | 16 | 9 | 60 | Fish/hunt/log-in | B.C. |
| Kwakiutl | 1986 | 12 | 1 | 23 | 40 | Road blockade | B.C. |
| Border protest | 1986 | 7 | 6 | 1 | 1,000 | March/demonstration | Ontario |
| Save dialect protest | 1986 | 6 | 25 | 1 | 12 | March/demonstration | Ontario |
| Peguis | 1986 | 12 | 11 | 1 | 125 | March/demonstration | Manitoba |
| Peguis | 1986 | 12 | 16 | 1 | 50 | Building occupation | Manitoba |
| Ontario legislature | 1986 | 10 | 29 | n.a. | 3,000 | March/demonstration | Ontario |
| Peguis | 1986 | 7 | 25 | 1 | 60 | Building occupation | Manitoba |
| Peguis | 1986 | 2 | 17 | 1 | 50 | Building occupation | Manitoba |
| Peguis | 1986 | 12 | 16 | | n.a. | Building occupation | Manitoba |
| Peguis | 1986 | 8 | 6 | n.a. | 50 | Building occupation | Manitoba |
| Mathias Columb | 1986 | 8 | 26 | 300 | n.a. | Boycott | Manitoba |
| Lubicon | 1987 | 12 | 16 | 1 | 24 | March/demonstration | Alberta |
| Diverse | 1987 | 8 | 13 | 10 | 4 | Other tactic | Sask |
| Peguis | 1987 | 1 | 29 | 41 | 600 | Other tactic | Manitoba |
| Lil'wat | 1987 | 10 | 15 | 1 | 25 | March/demonstration | BC |
| McLeod Lake | 1987 | 6 | 23 | 19 | 250 | Road blockade | BC |
| Port Alberni | 1987 | 7 | 7 | 1 | 100 | Fish/hunt/log-in | BC |

*Note: Name spellings reflect spellings at time of event*

The first columns in the table list the group name, the year the event started, the month and the day. The remaining columns show the duration of the event in days, the number of participants, the tactic used and the provincial location of the events. For example, the first event is a 1981 "building occupation" by the Sarcee/Tsuu T'ina First Nation. This was the first in a series of events in which band members took over Canadian Forces buildings that had been located on Tsuu T'ina lands. Thus, by 1989 *Windspeaker* would report that "more than 300 Sarcee Nation band members and supporters took a stand against the Canadian Forces Base in Calgary last Friday by blockading a military training bridge leading on to their land. They viewed it as a last-ditch effort to get the Department of National Defence (DND) to pay a leasing agreement and to clean up its on-reserve firing range" (Morrow 1989).

Over sixty-one days in 1985, members of two communities of the Haida nation (Masset and Skidegate) engaged in a road blockade to stop logging on their territory of Lyell Island on the south tip of Haida Gwai (then known in the non-Haida world as the Queen Charlotte Islands — this name change was also a result of resistance). *The Globe and Mail* reported that "Haida Indians stopped the chainsaws yesterday by blockading a road about ten kilometres from the logging contractor's Powrivco Bay camp on the south coast of Lyell Island" (1985: A5). On February 17, 1986, "About 50 members of Peguis Indian band yesterday occupied part of the regional offices of the federal Indian Affairs Department, forcing 20 staff members to be sent home for the day" (Moloney 1986). Table 1 is a snapshot of the database created to study resistance. The data continue until 2008. Information on more recent events, including the many Idle No More events have yet to be added, but plans are in progress to build on this foundation.

Table 2 shows another snapshot of the database for 1995, one of the peak years for mobilization of this kind.

**Table 2 Additional Events Documented in Resistance Database**

| Group Name | Year | Month | Day | Duration (in days) | Number of participants | Tactic | Province |
|---|---|---|---|---|---|---|---|
| Eel Ground | 1995 | 7 | 2 | 35 | 60 | Road blockade | Atlantic |
| Norway House | 1995 | 11 | 13 | 5 | 125 | March/demonstration | Manitoba |
| Gitksan | 1995 | 7 | 24 | 50 | n.a. | Road blockade | B.C. |
| Douglas Lake | 1995 | 5 | 24 | 14 | 200 | Road blockade | B.C. |
| Sundancers (Gustafsen Lake) | 1995 | 7 | 13 | 67 | 21 | Land occupation | B.C. |
| Nanoose | 1995 | 4 | 27 | 25 | 35 | Road blockade | B.C. |

| Group Name | Year | Month | Day | Duration (in days) | Number of participants | Tactic | Province |
|---|---|---|---|---|---|---|---|
| Gitksan | 1995 | 9 | 15 | 10 | n.a. | Rail blockade | B.C. |
| Penticton | 1995 | 10 | 26 | 66 | 30 | Other tactic | B.C. |
| Upper Nicola | 1995 | 5 | 3 | 1 | n.a. | Road blockade | B.C. |
| Adams Lake | 1995 | 7 | 20 | 5 | 11 | Hunger strike | B.C. |
| Hiawatha | 1995 | 9 | 1 | 4 | 20 | Road blockade | Ontario |
| Huron-Wendat | 1995 | 9 | 3 | 1 | 9 | Road blockade | Quebec |
| No specific group mentioned | 1995 | 2 | 6 | 3 | 12 | Other tactic | Ontario |
| No specific group mentioned | 1995 | 6 | 15 | 1 | 50 | March/ demonstration | Atlantic |
| Nuxalk | 1995 | 9 | 5 | 21 | 19 | Land occupation | B.C. |
| Eel Ground | 1995 | 7 | 7 | 30 | n.a. | Road blockade | Atlantic |
| Stoney Nation | 1995 | 11 | 23 | 1 | n.a. | Road blockade | Alberta |

Note: Name spellings reflect spellings at time of event

Members of the Upper Nicola band set up a blockade of a road leading into the Douglas Lake ranch to protect their fishing rights. As reported in *Windspeaker* (Russo 1995: 1), "An agreement signed by a federal agent in 1878 attested to the rights of the Upper Nicola Band to retain access to fish several lakes, including Minnie and Stoney Lakes. Minnie Lake is surrounded by private property owned by the ranch. Four Upper Nicola band members were arrested while fishing with gill-nets at Minnie Lake." When the Apex ski resort attempted an expansion, and the British Columbia provincial government backed the resort by claiming that "roads through reserves are no longer a fundamental Indian right and access is non-negotiable," (*Globe and Mail* November 27, 1995: A1) band members set up bunkers and checkpoints. Then band chief Stuart Phillip (currently the head of the Union of British Columbia Indian Chiefs) said that "Court rulings don't create Indian commitment ... The Apex road is Indian land and can never be taken, only shared" (*Globe and Mail* November 27, 1995: A5). Inalienable hunting rights were the subject of a seven–hour standoff and bridge blockade between hunters from Huron-Wendat who resisted attempts by Quebec game wardens to confiscate a moose they had killed in Laurentides Provincial Park (*Globe and Mail* September

4, 1995). I have constructed this database in the hope that it will prove to be useful, albeit for potentially different reasons, for both Indigenous and non-Indigenous peoples.[1]

First, the database draws attention to the scale of resistance during a specific time period. Resistance of this kind is not an isolated occurrence, but part of a larger Indigenous politics (see Alfred 1995; also Smith 1999; Alfred and Lowe 2005). Single acts of resistance taken together also constitute a broad, multinational coalition of Indigenous resistance. It is hoped that the contribution to knowledge about resistance that the database makes will be of use to Indigenous nations and groups as they engage in further mobilization. Although information about individual events may have been passed down within communities, this may not have occurred for all events, particularly for those that took place several decades ago and involved small numbers of participants. Although it is a database that can be used to generalize, each and every record in this database matters because each is an instance of action and political agency. The database can also be used as a means of drawing attention to the underlying issues about which the mobilization occurred. Non-Indigenous people need to know about and respond to these issues, especially if they seek to support Indigenous resistance, and to be aware of what their governments are supposedly doing on their behalf. Those individuals who mobilized did so both as direct action (see Blomley 1996) and with a view to garnering attention from outside communities, both Indigenous and non-Indigenous (Ramos 2006; 2008; Wilkes and Ibrahim 2013).[2] Of course, there may be other meanings to these events that derive from Indigenous worldviews. As Kelly Aguirre reminds us in Chapter Eight of this book, a blockade may be a "direct action" and at the same time a reinvention of centuries-old ceremonies and thus a spiritual event.

Second, resistance is important for Indigenous and non-Indigenous peoples alike because each instance of resistance reflects the courage of the group and of individuals. While some might say that engaging in resistance is not a choice but is a natural response to an attack on land, family, home and nation, this does not diminish the sacrifices activists make and the difficulties they confront. Activists do not always have the support of their communities, and endure racism and violence because, as Coulthard (2012) notes, "The Canadian state claims to hold a legitimate monopoly on use of violence." (Although I cannot speak for the individual motivations or to the individual experiences of those who partook in any given event, I attended several events as a supporter and observed the overtly racist and hostile reactions of some non-Indigenous people.)

Documentarian Alanis Obomsawin has discussed the difficulties faced by Warriors in relation to community support for the 1990 Siege at Kanehsatà:ke. The risks are considerable: in 1995, Ontario Provincial police killed Anthony Dudley George (see Edwards 2003). Standing up for what is right is to take the difficult path. But as a result of the actions of the groups and nations who have mobilized, what is clear is that several thousand people (or fewer) have often successfully resisted a much larger state of several million.

## Reflections on Research as a Scientific and Colonial Practice

In the years that have elapsed, I have had the opportunity to rethink several aspects of the process of publishing academic papers using this data. Research is not simply a mirror of the world out there; instead, it is an integral and often harmful enterprise (Deloria 1995; Smith 1999). One cannot simply send an academic journal a list of events and have it published. The events must be used to demonstrate some larger theoretical point or to test some empirical propositions. At least this is the assumption that underlies the discipline — sociology — and the professional identity — sociologist — that I hold. In what follows, I discuss the problems that arise (and thus critique my own work) when using sociological tools to explicate Indigenous resistance and/or in using this "case" to contribute to the larger socio-logical enterprise. I critique assumptions I have made about the commensurability of cases, critique assumptions about the transferability of theoretical concepts, and finally discuss the choice of language and geographic unit of analysis.

*Just Another Movement? Assumptions about Commensurability of Cases*
In an early paper, I compared resistance by Indigenous peoples in Canada to resistance by Native Americans in the United States (Wilkes 2004a). Drawing on sociological theorizing about the American Indian Movement as well as theorizing about the constitution of social movements more broadly, I concluded that events in Canada did not constitute a national social movement because there was a lack of social movement organization involvement and no national (that is, "Pan-Indian") collective identity. To situate resistance by the members of Indigenous nations in the sociological literature has meant assuming that the issues are simply another case of collective action with little difference from the women's, civil rights or Lesbian Gay Bisexual Transgender/Transsexual (LGBT) movements.

The focus on whether there was a Pan-Indian identity equated Indigenous nationhoods with the colonial Canadian federal state. That is, the Canadian federal state became the benchmark with which to assess identity for Indigenous communities. Instead, I should have seen that Indigenous resistance is already at the national level, as evidenced by the many different nations such as Cree and Anishinaabe that have mobilized. Moreover, I did not make sufficient connection to land, sovereignty, treaties, and colonialism, which together suggest a multinational resistance to colonialism, as manifest by the Canadian state and the Crown as the original signator to many treaties.

The application of a broad-based sociological and social movement perspective obscures the Indigenous rights that existed prior to the current nation-to-nation relationships among Indigenous peoples and between diverse Indigenous peoples and the Canadian state. Indigenous resistance is not about incorporation into an existing body politic within a rights-based framework, as Hayden King argues in Chapter Seven of this book. Attiwapiskat Chief Theresa Spence's rejection of this framework was evident when, during her 2012/2013 hunger strike, she insisted that Governor General David Johnson, as a representative of the Queen, be present at her meeting with Canadian government representatives. Indigenous resistance is about land, about resources and their stewardship, and about adherence to treaties and international agreements. Some would further argue that resistance is about inherent Indigenous rights to the land, which cannot be alienated through treaty or by another means. As François Paulette argued in the Royal Commission: "In my language, there is no word for surrender" (RCAP 1996).[3] These elements are obscured if viewed from a social movement perspective.

This point is well illustrated in Tuck and Yang's article titled "Decolonization Is Not a Metaphor" (2012). Here, these authors challenge the very foundation of the Occupy movement in the United States. When Occupy movement activists call for a redistribution of wealth from the 1 percent to the 99 percent, they completely miss that land is wealth and that Native American lands are already occupied (see also Barker 2012). Moreover, they miss a much more profound argument, which is not simply that the land is wealth, but that the land is life, part of the fabric of human and nonhuman relations in which many Indigenous peoples insist that we are all embedded (as the opening citation by Lee Maracle in Elaine Coburn's Introduction in this volume makes clear). "Occupy" disregards ongoing colonization within North America, but at the same time, it suggests an approach to the land that is arguably quite foreign to many Indigenous approaches that, in contrast with ideas of land as a resource or wealth, emphasize "respect" for the natural world (for various contested Nuu-chah-nulth interpretations of this principle, see Chapter Six in this volume). If a "normal" sociological approach would classify both Indigenous movements and the Occupy movements as "social movements," this obscures fundamental differences across them.

### Education or Assimilation?
### The Assumption that Theoretical Concepts are "Transferable"
There are also limits to the extent to which concepts, or at least some ways of measuring them, are transferable. In one instance, a paper compared the characteristics of First Nations that had engaged in mobilization with the characteristics of First Nations that had not engaged in mobilization (Wilkes 2004b). I drew on social movement theories of deprivation and resources, using such factors as education and unemployment as indicators of these concepts. What is/was the

problem with this work? Placing Indigenous resistance within a social movement framework assumed a uniformity of conceptual meaning across groups. Thus, a concept that had a particular meaning for African-Americans, for example, could also be applied to Indigenous peoples. The researcher simply has to identify variables that can be used to measure levels of deprivation and resources. In my case, I used the unemployment rate and percentage of the First Nation that had low education to indicate deprivation. Although they might make sense if one were studying racialized minority mobilization, their application for use in regard to resistance by Indigenous peoples is problematic.

Low education, for example, might indicate deprivation only if the standard of success is Western education with its emphasis on rank and status. For many individuals, withdrawal from the education system altogether might have occurred as a means of resistance. Clyde Tallio is a Nuxalk teacher, speaker for the hereditary chiefs, cultural leader and Honorary Visiting Scholar at the University of British Columbia. He is a leader in language revitalization efforts for his community. After a talk he gave at my department, he told me that although he had the opportunity to attend university, he decided that he would learn more by staying in his community and learning from his elders than by leaving his community to attend university. The university would always be there, but he realized that the elders would not. Thus, the fact that he does not have a university education reflects a rejection of the colonial education system entirely.[4]

Furthermore, it is difficult to know the extent to which the devastating impact of Indian residential schools is overlooked by such a definition. Low education could reflect a community that could keep more of its children out of residential schools. Thus, the measure of deprivation is an outside definition that may or may not be accepted and applicable to any particular community. For many Indigenous communities, a straightforward percentage accounting of the kind that I used may have obscured more than it illuminated.

Similarly, the census defines only those that were "without work, had looked for work in the past four weeks, and were available for work" as unemployed. A community could have a lower unemployment rate because everyone has given up looking for work, so people are more deprived with lower unemployment. Or a community could have lower unemployment if people are not "looking for work" because they are engaged in alternative means of living outside the "workforce." Dr. Taiaiake Alfred made a similar point in a conversation regarding a book chapter I was working on that used the census data to compare Indigenous and Non-Indigenous economic outcomes. So as not to misquote, I will repeat the resulting note that I included with that chapter:

The research provided in this chapter can be situated within a human-capital framework that assumes that all groups of people within a society have the same goals. As noted by Gerald Taiaiake Alfred, to focus solely on the socio-economic status of Indigenous peoples is to perpetuate an assimilationist model whereby Indigenous peoples are slotted into the capitalist wage economy. This model does nothing to address other areas such as language and culture, which also matter and which may be more important to Indigenous Peoples' overall social and psychological well-being. (Wilkes 2010: 327–328)

*Whose "Imagined Communities"?*
*The Use of Language and Geographic Units of Analysis*
As Patricia Monture (2010) has noted, languages suggest ways of thinking. English is noun-oriented, whereas other Indigenous languages are verb- or process-oriented. This difference has consequences for how resistance is understood (see also Alfred 2009; and Chapter One in this book, in which James Youngblood Henderson writes about learning English as "learning anguish"). But even when using English, as so many scholars have pointed out, no word selection used in the course of writing and discussing Indigenous resistance — "nation," "sovereignty," "treaty," "protest," "resistance," "claim" — has a universal agreed-upon meaning (LaRocque 2010; Simpson 2008; Stark 2008; see also Jennifer Adese's discussion of "sovereignty" in Chapter Five of this book). Each word has a complex set of meanings that can, in turn, shape the understanding of the larger subject matter. What does it mean to use the word "Indigenous" alongside "resistance"? Is "Indigenous" an adjective? Moreover, as Hayden King argues (in Chapter Seven of this book; also Coburn's Introduction), there are no "Indigenous peoples"; instead there are only Cree, Anishinaabe and Dene peoples, for example. The word "Indigenous" obscures the existence of multiple nations, multiple peoples, their distinct histories and present.

Similarly, the decision to define what does and does not constitute resistance is a political decision. The work that I do defines resistance as a particular kind of twentieth-century politics. There are many other kinds of actions or states that individuals can and do use that are also resistance that I do not include (see e.g., Blix et al. 2012). Moreover, this data and the census are noteworthy because for multiple First Nations, there was and continues to be a long-standing resistance against collecting this data. Statistics Canada (2011: 6)) defines these communities as "incompletely enumerated" because permission was not given by band councils to census enumerators to enter the reserve. In 2006, these refusals included Kanesatake, Doncaster, Kahnawake, Akwesasne, Walpole Island 46, Akwesasne (Part) 59, Rankin Location 15D, Goulais Bay 15A, Bear Island 1, Wahta Mohawk Territory, Big Island Lake Cree Territory, Saddle Lake 125 and Esquimalt. In hindsight, I defined "resistance" too narrowly and should have included "census refusal" as a category in the database of resistance "events." Moreover, many other forms of resistance are difficult to capture using the language of "events" such as maintaining Indigenous languages against efforts of forcible assimilation, hunting in traditional territories that have been renamed "national parks" or "private property" by the colonial state, and so on, that may not easily show up, except in outcomes such as language retention or arrest records related to "trespassing" and similar acts.

Furthermore, the terms used to describe resistance events such as "road blockades," "rail blockades," "land occupations" and "building occupations" are also political. Blomley (1996) notes that protest implies grumbling and proposes direct action as a better term (see also Vyce 2010). Why is occupying one's own land even "occupying"? Similarly, closing down a road on one's own land is not a "blockade." Why should individuals whose land has been stolen and occupied have to make land "claims" (Alfred 1999)? Such language repositions the colonial state as arbiter; but Indigenous peoples have inherent rights, not claims that depend upon "recognition" by the colonial state, the Queen or others.

Related and inseparably tied to language is geography. As Anderson (1991) noted in his book, *Imagined Communities*, censuses and maps were and are instruments of colonization. Tuhiwai Smith (1999: 80) has vividly described this dynamic: "They came, they saw, they named, they claimed." Thus, the discussion and conceptualization of geography, including geography as a "scientific" enterprise of geological surveying and so on, is tied to language. The description of First Nations as being "in" Canada or "in" British Columbia implies a particular meaning about land ownership and stewardship. The use of the term "in" implies that the First Nations are on top of or sitting on the "real" or rightful landowners: Canadians/ provinces. The Canadian state has superimposed itself on First Nations lands.

This language-geography interlinkage has huge implications for cross-national comparative work on resistance. Thus, what does it mean to group resistance events by province as I have discussed in previous papers? On the one hand, most treaties are signed with provincial representatives. Both visually and conceptually, this province-by-province framing suggests that the province is the "real" geographic level. This point was made by an audience member at a Toronto talk on the Nisga'a treaty that I attended who said that "It's always framed as if the Nisga'a are getting 10 percent of the territory of British Columbia. Why isn't it framed as if British Columbia is getting 90 percent of Nisga'a territory?"

## Conclusion: Indigenous Struggle as an Ongoing Political Project

In this chapter, my aim has been to provide an overview of Indigenous resistance to Canadian state colonialism and to describe the resistance dataset that I have created. At the same time, I have sought to reflect on how the mainstream sociological approach to Indigenous resistance that I have used obscures vital aspects of those struggles — and reproduces the colonial status quo. This critique can be used as a specific illustration of the extent to which colonial categories are ingrained parts of the conceptual apparatus and hence of the research enterprise more broadly. In the introduction to this book, Elaine Coburn suggests that her interest in Indigenous resistance and resurgence is "symptomatic" of the growing strength of Indigenous resistance in the current historical moment. It could be argued that the sociological approach is symptomatic of the normal scientific enterprise as bound up with colonial relationships and perspectives.

I outlined the logic behind the creation of a dataset that contains records of several hundred resistance events. It is my hope that the dataset will be of use to Indigenous struggles in some ways, including by adding to the knowledge that there have been many, many different ways that Indigenous peoples have acted out forms of self-determination over the last decades. At the very least, I hope that it informs a sense that Indigenous struggles are an ongoing political project of resistance, of which Idle No More is only the most recent manifestation. Then I provided three critiques that have arisen when conducting comparative sociological work using this dataset.

The first critique targeted the application of a theoretical model derived from outside Indigenous communities that served to reduce activism to another group seeking redress within a rights-based framework rather than a fundamental reimagining of Indigenous–Canadian state relationships. Related is that reducing real struggles to a dataset or to datapoints could be disrespectful to the struggles in that they are reduced to data objects. Several of the chapters in this book provide important frameworks for thinking about resistance (for instance, Jeff Denis's Chapter Nine of this book considers the four directions model for interpreting Indigenous struggles, and Kelly Aguirre argues in Chapter Eight that academic storytelling from Indigenous perspectives is both resistance to colonial academic storywork and resurgence or re-creation of Indigenous paradigms).

The second critique is that I have used discipline-derived theoretical concepts that may not have relevance or appropriately reflect the situation in particular communities. At worst, as with the example of school attendance, signs of "colonization" are actually resistance. One empirical lesson is that even if the resistance dataset documents hundreds of Indigenous "protest events," they may have been greatly underestimated (although of course there is always the critique that if resistance is everywhere, then it is nowhere). There may still be useful distinctions to make between more active "direct action" resistance and other kinds of resistance, such as withdrawing from and rejecting colonial institutions.

The third critique was that there are both political and theoretical implications of using a particular set of terminology, such as "blockade," and geographic boundaries, such as provincial boundaries, to discuss resistance. Such language arguably reifies the status quo and does not recognize the contested nature of ongoing Canadian occupation of Indigenous peoples' lands. The "scientific" language of sociology and geography is, in fact, saturated with political claims. What is the answer here? No word is without implications, and this is especially the case that words are located within language systems. As Kelly Aguirre explains in Chapter Eight of this book, "Names carry the record of our relations." Thus, while I cannot suggest that there is a correct set of words that ought to be used to discuss resistance, it is clear that language should be given greater consideration. As Alex Wilson observes, for instance, there is a difference between calling Theresa Spence a "chief," a colonial term for Indigenous political leaders, and calling her *Ogichidaakwe*, a holy woman (Simpson 2013).

Where to go from here? A number of years ago, I attended an equity and diversity teaching workshop at the University of British Columbia, the logic of which also applies to scholarship. Hoping to be given a set of "antiracist" teaching guidelines, the facilitator said that I was thinking about it the wrong way. "You don't get to be 'antiracist,'" she said. "Instead you should see it as a process." For non-Indigenous people, any attempt to "decolonize" one's thinking, actions and research is a process with no final "just," "correct," or "right" arrival point. Many, many mistakes will continue to be made. We are embedded in unequal relations of power. As long as they exist, it will require extra effort to think against the dominant social science paradigms, especially for non-Indigenous researchers who take them for granted. In taking on this self-reflexivity, it is hoped that research can be conducted so that it will in some small way contribute toward the objectives of those who have engaged in resistance.

## NOTES

1. Readers are welcome to obtain a copy of the entire database by contacting me at wilkesr@mail.ubc.ca. It should be acknowledged that such data could be used as part of the increasing surveillance of Indigenous communities, who are often conceived by the Canadian government as a security "risk" and even as terrorist threats (see Proulx 2014).
2. In this respect, one of the most telling images from the 1990 Siege at Kanehsatà:ke/ Oka Crisis shows warriors watching television news coverage of the blockade.
3. I thank Elaine Coburn for this point.

4. On October 27, 2014, Clyde Tallio granted me permission to recount this story and to use his name.

## References

Alcantara, Christopher. 2007. "Explaining Aboriginal Treaty Negotiation Outcomes in Canada: The Cases of the Inuit and the Innu in Labrador." *Canadian Journal of Political Science* 40, 185–207.

Alfred, Gerald (Taiaiake). 1995. *Heeding the Voices of Our Ancestors: Kahnawake Mohawk Politics and the Rise of Native Nationalism.* Toronto: Oxford University Press.

Alfred, Taiaiake. 2009. *Peace, Power, Righteousness: An Indigenous Manifesto,* 2nd ed. Toronto: Oxford University Press.

Alfred, Taiaiake, and Lana Lowe. 2005. "Warrior Societies in Contemporary Indigenous Communities." Report for the Ipperwash Inquiry. <attorneygeneral.jus.gov.on.ca/inquiries/ipperwash/policy_part/research/pdf/Alfred_and_Lowe.pdf>.

Anderson, Benedict. 1991. *Imagined Communities: Reflections on the Origins and Spread of Nationalism.* New York: Verso.

Armitage, Peter, and John C. Kennedy. 1989. "Redbaiting and Racism on our Frontier: Military Expansion in Labrador and Quebec." *Canadian Review of Sociology and Anthropology* 26, 798–817.

Barker, Adam J. 2012. "Already Occupied: Indigenous Peoples, Settler Colonialism and the Occupy Movements in North America." *Social Movement Studies* 11, 327–334.

Blix, Bodil Hansen, Torunn Hamran, and Hans Ketil Normann. 2012. "Indigenous Life Stories as Narratives of Health and Resistance: A Dialogical Narrative Analysis." *Canadian Journal of Nursing Research* 44, 64–85.

Blomley, Nicholas. 1996. "'Shut the Province Down': First Nations Blockades in British Columbia, 1984–1995." *BC Studies: The British Columbian Quarterly* 111, 5–35.

Coulthard, Glen. 2012. "Idle No More in Historical Context." *Decolonization: Indigeneity, Education & Society.* <decolonization.wordpress.com/2012/12/24/idlenomore-in-historical-context/>.

Deloria, Vine. 1995. *Red Earth, White Lies: Native Americans and the Myth of Scientific Fact.* New York: Scribner.

Earl, Jennifer, Andrew Martin, John D. McCarthy, and Sarah A. Soule. 2004. "The Use of Newspaper Data in the Study of Collective Action. *Annual Review of Sociology* 65–80.

Edwards, Peter. 2003. *One Dead Indian: The Premier, the Police and the Ipperwash Crisis.* Toronto: McLelland and Stewart.

*Globe and Mail.* 1995. (September 4).

____. 1995. (November 27).

____. 1985. (October 31).

Goddard, John. 1991. *Last Stand of the Lubicon Cree.* Vancouver: Douglas and McIntyre.

Goodleaf, Donna. 1995. *Entering the Warzone: A Mohawk Perspective on Resisting Invasions.* Penticton, BC: Theytus Books.

Irlbacher-Fox, Stephanie. 2012. "#Idle No More: Settler Responsibility for Relationship." December 27. <decolonization.wordpress.com/2012/12/27/idlenomore-settler-responsibility-for-relationship/>.

Kalant, Amelia. 2004. *National Identity and the Conflict at Oka*. New York: Routledge.

Lambertus, Sandra. 2004. *Wartime Images, Peacetime Wounds: The Media and the Gustafsen Lake Standoff*. Toronto: University of Toronto Press.

LaRocque, Emma. 2010. *When the Other Is Me: Native Resistance Discourse, 1850–1990*. Winnipeg: University of Manitoba Press.

Miller, John. 2005. "Ipperwash and the Media: A Critical Analysis of How the Story Was Covered." Report submitted to Aboriginal Legal Services of Toronto. <attorneygeneral. jus.gov.on.ca/inquiries/ipperwash/policy_part/projects/pdf/ALST_Ipperwash_ and_media.pdf>.

Moloney, Paul. 1986. "Band Protesters Allege School Cuts: Peguis Members Vow to Occupy Office Until $500,000 Deficit Addressed." *Winnipeg Free Press* 2 (February 18).

Monture, Patricia. A. 2010. "The Human Right to Celebrate: Achieving Justice for Aboriginal Peoples." In Leanne Simpson and Kiera Ladner (eds.), *This Is an Honour Song: Twenty Years Since the Blockades*. Winnipeg, MB: Arbeiter Ring Publishing.

Morrow, Jeff. 1989. "Sarcee Vow to Protect Land." *Windspeaker* 1 (July 7).

Niezen, Ronald. 2009. *Defending the Land: Sovereignty and Forest Life in James Bay Cree Society*, second edition. Upper Saddle River, NJ: Prentice Hall.

O'Bonsawin, Christine M. 2010. "'No Olympics on Stolen Native Land': Contesting Olympic Narratives and Asserting Indigenous Rights within the Discourse of the 2010 Vancouver Games." *Sport in Society* 13, 143–156.

Obomsawin, A., W. Koenig, R. Rochat, F. Grandmont, and C. Vendette. 1993. *Kanehsatake: 270 Years of Resistance*. Montreal: National Film Board of Canada.

Olzak, Susan. 1992. *The Dynamics of Ethnic Competition and Conflict*. Palo Alto, CA: Stanford University Press.

Pasternak, Shiri, Sue Collis, and Tia Dafnos. 2013. "Criminalization at Tyendinaga: Securing Canada's Colonial Property Regime through Specific Land Claims." *Canadian Journal of Law and Society/Revue Canadienne Droit et Société* 28, 65–81.

Proulx, Craig. 2014. "Colonizing Surveillance: Canada Constructs an Indigenous Terror Threat." *Anthropologica* 56, 83–100.

Ramos, Howard. 2006. "What Causes Canadian Aboriginal Protest? Examining Resources, Opportunities and Identity, 1951–2000." *The Canadian Journal of Sociology* 31, 2, 211–234.

RCAP (Royal Commission on Aboriginal Peoples). 1996. "Looking Forward, Looking Back." Ottawa: Minister of Supply and Services Canada. <aadnc-aandc.gc.ca/eng/11 00100014597/1100100014637>.

Russo, Gloria. 1995. "Douglas Lake Blockade Dismantled." *Windspeaker* 13, 3, 1. <ammsa. com/node/20579>.

Simpson, Leanne. 2013. "Fish Broth & Fasting." January 16. <dividednomore. ca/2013/01/16/fish-broth-fasting/>.

Simpson, Leanne, and Kiera Ladner. *This Is an Honour Song: Twenty Years Since the Blockades*. Winnipeg, MB: Arbeiter Ring Publishing.

Stark, Heidi Kiiwetinepinesiik. 2008. "Sovereignty." In *Encyclopedia of United States— American Indian Policy, Relations, and Law*. Washington, DC: CQ Press.

Statistics Canada. 2011. "Aboriginal Peoples in Canada: First Nations People, Métis and Inuit." National Household Survey 2011. Ottawa: Canada Minister of Industry. <12.

statcan.gc.ca/nhs-enm/2011/as-sa/99-011-x/99-011-x2011001-eng.pdf>.

Tuck, Eve, and K. Wayne Yang. 2012. "Decolonization Is Not a Metaphor." *Decolonization: Indigeneity, Education & Society* 1, 1.

Tuhiwai Smith, Linda. 1999. *Decolonizing Methodologies: Research and Indigenous Peoples.* London: Zed Books.

Turtle Island Network News. 2011. "Upping the Anti." Kanenhstation: The Protected Place. <turtleisland.org/news/news-sixnations.htm>.

Vyce, Amanda. 2010. "Protesting the 'Protest': Understanding 'Non-Native' Reactions and Responses to the Six Nations Land 'Occupation and Protest' in Caledonia, Ontario." Hamilton, ON: McMaster University.

Wadden, Marie. 1996. *Nitassinan: The Innu Struggle to Reclaim Their Homeland.* Vancouver: Douglas & McIntyre.

Wilkes, Rima. 2010. "Indigenous Peoples." In Barry Edmonston and Eric Fong (eds.), *The Changing Canadian Population.* Montreal: McGill Queen's University Press.

____. 2006. "The Protest Actions of Indigenous Peoples: A Canada-U.S. Comparison of Social Movement Emergence." *American Behavioral Scientist* 50, 510–525.

____. 2004a. "First Nation Politics: Deprivation, Resources and Participation in Collective Action." *Sociological Inquiry* 74, 570–589.

____. 2004b. "A Systematic Approach to Studying Indigenous Politics: Band-Level Mobilization in Canada, 1981–2000." *The Social Science Journal* 41, 447–457.

Wilkes, Rima, and Tamara Ibrahim. 2013. "Timber: Direct Action over Forestry and Beyond." In D. Tindall, Ronald Trosper, and P. Perrault (eds.), *First Nations and Forestry.* Vancouver: University of British Columbia Press.

Wilkes, Rima, and Danielle Ricard. 2007. "How Does Newspaper Coverage of Collective Action Vary? Protest by Indigenous Peoples in Canada." *Social Science Journal* 44, 231–251.

Chapter Five

# BEHAVING UNEXPECTEDLY IN EXPECTED PLACES
## FIRST NATIONS ARTISTS AND THE EMBODIMENT OF VISUAL SOVEREIGNTY

*Jennifer Adese*

In recent years, Indigenous peoples have harnessed the world's online power to take concerns about racialized representations of Indianness to a wider audience. Adrienne Keene's (2014) blog "Native Appropriations," for instance, exposes and interrogates derogatory, appropriative representations of Indigenous peoples by everyone and everything, ranging from small companies to larger corporations such as Walt Disney, to sports teams and hotel and restaurant chains. Indigenous people have used social media outlets such as Facebook and Twitter to effectively challenge fashion industries. Kim Wheeler, who is Ojibwe-Mohawk, successfully campaigned to have a "feather headdress" withdrawn from the shelves of the clothing chain H&M (CBC News 2013). Others confronted designer Paul Frank for throwing "Indian parties," resulting in an apology and then new partnerships with First Nations' artists such as Cree-Métis designer Candace Halcro (Allen 2013). Ian Campeau, better known as "Deejay NDN" of the DJ group A Tribe Called Red, drew on social media's organizing power, in concert with a formal human rights legal challenge, to end the racist and demeaning name of the Nepean "Redskins" football team (Wingrove 2013).

## Is it Worth Arguing Over "Tonto"?

Some argue that confronting such simple matters of "misrepresentation" is time poorly spent; there are more pressing, serious, and tangible threats to Indigenous lives. As this book attests, such threats include resource extraction, related environmental degradation and climate change, violence against Indigenous women and the overincarceration of Indigenous peoples. For instance, Chris Eyre, a Cheyenne and Arapaho film director, waded into the recent debates over the reboot of *The Lone Ranger*. The film, released in 2013, features Johnny Depp as Tonto, the Lone Ranger's "Indian" sidekick. Eyre argued that debating Depp's characterization, a pan-Indian composite that is "a pure invention of the Indian for the masses" is a "ridiculous use of our time" (Godreche 2013). Eyre concedes that it "could be dangerous if people believe that Natives are like that," but feels that Depp's caricature is so far off from Native realities as to be a nonissue. He maintains that confronting Native realities are more important. He suggests that discussing cases such as the court-supported adoption of Cherokee "Baby Veronica" by non-Indigenous parents (even though her birth father, supported by the Cherokee Nation, sought custody) would be more worthwhile (National Indian Child Welfare Association 2014). Thus, the assertion here is that our attention should be turned to more immediate, material forms of violence, rather than seeking to refute images of Indianness that are so fantastical they have no connection to actual Indigenous human beings.

In attending to representation, we cannot forget material violence against Indigenous peoples, but I think it unwise to abandon what the Facebook group F.A.I.R. Media (FAIR 2014) refers to as the "fair and accurate representation" of Indigenous peoples in public culture. Discourses of Indianness, whether constructed through the long history of traveler and exploration writing, academic writing or other visual media, are deeply intertwined with material concerns. They are both reflections and facilitations of the materiality of racialized power. They presume the validity of the colonizer's ways of knowing about Indigenous peoples and are manifestations of racist, so-called "knowledge systems" that have demeaned, degraded and been used to try to assimilate Indigenous peoples. That is, caricatures of Indigenous peoples have been drawn on to lend false legitimacy to imperialism and colonization; issues of representation cannot be decoupled from this legacy. Moreover, racialized representations of Indigenous peoples by non-Indigenous peoples reflect the very material reality that Indigenous peoples' self-representations remain marginalized in the production and wider circulation of discourses of Indigeneity.

In contemporary film, fashion, literature and art, representations of Indigenous peoples by non-Indigenous peoples are overwhelmingly driven by material concerns. As in the cases of *The Lone Ranger*, H&M, Paul Frank and the Washington

Redskins sport franchise, corporate entities transform contrived images of Indigenous peoples and cultures into saleable tangible and intangible products; they seek to derive maximum benefit from the commodification of and capitalization on all things "Indian." Meanwhile, they remain unconcerned about the racism inherent in what they create. In short, corporations and consumer societies adhere to nothing but neoliberal market logic dictating that what is good for the market trumps everything else. Thus, corporations respond to voices opposing racist imagery only if they are loud enough to threaten profit-making. Although the use of stereotypical and degrading images in product creation and marketing is not new, the globalization of world markets has resulted in the intensified and more widespread circulation of such images. Images born in earlier stages of colonization continue to be given new life through their circulation in consumer societies.

Further, the disregard of Indigenous voices in decision-making processes on Indigenous lands is anchored in an abiding devaluation of Indigenous existences. Indigenous peoplehood, whether Anishinaabe, Mi'kmaw, Inuit, Nehiyaw, Haudenosaunee, Michif, Dene or Kwakwaka'wakw, scarcely matters because settlers and the Canadian state rarely understand Indigenous peoples as human beings, much less as self-determining peoples. Cree-Métis scholar Emma LaRocque refers to this as the "dehumanization" of Indigenous peoples (2010). The denial of Indigenous peoples' collective autonomy that is the hallmark of colonization cannot be decoupled from entrenched racist thinking about us. If we are pictured as no more than grotesque caricatures such as Depp's "Tonto"; and our earth, air, water and animal relations as less deserving of respect and substantively equal treatment than peoples of European descent, we can be violated, discounted, ignored, commodified and consumed.

## The Legacies of Visual Imperialism

The denial of Indigenous peoples as human beings and the denial of our existences as coherent, collective, and self-determining peoples is a direct result of visual imperialism. Kathleen Kuehnast defines visual imperialism in relation to ethnographic film as "the colonization of the world mind through the use of selective imagery that acts as a representation of a dominant ideology or, as in many instances, a representation of the truth" (1992: 185). In other words, visual imperialism is the use of imagery to perpetuate what Michel Foucault refers to as a "regime of truth," a system by which what is posited as "truth" circulates. Each society has "types of discourse it harbours and causes to function as true" (Foucault 1979: 46). Visual imperialism expresses Eurocentric regimes of truth about Indigenous peoples in visual form.

Visual imperialism is the construction and exportation of visual representations of Indianness that facilitate the oppression of Indigenous peoples, thus advancing colonization and Canadian nation-building. At its origins, visual imperialism has been preoccupied with rendering visual the dichotomy between those figured as "civilized" and those figured as "savage," between the "superior" and the "inferior." As LaRocque argues (2010: 22), within early European representations Indigenous peoples have been "persistently portrayed ... in extremes as either the grotesque ignoble or noble savage." Women were polarized as "princesses" or denigrated "as sexually immoral and beasts of burden" (Fiske 2000: 12). Indigeneity was cut up and organized around dichotomies of sex and gender — male, female, masculine, feminine — with Indian men figured as depraved and brutal savages, or as heroic and sacrificing wisdom-keepers; and with Indian women represented as dirty, whorish and boorish, or pristine, innocent and in need of saving. By applying these categories to Indigenous peoples, colonizers tried to eliminate Indigenous understandings of sex and gender, and constructed heterosexist relations between Indigenous peoples that produced Eurocentric heteronormativity and those who would fall within that categorical space (Rifkin 2006).

People such as nineteenth-century artists Paul Kane and George Catlin fostered these ideas. They painted from imagination and the examples of living people, so that their work was taken to be precise, mimetic visual representations of Indians. Drawing from real meetings with Indigenous persons, they nevertheless drew on their imaginations to insert "clothing and artifacts foreign to the Indians in the paintings" (Francis 2004: 21). Often, they added "details of setting and landscape to highlight the romantic flavour of the scenes" (21). The result is a cache of visual narratives fusing reality and fantasy, but rooted in the painters' assumed ability, as inhabiting the civilized/superior side of the dichotomy to formulate visual truth regimes about Indigenous peoples and their lives.

In addition to artists, scientists participated in the colonial truth regime by "demonstrating" that Indians were innately inferior based on inalienable, biological characteristics that manifest themselves in "savage" ways of living, dressing, eating, and so on. Race-based conceptualizations of Indigenous peoples as Indians were positioned against the presumed normality, neutrality, civility, and purity of "Whites." While the notion that "race" is a scientifically sound method for human classification has been debunked, racial ideologies have been so entrenched that they remain intertwined with images of Indianness. LaRocque (2010: 22) refers to the system of racial discourse that perpetuates the innate inferiority of Indigenous peoples as "White North America's image machine." It is a machine produced by a colonial system that needs to prove Indian inferiority and that "hound(s) and haunt(s)" Indigenous peoples (22). To confront this, Indigenous peoples must "humanize the 'Indian' by, on one hand, de-normalizing the 'savage' view, and, on the other, putting forward Native peoples' humanity" through their writing and artistic engagements (LaRocque 2010: 11). It is thus vital to deconstruct the "Indian" whenever its presentation is in the hands of non-Indigenous peoples, just as it is critical to create affirmative images of Indigenous peoples, reflecting our humanity; neither of these should be considered secondary tasks in decolonization.

## The Visual Sovereignty of the Indigenous Artist

As in the past, Indigenous artists challenge colonial images, skillfully refracting racist imagery and so asserting what Michelle Raheja and Jolene Rickard have separately referred to as "visual sovereignty." Some artists deploy "new media technologies, [to] frame more imaginative renderings of Native American intellectual and cultural paradigms" (Raheja 2007: 1165–1166) that speak from Indigenous artists' own experiences. For example, Cree artist Kent Monkman (2014) paints compelling landscape paintings in the vein of Kane's historic landscape portraiture because Kane's work is now iconic as representations of a pre-Canadian landscape: of the earth as wild and empty land and Indigenous peoples as noble savages. Monkman mimics Kane's grand painting style in order to then radically Indigenize and queer the narratives produced by Kane's work. To do so, Monkman inserts his seminal figure, Miss Chief Eagle Testickle, challenging narratives of the past that are rife with White heteronormativity. In Monkman's paintings, Miss Chief, in hot pink stilettos, mesh, fringe, and shiny regalia, is subject and object, painter and model. She flouts the ways in which Indigenous peoples have been represented in gendered and heterosexist European race-thinking. Monkman also engages material culture, video and digital technologies, as in his presentation of the Boudoir de Berdashe, a full-size teepee installation — and the home of Miss Chief (National Gallery of Canada 2014). In this way, Monkman critically speaks back to the silencing of Indigenous peoples and visual imperialism's legacies (Monkman 2014).

Like Monkman, Shelley Niro, a Mohawk artist, confronts visual imperialism through her work. In particular, her photography and filmography challenge hypersexualized images of Indianness and the tradition of fixing Indigenous peoples to a past presence. She puts forth images of Mohawk women as "everyday" people and as consumers of popular culture (Niro 2014). By drawing on a multitude of resources and a number of representational strategies, artists such as Monkman and Niro challenge the confining tropes produced through the long history of dehumanizing Indigenous peoples through images.

Many Indigenous artists, working around the globe, critically confront legacies of Eurocentric visual imperialism; often, they address representations of Indianness as harmful misrepresentations of actual Indigenous peoples, responding to the ways that visual archives confine Indigenous peoples to the past. They draw on rich strategies to reflect humanized images of Indigenous peoples that are attentive to the complexities of Indigenous pasts and present realities. Here, I examine two works in greater detail, one by mixed media artist Rebecca Belmore (Anishinaabe) and the second by mixed media artist Terrance Houle (Blood). Belmore's Artifact #671B (1988) and Houle's Urban Indian Series (2007) direct attention to the seriousness of lingering racist and sexist imaginings of Indigenous peoples, raising awareness around their persistence in contemporary society. Houle and Belmore "represent back" and challenge White North America's image machine, but they also "write forward" (Cobb 2005: 128) by insisting on Indigenous visual sovereignty.

## On Colonialism and Sovereignty

So far, I have used the term "visual sovereignty" as though it were unproblematic. However, the term "sovereignty" has been subjected to extensive debate among Indigenous scholars. Its use in Indigenous context owes directly to Indigenous experiences with colonization. According to Alfred, colonialism is about "the complexities of the relationship that evolved between Indigenous peoples and Europeans as they came into contact" (2009: 45). The term refers specifically to the "development of institutions and policies by European imperial and Euroamerican settler governments towards Indigenous peoples" (2009: 45). Bonita Lawrence (2002: 26–27) extends the discussion of colonialism beyond references to institutions and policy relations by challenging historical narratives of early encounters as ones of mutual benefit and trade. She instead figures initial encounters along the eastern coast of Turtle Island as instances of "mercantile colonialism," a time in which "hundreds of trade ships of different European nations engaged in a massive competition for marks; an invasion instrumental in destabilizing existing intertribal political alliances in eastern North America." The result was the "almost inevitable" intensification of inter-Indigenous and Indigenous-European warfare.

Both Alfred and Lawrence indicate that peoples do not ultimately experience colonialism as theoretical frameworks. Instead, colonialism is "made real in the lives of First Nations people when these things go from being a set of imposed externalities to becoming causes of harm to them as people and as communities" (Alfred 2009: 45). Concrete imposed externalities include mechanisms such as the Indian Act, provincial liquor laws, national parks policies, game and resource management regulations, and health policies. The result is that colonialism has meant, as Alfred writes, "resource exploitation of indigenous lands, residential school syndrome, racism, expropriation of lands, extinguishment of rights, wardship, and welfare dependency" (2009: 43). It has manifested in individual and communal illnesses such as suicide and self-harm, family violence and lateral community violence and struggles with addiction. Indigenous peoples have been subject to processes of colonization and may feel the effects from colonization, but this does not mean that Indigenous peoples are colonized. We are not solely defined by the conditions to which we have been subjected.[1]

Given the diversity of Indigenous peoplehood, worldviews and experiences, however, it has not been easy for Indigenous scholars writing to trans-Indigenous and non-Indigenous audiences to identify English-language terms and conceptual tools that effectively "sum up" the fallout from colonial processes. Few terms can effectively condense and convey what it is that scores of distinct Indigenous peoples are respectively working to recover. As Indigenous peoples work to recover from the impacts of colonization, are Indigenous peoples decolonizing to assert autonomy? Self-determination? Nationhood? Sovereignty? Revitalization? Do these terms come close to articulating the many aims of decolonization and Indigenous peoples' movements for revitalization?

Indigenous scholars have long grappled with English-language terminology to assess its relevance for discussing the freedom that contemporary Indigenous peoples strive for. In Chapter One of this book, for instance, James (Sa'ke'j) Youngblood Henderson writes about this as the problem of being a split head and of using English in a way that enables transmission of Indigenous worldviews. Within such struggles, "sovereignty" has emerged as a popular yet contested term. Thus, some ask how this non-Indigenous monarchical-political concept, embedded in colonial legal and political discourse, has become the form of expression for Indigenous nationhood, when Indigenous nations have "had their own systems of government since the time before the term 'sovereignty' was invented in Europe." (Alfred 2007: 465).

Further, calling the colonial state to recognize Indigenous sovereignty reinforces colonial state power over Indigenous peoples asking for "recognition," as Hayden King argues in Chapter Seven of this book, and masks the reality that "sovereignty" is inextricably linked with centralized notions of power — supremacy, dominion, authority — antithetical to traditional Indigenous worldviews about governance. Indigenous collective organization involves "no absolute authority, no coercive enforcement of decisions, no hierarchy, and no separate ruling entity" (Alfred 2008: 56). Alfred pointedly reminds us of the divide between individualistic and hierarchical European conceptualizations of governance and decentralized, equitable Indigenous systems of governance. He cautions that Indigenous languages and ways of knowing must be at the core of what we do because to adopt Eurocentric concepts and processes further subjugates and devalues our own Indigenous systems.

Other Indigenous scholars, such as Amanda J. Cobb (2005: 123), argue that coercion is a contingent, not necessary aspect of sovereignty. In the context of "inter-sovereign relationships," particular states have behaved coercively — but sovereignty may be redefined to reject coercive interpretations and practices while ensuring consistency with "the sure knowledge of our own continuance" as

Indigenous peoples (2005: 131). As Cobb maintains, "we possess the power to reshape or transform the notion of sovereignty ... to fit our cultural needs and goals and are actively doing so" (2005: 126). Like Cobb, Rickard (2011: 469–471) views "sovereignty" as a site of possibility. For instance, Rickard remarks that although some scholars are "caught in a system of Western validation," two Haudenosaunee, Deskaheh and Sotsisowah adapted the concept of sovereignty to advocate for their communities. In such ways, sovereignty is not the exclusive purview of European and Eurocentric nations, but rather is about "both Western and Haudenosaunee ideas about law" (2011: 470–471). Rickard thus challenges the notion that our understandings of sovereignty should be derived from narrow, European legal-political interpretations.

An uncritical embrace of "sovereignty" may represent values not in keeping with traditional Indigenous worldviews; if some Indigenous peoples believe that sovereignty can be reworked, it may yet prove to provide a useful linguistic and conceptual space for those who remake it. Drawing on Beverly Singer, Cobb (2005: 127) thus observes an emergence of "cultural sovereignty." Museums have been "used as an instrument of colonization and dispossession," but may be transformed "into something else, in this case, into an instrument of self-definition and cultural continuance" (127). For her part, Singer uses "cultural sovereignty" to reflect pathways of revitalizing Indigenous lifeways. Both Cobb and Singer see "sovereignty" as useful for its adaptive possibilities outside of the political and legal realms.

In this, Rickard echoes many Indigenous scholars, including Vine Deloria Jr., Jack Forbes, Joanne Barker and Robert Allen Warrior, who have worked with the concept of "intellectual sovereignty." Intellectual sovereignty adopts the "singular idea of sovereignty as a legal construct" and transforms it in and through "multiple interpretations" (Rickard 2011: 471). This involves decolonizing "the theoretical and methodological perspectives used within analyses of indigenous histories, cultures, and identities" (cited in Rickard 2011: 471). Along similar lines, Rickard's and Raheja's framing of "visual sovereignties" recognizes the ways that Indigenous artists are affected by and challenge legacies of colonialism, rhetorical imperialism and visual imperialism through their artistic work.

In particular, Indigenous artists reject imperialism's claims to knowledge about their bodies. Visual artists simultaneously interrogate the mis/representation of their bodies as "Indian" bodies and offer their own understandings of their bodies in relation to space and place. By using "clothing, posture and the attitude of the photographic subject," Indigenous visual artists can and do "challenge stereotypical views of Indians as sad victims or noble savages" (Spears Bombay 2007: 134). Artists engage with many technical aspects of image-making, drawing on "practices like camera angles, distance from subject, pose, cropping and clothing" to "emphasize the humanity, individuality and authenticity of the Native people portrayed" (2007: 133). Given the canon of derogatory, contrived representations of imaginary Indianness, artists draw on visual expression to "simultaneously recognize Indigenous survivance while underscoring our colonial subjugation" by inverting colonial depictions of Indigenous bodies (Rickard 2011: 465). More than this, they assert Indigenous voice and visual sovereignty through the artistic conceptualization of theirs and other peoples' Indigenous bodies.

## Indigenous Resistance to Museum and Corporate Imperialism

### "The Spirit Sings"

Colonial images depict Indianness by confining First Nations peoples' bodies to pre- or early encounter time, reflecting expectations that Indigenous peoples would disappear from the earth through a "clash of cultures," forced assimilation policies, and processes of modernization and colonial nation-building. This colonial "truth regime" was evident in the Glenbow Museum's exhibition of First Nations, Inuit and Métis art, developed in 1988 to coincide with the Calgary Olympic Games. The initial title for the exhibit, "Forget Not My World: Exploring the Canadian Native Heritage" was interpreted by many Indigenous peoples as reflecting and reproducing the idea of the "vanishing Indian." Indeed, Ruth B. Phillips (2011: 63) writes that museum administrators at the Glenbow Museum felt that the initial title was "intriguing and catchy" and that it would "respond to a nostalgic evocation of the vanishing Indian idea." After much public opposition led by Indigenous peoples who rejected such framing, the exhibit was later renamed as "The Spirit Sings: Artistic Traditions of Canada's First Peoples."

"The Spirit Sings" was the flagship visual arts component of the Olympic Arts Festival and the "most ambitious and complex museum project ever undertaken in Canada" (oco'88 1988: 277). It opened its doors on January 14, 1988 and ran until May 1, 1988. The exhibit was reinstalled in Ottawa on the following Canada Day, July 1, for a five-month display. The popular exhibition cost more than two and a half million dollars and involved "627 rare Indian and Inuit art objects on loan from 82 lenders in 16 countries" and made claims that "two-thirds of the objects had never been seen in Canada before" (277). Statements such as these entrenched the narrative of vanished Indians, separating the material culture of Indigenous peoples in the past from Indigenous peoples in the present. Also, not all the exhibits were from the time prior to the formal existence of Canada, so Indigenous peoples made these objects; they had clearly seen them, but the description assumes that only the gaze of non-Indigenous Canadians "counts." If the Olympic organizing committee for the Calgary Olympics, "oco'88," and various media outlets considered the exhibit a resounding success, it faced sustained resistance from Indigenous peoples.

In particular, the Lubicon Lake Cree Nation and the acting Chief of the nation, Bernard Ominayak, opposed the exhibit's focus on a "pre-contact" past and the lack of "contemporary Native voice and presence" (McLoughlin 1993). The Lubicon contended that "the museum needed to promote, rather than deny, the relationship between the historical pieces and the realities of contemporary Native life" (1993). Part of those realities for the Lubicon is that the federal government consistently subverts its efforts to secure respect of and recognition for its land/environmental base, either through a land claim process or new treaty agreement. Because the Lubicon had not participated in the "numbered treaties" created throughout the prairies, recognition and rights (however problematically) affirmed through the treaty-making processes do not extend to the Lubicon or their lands. Without any obligation for consultation via pre-existing agreements, the Lubicon peoples' environments were, and continue to be, violated by oil sands expansion.

Since the 1950s, Shell Canada has been drilling in lands the Lubicon identify as their traditional territory. The oil drilling poses significant threats to the ecosystem and by extension to the survival of people who engage in hunting and trapping, both for subsistence and as a way of engaging with the wider Indigenous and Canadian economies (Sidsworth 2010: 52). Yet as a part of what the oco'88 branded "Team Petroleum'88," Shell Canada and the federal government cosponsored "The Spirit Sings." The oco'88 felt that Shell's financial sponsorship of the Games, its importance to the Calgary's economy and by extension to the city's identity, meant that Shell's sponsorship role was unproblematic. But the Lubicon challenged that it was highly inappropriate for Shell to sponsor "The Spirit Sings" while being directly "engaged in destroying the traditional economy and way of life of the Lubicon Lake Cree" (Trigger quoted in McLoughlin 1993). Ominayak (quoted in Wamsley and Heine 1996: 174) argued that the "irony of using a display of North American Indian artefacts [sic] to attract people to the Winter Olympics being organized by interests who are still actively seeking to destroy Indian people, seems obvious." At the heart of the matter, the Lubicon felt that the "presence of these oil corporations on contested indigenous territories, as well as the federal and provincial governments' unwillingness to engage in honourable treaty negotiations with the Lubicon Cree" reflected an ongoing commitment by the Canadian government to assimilate the Lubicon peoples (O'Bonsawin 2010: 147).

Representatives from the Glenbow Museum met with the Lubicon, who, according to exhibition curator Julia Harrison, had "no objection to the content of the exhibition but only to its sponsorship and association with the Calgary Olympics" (quoted in O'Bonsawin 2010). Indeed, Harrison even defended the sponsorship by suggesting "Museums, like Universities, are expected by the constitutions, to remain non-partisan." Curator Harrison's reply on behalf of the museum was that there was no "evidence that the public confuses corporate support for corporate policy"

(O'Bonsawin 2010). The Lubicon's retort was that by accepting Shell's sponsorship, the museum was anything but nonpartisan; it had taken a political stand in an ideologically powerful message clearly accepting Shell's violation of Indigenous peoples' lives. For the Lubicon, to claim to respect and honour Indigenous peoples through the exhibit while accepting sponsorship monies from a corporation directly contributing to the environmental genocide of Indigenous peoples was a decidedly politicized (and personal) act, regardless of public perception. The effect was that the "outward partnership displayed between corporate organisers and Aboriginal peoples" (Forsyth and Wamsley 2005: 236) at the Calgary Games only served as a "grim reminder of the weak attempts by Canadians to conceal historically oppressive relations that involved a difficult past and a tension-filled present."

### Belmore's Artifact 671B

The Lubicon were not the only voices of dissent. In fact, opposition to the rationale driving the structure of the exhibit and the serious problems of corporate oil sponsorship was widespread. One of the most provocative responses came from Anishinaabe mixed-media artist Rebecca Belmore. On January 12, 1988, Belmore debuted Artifact 671B, an embodied installation created and placed outside of the Thunder Bay Art Gallery just two days prior to the opening of "The Spirit Sings." Belmore's resistant artistic performance provided a counternarrative to Glenbow's romanticized Indians and the museum's ignoring the very real effects that Shell and other oil companies' rapacious greed had/have on the Lubicon and other Indigenous peoples. In full support of the Lubicon's resistance, Belmore envisioned her performative piece in conversation with the Lubicon Cree's call to boycott the Olympics and the torch relays, "respond[ing] to the hypocrisy of this supposedly celebratory exhibition and its relationship to the Olympics" (quoted in Martin 2012: 80). She decided that the Thunder Bay Art Gallery was a logical choice for the politicized performance, given the gallery's sizeable collection of Indigenous artwork and its path on the Olympic torch route.

In the installation, Belmore erected poles, mimicking an exhibition display case, with signs attached announcing "Glenbow Museum Presents" and "Artifact 671B-1988." Positioning herself within the "case," she sat "immobile, as an artifact, in −22°C weather for two hours on the frozen ground outside the Thunder Bay Art Gallery" (Martin 2012: 80). While hundreds of Thunder Bay area residents attended the Olympic flame's appearance as it passed through the city, local Indigenous students answered the call of the Lubicon and of Belmore by joining in the display. The students stood behind her "holding a banner that read 'Share the Shame'" (Belmore quoted in Martin 2012: 80).

Artifact 671B challenged the government's policy of non-negotiation with the Lubicon and the state's failure to address its complicity in ecological genocide and environmental racism. In her thoughtful reflection on Belmore's work, Rickard underscores how Artifact 671B effectively reveals contemporary capitalism's inherent contradictions. She writes that Belmore "revealed the duplicity of a company that provided corporate sponsorship of the Olympic exhibition, The Spirit Sings, which featured Canada's First Nations people, while securing drilling rights in the territories of outstanding Lubicon Cree land claims" (Rickard 2006: 2). Belmore (quoted in Martin 2012: 80) explains that the decision to engage was an easy one, writing that she "could not ignore the reality that objects made by our ancestors were vastly more desirable to the world than dealing with our present-day existence."

Like some of Belmore's other works, Artifact 671B plays on the fact that the "Native Indian is a marketable commodity" (Ryan 1999: 45). In fact, Belmore frequently acknowledges the complexities of the commodification of her body and being as an Indigenous artist. She engages in a satirical mimetic exercise that reveals the inherently racist dimensions of the commodification of Indigeneity, of a particular kind of "corporate colonialism." Through Artifact 671B, she uses her body in an act of visual sovereignty, mocking and so refusing the cultural, commercial exchange and marketing of Indigenous pasts and presents, and rejecting the ubiquity of corporate enterprise in the colonization of Indigenous peoples. Moreover, Belmore reveals how institutions (such as museums that are often seen as purely "cultural") participate and facilitate the corporate-driven exploitation of Indigenous peoples. With Artifact 671B, Belmore proposes an alternative vision of sovereign Indigeneity that refuses to be sold and refuses to be relegated to the historic memory of the museum. This connects to a larger refusal to be woven into Olympic performances of Canadian nationalism that hinge on the concealment of the brutality of colonialism and Canadian nation building.

In the years since Belmore's performance piece, which reveals the pervasive aggression of visual imperialist legacies and its entanglement with corporate colonialism, this corporate colonialism has only intensified. Corporations, the Canadian culture industry and the state collude to facilitate a mutual exchange of power, creating new initiatives that attempt to legitimate corporate incursions into and destruction of the lands wherein Indigenous peoples live. This corporate colonialism challenges Indigenous peoples' ability to uphold the original instructions given by their respective Creators to live in a respectful relationship with the land and all of Creation. To effectively abrogate Indigenous peoples' ability to uphold these "original instructions," to be caretakers of the land and its other inhabitants, corporations perpetuate dehumanized images of Indigenous peoples as Indians that are culturally "nice to look at" as part of the nation's past, but that are entirely irreconcilable with, and irrelevant to, the present.

*Houle's Urban Indian*

Like Belmore, Terrance Houle's artistic works challenge corporate, colonial visions of Indigeneity. In his Urban Indian Series portraits (Houle and Brown 2007), Houle highlights tensions produced when images associated with the past appear in a present in which they are projected as "not belonging." Houle was raised on his ancestral land on the prairies and in the city of Calgary. He is an artist, filmmaker, and performer whose work generally features Indigenous bodies — most often his own. In the Urban Indian Series, he plays on colonial misrecognitions of Indigenous identity, relationships to space and to markers of modernity that lingering racist attitudes view as irreconcilable with Indigenous peoples.

Houle defines the scope of the Urban Indian Series in his Artist's Statement, sharing that the Urban Indian Series is a comment on personal identity and cultural commodity in today's contemporary culture:

> Specifically, what is my culture as it compares to the mainstream under-standing of Native Peoples? My regalia is both a catalyst in the image, breaking up the sea of mundane western garb, and a representation that is part of my everyday, much like my culture, thus challenging the sugges-tion that I am out of place in a world that only identifies with conformity. The work serves to question ideas of tradition, identity and culture that are often negated or replaced by Western cultural standards. Also, in capturing the image of the "Indian" in portraiture and regalia, the Urban Indian Series seeks to comment on the historical relationship between photography and aboriginal identity. (2010)

In the Urban Indian Series, Houle offers a series of eight photographs of him-self, five of which I elaborate on here. In them, the Urban Indian is dressed in full grass-dance regalia, carrying out everyday activities that accompany life in urban space: getting dressed for the day (#1), kissing a person on the front porch of a home (#2), riding public transit (#3), talking on the telephone in an office (#4), sitting in a diner booth (#5), browsing CDs in a store (#6), buying groceries (#7), and taking a bath (#8) (Houle and Brown 2007).

In photograph #2 of the series, the Urban Indian is pictured standing opposite a young person holding a baby. Houle is ironically (but possibly nonironically) figuring a visual narrative of heteropatriarchal, nuclear family life wherein the "man" leaves for work as the breadwinner while the "woman" stays home. There is no reflection of the extended kinship networks that are a reality of many Indigenous peoples' family lives. Instead, the trio are alone on the front porch of a house, the open front doorway behind them. It appears that the Urban Indian is retreating backward down the stairs before leaving. The Urban Indian seems to have paused for the couple to have a fleeting "goodbye" kiss.

In Image #3, Houle is the primary subject, partially concealed by other figures while standing in a crowded bus, gazing out the bus window. The Urban Indian has left the family behind to join a crowd of commuters, so that the Urban Indian Series represents a "day in the life" of the Urban Indian. In the image, Houle stands out in his brightly coloured regalia, highly visible amid a sea of drab tri-tonal grey-, black-, and denim-clothed passengers.

The fourth image shows Houle in what is presumably an office. He sits behind a desk, still in his regalia, with a telephone to his ear. He reaches for a file as a pair of pale hands extends the documents and points at a particular line. Surrounded by scattered paper and stacks of office supplies, in the background we can see what looks like a miniature trophy atop Houle's desk. On the wall sits a poster of an entertainment wrestler.

Jumping to the seventh image, we see Houle, seemingly having finished work, shopping for groceries in a small store. With a green grocery basket slung over his right arm, extending his left arm out and his open palm lifting a small herb leaf, he leans over as if bending to smell the fresh herb.

The eighth and final image of the series shows Houle at what the viewer can reasonably assume is the end of his day, given the trajectory of images. Houle relaxes while reading a magazine among a sea of bubbles, next to a yellow-and-blue rubber ducky shower curtain. His regalia sits piled on the floor of the bathroom next to the bathtub as the Urban Indian relaxes while reading a magazine, laying in a sea of bubbles and next to a yellow-and-blue rubber ducky shower curtain; so ends the day in the life of an Urban Indian.

Shandra Spears Bombay argues that, "colonial meaning systems are not easily changed through guilt-inducing and/or educational efforts. However, it may be possible to shift the ideological position of the colonial viewer through trickier means" (2007: 133). Similarly, Walsh writes that "with great care, and awareness, we can transform the colonial gaze, with nudges or tickles, into another kind of gaze; one which sees us as we really are" (Spears Bombay 2007: 135). These are precisely the effects of Houle's images.

Whenever I have shared the Urban Indian Series, people respond with laughter. Some stifle their laughter, others are more obvious about it, but the images have yet to be met with silence. This anecdotal evidence suggests that viewers find something worth laughing at. An Indigenous person kissing someone goodbye or riding on a bus does not immediately sound as if it would be a cause for laughter, and yet people do laugh. When pressed about the source of their laughter, perceptions shift: They realize that their laughter is underpinned by a latent understanding that Houle's regalia-dressed Indian is present in a place not "traditionally" associated with Indianness: the city. Granted, certain regalia are reserved for ceremonial purposes rather than everyday wear. Yet clothing has a particular place within the colonizing mission. In the paintings of people like Kane, regalia is associated with a "pre-modern" Indianness; today, "traditional" Indigenous clothing is deemed incompatible with the contemporary moment.

Indigenous peoples and urban space have long been figured as antithetical to one another. Instead, European writers have pictured Indigenous peoples as "living in the countryside, in jungles, forests, the plains/pampas, or in small villages surrounded by mountains as in the Andes" (Forbes 1998: 15). As Susan Lobo and Kurt Peters identify (1998: 3), the rural/savage/Indigenous-urban/civilized/European dichotomy persists to this day as "a false expression" of the reality of life for Indigenous peoples. Houle's series directly confronts this false expression. Moreover, the juxtaposition of urban and Indian is punctuated by Houle's placing of himself in regalia. Regalia is confined to "traditional Indian" space and/or a particularly "cultural Indian" space through colonial policies.

Provisions to federal legislation, the Indian Act of 1876, dictated and attempted to control every aspect of First Nations' lives, including regulating First Nations' expressions through dance. Policymakers also developed rules and regulations concerning attire, often referred to as "Indian costume." Prior to 1933, the Indian Act criminalized any person with Indian status under the Indian Act who appeared at a festival, dance, or ceremony in regalia (Backhouse 2007: Chapter Three). The purpose of these legal regulations was to force Indigenous peoples to become European, although Indigenous refusal and the persistence of racial categorization nevertheless remained impediments to assimilation efforts. Banning traditional clothing through the Indian Act played an important part in this colonial effort. It is telling that status Indians could appear in "Indian costume," at colonizer-sanctioned events, however. For example, in 1894, the Canadian Pacific Railway (CPR) invited peoples from the Stoney reserve to dress in traditional clothing and to entertain travellers marooned in the town of Banff (Francis 2004: 179–181). First Nations peoples could thus dress in "Indian costume" in contravention of the Indian Act in more urbanized spaces, but only when mediated by Europeans to ensure the disconnect of Indigenous peoples and their regalia from meaningful ceremonial, spiritual and governance practices. These practices were rooted in ethics of love and sharing, often involving the "giving away" or "gifting" of food and material items to one another (see Pettipas 1994). This is an absolute contrast with current consumer-commodified visions of Indianness, which are about making profit for large corporations, fashion designers and so on.

In these ways, the Urban Indian Series resonates with Philip Deloria's book *Indians in Unexpected Places* (2004), in particular with an image titled "Red Cloud Woman in Beauty Shop, Denver 1941." In it, Red Cloud Woman sits beneath a hair dryer in a salon, receiving a salon manicure while wearing full powwow regalia. Deloria (2004: 4) argues that such an image is an off-putting one for non-Native people, challenging Euro-American ideas that Indians, signalled by Red Cloud Woman's body, her clothing and her braided hairstyle, are irreconcilable with modernity, symbolized by the beauty shop, hair dryer and manicure. The "vanishing Indian" discourse dictated that Indigenous peoples would not survive the onslaught of modern nation building; by implication, Red Cloud Woman "should not" be in the then-contemporary America of the beauty salon. Hence, the mere image of Red Cloud Woman defies racist colonial logics, showing that she and many others have thwarted their "tragic destiny" and survived unabated colonial oppression.

Red Cloud Woman wears regalia and clothing imagined through policy and imperialism as "pre-modern" while having a decidedly "modern" manicure. This jars because, as Deloria writes, "Even in the wake of decades of stereotype busting, a beaded buckskin dress and a pair of braids continue to evoke a broad set of cultural expectations about Indian people" (2004: 4). Countering expectations that imagine Indigenous peoples either in the past or in rural spaces closed off from so-called "mainstream" culture, Red Cloud woman's image shows a "traditional Indian" in contemporary consumer culture. She refuses assumptions that to fit into that life/world, she must forgo wearing regalia. This directly challenges the belief that Indigenous peoples, as imagined Indians, are incompatible with contemporary consumerism; it throws into question "common sense" notions of the irreconcilability of Indigenous peoples with the contemporary world. For new nations on Indigenous lands and for consumer society to flourish, so the thinking has gone, Indigenous peoples have to disappear, either as a natural product of "contact" or via successive waves of assimilation policies. Such policies assume that Indigenous peoples will concede to the superiority of Euro-American and Euro-Canadian ways of being.

Deloria's title for people such as Red Cloud Woman is "Indians in unexpected places." Red Cloud Woman is both "modern" and wears clothing that is "visibly Indian." She refuses to sacrifice her Indigeneity, against the colonial idea that real or imagined Indigenous peoples are unsuited to the contemporary world. In short, an Indigenous woman dressed in regalia, engaging in consumer culture, appears "out of place."

As American and Canadian societies desire the assimilation of Indigenous peoples, who are often figured by the media and governments as "problems" and socially dysfunctional burdens, the idea that Indigenous peoples become consumers — on their own terms — is also unthinkable. They are not the Indians that the colonizer imagined for the future because they remain Indigenous peoples while participating in contemporary life. Houle's Urban Indian, buying vegetables at the local grocery story and commuting through mass transit, is not the fixed figure of the colonial imagination, and the use of regalia is central to this repudiation. Regalia that (as Houle reminds us in the passage quoted previously) "stands in" for his culture is relevant to Indigenous lives in the present, something that is with him every day, whether it is visible to others or not. When the Urban Indian wears his regalia as a part of his every day, he reclaims it from the clutches of consumerist idolatry.

Houle's strategic representation of regalia reclaims it from colonialism's legacies and disrupts racist notions of the unsuitability for "traditional Indians" in the contemporary world. Houle's visible Indianness in the sites and spaces of capital is provocative. For those who have been indoctrinated to believe that Indigenous peoples look a certain way, what "makes sense" in the image is "the Indian." What is wrong or uncomfortable is the Indian in unexpected or un-Indian places: "the Indian" on the bus, "the Indian" having a bubble bath and "the Indian" at the grocery store. As David Theo Goldberg argues, understandings of space and of who belongs in certain spaces are steeped in racist discourses. He writes, "Racisms become institutionally normalized in and through spatial configuration, just as social space is made to seem natural, a given, by being conceived and defined in racial terms" (2002: 185). To unmap/denaturalize colonized and racialized spaces, we must "begin by exploring space as a social product, uncovering how bodies are produced in space and how spaces produce bodies" (Razack 2002: 17). Houle's illustrations effectively force us to "denaturalize geography" through denaturalizing Indians, undermining the "worldviews that rest upon" the construction of social space (Richard Philips, cited in Razack 2002: 5).

Put another way, Indigenous peoples "can't win for losing." Even when an Indigenous person is depicted as living in accordance with the ebb and flow of the daily life of Canadian consumer society — riding the bus, working in an office, shopping at the grocery store — we must do so as inconspicuously as possible (and in spite of persistent racism on the basis of appearances) because the image of the Indian is still irreconcilable with the place accorded to (and produced for) Indigenous peoples within contemporary colonial life. Houle's clothing, or perhaps he himself, belongs in a museum exhibit, not in the contemporary public. Houle thus effectively exploits the ruptures between false representations and presumptions of Indigenous reality and the reality of Indigenous peoples' ongoing relationship to rhetorical, visual and cognitive imperialism.

## Concluding Thoughts

If we agree with Cobb that sovereignty is "deeply and integrally related to what that nation believes, feels, and hopes about its identity and for its future" (2005: 118), we need to take artists seriously when we struggle for and imagine Indigenous sovereignties. Rickard (2006) reminds us that artists play a major role in publicly representing their respective Indigenous nations and Indigenous peoples more broadly. Along with legal-political, intellectual, cultural and other forms of sovereignty, visual sovereignty is a necessary strategy of resistance against the powerful representational work of colonization. Indigenous artists reflect their societies and the relations in which their peoples are entangled.

Rebecca Belmore's Artifact #671B and Terrance Houle's Urban Indian Series are two examples of the many Indigenous artists who resist the enduring racialization of Indigenous bodies. They draw attention to the circulation of racist imaginings of Indigenous peoples that undergird our continued dispossession. At the same time, their embodied narratives challenge Euro-normative assumptions about Indigenous peoples' place within current Canadian life. Through visual representation, artists validate Indigenous self-representation while asserting Indigenous presence on Indigenous lands in Indigenous terms. Conversely, although "the state removes and alienates an Indigenous peoples from their land and disrupts their connection," artists use their respective media to uncover and in some cases re-establish this connection (McLeod 2002: 37). By intervening in the representation of Indigenous bodies and in relation to Indigenous lands, artists cross into and make important interventions into legal-political struggles over land and the environment, and, in some cases, Indigenous nationhood.

It is this reality that makes the work of people such as Houle and Belmore so important, necessary and relevant. As with Monkman and Niro, they insert Indigenous peoples, often themselves, as movements of visual sovereignty that extends far beyond simply addressing discourses of Indianness. In self-aware, embodied rejections of such discourses, the artists become powerful forces in public education, although not reducible to acts of pedagogy. When asserting visual and material sovereignty through art, it becomes possible, as Gixtsan artist Wii Muk'willixw (Art Wilson) writes, to effectively educate people. At the same time, they express Indigenous self-determination in artistic realms. Houle and Belmore's art are practices of freedom, in which they tell "stories of injustice and resistance" while creating provocative "constant reminder[s] of the atrocities that have taken place" (Wii Muk'willixw 1996: 14). In short, the images created by these Blood and Anishinaabe artists confront the public face of Canada's neoliberal nation-state and the consumer capitalist order — highlighting their own experiences as First Nations' persons, they simultaneously insist on the depth and richness of Indigenous resistance and persistence.

## NOTES

1. I acknowledge the profound impact of Dr. Althea Prince (Ryerson University), who gave a talk at McMaster University while I was a university student. During the talk, Dr. Prince emphasized that although people who had been taken from the African continent and brought across the Atlantic Ocean had been *enslaved*, it was important to understand that they were not *slaves*. They were human beings first, people whose

lives were more than the conditions that they faced. Indigenous peoples are not only subjects of colonization; they are human beings first who are more than the sum of the colonial context.

## REFERENCES

Alfred, Gerald Taiaiake. 2009. "Colonialism and State Dependency." *Journal of Aboriginal Health*. Ottawa: National Aboriginal Health Organization (NAHO).

____. 2008. *Peace, Power, Righteousness: An Indigenous Manifesto*. Oxford: Oxford University Press.

____. 2007. "Sovereignty." In Phillip J. Deloria and Neal Salisbury (eds.), *A Companion to American Indian History*. Oxford: Blackwell Publishers.

Allen, Lee. 2013. "Put Some Beads on It: Paul Frank Native Designer Candace Halcro." <indiancountrytodaymedianetwork.com/gallery/photo/put-some-beads-it-paul-frank-native-designer-candace-halcro-150487>.

Backhouse, Constance. 2007. *Colour-Coded: A Legal History of Racism in Canada, 1900–1950*. Toronto: University of Toronto Press.

CBC News. 2013. "H&M Pulls Feather Headdresses from Canadian Shelves." August 9. <cbc.ca/news/canada/h-m-pulls-feather-headdresses-from-canadian-shelves-1.1327036>.

Cobb, Amanda J. 2005. "Understanding Tribal Sovereignty: Definitions, Conceptualizations, and Interpretations." *American Studies Journal* 46, 3–4 (Winter).

Deloria, Philip J. 2004. *Indians in Unexpected Places*. Kansas City: University Press of Kansas.

FAIR (For Accurate Indigenous Representation). 2014. *F.A.I.R. Media*. <Facebook.com/realIndigenous>.

Fiske, Jo-Anne. 2000. "By, For, or About? Shifting Directions in the Representations of Aboriginal Women." *Atlantis* 25, 1.

Forbes, Jack. 1998. "The Urban Tradition Among Native Americans." *American Indian Culture and Research Journal*. 22, 4.

Forsyth, Janice, and Kevin B. Wamsley. 2005. "Symbols Without Substance: Aboriginal Peoples and the Illusions of Olympic Ceremonies." In Kevin B. Wamsley and Kevin Young (eds.), *Global Olympics: Historical and Sociological Studies of the Modern Games* 3. Oxford: Elsevier Press.

Foucault, Michel. 1979. "Truth and Power: An Interview with Alessandro Fontano and Pasquale Pasquino." In M. Morris and P. Patton (eds.), *Michel Foucault: Power/Truth/Strategy*. Sydney: Feral Publications.

Francis, Daniel. 2004. *The Imaginary Indian: The Image of the Indian in Canadian Culture*, second edition. Vancouver: Arsenal Pulp Press.

Godreche, Dominique. 2013. "Director Chris Eyre: Debating Tonto Was 'A Ridiculous Use of Our Time'." *Indian Country Today* (November 30). <indiancountrytodaymedianetwork.com/2013/11/30/director-chris-eyre-debating-tonto-was-ridiculous-use-our-time-152499>.

Goldberg, David Theo. 2002. *The Racial State*. Malden, MA: Wiley-Blackwell.

Houle, Terrance. 2010. "Artist Statement." *HIDE: Skin as Material and Metaphor*. New York: National Museum of the American Indian George Gustav Heye Center. <nmai.si.edu/exhibitions/hide/terrance.html>.

Houle, Terrance, and Jarusha Brown. 2007. *Urban Indian Series No. 1–8.* <terrancehouleart.com/givn-r.html>.

Keene, Adrienne. 2014. *Native Appropriations.* <nativeappropriations.com>.

Kuehnast, Kathleen. 1992. "Visual Imperialism and the Export of Prejudice. An Exploration of Ethnographic Film." In Peter Crawford and David Turton (eds.), *Film as Ethnography,* 183–196. Manchester, UK: Manchester University Press.

LaRocque, Emma. 2010. *When the Other Is Me: Native Resistance Discourse, 1850–1990.* Winnipeg: University of Manitoba Press.

Lawrence, Bonita. 2002. "Rewriting Histories of the Land: Colonization and Indigenous Resistance in Eastern Canada." In Sherene H. Razack (ed.), *Race, Space, and the Law: Unmapping a White Settler Society.* Toronto: Between the Lines.

Lobo, Susan, and Kurt Peters. 1998. "Introduction." *American Indian Culture and Research Journal* 22, 4.

Martin, Lee-Ann. 2012. "Out in the Cold: An Interview with Rebecca Belmore." *Canadian Art* 78–81. <canadianart.ca/features/2012/03/06/rebecca-belmore-out-in-the-cold>.

McLeod, Neal. 2002. "nêhiyâwiwin and Modernity." In Patrick Douaud and Bruce Dawson (eds.), *Plain Speaking: Essays on Aboriginal Peoples & the Prairie.* Government of Saskatchewan: Canadian Plains Research Centre.

McLoughlin, Moira. 1993. "Of Boundaries and Borders: First Nations' History in Museums." *Canadian Journal of Communication* 18, 3.

Monkman, Kent. 2014. *Kent Monkman.* <kentmonkman.com>.

National Gallery of Canada. 2014. "*Boudoir de Berdashe* by Kent Monkman." <gallery.ca/en/see/collections/artwork.php?mkey=194076>.

National Indian Child Welfare Association. 2014. "Adoptive Couple v. Baby Girl: Information and Resources." <nicwa.org/BabyVeronica>.

Niro, Shelley. "Shelley Niro." <Shelleyniro.ca>.

O'Bonsawin, Christine M. 2010. "'No Olympics on Stolen Native Land': Contesting Olympic Narratives and Asserting Indigenous Rights within the Discourse of the 2010 Vancouver Games." *Sport in Society* 13, 1.

OCO'88. 1988. *XV Olympic Winter Games Official Report.* Calgary, AB: XV Olympic Winter Games Organizing Committee.

Pettipas, Katherine. *Severing the Ties that Bind: Government Repression of Indigenous Religious Ceremonies on the Prairies.* Winnipeg: University of Manitoba Press.

Phillips, Ruth B. 2011. *Museum Pieces: Towards the Indigenization of Canadian Museums.* Montreal: McGill-Queen's University Press.

Raheja, Michelle. 2007. "Reading Nanook's Smile: Visual Sovereignty, Indigenous Revisions of Ethnography, and Atanarjuat (The Fast Runner)." *American Quarterly* 59, 4.

Razack, Sherene H. 2002. "When Place Becomes Race." In Sherene H. Razack (ed.), *Race, Space and the Law: Unmapping a White Settler Society.* Toronto: Between the Lines.

Rickard, Jolene. 2011. "Visualizing Sovereignty in the Time of Biometric Sensors." *South Atlantic Quarterly* 110, 2.

____. 2006. "Rebecca Belmore: Performing Power." *Catalogue "Rebecca Belmore Fountain."* Kamloops Art Gallery, The Morris and Helen Belkin Art Gallery. Vancouver: University of British Columbia.

Rifkin, Mark. 2006. "Romancing Kinship: A Queer Reading of Indian Education and

Zitkala-Sa's American Indian stories." GLQ: A Journal of Lesbian and Gay Studies 12, 1, 27–59.

Ryan, Allan. 1999. *The Trickster Shift: Humour and Irony in Contemporary Native Art.* Vancouver: University of British Columbia Press.

Sidsworth, Robin. 2010. "Aboriginal Participation in the Vancouver/Whistler 2010 Olympic Games: Consultation, Reconciliation and the New Relationship." LLM thesis. Vancouver: University of British Columbia.

Spears Bombay, Shandra. 2007. "Re-Constructing the Colonizer: Self-representation by First Nations Artists." *Atlantis* 29, 2.

Wamsley, Kevin B., and Mike Heine. 1996. "'Don't Mess with the Relay — It's Bad Medicine': Aboriginal Culture and the 1988 Winter Olympics." In Robert K. Barney et al. (eds.), *Olympic Perspectives: Third International Symposium for Olympic Research.* London, ON: University of Western Ontario.

Wii Muk'willixw. 1996. *Heartbeat of the Earth: A First Nations Artist Records Injustice and Resistance.* Gabriola Island, BC: New Society Publishers.

Wingrove, Josh. 2013. "Ottawa Football Team to Seek New Name After Racism Complaint." *Globe and Mail*, September 20. <theglobeandmail.com/news/national/ottawa-team-to-seek-new-name-after-racism-complaint/article 14431430>.

Chapter Six

# ABORIGINAL ECONOMIC DEVELOPMENT AND LIVING NUU-CHAH-NULTH-AHT

*Clifford (Kam'ayaam/Chachim'multhnii) Atleo*

This chapter examines the prospects of and challenges to living Nuu-chah-nulth-aht in contemporary times. At the heart of this examination is how Nuu-chah-nulth people struggle to maintain their identities and livelihoods in the context of rampant neoliberal economic development. Nuu-chah-nulth people have endured generations of colonial occupation and economic oppression, but of particular interest to me is the more recent challenge presented by the neoliberal development paradigm, which emphasizes individuality and self-reliance. There is nothing inherently wrong with concern for individuals or their capacity for self-reliance, but individuality at the expense of the collective can be problematic for Indigenous communities. Neoliberalism can also lead to changing conceptions of Indigenous identities that Isabel Altamirano-Jiménez describes as a descent into "market citizenship," which allows for shallow cultural recognition while subsuming Indigenous values to market demands (Altamirano-Jiménez 2004). Nuu-chah-nulth people have deployed various adaptive strategies since contact, but the question is whether recent strategies successfully integrate new practices into Nuu-chah-nulth ways of being or whether these new practices fundamentally transform those ways of being. I look at several examples of resistance, adaptive practices, some controversial practices and resurgence to assess their implications for community revitalization.

First, I must provide a brief summary of the Nuu-chah-nulth people and situate myself as a member/author accordingly. There are more than 9,300 registered

Nuu-chah-nulth-aht, traditionally located on the west coast of what is now commonly known as Vancouver Island, British Columbia, Canada. The Nuu-chah-nulth people are also closely related to Kwih-dich-chuh-ahtx (Makah) of Neah Bay on the Olympic Peninsula in Washington State. Since contact, we have become more widely dispersed, especially toward urban areas such as Vancouver, Victoria, and Seattle. Nuu-chah-nulth people share many commonalities with our Kwakwaka'wakw and Coast Salish neighbours, but we are distinct in many ways as well, including being the only coastal peoples to have traditionally hunted for whales. I am Tsimshian on my mother's side, with relatives from Kitselas, Kitsumkalum and Lax Kw'alaams. On my father's side, I am Nuu-chah-nulth-aht from Ahous.[1] My Nuu-chah-nulth name is Chachim'multhnii or "One who does things properly" and I am from the house of Klaq-ish-piilth. Although I grew up mostly in the city of Vancouver, I have also lived and worked in Nuu-chah-nulth communities, so my perspective is that of an insider with a vested interest in the questions and issues considered here.

I begin with a brief look at the political economy of Nuu-chah-nulth peoples, which focuses on our connection to and reliance on the ocean and rivers and all the life within. I then take a broader look at Aboriginal economic development trends, including advocating people and institutions. What follows is an examination of Nuu-chah-nulth community efforts to come to grips with changing economic circumstances and market pressures. I discuss the ways in which some economic projects have attempted to draw upon Nuu-chah-nulth teachings and guiding principles. I then take a step back to critically analyze the challenges of revitalizing traditions, paying special attention to practices that might reinforce exploitative and patriarchal relations. Finally, I look at some encouraging examples of young families who have made significant efforts to return home to reconnect to our lands and waters in a way that I describe as living Nuu-chah-nulth-aht.

## Economic Life in Nuu-chah-nulth Territories

Like many coastal areas at present, unemployment and poverty are high among Nuu-chah-nulth people in Clayoquot Sound, home to the Hesquiaht, Ahousaht, and Tla-o-qui-aht. Of course, this was not always the case.[2] At the height of our participation in the West Coast commercial fisheries, there were more than two hundred fishing vessels in the Nuu-chah-nulth fleet. A common name for coastal Indigenous peoples was "saltwater people," such was our connection to and dependence upon the sea. Today, there are about a dozen Nuu-chah-nulth boats making a living commercial fishing, although the *Ahousaht et al. v. Canada* case (BCCA 2013) has the potential to make some changes on this front. Historically, Nuu-chah-nulth communities thrived off the bounty of the sea. After contact with

European and American trading ships, my ancestors also hunted and traded sea otters and seals. Even though many traditional practices morphed into adaptive commercial practices over the generations as money became increasingly important, it was not that long ago when every family was involved in fishing. Sadly, we can no longer accurately say that we are saltwater people. Today's reality, like that of many Indigenous communities in this country, is that we no longer have a direct relationship with our lands and waters for our sustenance, but instead participate in the wage economy and buy most of our food from grocery stores.

There are now more Ahousaht working for the fish farm companies than there are those still fishing for wild salmon. Industrial finfish aquaculture has taken over as the primary employer in Ahous territories. The fish farm industry is controversial, with critical concerns over ecosystem and employee health, as well as wild salmon health via transmittable parasites and diseases. There are also concerns over escaped farmed Atlantic salmon colonizing wild Pacific salmon habitat. The fish farm debate has both local and global implications. Many of the companies are from Norway and Chile. Farmed salmon, which are still carnivorous fish, are fed fish oil and ground up fishmeal derived from other wild fish, usually small forage fish from other parts of the world. It takes several pounds of mashed up forage fish to produce one pound of farmed salmon. This flies in the face of one of the industry's main arguments, which is that they are only meeting a growing world demand for affordable seafood. The truth is that they are producing a highly profitable product to a relatively affluent market (mostly the United States) and putting wild fish species at risk. It is a tragic irony that in the space of one or two generations, so many Nuu-chah-nulth-aht have gone from fishers to farmers of fish.

Atlantic salmon aquaculture is not the only controversial development in our territories. Logging has long been a source of conflict with Settler governments and corporations. A dispute over industrial logging practices and the provincial government's failure to consult Nuu-chah-nulth nations in Clayoquot Sound culminated in "The War in the Woods" of 1993, the largest demonstration of civil disobedience in Canadian history. Nuu-chah-nulth communities directly affected by the logging and thousands of Settler Canadians working with environmental nongovernmental organizations (ENGOs) peacefully fought the provincial government, the logging companies, and police. The outcomes are worth noting—environmentally, politically and economically. Due in large part to Nuu-chah-nulth lobbying and legal injunctions, ENGO support and public protest, much of the old growth forests in Clayoquot Sound were (provisionally) protected. Forest companies consequently logged other areas more intensively, which only highlights the importance of hishookish tsa'walk ("everything is one") and the need to coordinate with our neighbours as well as questioning the dominant economic system. Politically speaking, the protests and injunctions created space in the public imagination, contributing to the British Columbia Treaty Process. Unfortunately, that space shrunk rather quickly, and although five Nuu-chah-nulth communities (Maa-nulth Treaty Society) did conclude a comprehensive claim agreement in 2007, the majority of the communities' negotiations have stalled or broken down. There is insufficient space here to critique the B.C. Treaty Process, but my concerns centre on drastically different conceptions of land ownership that expose our traditional territories to privatization and potential loss.

Cooperation between Nuu-chah-nulth-aht and ENGOs has not always been harmonious, either. For instance, there were significant tensions between the Nuu-chah-nulth communities and the ENGOs involved in the Clayoquot Sound dispute. Their strategic alliance was short-lived, with Nuu-chah-nulth Tribal Council chairman George Watts accusing the ENGOs of "neocolonialism" in 1994 and the banning of Greenpeace in 1996 (Braun 2002: 107–108). The Clayoquot Sound disputes did usher in a new era of consultation and attempts to include Indigenous input into ecosystem management and economic projects. Although these early consultations were met with considerable optimism, many now regard these efforts as wholly inadequate compromises that failed to recognize true Nuu-chah-nulth self-determining autonomy. I examine these efforts in the following text. At present, there are also several mining proposals for gold and copper that threaten the ecological and political peace.

Another notable change in recent economic development projects is the increasing participation and involvement of Nuu-chah-nulth communities working with outside companies. This has extended beyond the government duty to consult on planning matters and into the realm of economic partnerships. Local First Nations have signed benefit/partnership agreements with fish farm companies operating in their territories, which have proven controversial within those communities as well as with their other Nuu-chah-nulth and Settler neighbours. Many local leaders will tell you that they are merely looking out for the day-to-day needs of community members who now need to participate in the wage economy to feed their families. They argue that these benefit/partnership agreements create jobs and allow for some Nuu-chah-nulth input into the projects' environmental standards. Because these agreements are confidential, hidden even from most community members, I have no way of knowing what was agreed to or how true the companies have been to those agreements.

A Vancouver-based company, Imperial Metals, is also looking at two potential mining projects in Clayoquot Sound, again with the hopes of First Nation participation and endorsement. One might consider this recent, more collaborative approach as a sign of economic justice for Indigenous people, but it is fraught with problems. Certainly, the economic history in Clayoquot Sound has been predominantly one of outsiders exploiting local resources, while leaving very little benefit and a lot of mess for Nuu-chah-nulth-aht. However, it is important to remember the necessity that has brought about these collaborations in the first place. During the colonial process of Indian reserve allocation, Nuu-chah-nulth nations, along with their coastal neighbours, were confined to very small parcels of land. The colonials argued that it was because of our reliance on the oceans and rivers that we did not need large parcels of land (Harris 2001: 45). The argument was that we would always have access to seafood and would not have to take up the more sedentary agrarian ways of the newcomers. Yet as the last century of colonial occupation has unfolded, we have gradually lost access to our traditional livelihoods to the point now where our reality is near-complete alienation from our lands and waters. This is not only true of the majority of Nuu-chah-nulth people who now live in cities away from their homelands but also the existence of our people at home on our small reserves. Our compliance and cooperation with industrial–scale economic development in our territories seems inevitable given our loss of access to traditional and adaptive ways of life. As S'ake'j Youngblood Henderson puts it in Chapter One of this book, we have become dependent on cash, but our dependency on the cash economy is predicated on our alienation from our homelands and waters.

Historically, with such abundant access to seafood, we never considered ourselves poor. My father remembers the first time the Indian agents brought canned meat to the village around the middle of the last century. They brought cases of it because they thought we were poor by Western standards. Our initial response was to laugh, but my father said that eventually some of our people began to take the meat, and he feels we have only gone downhill from there in terms of community self-sufficiency. Western conceptions of wealth and poverty, as well as political and economic pressure, have all contributed to a loss of access to our traditional foods. Simply put, we have been starved into submission and must now compete in the wage economy to feed our families. The ongoing alienation from our lands and waters has also had another impact. Where we once saw animals as relatives worthy of respect, we now increasingly see resources for harvesting and sale. Our relations with our territories have been fundamentally transformed. This is not to say that efforts have not been exerted to maintain our Nuu-chah-nulth values and principles, but that they have, at the very least, come under considerable strain. This is a consistent experience in many Indigenous communities across North America, part of a paradigm shift that has laid the way for what I refer to as Aboriginal economic development.

## Aboriginal Economic Development

In British Columbia, a number of people, publications and institutions have come to epitomize Aboriginal economic development (AED). I use the term "Aboriginal" intentionally. It carries with it specific legal and political meanings in Canada that are significant to my analysis. "Aboriginal" is a legal term used by Canadian political, bureaucratic and legal institutions to identify status and non-status Indians, Inuit and Métis peoples within the confines of Aboriginal and constitutional law. It is also used in academic circles to highlight a particular form of identity, indicating a collaborative and acquiescent posture toward state efforts at assimilation (Alfred and Corntassel 2005). In this context, Aboriginal economic development is less critical of Western forms of political and economic organization such as neoliberal-democracy and capitalism. It does not seek drastic change, but rather seeks to fit in to existing political and economic frameworks. I do not mean to suggest that all practitioners of AED do not have criticisms of mainstream politics and economics, nor that they do not believe that they have the best interests of their communities at heart. Some believe that we can adapt to capitalism; indeed, they believe that this adaptation is necessary for us to survive and flourish.

Many AED proponents believe that capitalism can be Aboriginalized and accommodated within Indigenous worldviews. David Newhouse calls this "capitalism with a red face" (2000), Duane Champagne calls it "tribal capitalism" (2004) and Robert Miller uses the term "reservation capitalism" (2012). But perhaps the most influential academic work in this area springs from the Harvard Project on American Indian Economic Development, founded in 1987 by Stephen Cornell and Joseph P. Kalt. They popularized the "nation-building" approach, which prioritizes "de-facto sovereignty," achieving a "cultural match" between specific capitalist and political institutions and Aboriginal values, and the establishment of stable governing institutions (Cornell and Kalt 2003: 10–20). They discourage the idea of simply starting businesses; instead, they encourage Native communities to "build an environment that encourages investors to invest, that helps businesses last, and that allows investments to flourish and pay off" (8). At the end of the day, Indigenous cultures and values are secondary to stable and predictable governing institutions that encourage foreign direct investment. I cannot fault Cornell and Kalt for uncovering the obvious requirements for "success" in competitive capitalist markets, but I do feel that more time should be spent critiquing the economic system and understanding the implications for Indigenous community wellness. Needless to say, the ideas coming out of the Harvard project are popular in many Native communities in Canada and the United States, and have expanded academically to places like the Native Nations Institute at the University of Arizona (Native Nations Institute).

Closer to home, influential advocates for AED include Tsimshian lawyer, Calvin

Helin and Osoyoos Indian Band Chief, Clarence Louie. Helin has published two books about economic development and has recently moved into the self-help genre that is entirely consistent with neoliberal precepts. Such views take for granted the natural world as a resource to be exploited and assume that economic growth and profits improve the well-being of communities. At the same time, such approaches abstract from the ecological and social relations in which all human beings are embedded. Instead, "self-help" emphasizes that human beings, understood as atomistic rational individuals, are personally responsible for their fates. Helin offers valid critiques of First Nation economic dependence and governance, but he does not apply the same level of criticism toward his preferred solution of capitalism. He believes that capitalism can be Aboriginalized to include enough Aboriginal values to offset any potentially negative consequences.

Others, notably Clarence Louie, use neoliberal rhetoric to reinforce the idea of individual responsibility while reifying capitalist economics. For instance, Louie states: "If your life sucks, it's because you suck" and "It's called the economy, stupid." He is known for his blunt and controversial rhetoric, but he also hits close to home with phrases such as "Economic development is how we hunt today. If you call yourself a leader, give all your people the chance at the dignity of a job, equal opportunity and the individual responsibility to earn a living" (Helin 2006: 235). Some people hesitate to argue with these assertions because they use nationalistic and traditional-sounding rhetoric, but Louie conflates nation and tradition with the inevitability of capitalism and neoliberal self-reliance. He's not an overt champion of capitalism, but his worldview and assumptions certainly take it for granted. Louie sees himself as a pragmatist and is consequently a darling of the right-wing elite in Canada. Neither Helin nor Louie offer any substantial concerns over the inherent destructiveness of capitalism. Consequently, we are left with an uncritical program selling capitalist development as the lesser of evils; the only other option implicitly being ongoing misery and struggles for survival.

As far as I can tell, AED proponents genuinely believe that what they are doing is either consistent with their Aboriginal values or, at the very least, a pragmatic necessity. I am not so certain about the former, but openly acknowledge the significance of the latter. I am not trying to vilify these leaders, although it is perfectly within my place to submit their words and actions to critical examination. My primary concern about AED is the implicit acceptance of the capitalist economic framework, a lack of criticism of its inherently exploitative and destructive nature, and the subsequent impacts on Indigenous cultures and communities. At its most basic, mainstream economic development requires incessant growth. I am not an economist, but I understand that "healthy" economies grow at about 3 percent per year. This might sound modest, but year after year, the capitalist necessity of never-ending economic growth takes its toll on Mother Earth. It seems incredible to me that it is necessary to assert the self-evident fact that we live on a finite planet. The current economic doctrine is not sustainable. At some point, we will have extracted too much, polluted too much and not given enough back. This critique of mainstream economics and AED is entirely consistent with my understanding of the Nuu-chah-nulth principles of iisaak ("respect") and hishookish tsa'walk ("oneness"). So what has been happening in our homelands lately?

## Nuu-chah-nulth Life

As previously noted, Nuu-chah-nulth people have a relationship with the sea and seafood going back as far as anyone can remember. Some have argued that the rich cultural and artistic traditions that the Northwest coast has become known for can be attributed to this abundance of seafood. Nuu-chah-nulth peoples moved with the seasons to gather food. Our diets consisted of fish, including salmon, halibut, cod and herring. We also feasted on herring, salmon roe and shellfish. A common expression among coastal peoples, "When the tide is out, the table is set," refers to our access to clams, mussels, sea urchins and other life from the foreshore. We also gathered vast amounts of food on land, including berries, roots, and plants as well as deer and elk. Perhaps most noteworthy in distinguishing ourselves from our neighbours, however, was our hunting of whales.

As far as I know, my great-great-grandfather Keesta was the last Ahous chief to capture a whale near the end of the nineteenth century. It has been well over one hundred years since our family prepared, hunted, captured and feasted on a whale. My understanding is that largely due to industrial-scale whaling by foreigners and the decimation of whale populations in the Pacific, Nuu-chah-nulth whalers voluntarily ceased their traditional hunts. Of course, our close relatives the Kwih-dich-chuh-ahtx captured a whale, first in 1999 in accordance with a treaty with the United States and with much community celebration, and then more controversially in 2007, while under increased legal and public pressure (Coté 2010: 115–192). Despite the passage of time, whale hunting and whaling culture still play a prominent role in the imagination of Nuu-chah-nulth peoples. Recent books by Nuu-chah-nulth scholars highlight the centrality of whaling to our peoples (Atleo 2005; Coté 2010). Atleo speaks mostly of the historical significance of whaling — the preparatory traditions, protocols and petitions — and emphasizes our relations with the whales and all life. Coté emphasizes the contemporary relevance of whaling to Nuu-chah-nulth and Kwih-dich-chuh-ahtx.

Umeek reminds us that whales are "great personages who require great respect and an appropriate ceremonial recognition for their important role in the mysteries of life" (Atleo 2005: 114). Every family member played a role in these preparations and protocols. Kwih-dich-chuh-ahtx leader Keith Johnson stated in an open letter,

"Whaling has been part of our traditions for over 2,000 years" and that the Makah revival of whaling was part of a community effort at addressing health and diet concerns, as well as cultural pride and discipline (Sullivan 2000: 13–14). Coté emphasizes the importance of oral traditions and storytelling in Nuu-chah-nulth cultural perpetuation. In her analysis, despite the overall cessation of whaling, our rich whaling traditions have been kept alive through our stories, songs, dances, place names and naming of family members (Coté 2010: 69–114).

Nuu-chah-nulth people also participated in hunting for sea otter pelts for trade and seal hunting in the Pribilof Islands in the Bering Sea. There has been no confirmation of any Nuu-chah-nulth people joining the industrial whaling fleets, perhaps because whaling was a privilege/responsibility of the Ha'wiih. With the end of the traditional whale hunts, commercial fishing gained in importance for Nuu-chah-nulth villages. My father grew up fishing with his father, and I spent several summers as a teenager fishing with my uncles and cousins. As previously mentioned, the Nuu-chah-nulth fishing fleet numbered around two hundred boats at its peak. Every family was directly connected to commercial fishing, in what I interpret as an adaptive way of life. Changes to fishing regulations and the fishing industry started to negatively affect our participation, however, and today there are only about a dozen boats in the Nuu-chah-nulth fleet, despite a recent court victory in favour of an Aboriginal right to fish commercially. The federal government sought leave for appeal to the Supreme Court of Canada, but was denied in 2014. Details are still being negotiated of what this legal affirmation of the Nuu-chah-nulth right to fish means in practice. At present, the Canadian Department of Fisheries and Oceans has allocated a specific number of fish that can be caught by Nuu-chah-nulth fishers under the new arrangement. Time will tell how this plays out in negotiations and on the water, but for the time being, we are seeing a modest increase in Nuu-chah-nulth fishers taking advantage of the court decision.

Certainly, some would argue that our people engaging in commercial fishing might run counter to Nuu-chah-nulth principles, and I think that there is some merit to this concern. I do see a difference, however, between small entrepreneurial engagements with markets on our own terms and the industrial scale exploitation that commercial fishing and salmon farming has recently become. When explaining this to Canadians, I liken it to the small family farm versus large agri-business. At least the former attempts to sustain local families, whereas the latter prioritizes profits for large international corporations. In the next section, I consider specifically what critically engaging with Nuu-chah-nulth traditions means. What constitutes adaptation and what constitutes cooptation into colonial-capitalist relations? What are the bases on which we can practically answer that question as we seek to enact self-determination? I argue that a critical engagement with our "traditional" practices does suggest some principles to help us answer these questions.

## Critically Engaging Nuu-chah-nulth Traditions

Canadian colonization, including laws and policies designed to dismantle Nuu-chah-nulth community governance, cultural and religious institutions, and the experience of residential schools have severely disrupted and damaged our traditional and adaptive ways of living. That said, our stories carry on, and many "traditional" practices do as well. With respect to political and economic organizing, Nuu-chah-nulth-aht still struggle to live in ways that respect our teachings. Although it is an understatement to say that times have changed, many of us still believe that our traditional teachings can instruct us through these processes of change. What I propose is a critical engagement with tradition to identify the principles in our ways of living that can guide a revitalization of those ways, as well as new ways that are nonetheless consistent with Nuu-chah-nulth principles and values.

I suggest a critical approach for a number of reasons. Vine Deloria, Jr. pointed out that the experience of boarding schools in the United States, like that of residential schools in Canada, led to major disruptions in Indigenous cultural continuity (Deloria 2004: 5). Essentially, it has become impossible to know exactly how things were precontact, but Deloria felt that many remnants remained, including oral traditions and Settler anthropological accounts. Leroy Little Bear has referred to the present predicament of colonialism in Canada as "jagged worldviews colliding." Government policies attempted to eradicate Indigenous worldviews, but they ultimately failed, and instead we were left with a reality that was neither entirely Indigenous nor Eurocentric (Little Bear 2000: 84). What remains are the oral histories and origin stories that have been passed down through the generations (some of which have been written down) and early anthropological accounts. I believe that we have to approach these sources critically and carefully. The goal is not to decipher "pure" Nuu-chah-nulth practices, but to identify core beliefs and values that have stood the test of time. Many of the traditions are important because they have retained relevance to subsequent generations, but they may also contain elements that are not presently desirable, such as patriarchy or exploitative relations.

I also believe that the early anthropological accounts of Nuu-chah-nulth life need to be engaged critically. Citing early colonial and Settler texts, Richard Inglis and James Haggarty refer to a number of anthropologists and historians who attempt to piece together traditional Nuu-chah-nulth life based on the early recordings of people such as Captain Cook and Mowachaht captive John Jewitt. However, they warn that "by assuming that these early descriptions reflect traditional cultural patterns, anthropologists and historians have misinterpreted the magnitude and intensity of cultural change in the first decades of recorded history in Nootka Sound" (Inglis and Haggarty 2000). Our lives began to change immediately as imperial powers such as Great Britain and Spain vied for control over colonial trade. The interference of emerging colonial powers such as Canada and the United States soon followed. We should not dismiss such accounts out of hand, but we should apply all our critical faculties and compare them with our interpretations and our relevant circumstances. This includes an appreciation of our cultures and societies as dynamic rather than static and frozen in time at contact, as described in the first, early European accounts of us. Moreover, it means taking our own sources of histories and knowledge seriously.

Another fruitful approach might be to take those Nuu-chah-nulth principles that have the most obvious community consensus and build from there. The two principles that immediately come to mind are hishookish tsa'walk and iisaak. The first is often translated into "everything is one" and the second as "respect." There are both simple and complex interpretations of these principles, but I think they are both foundational in guiding our present actions. Hishookish tsa'walk is an affirmation of the unity of creation and that everything is connected. Nothing we do takes place in a vacuum, and there are consequences of our words and actions that are not always readily apparent. I take this principle to urge caution and thorough deliberation before acting; it might also imply a willingness to be flexible and change approaches when there are unanticipated negative consequences of even the most carefully planned decisions. This cautionary approach applies to us as individuals as well as communities. As individuals, many of us have been taught to be careful what we say because once our words have left us, they often travel far and wide and we remain accountable for their impacts and even interpretations. As communities, we are presented with many political and economic decisions. Elected leaders undertake most of these decisions today, but in many Nuu-chah-nulth communities, the hereditary leaders (Ha'wiih) still carry influence, and so do community members in some cases.

Iisaak is another commonly invoked Nuu-chah-nulth principle that means "respect." It has been described to me in a way that closely follows hishookish tsa'walk, in that we are to respect all things, including our relatives, strangers, leaders, children, elders and all of creation. The latter includes our animal relatives as well as the plants and trees; and the earth, sun and water that sustain them. Although Nuu-chah-nulth-aht take plants and animals for sustenance, it is in keeping with the principle of iisaak that we do not take more than the community requires and that we do everything in our power not to endanger whole species recklessly. The health of our ecosystems and all its inhabitants is directly related to our health. As human beings, we hold the responsibility to care for our homelands, something Nuu-chah-nulth-aht have done for thousands of years. As I alluded to in the fish farm and mining examples, it is evident that our leaders find themselves in challenging circumstances. Not all the community economic projects have been as controversial, though. There are examples of Nuu-chah-nulth economic development that do attempt to respect these two basic principles.

## Contemporary Nuu-chah-nulth Economic Development

After the events of Clayoquot Sound in 1993 and through the B.C. Treaty Process, several communities, including Ahousaht, negotiated for government resources to develop economic opportunities in the region. This process included a planning board with Nuu-chah-nulth and government representatives designed to give us meaningful say in resource development and to avert the confrontations of the past. A scientific panel was also created that included Canadian scientists and Nuu-chah-nulth representatives that included our first doctoral recipient (Umeek) and other knowledgeable elders. The scientific panel attempted to give equal weight to Western science as well as traditional ecological knowledge. One example of their outcomes was a recommendation that logging in old growth forest areas be conducted selectively and every three hundred years to ensure that there would always be old growth forests. Current government and corporate models on Vancouver Island call for logging every fifty years or so. One of the outcomes of the treaty interim measure agreements was the creation of Iisaak Forest Resources Ltd. Initially, this was a joint venture with Weyerhauser, a large multinational forestry company. Since 2005, Iisaak has been wholly Nuu-chah-nulth–owned. Iisaak claims to follow the recommendations of the Clayoquot Sound Science Panel, which include the promotion of biodiversity, watershed integrity and overall ecosystem health. Potential conflict is looming, however, as Iisaak must now look to previously protected old growth areas in Clayoquot Sound to remain viable. What counts as "viable" is complicated both by capitalist market demands and contemporary environmental efforts to preserve all the old growth trees in the sound. Despite many peoples' best efforts, there are pronounced disconnects between Nuu-chah-nulth–centric forestry practices and mainstream economic, political and environmental frameworks.

In addition to the larger First Nation–run projects, scores of individual Nuu-chah-nulth-aht have prospered as entrepreneurs, often with the initial support of the Central Region Board and/or the Nuu-chah-nulth Economic Development Corporation. Those companies are wide-ranging, from tourist operations to art galleries to construction, legal, health and wellness services, financial and consulting services. My primary interest here, however, is in the projects that are directly tied to the land and sea and our responsibilities to future generations. One cannot fault entrepreneurial efforts to support one's family. Everyone does the best they can, but I am particularly interested in ventures that purport to uphold Nuu-chah-nulth values and beliefs. This is no easy task in today's predominantly capitalist economy. Canadian society, along with much of the neoliberal world, has excelled at segmenting our daily lives and partitioning our political lives from our economic, social, cultural and religious lives. Many Indigenous people have come to accept the fact that politics and business should not mix or that our personal lives are separate from our work lives. I argue that such partitioning goes against the principle of hishookish tsa'walk, a principle that refuses segmented existences and insists that we cannot separate out aspects of our lives as sealed off political, economic, social, cultural and religious compartments. I am not denying that traditional and contemporary Indigenous realities were and are complex; on the contrary, I am affirming that complexity, including the impossibility of isolating the political and economic from other aspects of our everyday lives. Moreover, if colonial capitalism pretends that each domain is hypersegmented, it is not true in fact. Instead, political power and capitalist economic imperatives, including the profit motive, tend to overrule all other values. One of my intentions here is to re-blur the lines of distinction between the discrete segments. I am interested in Nuu-chah-nulth people who seek to reintegrate their traditional and revitalized values into all aspects of their lives; people who are attempting to live Nuu-chah-nulth-aht.

## Living Nuu-chah-nulth-aht

Understanding the need for resistance and resurgence can be pretty depressing. When mere survival is cause for celebration, I can appreciate the desire for a bright side. I have always resisted providing one if I had not indeed found one. However hard the truth is, it must be faced. Gladly, I conclude here with a story of true inspiration in Nuu-chah-nulth territories. Naas-a-thluk (John Rampanen) is Ahousaht and Tla-o-qui-aht. He and his family have been reconnecting with their ancestral lands for more than ten years. Beginning in 2003, they started returning to Seitcher Bay, initially for short visits, but over the years have developed a more permanent presence there for the first time in nearly one hundred years. Seitcher Bay is not part of an official Indian reserve, but simply connected to their family history and no less legitimate in Naas-a-thluk's mind. Indeed, our connections with territories have never been limited to "reserves" carved out for us by a colonial government that has long wished for and aggressively sought and planned for our disappearance. Naas-a-thluk's reconnection is intriguing to me for a number of reasons. Over the years, many people, both Indigenous and non-Indigenous, have taken to saying that "you cannot go back." The implication is that traditional Indigenous ways of living are antiquated and no longer relevant or realistic. Along with this sentiment comes the notion that every culture evolves, and in neoliberal terms that usually means liberal-democracy, bureaucratized institutions and capitalism. The language of "going back" is premised on a linear language of progress and forward thinking that assumes that Indigenous ways of living are merely historical. Against such assumptions, the Seitcher family has made a conscious decision to revive old ways as well as experimentally create new ways rooted in Nuu-chah-nulth worldviews and principles on their ancestral lands.

Naas-a-thluk and his wife have eight children and spent some time living in the city of Vancouver prior to moving back to Nuu-chah-nulth territories. Both were active in the Native Youth Movement in the 1990s, and Naas-a-thluk was also a member of the West Coast Warrior Society, a group of mostly young Nuu-chah-nulth men that helped defend Indigenous lands, waters and ways of living. In British Columbia, they responded to calls from the Cheam and WSÁNEĆ First Nations in support of their respective salmon fisheries and they also travelled as far as the Mi'kmaq community of Esgenoôpetitj (Burnt Church) in New Brunswick. Despite a life of political and physical activism, living in the city took its toll. A logical and spiritual conclusion of their activism became increasingly clear: a return home. Naas-a-thluk shares that his family has long had a history as healers and "prayer warriors," and that Seitcher Bay is significant to them because it is regarded as a place of healing and regeneration. Many of his family members have assumed contemporary roles such as social work, counseling, and political leadership as well as witwaak ("warriors/protectors"). Naas-a-thluk believes that the responsibilities of the witwaak are to provide protection and security for the people and the land. Witwaak are also tasked with upholding Nuu-chah-nulth principles and laws. Although Nuu-chah-nulth societies afforded great respect and recognition for the Ha'wiih and their responsibilities, no one was above the law, and there are several stories that tell of the consequences of transgression, even for Ha'wiih.

I ran into Naas-a-thluk at my favourite Chinese restaurant in Port Alberni a few years ago and I asked him how things were going and what he was up to. He said his family was attempting to eat a strict traditional diet. This diet required that they not only fish, hunt, and gather but also preserve and learn more about our traditional foods, especially those that have fallen from favour in recent times. I asked if he was taking a break because we were both picking up take-out food at the time, and we laughed. I share this story because most of our people can relate. Naas-a-thluk and his family had many ideals in mind as they proceeded to live Nuu-chah-nulth-aht, but we all confront contemporary colonialism within ourselves and in the broader community. Returning to traditional principles and reviving practices is a learning process that is also full of obstacles, especially because colonialism in a Nuu-chah-nulth context has alienated us from our lands, waters and traditional livelihoods.

Naas-a-thluk said that something else they were experimenting with was trading food from the West Coast for food from the territories of his wife's people: Nehiyawak (Cree). This food might include buffalo, moose, caribou and inland whitefish. Historically, Nuu-chah-nulth-aht traded extensively with neighbours with whom they maintained friendly relations. The "grease trail" is a common term on the West Coast used to describe the trade networks that extended from Alaska to northern California to Alberta. The term is mainly connected with the trading of oolichan oil, but it also included many other territorially unique items and foodstuffs.

There are now four cabins at Seitcher Bay, which allows for family members to spend more and more time on the land, and Naas-a-thluk's family has plans to build a longhouse. The family's ongoing projects include carving a dugout canoe, continued learning of and harvesting traditional foods and medicines, and language revitalization through immersion. These efforts extend beyond the Seitcher family as other families from Ahousaht, Tla-o-qui-aht and Tofino have shared and supported their endeavours. Indeed, one of the important elements of Naas-a-thluk's family efforts is that they inevitably involve other people because they talk with others in the community to relearn and innovate traditional practices. The example of Seitcher Bay is inspiring, and in my view an honest attempt to live Nuu-chah-nulth-aht. I cannot help but admire their approach, which is open and flexible, but rooted, as best as they can determine, in Nuu-chah-nulth teachings. Naas-a-thluk has often stated that modern urban living and the pressures of consumer-oriented lifestyles are hard on everyone, particularly Nuu-chah-nulth-aht, for whom contact and colonization is such a recent experience. We still remember many of the old ways, and not all our teachings are lost. Revitalizing our communities in a principled way on the land and sea requires critical thought and praxis, and a willingness to experiment and make mistakes. Some of our traditional practices have stayed alive, some have been revived and some have died, and that is something that we live with.

During the course of research for my master's degree, I came across small–scale organic gardens in Nuu-chah-nulth territories. Several West Coast communities were accessing grants from the First Nations Agricultural Association to build their own community gardens. I should not have to tell you that agriculture has a contentious history among Indigenous peoples in this country. Not only were families forced to give up seminomadic lives in favour of Eurocentric sedentarization and agriculture but most residential school experiences also included hard farm labour, among other negative associations. To my initial surprise, I visited gardens in Tla-o-qui-aht and Ahousaht that were being tended to by enthusiastic community members. Perhaps enough time since the residential school had passed that these people were able to adapt small-scale agricultural practices on their own terms. Perhaps it was because these were community-driven efforts, people were genuinely excited about producing their own food in new ways. In Ahousaht, the main organizer was Harvey Robinson, my uncle with whom I first learned to fish when I was thirteen. His description of the Ahousaht garden experience was full of experimentation, mistakes and learning. I realized that we did not need to strictly tie ourselves to all traditional practices, but that we could critically engage our traditional principles to revive desirable old practices and inform new ones. We could still honour iisaak and hishookish tsa'walk in new forms, even in an activity such as organic gardening that is far from our original saltwater ways of living. In many ways, this is necessary. Breathing life into our culture and fulfilling our sacred obligations requires creativity and flexibility.

Much of the Indigenous-Settler relational discourses over the last century have focused on Aboriginal rights and the shaping of Aboriginal claims to fit Canadian legal, political, bureaucratic and economic logics. I fear that we have lost our way down this schizophrenic path of assimilation and racism. Our populations were decimated, mostly due to the lack of immunity to foreign diseases, but also to deliberate colonial violence, and we have been dispossessed of our lands and livelihoods. Residential schools taught us that we were inferior and that the ways that served us for thousands of years were evil. "Going back," which is at the same time a way of going forward, is hard precisely because so much effort was made to dislocate us from our lands, waters and traditional livelihoods to make way for colonial settlement and development. On many counts, we have stemmed the tide of defeat and we are making recoveries in many areas. Our populations are rebounding, and many young people like Naas-a-thluk and his family are relearning old ways and developing new ways consistent with traditional teachings. They have pushed aside concerns over Aboriginal rights and instead take seriously our Indigenous responsibilities. Nuu-chah-nulth culture is not simply something we are born into and experience; it is also an obligation to carry on, revive and rebuild.

## NOTES

1. "Aht" is to be from or of a place, so although people currently consider Ahousaht to be a place, it is actually Ahous, and a person from there is Ahousaht.
2. Unemployment is an unavoidable a contemporary reality for the Nuu-chah-nulth (as for many other Canadians). Nonetheless, the concepts of employment/unemployment are complicated for many Indigenous peoples. Our ancestors certainly "worked" for a living. But "unemployment" today takes on new meanings in the context of capitalist wage economics and given differing conceptions of prosperity/poverty between Indigenous peoples and other Canadians.

## REFERENCES

Alfred, Taiaiake, and Jeff Corntassel. 2005. "Being Indigenous: Resurgences against Contemporary Colonialism." *Government and Opposition* 9.

Altamirano-Jiménez, Isabel. 2004. "North American First Peoples: 'Slipping up into Market Citizenship?'" *Citizenship Studies* 8, 4 (December).

Atleo, Umeek E. Richard. 2005. *Tsawalk: A Nuu-chah-nulth Worldview.* Vancouver: University of British Columbia Press.

BCCA. Ahousaht Indian Band and Nation v. Canada (Attorney General). 2013 British Columbia Court of Appeal (BCCA) 300 (CanLII). <canlii.ca/t/fzgp9>.

Braun, Bruce. 2002. *The Intemperate Rainforest: Nature, Culture, and Power on Canada's West Coast.* Minneapolis: University of Minnesota Press.

Champagne, Duane. 2004. "Tribal Capitalism and Native Capitalists: Multiple Pathways of Native Economy." In Brian Hosmer and Colleen O'Neill (eds.), *Native Pathways: American Indian Economic Development and Culture in the Twentieth Century*. Boulder: University Press of Colorado.

Cornell, Stephen, and Joseph P. Kalt. 2003. "Sovereignty and Nation-Building: The Development Challenge in Indian Country Today." *American Indian Culture and Research Journal* 22, 3.

Coté, Charlotte. 2010. *Spirits of our Whaling Ancestors: Revitalizing Makah and Nuu-chah-nulth Traditions*. Seattle: University of Washington Press.

Deloria, Jr., Vine. 2004. "Philosophy and the Tribal Peoples." In Anne Walters (ed.), *American Indian Thought*. Malden, MA: Blackwell.

Harris, Douglas C. 2001. *Fish, Law, and Colonialism: The Legal Capture of Salmon in British Columbia*. Toronto: University of Toronto Press.

Harvard Project on American Indian Economic Development.

Helin, Calvin. 2006. *Dances with Dependency: Indigenous Success Through Self-Reliance*. Vancouver: Orca Spirit Publishing & Communications.

Inglis, Richard, and James C. Haggarty. 2000. "Cook to Jewitt: Three Decades of Change in Nootka Sound." In Alan L. Hoover (ed.), *Nuu-chah'nulth Voices, Histories, Objects and Journeys*. Victoria: Royal British Columbia Museum.

Little Bear, Leroy. 2000. "Jagged Worldviews Colliding." In Marie Battiste (ed.), *Reclaiming Indigenous Voice and Vision*. Vancouver: University of British Columbia Press.

Miller, Robert. 2012. *Reservation "Capitalism": Economic Development in Indian Country*. Santa Barbara, CA: Praeger.

Native Nations Institute. <nni.arizona.edu/>.

Newhouse, David. 2000. "Modern Aboriginal Economies: Capitalism with a Red Face." *The Journal of Aboriginal Economic Development* 1, 2.

Sullivan, Robert. 2000. *A Whale Hunt: Two Years on the Olympic Peninsula with the Makah and Their Canoe*. Toronto: Scribner.

Chapter Seven

# THE PROBLEM WITH "INDIGENOUS PEOPLES"
## RE-CONSIDERING INTERNATIONAL INDIGENOUS RIGHTS ACTIVISM

*Hayden King*

With a general failure of national, state-based efforts to achieve Indigenous–Settler reconciliation, Indigenous communities and groups have increasingly turned to the international in their activism. Global institutions, nongovernmental organizations (NGOs), and trans-state alliances have become hopeful avenues to bypass state negotiation channels, work toward collaborative Indigenous resistance, and offer a potential engine for incremental change toward the reclamation of land and territories and realization of self-determination. Faith in the international rights regime was affirmed in 2007 when nearly 150 states endorsed the UNDRIP, the United Nations' Declaration on the Rights of Indigenous Peoples (UNHCR 2007). Despite the notable late endorsement from the United States, Canada, Australia and New Zealand (Settler states home to millions of Indigenous peoples), the UNDRIP has to be considered a significant accomplishment, if only for transforming Indigenous peoples "from objects of international law to subjects" (Venne 1999: 119). Yet there are also threats to consider when struggling for rights under the current (but very old) international society paradigm. Foremost among these threats are the potential validation of the ideas and institutions that continue to oppress Indigenous peoples, the reification of the state as the arbiter of Indigenous rights and narrow applicability of rights claims that result from pan-Indigenous resistance.

Although it is undeniable that rights activism globally though international institutions is an example of resistance, it cannot allow for the resurgence of Indigenous nations and the required accompanying self-determination.

Jeff Corntassel offers elaboration. He argues that the rights-based approach is premised on "state-centered processes that prioritize the legitimization of Settler occupation of Indigenous homelands" (2012: 94). He suggests that rights rhetoric is organically tied to the artificial political creation of states, and that rights are made conditional upon protection of Settler occupation. In contrast with such rights-based resistance, resurgence focuses on the "re-emergence of Indigenous cultural and social institutions" (2012: 97) and emphasizes *responsibilities* to the land rather than rights or entitlements (to land or otherwise). Taking direction from Corntassel's distinction, this chapter seeks to more clearly understand how rights-based activism in the international context legitimizes Settler occupation and how it can even work against the realization of resurgence.

There are four relatively straightforward arguments here. First, investigating the historical trajectory of international law as it applies to Indigenous peoples reveals that from its origins the system has aided imperialism, colonialism and Settler colonialism by formally denying Indigenous humanity and then absorbing Indigenous ideals into alien political relationships articulated in a state. This absorption is based on the belief in the inhumanity of Indigenous peoples — at best, their lack of civilization. Second, drawing on the history of Indigenous resistance to international law as well as evidence from the negotiations and implementation of the UNDRIP, Indigenous activism in the international system can be characterized as practicing the politics of recognition; a self-defeating reinforcement of the state's capability to regulate the scope of Indigenous rights. Third, with the emergence of the concept of "Indigenous peoples" in the lexicon of human rights, international institutions, activists and academics have increasingly appropriated the term. It has become a shared rallying call for marginalized peoples to articulate their concerns, interests and demands, but one that results in an insubstantial pan-Indigenous homogenization. Finally, considering the problematic nature of Indigenous people's recent membership into international society, I reflect on the utility of resurgent practices of international relations among Indigenous nations rooted in authentic diplomatic traditions, independent of the rights discourse. The ideas in this chapter reflect an earnest attempt to engage in productive dialogue with Indigenous activists and intellectuals on the scope and nature of resistance to Settler colonialism and imperialism.

## The Ongoing Inhumanity of Indigenous Peoples
## in International Law and Society

Tracing the international law paradigm relating to Indigenous peoples corresponds to the emergence of international law. The two broad trends are intertwined, born from the same provocation: contact between Indigenous peoples in the Americas and European would-be colonizers. While there is much theoretical debate about the emergence of international society among scholars of international relations and international law, a key benchmark in its European evolution revolves around the mitigation of conflict between competing colonial powers after 1492. From this turning point in world history, international law would only seek to destroy Indigenous peoples and nations. And then when destruction failed, to absorb those who resisted by attempting to transplant foreign universal norms of the good life through a narrow conception of political community, the unitary state. Charting the history of the application of international law should serve as the first warning to Indigenous activists about the utility of international law and human rights protections in their campaign for autonomy and resurgence.

That history inevitably, but disappointingly, begins with Christopher Columbus. With the news of his unlikely arrival in the Caribbean, subsequent Spanish and Portuguese explorers raced to discover new "New Worlds." In their haste, an unresolved debate re-emerged on the "rights" of colonial powers: Who should be considered the legitimate sovereign in the newly acquired territories? In 1491, the law governing exploration and colonization was the Papal Bull *Romanus Pontifex*, which had granted all lands west of the Iberian Peninsula to Portugal — at a time when the collective European imagination ended at the Canary Islands (Muldoon 1994). In 1492, *Romanus Pontifex* was challenged by Spain on the basis that the Bull did not cover the discovery of new peoples as opposed to simply new land. A year later, and after vigorous Spanish lobbying, the Pope issued a series of new conventions to guide relations in a trans-Atlantic world (Venne 1999). The most important of these Papal Bulls, *Inter Caetera divinai,* would come to be known as the infamous Doctrine of Discovery.

Aside from allowing Spain legal access to the Americas, the Doctrine also conferred the power to "colonize, civilize and Christianize the 'well-disposed' inhabitants of the New World" (Williams 1992: 81). The Doctrine stipulated that any lands discovered by Christian nations could be legally claimed and possessed if no Christians could be found. Any non-Christian peoples "discovered" would be placed under the guardianship of the Pope via the discovering-Christian nation. This foundational component in the new legal framework among Christian nations legitimized the legal theft of entire continents and the enslavement and death of millions. In the centuries that followed, "no state in Europe contested the Doctrine of Discovery. Every subsequent European state that moved onto the lands of Indigenous peoples used the Doctrine to assert their jurisdiction" (Venne 1999: 4). The most prominent examples of this continuity come from England and later English colonies in which Discovery was used as the principal argument for English sovereignty in the face of competing European claims (Miller et al. 2010).

As international law moved beyond strict Christian influence and through the corresponding evolution of the equally exclusionary state-centric system, Indigenous peoples — as they were imagined and described by Europeans — remained an influence on the thinking and theorizing about political community, war, peace and so on. After studying the causes of war and peace among peoples, and after reading travelogues of early explorers, settlers and priests in North America, Thomas Hobbes famously articulated assumptions about life in the state of nature as "nasty, brutish and short." He imagined the "state of nature" as a place in which individuals ruthlessly compete with one another, without laws, without order, and without meaningful relationships aside from exploitation. Hobbes concluded that the international arena might closely resemble this scenario: a lawless and anarchic environment.

Given anarchy as the guiding principle of political relationships between peoples, international relations must then require elaborate institutional arrangements to provide defense in a lawless world: strong states. These communities must also have "government, sovereignty, territory, and population. Any unit which does not display these qualities ... does not qualify" for participation in international relations. States are reified as the "the supreme normative principal of the political organization of mankind" (Bull quoted in Shaw 2002: 63). In other words, geographic containers with rigid borders, exclusive government powers and exclusively held sovereignty are necessary and desirable for political community among humans and represent common sense politics in an anarchic world.

This reading of international law and society depicts an operation that first excluded Indigenous peoples from the legal conception of humanity and then used that nonhuman savagery as the justification for the evolution of the state, which only further alienated Indigenous peoples from European notions of community. The state doubles down on the exclusion of Indigenous peoples from humanity generally in ways at once straightforward and explicit, subversive and nuanced. This includes the concrete exercise of state power over Indigenous peoples, primarily through the absorption of Indigenous peoples. At the same time, the exclusive theorization of formal politics and governance through the historically specific, contingent body of the state is a discursive justification for marginalizing and excluding Indigenous peoples from international politics on their own terms. This exclusion is represented symbolically in European cartography, as James (Sa'ke'j) Youngblood Henderson demonstrates in his deconstruction of the universally familiar geopolitic map. He notes that "humanity is viewed as a set of political states, with Europe at the centre of the planet. The map does not reveal human or ecological diversity" (2008: 19). For Indigenous peoples who have never expressed political community as a geographic container with exclusive sovereignty historically or in contemporary times, the result is marginalization at best.

Of course, despite this wilful ignorance, Indigenous peoples actually do have perspectives on political community, and not surprisingly, they clash with the "common sense" Eurocentric vision. Taiaiake Alfred offers the following alternative or exceptions to the accepted rule of political community:

> Indigenous perspectives offer alternatives, beginning with the restoration of a regime of respect. This ideal contrasts with the statist solution, still rooted in a classical notion of sovereignty that mandates a distributive arrangement but with a basic maintenance of the superior posture of the state. True Indigenous formulations are non-intrusive and build frameworks of respectful co-existence by acknowledging the integrity and autonomy of the various constitutative elements in the relationship." (2005: 46)

For Alfred, there is no such thing as the state in a Mohawk (or Haudenosaunee) articulation. Even the notion of sovereignty, the idea of a central authority enforcing its rule through what is essentially coercion, would not be permitted. As Alfred notes, *sovereignty* is not a Mohawk word; it's not an Anishinaabe word nor Mushkegowuk. There is no translation. It is generally not applicable to Indigenous notions of political community.

Beyond broad conceptual incompatibility over ideas as central to European political theories as the state and sovereignty, there are a number of related ideational and material challenges for Indigenous peoples. With reference to Stam and Shohot (2012), I elaborate on the six basic ways that Indigenous political communities contrast with the notion and realities of the state. First, Indigenous governance predates the emergence of states (of course, European states did not always exist, either, but are a centuries-old contingent political development). Second, Settler colonial states have crafted their images of states in opposition to Indigenous peoples, understood as threats or examples of undesirable difference. Third, Settler-states have been possible only through the theft of Indigenous territories, so their existence is premised on the dispossession of Indigenous peoples. Fourth, many Indigenous peoples reject the concept of a state to organize their societies, arguing that Indigenous self-determination implies radically different forms of governance. Fifth, Indigenous territories often cross state borders: for example, the Yanomami in Brazil and Venezuela; or the Lakota, Salish, Blackfoot and so on in Canada and the United States. Hence colonial states disrupt Indigenous governance and Indigenous political communities. Finally, Settler colonialism has displaced peoples belonging to Indigenous nations throughout the globe, whether as the result of forcible relocations, dispossession through development "projects" and processes, through adoptions into non-Indigenous families living outside of Indigenous homelands and so on. Not only is the state antithetical to Indigenous peoples in its very constitution but the existence of states also then truncates Indigenous political relationships.

If international law supports or is embedded in the creation and maintenance of the state, how can it be used to "transcend" its most salient feature? Consider that the League of Nations and the United Nations, finance and trade institutions, security regimes, bilateral or regional partnerships (and all the norms, conventions or laws that emanate from them) privilege the state as the primary actor. It is referenced in charters, constitutions and terms of reference. The state and international law and society generally continue to express what Anghie (2007) calls the "dynamic of difference," a logic that extinguishes alternative understandings and practices of the international. From Spanish colonization and the emergence of the state to the discipline of "Third World" countries following the "decolonization" era and continuing with the contemporary "War on Terror," each instance is an extension of this inaugural act of dispossession, the alienation of Indigenous peoples from the land and the expunging of their nonstate political relationships. Conformity to this international architecture presumes European law and the state system; engaging with this architecture necessarily means surrendering to the laws and institutions that create and legitimize the situation Indigenous peoples now face.

### The Doctrine of Discovery, UNDRIP, and the Politics of Recognition

In the face of this hostile history of international law, Indigenous peoples have nonetheless continued to turn to the international arena for redress. This resistance is very old, beginning soon after the Doctrine of Discovery was applied and continuing into the present. Whatever it has accomplished, it has certainly forced states and institutions to acknowledge the agency of Indigenous peoples. Yet these efforts have been co-opted, trapping Indigenous peoples in the self-defeating politics of recognition — what Glen Coulthard refers to as simply reproducing configurations of colonial power (2007). It is the state, after all, that must recognize rights and thus can modify or restrict them. This pattern is demonstrated in the very long Indigenous rights negotiation process (dating back 460 years) as well as the much more recent trends in implementation; implementation that is always partial and always premised on the permanency of Settler occupation and unrestricted access by the state and capitalist enterprises to Indigenous lands and waters. This compromised outcome is the predictable consequence of using colonial international laws as the primary vehicle to express Indigenous diplomacy.

Beyond immediate on-the-ground physical resistance to the genocidal Doctrine of Discovery, origins of this formal struggle can be traced to 1550, which is the same era during which the politics of recognition first failed. In the city of Valladaloid, Spain, Indigenous-proxy and former Bishop of Chiapas Bartolomé de las Casas debated the "Indian Question" with Spanish theologian and lawyer Juan Sepúlveda. More specifically, Spain and Portugal (with their contemporary colonial empires looking on) sought to determine whether the brutal treatment of Indigenous people in Central and South America could be reconciled with justice. Sepúlveda, employing interpretations of Aristotle and Plato, asserted that there was a hierarchy of races, with Spaniards and other Europeans at the top. Indigenous peoples were subhuman, so they could be treated with violence and extreme cruelty until they were fit to become civilized. Meanwhile, las Casas tried to prove that Indigenous peoples had souls and that their violent colonization was contrary to Catholic law (Berger 1999). While his appeal resonated with some, Sepúlveda won the debate, setting established policy and discourse about Indigenous peoples for the next four centuries.

It took until 1957 for the international community to once again revisit the Indian Question. It was the International Labour Organization (ILO),[1] an agency within the UN concerned not only with workers' rights but also social justice generally, that debated and eventually passed Convention 107: *The Indigenous and Tribal Populations Convention*. As the ILO put it, the Convention was necessary because there were Indigenous "populations which are not yet integrated into the national community and whose social, economic or cultural situation hinders them from benefiting fully from the rights and advantages enjoyed by other elements of the population" (ILO 1957: Article 2, 1). "Integration" was the key word here — the Convention sought to protect Indigenous peoples by having them assimilate into the dominant populations of states. Indigenous activists criticized the document, suggesting that "rather than providing a source of rights for Indigenous peoples seeking to retain their territorial, political, social, and cultural integrity, the instrument legitimizes the gradual extinction of Indigenous peoples" (Venne 1999: 123).

It would take three more decades of struggle before some semblance of success. Following the disappointing Convention 107, as well as Convention 169 (which is discussed in the next section), the UN extended an invitation to a Working Group on Indigenous Peoples (UNWGIP) in the hope of creating a more appropriate legal tool. It declared success in 2007 with the UNDRIP, which earned the support of 142 countries. Attempting to reconcile the previous poor efforts, the preamble of the document states that all doctrines, policies and practices based on or advocating superiority of peoples or individuals on the basis of national origin or racial, religious, ethnic or cultural differences are racist, scientifically false, legally invalid, morally condemnable and socially unjust ... that indigenous peoples have suffered from historic injustices as a result of colonization and dispossession of their lands, territories and resources, thus preventing them from exercising, in particular, their right to development in accordance with their own needs and interests. (UNHCR 2007: Preamble)

It then goes on for forty-six Articles, espousing rights to define membership and identity, rights to have previous poor treatment redressed, and the right to revitalize traditions and cultures. The Declaration affirms rights to participate in colonial governments that make decisions that affect Indigenous peoples and their own governance systems, the right to self-determination (UNHCR 2007).

The Declaration has been a widely heralded success that was celebrated by Indigenous peoples around the world and also by scholars. The First People of the Kalahari said, "we are really very happy and thrilled to hear about the adoption of the Declaration. It recognizes that governments can no longer treat us as second-class citizens." Kenya's Ogiek tribe declared that "with the adoption of the Declaration, the lives of indigenous peoples will be improved on an equal footing with the rest of world citizens" (*Survival International* 2007). James (Sa'ke'j) Youngblood Henderson argues that "the Declaration is a major step toward establishing a normative vision. It seeks to eliminate the human rights violations suffered by Indigenous peoples and the nation-states justification for their oppression" (2008: 23). Likewise, Marshall Beier suggests that it is among "the global political initiatives enacted by Indigenous peoples that have affected outcomes on a range of important issues and in a manner without historic precedent" (2010: 176). Indigenous peoples finally convinced states to acquiesce some degree of sovereignty and permit international Indigenous rights.

Yet there is an important qualification to the effectiveness of this campaign. As Beier hints, these initiatives are "limited only by states' willingness to recognize them across different sites and moments of the colonial encounter" (2010: 177). This caveat reaffirms that states remain the arbiter of success of any rights activism. Any agency Indigenous peoples possess is tempered by the reality that the exercise of this agency is ultimately "permitted" — or not — by the states in which they reside. Coulthard warns of the futility and dangers of struggling for domestic Aboriginal rights in Canada through the kind of "politics of recognition" elaborated and defended by Canadian philosopher Charles Taylor. According to Taylor's formulation (1994), Indigenous peoples represent a culturally distinct but threatened minority in Canada that deserves "recognition" for this special status via unique rights. But as Coulthard (2007: 446) warns, it can only

> address the political economy of colonialism in a strictly "affirmative" manner: through reformist state redistribution schemes like granting certain cultural rights and concessions to Aboriginal communities via self government and land claims processes. Although this approach may alter the intensity of some of the effects of colonial-capitalist exploitation and domination, it does little to address their generative structures, in this case a racially stratified capitalist economy and the colonial state.

Adapting Coulthard's critique to the UNDRIP reveals starkly similar patterns. Charmaine Whiteface, Spokesperson for the Sioux Nation Treaty Council at the UNWGIP and Working Group on the Draft Declaration provides some insight into how the politics of recognition functioned throughout work on the UNDRIP. Her account (2013) of the ten years of negotiations between submission of the original text to the Human Rights Council and the final version endorsed by the UN General Assembly is revealing.

During discussions, English-speaking states frequently objected to the draft Declaration and ultimately forced rewrites of forty-three of the forty-six Articles to dilute them. In the editing process, terminology and whole sections placing obligations on states to enforce the Declaration's stipulations were deleted (Articles 12, 16, 21, 22, 26, 27, 37, 45). They even removed two Articles — the original Articles 8 and 11 — that apparently went too far for state representatives. In nearly as many cases, limits were placed on the potential exercise of Indigenous rights (Articles 4, 7, 16, 18, 19, 24, 29). These changes were made despite boycotts and hunger strikes by Indigenous delegates. But the most damaging were the changes made to the last article, Article 46. The original text stated, "Nothing in this Declaration may be interpreted as implying for any State, people, group or person any right to engage in any activity or to perform any act contrary to the Charter of the United Nations." The revised Article 46, (1) in part stipulates that

> nothing in this Declaration may be interpreted as implying for any State, people, group or person any right to engage in any activity or to perform any act contrary to the Charter of the United Nations or construed as authorizing or encouraging any action which would dismember or impair, totally or in part, the territorial integrity or political unity of sovereign and independent States.

The key additions here are "territorial integrity or political unity of sovereign and independent States" that, as Whiteface observes, "puts the political and territorial integrity of States first and foremost" (2013: 105). But the article goes even further, giving states a back door out of the Declaration by excusing any of the content they disagree with as a threat to "territorial integrity or political unity," however they choose to define it. Upon endorsement of the UNDRIP, Australia's then–Prime Minister Kevin Rudd noted that the government's concerns with the "free, prior and informed consent" elements of the Declaration, primarily Article 20, would be "interpreted in accordance with Article 46" (Australian Ministry of Families, Housing, Community Services & Indigenous Affairs 2009).

This speaks to a second danger inherent in the politics of recognition and so evident in the aftermath of the formal adoption of the Declaration: implementation. Similar to the negotiations, states have been able to assert their own perspectives to maintain the *status quo ante*. In her work around states' implementation of the UNDRIP, Sheryl Lightfoot has noted that upon ratification, many have asserted "qualifications and exclusions (which) wrote down the content of international Indigenous rights norms so that they were already in alignment with the legal and institutional status quo making further implementation efforts unnecessary" (2012: 116). Canada, for instance, released a formal statement of support for the Declaration. The government endorsed the UNDRIP as an important "aspirational document," but added that "the Declaration is a non-legally binding document that does not reflect customary international law nor change Canadian laws" (AANDC 2010). Lightfoot argues that Canada sought to "domesticate Indigenous issues, maintain the status quo in terms of policy, law and institutional structures" (2012: 115). In Lightfoot's work, each of the other previously hesitant endorsers, former English colonies Australia, New Zealand and the United States, all recognized the opportunity and echoed similar pre-emptive aversions.

In both the drafting of the Declaration and its implementation, states regulate their obligations and offer "legal" interpretations meant to ensure that Indigenous rights do not challenge any fundamental aspect of their current colonial relationship. Indigenous peoples might be able to affect a modicum of change via absorption, but it is always after the fact. Put another way, practicing the politics of recognition forces Indigenous peoples to accept their colonization and seek limited "rights" as redress within the colonial framework. This ultimately affirms the legitimacy of the Settler state and the discourses through which it articulates itself. Indeed, there have been few indicators of concrete benefits. As Corntassel notes of LEKWUNGEN land–based economic practices that violate federal and provincial laws in Canada, "the (international) rights discourse does little to assist (their) everyday acts of resurgence" (2012: 93). Moreover, considering the evolution of the rights discourse sketched here, I would argue that the situation in which the LEKWUNGEN community members have found themselves results from a colonial system of international law and the emergence of the state: They have signed into

Declarations that presuppose international law, the state and so their own dispossession. At best, the rights discourse offers limited support in those everyday acts of resurgence; and at worst, it will extinguish them.

## Implications of the Elastic Conceptualization of Indigenous Identity

The third feature of this critique moves away from institutions such as international law and the state and toward identity. It is concerned with the consequences of organizing global resistance through pan-Indigenous channels. Throughout the evolution of the UNWGIP and discussions on the UNDRIP by member states of the UN, the broad conceptualization of Indigenous identity has become a powerful rallying point for marginalized communities and individuals around the globe. The term "has been transformed from a prosaic description without much significance in international law and politics, into a concept with considerable power as a basis for group mobilization" (Kingsbury 1998: 414). Indeed, the Indigenous human rights discourse among activists and scholars has the tendency to stretch the concept of "Indigenous peoples." But the consequences are not a beneficial unification of diverse Indigenous peoples in a worldwide movement against colonization. Instead, the risk is that the concept becomes so elastic that it loses shape and becomes devoid of real substance. In fact, pan-Indian organizing under the identity category could further erode the elements of Indigenous societies that make them unique: sophisticated and alternative notions of political community.[2]

Returning to the history of rights activism reveals that legal interpretations of what it means to be "Indigenous peoples" has been an ongoing debate. Following the aforementioned integrationist Convention 107, the next attempt at protecting Indigenous peoples' rights occurred in 1989 when the ILO crafted Convention 169. And indeed the latter convention went much further than 107, even addressing the notion of self-determination for Indigenous peoples, promoting "the full realization of the social, economic and cultural rights of these peoples with respect for their social and cultural identity, their customs and traditions and their institutions" (ILO 1989: 5 Article 2, ii, b). Yet, in an equally laughable parallel to the earlier incarnation, it contained this passage: "The use of the term peoples in this Convention shall not be construed as having any implications as regards the rights which may attach to the term under international law" (1989: Article 1, 3). The Convention included a technicality that allowed states to skirt the content of the Convention by declaring Indigenous peoples nonpeoples and thus once more nonhuman in a legal sense, internationally.

It is no surprise, then, that throughout the negotiations on the UNDRIP ten years later, one of the most controversial topics was the definition of Indigenous peoples. That is, how are Indigenous peoples defined, what are the parameters of this concept, who qualifies as an Indigenous person? In 1986, a few years before Convention 169, the United Nation's Special Rapporteur Jose Martinez Cobo wrote the most frequently used definition of Indigenous communities, peoples and nations. He described them as

> those which, having a historical continuity, with pre-invasion and post-colonial societies that developed on their territories, consider themselves distinct from other sectors of the society now prevailing in those territories or parts of them. They form at present non-dominant sectors of society and are determined to preserve, develop and transmit to future generations of their ancestral territories, and their ethnic identity, the basis of their continued existence as peoples, in accordance with their cultural patterns, social institutions and legal systems. (Cobo 1998, quoted in Keal 2003: 7)

In his reading of Cobo's definition, Paul Keal (2003) notes that this definition can actually apply to a very broad range of humanity who have histories, relations and worldviews quite unlike the Maliseet, Sami and other original peoples. This leaves the claims to Indigenous rights vulnerable to manipulation, although the intent was to ensure that "Indigenous" remains a self-identifiable category, open for individuals and collectives to adopt based on their unique circumstances (Hartley et al. 2010). The consequence has been an unsettling tendency to co-opt, universalize, and indeed manipulate definitions of the "Indigenous." Courtney Jung provides an example with reference to resistance to globalization:

> Indigenous identity is portrayed as ancient, communal, traditional and moral, able to draw on a wealth of inherited wisdom to operate in organic sympathy with the earth. Globalization is its constitutive opposite: atomizing and amoral, leaving in its wake the detritus of unemployed labour, depleted resources, and degraded environments ... Indigenous identity is a resource that allows millions of the world's most dispossessed to challenge the terms of their exclusion. (2008: 11)

So the result has been numerous diverse peoples employing the term for their own unique circumstances, antiglobalization or otherwise. This echoes enlightenment-era appropriation of Indigenous "histories" for the purposes of praising or critiquing European society. But the implication, in some cases, is the erosion of authentic Indigenous identities and desires.

It is difficult to empirically evaluate the results of the deployment of the term "Indigenous." In one of the few robust case studies of an Indigenous community/people consciously articulating their campaign under the banner of "Indigenous peoples," Dorothy Hodgson's work (2011) with the Maasai of eastern Africa (Tanzania) reveals some negative consequences. Since the 1980s, the Maasai had participated in the UNWGIP and contributed to the creation of the UNDRIP. With apparent success at the UN, they reoriented their resistance to the state, beginning to define themselves as Indigenous, as opposed to previous understandings based on ethnicity or livelihood as pastoralists. They joined what they hoped would be a collective of transnational activists with significant lobbying power. They thought that "mobilizing around the label 'indigenous' implied that members shared common interests because of their common identity," but it was "an assumption that may have reflected more rhetoric than reality" (2011: 142). The Maasai realized that the more dominant Indigenous peoples who already had some form of land rights, whether in North Africa or North America, were able to steer the rights agenda in their favour. Moreover, as more and more people and groups in Tanzania began identifying as "Indigenous," the Maasai found the term inoperable in their discussions with the state due to its widespread and contrasting uses. Although it's true that the Declaration makes space for unique cultural, social and land rights; and the Maasai benefitted from resources and extra-state NGO support; Hodgson found that they were unable to use the international rights discourse effectively to satisfy their specific goals and ultimately abandoned the term "Indigenous peoples" altogether, drawing back from international rights activism in frustration. This is a unique case with its own circumstances, but nonetheless instructive for understanding some of the perverse, unintended consequences of abstract ideas of the "Indigenous."

Indigenous and marginalized peoples' demands for global structural change often begin with calls for global solidarity. Yet too often, this process ultimately also engenders sameness. Makere Stewart-Harawira, who has contributed immensely to the literature of Indigenous peoples and globalization, argues for "traditional Indigenous ontological principles [to] provide a framework and context for the development of a socio-political-economic ontology of the possible" (2005: 250). Elsewhere, she writes that "we are called to re-weave the fabric of being in the world into a new spirituality grounded and feminine-oriented political framework and process of 'being together in the world.' In that process, we are invited to deeply embrace the other, who is after all, the Elders teach us, Ourself" (2007: 136). But in Stewart-Harawira's calls for the dismantling of the self/other dichotomy as a basis for systematic change, she neglects to navigate the diversity of nations and corresponding visions of the future. This is true even as her own normative vision hints at gender inequalities and differences within "Indigenous" communities.

The fact is that Maori, Maasai and Masyarakat Adat (among others) do not share the same ontology or normative hopes. In many cases, despite overwhelming consensus on the nature of the problem and/or desire to simply get free, there is little to unite Indigenous understandings of a potential post–Settler-colonial world. So theorizing about the alternatives in a general way actually does a disservice to those people by conflating Indigenous cultures, values and nations into one homogenous view of change. Even the simple call for global transformation via solidarity seems like overstretching without a corresponding consensus on the direction of that change. In fact, an example of the result of this process is the inert UNDRIP. And even beyond static legal instruments, the conflating consequences of pan-Indigenous resistance are reflected in the activism of the Maasai, whose deployment of the discourse produced few results and instead marginalized them in their own struggle, both internationally and within Tanzania.

## The Resurgence of Indigenous International Relations

It is undeniable that Indigenous peoples from all over the globe find value in pursuing some semblance of autonomy through the international rights architecture. There are even those who might be content with rights secured through their negotiations with states and institutions. This critique is not meant to disparage those people or communities, nor is it designed to provide prescriptions for resistance. Instead, this chapter simply seeks to draw broad cautions around international rights activism and its potential as an avenue for resurgence or fundamental change. In light of this reading of the emergence of international law as a colonial accomplice, international rights activism as self-defeating politics of recognition, and the elastic concept of Indigenous peoples as insubstantial pan-Indianism, Indigenous resistance via the international society constructed by Eurocentric values and interests arguably both reinforces Settler occupation of Indigenous lands and disempowers authentic Indigenous alternatives.

A common theme here has been the inability to overcome the dynamics of difference and assert the re-emergence of Indigenous cultural and social institutions. In her critique of antiglobalization social movements, Radha D'Souza argues that activists generally are facing a crisis because of "their inability to develop conceptual resources to advance ideas about human emancipation, liberation, and self determination" (2010: 227). In fact, the language and concepts heretofore simply mirror "the conceptual repertoire of philosophical liberalism" (2010: 230). The result is a poverty of imagination about alternatives.

As I have argued in this chapter, as long as Indigenous activists are deploying rights discourse, they are trapped in the constraints of the state, sovereignty and anarchy as conceptual and ultimately material realities. So a potential escape might be the focus by Indigenous peoples on elaborating on what resurgence actually means as it applies to their specific context. From an Anishinaabe perspective, the cultural and political tradition I come from, notions of political community, the international and diplomacy are beyond the conceptual lexicon of the more orthodox international discourses discussed throughout this chapter. There is the story of our first treaty, an agreement between the deer, moose and humans that would govern our relationships for centuries. That arrangement saw the hooved creatures sacrifice themselves to feed, clothe, provide tools and educate humans. In return, humans would have responsibilities to maintain the integrity of their homes and avoid wasting their flesh (Borrows 2002; Simpson 2013). There is also the story of the birth of the Grandfather Drum: a narrative that demonstrated the drum's capability to diffuse seemingly endemic conflict between the Ojibwe and Dakota throughout the eighteenth and nineteenth centuries in the southwestern Great Lakes area. By reconnecting men to compassion and empathy, the drum offers peace (women had never lost this connection) (Witgen 2007; Vennum 2009). And, of course, there is the multinational resource-sharing pact known as the *Dish With One Spoon*, a metaphor that recognizes shared and overlapping jurisdiction and access to resources in modern day southern Ontario between the Anishinaabe and Haudenosaunee, among others (Hall 2003).

As even this exceedingly brief survey of authentic Anishinaabe international relations suggests, in our political worldviews, the state and sovereignty melt away. Ideas of anarchy as synonymous with the absence of the state and of international society, as conceived as an interstate system around individual liberal rights, play no role in Anishinaabe political relations. The pursuit of this Indigenous reconceptualization of the international on a broader scale might offer Indigenous peoples diverse, unique, but very old renewed visions of emancipation and political relationships. They can be employed to rebuild diplomacy among Indigenous nations, leading to a new understanding of the limits of possible and/or global Indigenous solidarity. Used in conversation with colonial institutions, they may cause a shift in discourse and even practice. In recentering and using diverse Indigenous politics and imaginations, this process would avoid the colonial–inspired international law that truncated Indigenous nations in the first place. We would abandon the distracting politics of recognition and sidestep pan-Indigenous homogenization. Of course, this route to resurgence also requires action. Revitalizing concepts is one thing; living them is the all-important other. In the realm of international society, there may be no more empowering resistance.

## NOTES

1.  Despite its name, the ILO is actually a tripartite organization giving "equal voice" to employers, governments and workers.
2.  I distinguish between the use of the term "Indigenous" to describe the diverse, broad spectrum of land-based peoples subject to colonial domination and the concept of "Indigenous" as an avenue to political action and change.

## REFERENCES

AANDC (Aboriginal Affairs and Northern Development Canada). 2010. "Canada's Statement of Support on the United Nations Declaration on the Rights of Indigenous Peoples." November. <aadnc-aandc.gc.ca/eng/1309374239861/1309374546142>.

Alfred, Taiaiake. 2005. "Sovereignty." In Joanne Barker (ed.), *Sovereignty Matters: Locations of Contestation and Possibility in Indigenous Struggles for Self-Determinism.* Lincoln: University of Nebraska Press.

____. 1999. *Peace, Power and Righteousness: An Indigenous Manifesto.* Oxford: Oxford University Press.

Anghie, Antony. 2007. *Imperialism, Sovereignty and the Making of International Law.* Cambridge: Cambridge University Press.

Australian Ministry of Families, Housing, Community Services & Indigenous Affairs. 2009. "The Declaration on the Rights of Indigenous Peoples." March. <jennymacklin.fahcsia. gov.au /statements/ Pages/ un_declaration_03apr09.aspx>.

Beier, Marshall. 2010. "At Home on Native Land: Canada and the United Nations Declaration on the Rights of Indigenous Peoples." In Marshall Beier and Lana Wylie (eds.), *Canadian Foreign Policy in Critical Perspective.* Don Mills, ON: Oxford University Press.

Berger, Thomas, R. 1999. *A Long and Terrible Shadow: White Values, and Native Rights in the Americas Since 1492.* Seattle: University of Washington Press.

Borrows, John. 2002. *Recovering Canada: The Resurgence of Indigenous Law.* Toronto: University of Toronto Press.

Corntassel, Jeff. 2012. "Re-envisioning Resurgence: Indigenous Pathways to Decolonization and Sustainable Self-Determination." *Decolonization: Indigeneity, Education & Society* 1, 1.

Coulthard, Glen. 2007. "Subjects of Empire: Indigenous Peoples and the 'Politics of Recognition' in Canada." *Contemporary Political Theory* 6.

D'Souza, Rahda. 2010. "Three Actors, Two Geographies, One Philosophy: The Straightjacket of Social Movements." In Sara Motta and Alf Gunvald Nilsen (eds.), *Social Movements in the Global South: Dispossession, Development and Resistance.* New York: Palgrave Macmillan.

Hall, Anthony J. 2003. *The American Empire and the Fourth World.* Montreal: McGill-Queens University Press.

Hartley, Jackie, Paul Jofee, and Jennifer Preston (eds.). 2010. *Realizing the UN Declaration on the Rights of Indigenous Peoples.* Saskatoon: Purlich.

Henderson, James (Sa'ke'j) Youngblood. 2008. *Indigenous Diplomacy and the Rights of Peoples: Achieving UN Recognition.* Saskatoon, SK: Purlich.

Hodgson, Dorothy L. 2011. *Being Maasai, Becoming Indigenous: Post-Colonial Politics in a Neoliberal World.* Bloomington: Indiana University Press.

International Labour Organization (ILO). 1989. "Convention 169: Convention Concerning the Protection and Integration of Indigenous and Other Tribal and Semi-Tribal Populations in Independent Countries." <ilo.org/ilolex/cgi-lex/convde.pl?C169>.

____. 1957. "Convention 107: Indigenous and Tribal Populations Convention." <ilo.org/ ilolex/cgi-lex/convde.pl?C107>.

Jung, Courtney. 2008. *The Moral Force of Indigenous Politics: Critical Liberalism and the*

*Zapatistas*. New York: Cambridge University Press.

Keal, Paul. 2003. *European Conquest and the Rights of Indigenous Peoples: The Moral Backwardness of International Society*. New York: Cambridge University Press.

Kingsbury, Benedict. 1998. "'Indigenous Peoples' in International Law: A Constructivist Approach to the Asian Controversy." *American Journal of International Law* 92, 3, 414–57.

Lightfoot, Sheryl. 2012. "Selective Endorsement Without Intent to Implement: Indigenous Rights and the Anglosphere." *The International Journal of Human Rights* 16, 1.

Miller, Robert, et al. 2010. *Discovering Indigenous Lands: The Doctrine of Discovery in the English Colonies*. Oxford: Oxford University Press.

Muldoon, James. 1994. *The Americas in the Spanish World Order: The Justification for Conquest in the Seventeenth Century*. Pittsburgh: University of Pennsylvania Press.

Shaw, Kerena. 2002. "Indigeneity and the International." *Millennium Journal of International Studies* 33, 55.

Simpson, Leanne. 2013. *The Gift Is in the Making*. Winnipeg, MB: Albeiter Books.

Stam, Robert, and Ella Shohot. 2012. "Whence and Whither Postcolonial Theory?" *New Literary History* 43.

Stewart-Harawira, Makere. 2007. "Indigenous Feminism as Resistance to Imperialism." In Joyce Green (ed.), *Making Space for Indigenous Feminism*. Black Point, NS: Fernwood Publishing.

____. 2005. *The New Imperial Order: Indigenous Responses to Globalization*. Wellington, NZ: Huia.

*Survival International*. 2007. "Jubilation as UN Approves Indigenous Peoples Declaration." <survivalinternational.org/news/2501>.

Taylor, Charles. 1994. "The Politics of Recognition." In Amy Gutmann (ed.), *Multiculturalism and "The Politics of Recognition."* Princeton, NJ: Princeton University Press.

UNHCR (United Nations High Commissioner for Human Rights). 2007. "The United Nations Declaration on the Rights of Indigenous Peoples." <ohchr.org/EN/NEWS EVENTS/Pages/DeclarationIP.aspx>.

Venne, Sharon Helen. 1999. *Our Elders Understand Our Rights: Evolving International Law Regarding Indigenous Peoples*. Penticton, BC: Theytus Books.

Vennum, Thomas. 2009. *The Ojibwa Dance Drum: History and Construction*. St. Paul: Minnesota Historical Society Press.

Whiteface, Charmaine. 2013. *Indigenous Nations' Rights in the Balance: An Analysis of the Declaration on the Rights of Indigenous Peoples*. St. Paul, MN: Living Justice Press.

Williams, Robert. 1992. *The American Indian in Western Legal Thought: The Discourses of Conquest*. Oxford: Oxford University Press.

Witgen, Michael. 2007. "The Rituals of Possession: Native Identity and the Invention of Empire in Seventeenth-Century Western North America." *Ethnohistory* 54, 4.

Chapter Eight

# TELLING STORIES
## IDLE NO MORE, INDIGENOUS RESURGENCE AND POLITICAL THEORY

*Kelly Aguirre*

In the winter of 2012, Theresa Spence, elected Chief of the Attawapiskat First Nation, was engaging in a hunger strike and ceremonial fast for her people in view of Parliament Hill on the Ottawa River. The Federal Omnibus Budget Bill C-45 threatened the further erosion of Indigenous inherent, constitutional and treaty rights centred in land and water. That winter, what came to be known as the Idle No More (INM) movement thundered over the snowy lawns of Canadian legislatures, in crowded shopping malls, across major highways, through social media and from thousands of hearts beating, it seemed, in unison. These places resounded with the drum. These practices resounded with story. Not one narrative, but many stories with diverse meanings. Recounting them provokes significant questions for Indigenous scholarship and the role of academics as storytellers. They are questions about the telling and retelling of stories about Indigenous self-determination and decolonization, what this may mean, where this is to be found and how this comes to be. They are about the difficult process of relearning our own stories, internalizing them, as well as challenging and dislodging those that have been imposed on us. They are also about acknowledging the stories of others that speak to us but don't fully convey our own experiences and intentions.

As a young scholar, I acknowledge my position. I'm still learning how to speak and to listen, what it means to inhabit language, to engage responsibly in what Jo-Anne Archibald calls "Indigenous storywork" (2008). Storywork is a mode of knowledge (re)production and transmission centred in the responsibilities of storytelling that also acknowledges and draws out the narrativity of all knowledge practices.[1] It includes Western academic political theory, a form of storytelling that, even at its most unconventional, continues to have a fraught relationship with Indigenous ways of knowing that trouble its authority to define the boundaries, substance and form of both politics and theory. Some characterizations of transformative action are inadequate or even complicit in ongoing dispossession by describing Indigenous practices to align with their own projects and projections. That is, some conceptual languages can appropriate or filter our voices, reforming Indigenous subjectivities to reflect back the ideals or more often *failed* ideals of others. INM brings some of the contours of this problem into focus, particularly what's invoked when its complex practices are aggregated as a unique movement or moment, and described either as a kind of recognition politics or a new form of anticolonial resistance.

In this telling, I aim to honour the collective storywork of many generations of Indigenous thinkers to suggest INM as an expression of the renewal cycles of *decolonial resurgence*. The community of scholars forwarding the concept of resurgence indicates a kind of epistemic shift in storytelling on and of self-determination. By *epistemic*, I mean our approach to sources of knowledge, methods, scope and validity. This is a turn away from seeking legitimacy and accommodation through political discourses and structures complicit in foundational and ongoing violences. Yet crucially it is also a move toward once again focusing on those relationships that constitute Indigenous nations and communities, affirming the vitality of their cultural lifeworlds. This shift is effectuated by upholding stories of resistance *to* and resilience *through* violence, but crucially those that also regenerate and *refigure* still existing, particular and substantive alternatives to colonial forms of relationality. That is, stories that don't just anticipate future possibilities or prescribe aspirations for all peoples according to utopian, generalized or abstract ideals. For me, resurgence involves a reorientation in ways of knowing, living more fully *again* from within Indigenous knowledge systems. Decolonization not only requires confronting and dismantling structures of colonial power but also a pervasive *coloniality* that renders Indigenous ways of being *and* knowing dependent on external "recognition" and so consistently denied.[2] Self-determination isn't contingent on the sanction of the Settler-State, the approval of Canadian public opinion or the definitions of Eurocentric political theory. Rather, it's enacting the substance of a self-determining existence for specific peoples through re-engaging in the practices that sustain us as such.

The practices of INM in their greatest visibility and in their as-yet-unknown reverberations can be seen as an instantiation of this epistemic shift and also part of a long continuity. INM challenges us as scholars to apprehend how the exercise of self-determination is actuated and made immanent in myriad interconnected practices normatively grounded in Indigenous understandings of freedom, responsibility and what it is to live a good life. Reflection on the stories we tell of such practices, *how* and *where* they are repeated or transcribed, for what and whose purposes, is important for awareness of our own forms of enactment. Along with unsettling the privilege of academia as a legitimating source of political theory that marginalizes traditional intellectuals, there's the question of disclosing Indigenous knowledge practices in ways that render them intelligible or even amenable to foreclosure or reformation by colonial power, sometimes in insidious ways and sometimes through those perceived as allies.

## Colonial Violence and Apologism

> Our culture and identity has the power to sustain us in difficult times and in my opinion, this is the core around which we should rise up and defend our lands, waters and peoples. The sooner we stop orienting ourselves around the laws, policies and media releases of the Canadian government, the stronger we will be in our resistance. Canada requires our participation in their processes to validate their ongoing oppression of our people — we can choose to withdraw and demand better.
>
> —*Palmater 2013*

Many practices of INM seem to reject conduits for the expression of Indigeneity and Peoplehood endorsed as legitimate by and within the Canadian Settler-State formation for the last forty years. Such approaches have involved seeking a recognition of nationhoods through rights and title adjudication or claims-making, primarily through representational organizations and governing structures such as the band councils and Assembly of First Nations or contemporary treaty groups. The established judicial and institutional processes they engage in are aimed toward an ultimate "reconciliation" with Canadian sovereignty rather than a deconstructive reckoning of that sovereignty, which is simply assumed. Yet can INM really be seen as manifesting a turn away from recognition politics when many practices appeared, such as demonstrations, directed toward "resetting" the relationship with Canada (see Alfred and Rollo 2014)? Indeed, initial organizing was responsive to Bill C-45 and the relegation of reserves such as Attawapiskat and the bodies of Indigenous women such as Theresa Spence as zones of permanent emergency, subject to a simultaneous scrutiny, exploitation, abjection and neglect. Both are treated as permissible sites for the exercise of sovereign exceptionalism toward Indigenous nations, just as Bill C-45 also renders Indigenous territories and authority violable. We said this must end with us.

As INM organizer and writer of the Afterword of this book Alex Wilson observes, the rallying points of violence against the land and Indigenous women provided "the impetus to a sudden rise in resistance," but there was also "a sudden rise of interest in a movement that's based on broad-scale community building" (Wilson quoted in Schwartz 2013). Indigenous activism is frequently portrayed as precipitated only by immediate threats and as event-oriented, suggesting a limited reactive agency tied to the Colonizer's initiative. However, acts of incursion, such as bringing the drum into Settler spaces imposed over Indigenous places, don't simply defer to the State's power through protest. As gatherings of reoccupation, they assert Indigenous presence, and as practices with and for the land, they're in continuity with all other land-based practices. They expose colonial violence, but exceed the bounds of resistance alone insofar as they embody Indigenous ways of being.

Indigenous storywork with practices such as those of INM must face Settler apologism about the colonial reality. This revisionism paints truth-telling on the Canadian national mythos as "academically-generated 'narratives' of colonialism, racism and genocide" that are an "abuse of reality," as pundit Rex Murphy (2013) derisively commented on Elsipogtog First Nation's blockade against fracking exploration on their territories. This echoes Prime Minister Stephen Harper when he remarked at the 2009 G20 Summit that Canada has "no history of colonialism" — the year following his delivery of the federal government's apology for the Indian residential schools. Contrary to but indirectly attested by Murphy and Harper's rhetoric, Indigenous peoples here remain embedded in systematic relations of colonial power that can be identified over the last century as a kind of *internal colonialism*, the attempted minoritization and domestication of Indigenous nations within the Settler-State. This system's impetus remains the nations' dispossession and displacement, an ongoing and insatiable capitalist accumulation of land augmented with the imperatives of Settler nation-building. The operation of colonial power involves what James Tully describes as concrete "structures of domination" and also a disciplinary regime, those "techniques of government," which include the "totality of modifiable discursive and nondiscursive ways and means used in strategies for guiding the conduct, directly and indirectly, and responding to the resistance of indigenous peoples" (2000: 38). *Discursive* refers here to the whole assemblage of narratives and communicative practices conceptualizing and codifying Indigenous-Settler relations. For example, the popular tale of denial retold by Murphy and Harper that repudiates narrativity, including its own — suggesting what can validly be told and how. These disciplinary moves intersect with the lived experience of colonial structures that, while repressive, don't totalize Indigenous peoples' agency.

A narrative of anticolonial resistance might be offered as an antidote to one of denial and apologism. Like many others, I've found inspiration as a storyteller in psychiatrist and revolutionary Frantz Fanon and his writings on Algerian independence, race and struggles for recognition. His words are searing, shattering and quickening, and have been crucial to me. But I've had to come to grips with the limitations in his insights for Indigenous practices. Fanon's work continues to provide a go-to decolonization lexicon for many Indigenous scholars and activists. Beyond diagnoses of colonial trauma and the defense of counterviolence, I think the ongoing appeal of his story comes from alignments in his depiction of decolonial action with the praxis-centeredness of Indigenous knowledge systems, but this is also where his words falter for me. We must be mindful of what we invoke when drawing on the stories of others, what we bring into being with our words, because every word itself carries story, and they are never only ours. Although some words, borrowed or embraced, can nourish us, they may not fulfill our needs. Scholarly naming of practices aren't unilateral acts on words where only our intentions as individuals matter. Names carry the record of our relations. They are genealogy. We have to consider how they are received or can be disfigured, and fundamentally that naming is creative and re-creative action. Unpacking some of Fanon's words, applied in the context of INM, suggests that telling of Indigenous practices as *anticolonial resistance* may sometimes distort more than illuminate.

## Heartbeat Drum Is on the Ground

Anticolonial thinkers of Fanon's generation wrote primarily from the experiences of African decolonization in the mid-twentieth century, yet their work can be marshalled for an incisive interpretation of colonial power's response to Indigenous action here. They suggested that material and symbolic exploitation requires the neutralized existence, not disappearance of an inferiorized Other, despite the occasional emergence of efforts to assimilate or modernize "the Native" (Sartre 1992: xxvii; see also Cabral, 1979: 40; see also, for example, Memmi 1992; Sartre 2001). Colonialism structurally relies on maintaining Dependent Colonized/Governing Colonizer identities, which are constituted through mutual recognition as such.[3] However, explicitly genocidal policies have also served Canadian nation-building projects since 1867. It can be asserted that a now diverse settler majority wants to shed its Colonizer identity and establish claims to the land through the destruction of Indigenous societies and their own nativization — for example, through popular stories of benign Indigenous inheritance, founding or exchange. There seems a simultaneous desire for both the eradication and subsumption of "the Native," producing alternating drives in the record of Canadian Indian Policy.[4] In (mostly) un-treated B.C., this has cultivated an "internal Otherness" that retains the unsettling "spectre" of nationhoods (Day and Sadik 2002: 5). A consequence is that the ongoing presence of Indigenous peoples is perceived as both anachronistic (as Jennifer Adese underlines in Chapter Five of this book) and threatening. This results in paranoia of Indigenous agency exposed by the State's use of blunt force and demonization of self-defense when it is unequivocally demonstrated to Settler perception, particularly to block access to territory.

Settler paranoia isn't abstract. The stakes are revealed when the flow of Capital is disrupted. Look at State responses to *demonstrations* such as the Kanien'kehaka of Kanesatake's stand at Oka in 1990, the Mi'kmaq of Elsipogtog's in 2013 or even flash mob round-dances in retail centres. Indigenous difference is registered by Settler desire as harmlessly folkloric when performed through practices such as dance and drum only as this suits. For Fanon, awareness of the contradictions in the Colonizer's precarious reliance on Native Otherness for their identity and position in a political economy based on "accumulation by dispossession" (Harvey 2004) provides openings for the Colonized to take up their human potential as agents of Historical change (Fanon 2004: 155). In moments of crisis, the Native can seize this opportunity by returning the Colonizer's objectifying gaze and meeting violence with cathartic counterviolence, "the ultimate praxis" (Fanon 2004: 44; also 1, 10). Decolonization requires us to first assume and reverse the asymmetrical Colonizer/Colonized binary, to gain a position of dominance from which we might eventually break it down. In terms of strategy, a self-aware leadership eradicates ambiguities or internal dissension to forward a single oppositional Native bloc capable of challenging the colonial order on its own scale, appropriating the Colonizer's tools and aspirations to be redeployed against them. The immediate and temporary aim is to replace or become the State rather than dismantle it. Native nationalism will then somehow fall away, and eventually a revolution for universal emancipation will commence (Fanon 1968: 244).

In my view, Fanon's narrative of anticolonial resistance can't account for non-violent, nonhierarchical and many-sided mobilizations with diverse aspirations for diverse nations such as INM's. It can't acknowledge the full array of decolonial practices Indigenous people engage in beyond those overt "demonstrations" of agency. It's also a narrative that accepts the destruction of distinct Indigenous societies, their reconstitution as "Colonized Natives" and eventual postcolonial reformation as *new* people(s) — if not its predestined inevitability (Fanon 2004: 50). For Fanon, the Third World would eventually initiate a dialectical transition beyond the liberal-Capitalist state system and unify all people to realize the belief in a shared humanity, not the false prophets of the West. National liberation and decolonization are just episodes in a linear progression toward this ideal, and mobilization around *Nativeness* is only ideological and instrumental. This is problematic to any understanding of Fourth World freedom centred in regenerative concepts of Indigeneity — and the continuation of distinctive nationhoods, homelands and traditional cultures.

Interrogating Fanon's limits further can shed some light on the complications in depicting INM as an unprecedented "Historical Moment" and "Native Movement" out of idleness made up of protest events. *First*, what's recognized as an anticolonial political act tends to exclude customary practices such as drumming and delink them from explicit confrontations with colonial power. *Second*, those acts that narrowly qualify, if they visibly signify as oppositional, can be discredited by the same criteria as spontaneous, momentary, disorganized, emotional and reactive. These labels have long been used to dismiss Indigenous practices as prehistoric, nonpolitical, ineffective and immature. The criteria for authentic action and change in "classic" anticolonial theory emerges from utopian — or more, Euro-topian — views of history, agency and world formation. These criteria don't engage Indigenous perceptions of time, place, movement and creativity, and so the nature of specifically Indigenous forms of resistance and transformation. I'll attempt to address these two linked issues of anticolonial storytelling in reference to INM here.

While Fanon eloquently described the disfiguration of colonized peoples' pasts to fabricate the dependent and anachronistic Native in the Colonizer's stories, he saw their "cultural alienation" as effectively achieved (Fanon, 2004: 149). The work of so-called Native intellectuals only valorizes the past to help unite people in the service of a modernizing nationalism. Meanwhile, the frequently clandestine engagement in "precolonial" customs such as ceremonial dance is deemed to only stage revenge fantasies, performing resentment in avoidance of the *real* praxis of a violent faceoff. Dance and song is dismissed as only the ritualized trappings of obsolete cultures; the wider systems of relationality these practices were once integral to sustaining having been irreversibly fractured. Commitment to what Fanon calls an "inventory of particularisms," or the "mummified fragments" of customs amounts to going through a catalogue of empty motions, as the living multiplicity of cultures they once expressed aren't recoverable (Fanon, 2004: 160). In this regard, Fanon tended to corroborate characterizations of Nativeness and traditionalism as stagnating, though the blame was shifted in his account. For example, he acknowledges that the "reproach of inertia constantly directed at the Native is utterly dishonest" because in his view it's only a result of colonial interference. Indeed, the category of "Native" itself only comes into being with it (Fanon 1994: 34). However for Fanon, colonized peoples who continue to practice traditional dance, singing and ceremony in the face of oppression are still *idle*, only becoming authentically active again when resistance is openly antagonistic — competition for control with an enemy over government, resources, property. In short, they're active when their praxis is *recognizable* to modern Euro-Western definitions of politics and power as a struggle for domination.

For Fanon, Native stagnation is perpetuated by emphasizing cultural *content* over *form*. To him, culture's living essence is the energy of forward motion, a constant production of newness toward fulfilling our supposedly distinctive human nature as creative beings (Fanon 1968: 247). Yet content and form are inextricable for Indigenous cultures. Peoplehood is (re)produced in particular *traditional practices*. Culture isn't the "opposite" of customs, in which attempting to "stick to tradition or reviving neglected traditions" through their repetition is to "go against history" and "one's people," to be stymied in the past (Fanon 2004: 160). Instead, as Kainai elder Leroy Little Bear relates, repetitive practices such as singing, dancing and all forms of storytelling maintain the integrity of a people's distinctive lifeworld (Little Bear quoted in Henderson 2000: 248). This is part of their responsibility to contribute to the diversity of Creation, discerning and (re)making patterns out of flux. Creation is not an initiating event in a chronological sequence, but an ongoing process of renewal in which humans are only a part. We are unique agents among a multiplicity of equally integral forces, spirits, beings. We're created and also necessarily self-(re)creating in a system of interdependence, not at the centre or apex of a hierarchy. This also indicates Indigenous notions of movement and time as nonlinear, nonfixed and noncumulative. Tradition is understood to involve both continuity and motion; it doesn't imply invariance but adaptation. Without renewal, particular combinations of energy that form the reality of a people's exist-ence will dissipate into the flux (Little Bear 2004: 27). Indigenous lifeworlds are sustained and affirmed through customary practices aligned with the earth's cyclical dynamism and evoke both a sense of enduring being and continuous becoming.

## How Do We Tell of the Drum?

The practice of dance and drum is testament to the failure of colonial totaliza-tion, not evidence of it. So how do we tell of the drum? When youth Donna Cook addressed a student–organized INM gathering on January 26, 2013 at the B.C. Legislature, she said unequivocally that our "weapon of choice is the drum" (Cook quoted in Lavoie, 2013). What I heard standing behind her that day was an expression of drumming as a decolonial practice that can't be neatly categorized or encapsulated as resistance alone, although it is that, too. For Fanon, the decisive moment in what he sees as only mimicking direct action through dance and other "ritual" comes with coercive violence (Fanon 2004: 20; see also Coulthard 2007: 454; Gibson 1999: 415). It's when the Native's drum is answered by the Colonist's gun. But what does the image of a line of Mi'kmaw women, drums raised toward a line of armed soldiers at Elispogtog reveal? The threat that the ban of drums, regalia and Potlach under the Indian Act attempted to suppress is nothing other or less than that of Indigenous lifeworlds. Drumming is constituent of *AlterNatives* to capitalist and Settler-Colonial exploitation (to borrow the phrase from a mentor, Kiera Ladner). This is the sense in which the Drum has been weaponized. Customs that may be compartmentalized as nonpolitical or nonmaterial to neutralize their significance are actually undifferentiated from or contiguous with a people's modes of governance, production and exchange; their way of being with/in their homelands. Drumming as a practice can't be isolated, but is always connected to the life of the people and the land. It is the heartbeat of nations and of our mother Earth. Each drum's beat resonates, joins the resonance of all others before it and into the next generations. The drum is a living heart, and as the proverb goes, a nation is not conquered until the hearts of its women are on the ground. The actions at blockades aren't born from being reduced to a desperation that only counterviolence can heal, but love. The women of Elispogtog have their hearts raised before the Colonist's guns.

Here I need to speak to the gendered dimensions of discounting customary practices in narratives of anticolonial resistance. The leadership roles of women at the frontline of confrontations connect to those as cultural knowledge holders integral to sustaining Indigenous life on all "fronts." This may be through everyday practices that aren't directly responsive to colonial power, such as medicine and healing; food cultivation; harvest and preparation; language, beadwork or childcare with children and youth as learners; and also as decision-makers, law and protocol carriers. Taken as emblematic of anticolonial confrontation, the infamous photo of Cloutier and Laroque's standoff at Oka, locked in a masculine binary of two enemy warriors, renders this invisible. Ellen Gabriel served as a spokesperson at Oka, but it's not her image that endured in Canadian popular memory. Scenes at the blockade by Elispogtog such as the drummers or Amanda Polchies kneeling and raising an Eagle Feather to heavily armed RCMP trouble the image of male protagonists in resistance stories. As Audra Simpson recently elucidated, perceptions that Theresa Spence's hunger strike was "unsuccessful" because she *survived* it, points to femicide as a key colonial technique of governing toward the elimination of Indigenous nationhoods (A. Simpson 2013). The abusive public commentary on her physical body as a Native woman *and* leader takes on significance beyond the appalling immediate. Disparaging women's influence in and *embodiments* of the life of their nations, imagining us as only passive media for exploitation, connects intimately to disassociating customary practices from acts of "political" resistance. Anticolonial storytelling can reproduce such erasures and the gendered violence women experience for their identification with and guardianship of traditional knowledge, governance and the land.

The second problem of anticolonialism in how we tell of INM is around our relations with time and place/space. As a Marxist committed to agency, Fanon wasn't a fatalist, but still understood anticolonial action within a concept of universal historical time. He saw decolonization movements as necessarily cohesive and progressive struggles within a trajectory that in liberating the Colonized, advances the freedom of all. The Colonizers persist in a lie that they're the only ones who can "make History" in this way, and the Colonized shatter this deception through violence (Fanon 1968: 14–15). Fanon saw violent anticolonial action as "living within history" against colonialism's basic *spatiality* (Fanon 1968: 147). Anticolonial violence destroys the social and geographical partitions of the colonial order and is "temporalizing," initiating Colonized peoples' re-engagement with History as subjects rather than passive victims. Subjecthood is immobilized by the *internments* of colonization, such as relegation to Native spaces, such as reservations, and the conflation of identity with its object of control: the land (Fanon 2004: 14–15). This is also cultural *internment* — burial in the past. For Fanon, violent uprising produces an "unstable, critical and creative moment of negativity and transcendence" (Gibson 1999: 411). The Colonized can shed their own objectified *being for* (an)Other — that is, existence *for* the Colonizer, to serve as their foil — and initiate a self-determining condition of *becoming*. Although this may involve redeeming stories of precolonial life, any attempt to recuperate that life would be regressive because decolonization requires us to work in the present, looking forward to the future.

Glen Coulthard suggests the limits of Marxist time/place distinctions when applied to Indigenous contexts (Coulthard 2010).[5] It's been observed that Fanon recognized the ongoing theft of land rather than time as fundamental to *colonial* dispossession (and so the locus of struggle). This is distinct from a more conventionally Marxist emphasis on the exploitation of labour (Sekyi-Otu 1997: 77; Kulchyski 2005: 88). However, the stakes here go far beyond a simplistic materialist view affirming that for colonized peoples the "most essential value, because the most concrete is first and foremost the land" (Fanon 1968: 44). Indigenous decolonial practices express a reactualization of what Coulthard calls "grounded normativities," patterns of life derived from interdependency with homelands. Leanne Simpson articulates this clearly in her essay "Aambe! Maajaadaa! (What #IdleNoMore Means to Me)": "I stand up anytime our nation's land base is threatened because everything we have of meaning comes from the land — our political systems, our intellectual systems, our healthcare, food security, language and our spiritual sustenance and our moral fortitude" (L. Simpson 2012). Practices associated with INM such as drumming at sites of reclamation such as PKOLS in WSÁNEĆ can be seen as despatializing in their disruption of arbitrary geographies and boundaries imposed on Indigenous peoples, which is tied to the de- and reterritorialization of occupied lands as Settler spaces.[6] As practices, however, not just independent acts or protest events, they're profoundly about being *and* becoming *in/of* a place, the restitution of a form of subjectivity constituted by the integral connection with your particular homelands through time. This implies situatedness in a confluence of constantly negotiated relationships, humans' relations with animal people, plant people, earth people, spirit people; all beings that make up what I might imperfectly call a kinship ecology of Creation. Ethics of responsibility between these relations are carried in the dynamic practices of customary lifeways. Interdependence with the land is the source of AlterNative normative systems — understandings of what are good, respectful, just relations and conduct. There's an obligation to sustain these systems though repetitive traditions on the land, which are all themselves knowledge practices oriented to continuity as peoples that don't preclude but incorporate transformation. In light of this, the re-enactment of the signing of the North Saanich Douglas Treaty at PKOLS on May 22, 2013 wasn't commemoration of an event, but a renewal calling on the treaty partners to meet their obligations. It animated a story of that Indigenous place.

"Historicizing" Indigenous agency raises the problem of gesturing to a unilinear concept of History used in colonial governance. This concept has cast Indigenous societies in lethargic backwardness and colonialism itself as past episodes of colonization rather than as persistent processes replicating violent structural practices and relationships of domination. Describing INM as a single Revolutionary Movement and Historic Moment of "revival" in Indigenous activism with broad strokes doesn't address the many AlterNative, contested histories of Indigenous-Settler relations that trace vitality and continuity in Indigenous praxis. From a Fanonian perspective, INM could be deemed a disruptive break in complacency, providing a short-lived opening for radical transformation. The definitive anticolonial Moment comes when there's an outrage, causing anger to erupt from festering resentment. The resulting crises are sporadic and fragile catalysts, opportunities to foment true revolution, missed if not grasped while the iron is hot. INM has been perceived to be trapped in such a moment, defined by opposition to a set of federal legislation and the particular government behind it and so unsuccessful (Coulthard 2013). Indeed, the visibility of mass gatherings has declined since the winter of 2012–13, but this just defers to the spectacle of the event (Palmater 2013). In dominant media, Indigenous activism is portrayed as a loose chain of clashes, somehow spontaneous and disjointed incidents, outside the broader context of dissent and community defense, in specific and long-standing struggles with the corporate and state engines of their dispossession. Media coverage of INM and Elispogtog evoke dramatic confrontation, Red Power and the American Indian Movement, Oka, Grassy Narrows, Burnt Church, Restigouche; while images of seized weaponry, destroyed police or military equipment and arrests feature prominently, criminalizing supposedly irrational and inconvenient Indigenous counterviolence. These aren't deemed traditional practices of protection borne from responsibility to each other as links in the chain of intergenerational embraces, as Leanne Simpson so eloquently references the Anishinaabe concept of *kobade* to describe nationhood (L. Simpson 2013a). Yet this is likewise distant from Fanon's evocative description of the anticolonial actor as a "violent link in the great chain, in the almighty body of violence rearing up in reaction to the primary violence of the colonizer" (Fanon 2004: 50).

## We Have Never Been Idle

It's important here to address what's happened since the winter of 2012, in particular the contentious transition from Idle No More to the Indigenous Nationhood Movement called for by some organizers, and the divergences between visions of decolonization such reframing of the INM stories indicate. This divergence can be compared to Fanon's depiction of Native efforts to end "certain definite abuses" by pursuing limited domestic legal rights, for example, which Fanon says can suck us into "the confusion of neoliberal universalism" before the necessary turn to nationalist politics (Fanon 1968: 148). It certainly suggests a disconnection from the reconciliation and recognition politics that major organizations such as the AFN have invested in since the 1970s, and is perhaps the end of an era of accommodation and constitutionalism. Nonetheless, appeals to galvanize around *nationhood* aren't about Native nation-building in Fanon's terms, but the regeneration of many original nationhoods. Yet we should be cautious about how we aggregate the diversity this poses under any banner, no matter the acronym. Some may see a troubling liberal co-optation of people "newly politicized" by INM, but not everyone agrees on what integrity entails. Aside from underappreciating everyday resistance and practices of self-determination, and that to be Indigenous is to *be* political, focusing on fissures can disempower our stories. At the forum "Where Do We Go From Here?" on January 16, 2013 at the University of Victoria, Taiaiake Alfred, a proponent of the shift to the Indigenous Nationhood Movement, discussed the depiction of disagreement in and around INM as weakening divisiveness (see also King 2013). Any notion of the necessity for unity under one strategic program of decolonization would have us see INM as a single movement now splintered by disputes over leadership and "ownership." However, dissonance doesn't signal a loss of momentum or cohesion, but rather outgrowth that comes with an experience of profound solidarity against *arbitrary* divisions. The drum's beat resonates in all directions. No energy is ever lost or destroyed, but is reconstituted in other forms. I believe INM's energy has been in stories and their proliferation; we take hold of them and they take hold of us, sometimes in unexpected, but never irrelevant or insignificant ways. I don't aim here to suggest the truth of any one (or *anyone's*) story over another. INM was always and still is many stories, braided together. They are all stronger for this.

A December 20, 2012 briefing to then-Minister for Aboriginal Affairs John Duncan states that INM is "quite different from what we've seen before in terms of activity and rhetoric," revealing concern with INM's sea-change potential (quoted in Press and Woods 2013). As Jarrett Martineau observes in Chapter Ten of this book, with the globalization of social media, channels and platforms of communication have changed and multiplied, and how we share and act through our stories has adapted (#INM) in ways Martineau doesn't always see as benign. But INM is anything but new, unprecedented or exceptional. Understood as *resistance* INM is part of a story of survivance begun more than five hundred years ago, when strangers arrived on our shores. As an expression of Indigenous vitality, INM as *resurgence* is part of a story from time immemorial. It is neither the beginning nor end of these stories. Colonial narratives would have us believe in their termination. However, so too would an anticolonialism that seeks to ultimately end difference by projecting a universal vision of emancipation. More, resistance understood only as an opposition that redeploys colonialism's structural, physical and discursive violences defines us according to this relationship. Resurgence defines us by the substance of our alternatives. As Alfred and Jeff Corntassel suggest:

> There is a danger in allowing colonization to be the only story of Indigenous lives. It must be recognized that colonialism is a narrative in which the Settler's power is the fundamental reference and assumption, inherently limiting Indigenous freedom and imposing a view of the world that is but an outcome or perspective on that power. (2005: 601)

Fanon once said that he didn't "want to sing the past to the detriment of my present and my future" (Fanon 2008: 201). INM didn't sing a "new" song; it sang connections through past, present and future. We can see this in what's sometimes known as the "Constitution Song." The song has origins as a bone-game song here on the coast; it was taken up in the context of resistance to the exclusionary 1981 Constitutional Patriation process and sung again in 2012. The context of the singing may have shifted, but the song remains the same. Never just an oppositional statement — it was always an affirmation of self-determination.

While Fanon appreciated the materiality of traditional practices that comprise AlterNative normative systems as a Marxist (see Gibson 1999: 418), he didn't see existing immanently in their stories what Johnny Mack refers to as "different conceptions of what it means to be human, to live as a community, to live in relation to the land" (2011: 297). As Coulthard points out, Fanon saw "cultural self-recognition" as instrumental to decolonization, but Indigenous decolonial practices such as those of INM "articulate a far more substantive relationship between identity and freedom insofar as they are attempting to critically reconstruct and redeploy previously disparaged traditions and practices in a manner that consciously seeks to prefigure a lasting alternative to the colonial present" (2008: 199). This use of the word *prefiguration* was a revelation for me as a way to describe resurgence through practices of self-determination beyond the terms of recognition. Such practices constitute the ends they seek to bring about; they bring into effect the decolonial forms of life sought in the process of decolonization itself by enacting them.[7] Indigenous prefiguration is about the *resurgence* of traditional practices that form established alternatives — not anticipation of a future socialist utopia or revolutionary inauguration of an entirely new way of life. Tradition is engaged not to recuperate the past, but to *renew*, a life-giving force that sustains peoplehoods and also *re*-creates non-Capitalist, non-Sovereign Statist, non-Imperial relationality between all beings and the land. There's a difference between complete reconstruction, the radical break of revolution and the *regeneration* of lifeways that have always existed. Decolonization doesn't exceed these practices. It's in them. This is why *refigurative* may actually be a better term to associate with resurgence than *prefigurative*. The "alternative forms of production and reproduction or alternative conceptions of nature-society relations" beyond Capital and State sought by Marxists (Karriem quoted in Carroll 2010: 179) have already been successfully created. They've been diminished under constant assault, *but remain unextinguished*.

The idea of *refiguring* a self-determining life through our practices helps to understand their connection. If we can rhetorically differentiate practices of resistance from resurgence in terms of emphasis and orientation, externally to colonial relations or inwardly to those relations that strengthen peoplehood, *refiguration* suggests that they're not distinct activities. Nor does resurgence come after resistance as a stage — they have been and are inseparable and are often contiguous. Customary practices in many forms have been resistive in that they produce AlterNatives to capitalist-colonial relationships. What have been externally "recognized" acts of resistance are not only oppositional but can also be understood as traditional because they enact responsibiliteis of Indigenous nationhood.[8] Through a continuity of practices from blockades, rallies and marches, to treaty and legal pursuits, to tanning hide, to language use, to drumming, Indigenous peoples have never been idle.

## Feasting and Fasting, Always Dancing

Antonio Gramsci described Marxism as the "philosophy of praxis," but this is a better claim for Indigenous knowledge and normative systems. Stories of practices generate philosophy; the values that philosophy describes are animated through practice. Many Indigenous thinkers such as Little Bear and Johnny Mack perceive customary practices of identity and community, whether from beadwork to fishing, narratively — they express a people's stories. This is why Mack stresses that the institutionalization of colonial narratives calls for Indigenous nations to reorient within their own "storied practices," regaining a subject position outside the limits of such narratives and thus the perspective necessary to assess different approaches to reshaping relations with Settlers (2011). For example, in his conversations with the elder Wickaninnish, Mack learned that preparations involved in a chiefly feasting process have a regenerative potential. He advocates *h'onquist* (reorienting) back to such practices rather than pursuit of external recognition. Relationship, agency, identity as it is known for Nuu-chah-nulth-aht, is reinforced through the practice of feasting (2011: 304–5):

> [Our People] tend to understand the world as a series of relationships between performative agents. We understand things through what they do rather than identifying any particular essences of their being ... We say that we are Nuu-chah-nulth and that there is a story to that identity. And that is a story of practice ... Thus, though we may not know how to build our canoes or paddle them now, we have reason to hope that this knowledge will return if we embed ourselves in the kind of practices that generated it.

We must re-engage such storied practices amid the scarcity and losses of colonialism. Reflecting on this, we can see Chief Spence's "individual hunger strike" (as it was depicted in mainstream media), both the solidarity and attempted discrediting it elicited, in its full context as the relational practice of a traditional fish broth fast. Leanne Simpson describes the significance for her as evoking an imposed diet in a time of human-made famine, the hardship in a homeland's bounty stripped away and appropriated. There is sacrifice, but also resilience. Fish broth isn't a cheat; it is survivance. For Simpson in this storied practice, Spence was not an elected leader in an oppositional political maneuver acting alone, but *Ogichidaakwe*, a holy woman in ceremony with her people (L. Simpson 2013b). This is understood by those for whom she undertook this responsibility, and the support owed her on this difficultly chosen path is the reciprocity of a gift. Indeed, James (Sa'ke'j) Youngblood Henderson cautions that we not seek the meaning of our stories exactingly and absolutely as objects, but rather to see them as gifts, offering a teaching and a choice, the significance of the exchange varying with the practitioner or participant. Stories offer guides, not prescriptions. They're about relationships and "processes of knowledge" (Henderson 2000). What does Theresa Spence teach through her leadership? The lesson I learned from her story is a vision of self-determination and the role of women as fulcrums that balance and connect their peoples. I also learned that my body is a place for self-determination and that this is threatening to the patriarchal, heteronormative and misogynistic pillars of colonial rule and internalized strains of gendered and sexualized oppression. For this, I thank her and retell this story of which I am now a part.

Fanon's depiction of cultural deprivation suggests that the context in which we might fully assume the forms of subjecthood our storied practices entail has been demolished. Indeed, Mack is concerned that the degree to which colonialism has "reformed our subjectivities, changing the way we understand and respond to the world" makes it difficult to conceive rejecting the liberal political-legal institutions that have attempted to enclose us (Mack 2011: 299). I recall a personally affecting comment Alfred made once that "we can no longer say we stand firmly on Turtle's back".[9] Yet INM and Leanne Simpson remind us that while rooted, we — all Indigenous people — have never only stood, but have always *danced* on our Turtles' backs — through times of feasting and fasting, in the winter of 2012, as every winter before. Tradition and identity aren't static, and this is where demands for authenticity that essentializes "cultural integrity" in terms of haves and have-nots can actually deny the possibility of resurgence. That said, all our dances are in some form ones of reconnection, to a resolute sense of being, to foundations destabilized by colonialism. So for me, a first step is affirmation that alternative ways of life are still possible, to regenerate and refigure, to honour our pasts, meet our present needs and protect our futures. Indigenous intellectual resources are alive, rich and necessary to see practices such as those of INM as resurgent and decolonial, not only resistive and reactive.

## What Are Our Roles as Storytellers?

Resurgence for me involves recentering within Indigenous knowledge practices, but what does it mean for Indigenous academic production? How is our work as scholars implicated, or not, in the critical shift on the ground many of us perceive and are attempting to describe and interpret? What are Indigenous scholars' obligations as storytellers in relation to resurgence? Theresa Spence and INM's lesson for me is modeling the stories we tell and retell. Can modes of expression used to communicate with State institutions for the past half-century or so — courts, government, education, justice, healthcare and so on —facilitate Indigenous *storied practices* and pre-/refigure self-determination? This question challenges occupations, particularly academics, lawyers and politicians, committed to translating and transliterating Indigenous stories into the language of these still-colonial institutions. This includes projects of "Indigenizing" law, politics, political theory, the Academy that wrestle with their distortion and appropriation. There's much in the power of names and naming. We can't overemphasize the importance of attempting to resignify concepts such as sovereignty away from the Imperial lexicon to reflect nonhierarchical, nondominating or noncoercive Indigenous meanings. This isn't a sufficient critical activity in itself. As Indigenous scholars, our work between worlds can't assume a power vacuum in this interstitial space. As allied thinker James Tully suggests, theory can be understood as a critical practice, but resurgence's greater disruption of epistemological authority is to challenge academics to understand practice *as* theorizing in Indigenous normative and knowledge systems. This broadens the field of whom we hold up as theorists and intellectuals, provoking us to prioritize practitioners of Indigenous knowledge, not trained academics (L. Simpson 2011). What then should change in the aims of our scholarly storywork?

In retelling stories such as those of Theresa Spence or INM, I see a role of Indigenous academics as imperatively looking to Indigenous knowledge, respected on its own terms, as the foundation for our understandings of self-determination. So how might we engage self-consciously in this process? We can begin by not describing Indigeneity in ways that imply the Settler sociopolitical order's forms can simply be "filled by Native substance" (West 1995: 280, 289). We can take the inextricability of form and substance seriously. Vine Deloria Jr. once argued that making the potential for *intellectual* self-determination a preoccupation is tantamount to tilting at "windmills in the mind" (1998). I take this as a provocation to be self-reflexive on the distraction of theoretical *abstraction*. Self-determination appears ungraspable when alienated from its "meaning in practices" to particular peoples. We must do more than seek to change the conceptual terms of generalized discourses to actualize reconnection with lands and lifeways. Yet colonialism comprises structural and material power relations as well as cultural and cognitive imposition, so decolonization isn't restricted to self-government and redistribution but also involves addressing "colonial power-knowledge" (Doxtater 2004) — as in dichotomous thinking on theory and praxis. Reclamation of Indigenous authority on the (re)production of knowledge that shapes Indigenous lives and frames Indigenous aspirations is necessary to topple "intellectual imperialism" (Waziyatawin 2004). This is where we have a role: to use our privilege in the houses of power-knowledge toward disassembling that imperialism and, by extension, our own privilege.

This involves considering how self-determination is enacted outside depictions in the Academy: scrutinizing its representations in the authoritative discursive formations through which such institutions function, how Indigenous storied practices elude them and thus also the defensibility of scholarly work as an appropriate medium for their expression. That is, to ask whether, in Audra Simpson's phrasing, to make ourselves intelligible to "the imperial ear" or "discernible" to its gaze (A. Simpson 2007a, 2007b) or rather refuse to render our difference cognizable to the Liberal-Capitalist-Colonial order. Resurgence's refusal of recognition isn't to seek or celebrate incoherence for its own sake, nor is it to be incomprehensible to "the Colonizer" or Colonial order by juxtaposing an equally imprecise Indigenous Otherness. Instead, it's to be coherent according to our own stories — decentering the colonial implies a recentering. However, there are many practical questions about averting disciplinary representation of storied practices such as those of INM to avoid capturing and fixing the knowledges they regenerate through documentation, revealing or exposing them, and so contradicting an intended defiance of colonial surveillance and demands for verification.

In a 2013 interview, Ovide Mercredi reflected on his life as a student, activist and leader. He saw his time as AFN Grand Chief mostly characterized by grievance and petitioning, but suggested the youth leadership of INM has shifted to enaction: "They're just going to do it. Where they see oppression, they're going to fight it. Where they see poverty, they're going to change it. Where they see poor housing, they're going to improve it. Where they see bad education, they're going to make it better" (Mercredi quoted in Chalmers-Brooks 2013: 13). This echoes INM organizer and media personality Wab Kinew, who half-humorously suggested that a "just do it" practice-based understanding of self-determination is re-emerging, led by Youth and women, and guided by elders (#J16 Forum UVic). The Nishiyuu Walkers' 1600 km journey on foot to Ottawa for their Cree community of Whapmagoostui and all Indigenous nations inspired by Theresa Spence's fast are emblematic of this leadership. These youth showed the spiritual and ethical conviction that they're capable of making change. As a traditional teacher and friend imparted to me when he sensed my own uncertainty, the courage of leadership is in humility and acceptance of taking direction from the people. As Alex Wilson also emphasizes in the Afterword in this book, it is a responsibility given, not taken or assumed, and all have the capacity for leadership should they be called upon because it takes many forms. Though some are asked to bestow their gifts to light fires, others are tasked as firekeepers, and both roles are equally important. We all have many roles, but as scholars I have come to see one of these in some sense to be firekeepers — to help keep the flame for those who have reignited it, taking direction from Indigenous knowledge holders and practitioners such as Chief Spence and the Nishiyuu Walkers. Recounting the stories we're enmeshed in and weaving them together as the strands of decolonization narratives is a worthy practice and one we can do responsibly until we can more fully live our freedom again.

## Call to (En)action

Resurgence attends to and affirms everyday forms of resistance and practices of self-determination, but focusing inward on the reconstitution of Indigenous societies isn't a call for conservative gradualism, abandoning externally oriented or assertive tactics of decolonization. For example, we need barricades that target the flows of Capital feeding the engines of ongoing dispossession. Confrontation with the Corporate State is inevitable and necessary, and it's here that alignments with Settler and non-Indigenous social movements arise. The distinction between transfiguration and transformation speaks to the divergence of decolonial practices for Indigenous peoples and those of Settlers, as well as the problem posed for alliances in the ongoing reductionist, flattening and universalizing tendencies in some of these social movements. Indigenous peoples do have a lot to offer everyone in terms of functional alternatives to the liberal Capitalist State order. However, the epistemic shift of resurgence is to declare Indigenous theory/practices not be judged by what they can contribute to other struggles, nor to be preoccupied with describing our projects in the terms of other theoretical traditions. Instead, we focus on relevance to Indigenous freedom without apology. Indigenous resurgence is about the trans*figurative* potential in diverse, already existent though repressed lifeways for Indigenous peoples. Settler society requires radical trans*formation* or metamorphosis — revolution — to support the structural and material context of decolonization and sustain a decolonial form of relationality with Indigenous peoples. But this project of liberation must be led by Settlers for themselves, addressed to the structures and relations in which they're complicit and benefit from. This complicity arises from the displacement of Indigenous peoples here regardless of intent, origin or marginalization within a now diverse Settler society as relative newcomers, refugees, people of colour, religious or ethnic minorities, and so on. This material fact is how the Settler/Indigenous division continues to be experienced and must be negotiated accordingly. This negotiation and its commitments will be complex and layered for those like myself whose own displacements straddle Indigenous and Settler identifications, but difficulty can't be an excuse for avoidance. We must come to grips with being *unsettled*.

This isn't to redraw repressive divisions in the shared interests and intersections with non–First Nations antioppressive, antiracist, anticapitalist, anarchist, socialist, feminist, queer and (im)migrant movements. Nor to do so with inter-national or inter-continental Indigenous movements, in which critical conversations are needed along linguistic and state borders. There's strength in difference, in working alongside without the impetus to absorb, while also not precluding internal engagements with difference along lines of gender, sex, race, class, dis-/relocation and (dis)ability as requisite elements of resurgence and self-determination (see Kidane and Martineau 2013). The kinship relations within and between Indigenous peoples and their homelands are prioritized, but none of these relationships is closed or given. We're in a nexus of effect and responsibility with all Creation. No more has this been evident than in this age of human-made adversity and environmental catastrophe, and in this INM has acted not just for the Fourth World but also for our shared Earth. Indigenous resurgence and Settler revolution both will provide the context for a true mutual flourishing with our shared mother. Surely this is a call to (en)action for us all.

In her important intervention, *Dancing on Our Turtle's Back*, Leanne Simpson reminds us that rather than storytelling as escapism, it is "a lens through which we can envision our way out of cognitive imperialism, where we can create models and mirrors where none existed, and where we can experience the spaces of freedom and justice" (L. Simpson 2011: 33). The INM practices tell (re)Creation stories that affirm our responsibilities, and we can recall our experience of freedom through them. Here I recall Jeff Corntassel on the importance of witnessing.[10] Anyone who participated in INM rallies, marches or forums will remember how they felt. We were present for the unfolding of these stories, are part of them and as gifts carry the obligation to retell them. Storytelling is not empty repetition but a relational practice — it is where we come alive as peoples. Resurgence is about a reorientation to living from within our own stories once again. The most troubling passage for me in *Wretched of the Earth* has always been Fanon's depiction of a gathering to dance. He wrote that with their "back to the wall," a knife to the throat, the Native is "bound to stop telling stories" (Fanon 2004: 20). What the practices of INM, the journey of Nishiyuu, the Kwakwaka'wakw copper-breaking ceremony on the steps of Victoria's colonial seat, the WSÁNEC-led campaign to reclaim the sacred mountain PKOLS; what these profoundly decolonial practices tell me is that with our backs to the wall, we must never stop telling stories.

## NOTES

1  Storywork requires us to locate ourselves and thereby our responsibilities as storytellers. This is inevitably a story about me. I've been living on the unceded territories of the LEKWUNGEN and WSÁNEC for more than four years. I must raise my hands to the peoples, ancestors and beings of this land that teach me every day. I'm Nahua (with some Nuu Savi Mixtexa ancestry) and my birthplace is México Tenochtitlan. My father's family is originally from Acatlan, Jalisco and Juajuapan/Nuu Dee, Oaxaca. My Abuela Cipriana was a respected *curandera*, gifted in traditional medicine, and she walks with me. I grew up in Winnipeg Treaty 1 territories among my mother's family, second-generation settlers of Welsh-speaking Cymry and German-Russian descent. I speak from my outside/insider position as an allied mestiza woman who displacement displaces in turn. My experience growing up a racialized "Native immigrant in Settler Canada" has produced both the deep sense of affinity and also difference that impels me along this path. My role as a graduate student in political theory embedded in the university and as a participant in Idle No More also indelibly informs my observations here. All mistakes are my own. These are the threads of my *huipil*, still being woven.

2  The work on coloniality of knowledge by Latin American scholars Anabel Quijano and Walter Mignolo, among others, speaks to this.

3  See Coulthard's (2014) important critiques of recognition politics using Fanon, explored in the longer draft of this chapter. The final edited version emphasizes my critical reading of Fanon.

4  See, for example, Tobias 1991 and Tully 2005. The drive for access to territory produces what Patrick Wolfe calls *the logic of elimination* as the organizing principle of settler society and its relationship with Indigenous peoples, though this does not always

manifest straightforwardly as genocide. Strategies toward the diminution, dissolution and replacement of Indigenous societies can involve their reconstitution and integration through various forms of "resocialization" and "biocultural assimilation" into the new society, but also the neutralization, minoritization and symbolic appropriation of Nativeness because total erasure may conflict with the needs of Settler nationalism (Wolfe 2006: 388).

5    Discussing eminent Nebraska thinker Vine Deloria, Coulthard (2010) suggests that

> it is a profound misunderstanding to think of land or place as simply some material object of profound importance to Indigenous cultures (although it is this, too); instead it ought to be understood as a field of relationship of things to each other. Place is a way of knowing, experiencing and relating with the world — and these ways of knowing often guide forms of resistance to power relations that threaten to erase or destroy our sense of place.

6    Marxist geographer David Harvey has argued that "primitive accumulation" or appropriation of land is not a stage in the development of capitalism, but its perpetual condition of ravenous expansion, part of a broader "accumulation by dispossession." De-/reterritorilization is appropriate in several senses to describe its effect here, including the removal of already-present territorial or "governing" order and inscription of another, as well as the subsequent alienation of "Native labour" from their attachments to land and disrupting the continuity of Indigenous modes of production. I understand *space* as the generalizable projection of an area between dimensional points, empty of meaning against *place*, imbued with human meaning. This is pertinent to the application of the "spatial abstractions of the modern nation-state" (Sparke 2005: 49) over Indigenous places and their co-constitutive relation with collective identity. That is, the abstraction of Indigenous cultural identities from their homelands into a virtual space of recognition devoid of implications for addressing dispossession.

7    Italian Marxist Antonio Gramsci suggested prefiguration to mean designing popular institutions and organizations such as cooperatives to integrate a nascent revolutionary politics in the everyday of the worker and avoid reproducing authoritarianism. This establishes the context for a move beyond counterhegemony and a cycle of domination. A call to prefiguration can be read in Fanon's depiction of breaking the link of tradition and resistance following the "fighting" stage of nationalism in anticolonial struggle (see Gibson 1999: 419–20). For Indigenous peoples, this does not come in the break from tradition, but as a strengthening of these links.

8    David Lynes suggests that resistance to colonialism can imply a "debilitating dialectic" between cultural and political imperatives (Lynes 2002: 1043) and thus the longer the tradition of resistance, "the greater the need to represent this resistance as itself part of the evolving nature of the cultural tradition to be affirmed" (1061).

9    He made this comment at the First Annual Meeting of the Native American and Indigenous Studies Association in Minneapolis in 2009.

10    During the roundtable "Settler Colonialisms: Solidarities, Territorialities and Embodiment" as part of the workshop "Anti-Racist and Indigenous Politics in Canada: Divergence and Convergence." Congress at University of Victoria, June 4, 2013.

## REFERENCES

Alfred, Taiaiake, and Jeff Corntassel. 2005. "Being Indigenous: Resurgences against Contemporary Colonialism." *Government and Opposition* 40, 4.

Alfred, Taiaiake and Tobold Rollo. 2014. "Resetting and Restoring the Relationship Between Indigenous Peoples and Canada." In Kino-nda-niimi Collective (ed.), *The Winter We Danced*. Winnipeg, MB: Arbeiter Ring Publishing.

Archibald, Jo-ann. 2008. *Indigenous Storywork: Educating the Heart, Mind, Body, and Spirit*. Vancouver: University of British Columbia Press.

Cabral, Amilcar. 1979. "National Liberation and Culture [1970]." Translated by Michael Wolfers. In Amilcar Cabral, *Unity and Struggle: Speeches and Writings of Amilcar Cabral*. New York: Monthly Review Press.

Carroll, William K. 2010. "Crisis, Movements, Counter-Hegemony: In Search of the New." *Interface* 2, 2.

Chalmers-Brooks, Katie. 2013. "The Great Equalizer." *On Manitoba* (Fall). <http://issuu.com/umanitoba/docs/onmb_fall_2013/12>.

Coulthard, Glen. 2014. *Red Skin, White Masks: Rejecting the Colonial Politics of Recognition*. Minneapolis: University of Minnesota Press.

____. 2013. "Past and Present: the First Nations Quest for Justice in Canada." *Singing a New Song: Creating a Renewed Relationship with First Nations*. Conference. Victoria, BC: Parish of St. John the Divine (April 26).

____. 2010. "Place against Empire: Understanding Indigenous Anti-Colonialism." *Affinities* 4, 2.

____. 2008. "Beyond Recognition: Indigenous Self-Determination as Prefigurative Practice." In Leanne Simpson (ed.), *Lighting the Eighth Fire: The Liberation, Resurgence, and Protection of Indigenous Nations*. Winnipeg, MB: Arbeiter Ring Publishing.

____. 2007. "Subjects of Empire: Indigenous Peoples and the 'Politics of Recognition' in Canada." *Contemporary Political Theory* 6, 4.

Day, Richard J.F., and Tonio Sadik. 2002. "The B.C. Land Question, Liberal Multiculturalism, and the Spectre of Aboriginal Nationhood." *BC Studies* 134.

Deloria Jr., Vine. 1998. "Intellectual Self-Determination: Looking at the Windmills in Our Minds." *Wicazo Sa Review* 13, 1.

Doxtater, Michael G. 2004. "Indigenous Knowledge in the Decolonial Era." *American Indian Quarterly* 283, 4.

Fanon, Frantz. 2008. *Black Skin, White Masks*. Translated by Richard Philcox. New York: Grove Press.

____. 2004. *The Wretched of the Earth*. Translated by Richard Philcox. New York: Grove Press.

____. 1994. *Toward the African Revolution*. Translated by Haakon Chevalier. New York: Grove Press.

____. 1968. *The Wretched of the Earth*. Translated by Constance Farrington. New York: Grove Press.

Gibson, Nigel C. 1999. "Radical Mutations: Fanon's Untidy Dialectic of History." In Nigel C. Gibson (ed.), *Rethinking Fanon: The Continuing Dialogue*. Amherst, NY: Prometheus Books.

Gramsci, Antonio. 1971. *Selections from the Prison Notebooks*. Translated by Quinton Hoare and Geoffrey Nowell Smith. New York: International Publishers.

Harvey, David. 2004. "The 'New' Imperialism: Dispossession by Accumulation." *Socialist Register* 40, 63–87.

Henderson, James Sa'ke'j Youngblood. 2000. "Ayukpachi: Empowering Aboriginal Thought." In Marie Battiste (ed.), *Reclaiming Indigenous Voice and Vision*. Vancouver: University of British Columbia Press.

Kidane, Luam, and Jarret Martineau. 2013. "Building Connections Across Decolonization Struggles." *ROAR Magazine* (October 29). <roarmag.org/2013/10/african-indigenous-struggle-decolonization/>.

King, Hayden. 2013. "We Natives Are Deeply Divided. There's Nothing Wrong with That." *Globe and Mail,* January 9. <theglobeandmail.com/commentary/we-natives-are-deeply-divided-theres-nothing-wrong-with-that/article7096987/>.

Kulchyski, Peter. 2005. *Like the Sound of a Drum: Aboriginal Cultural Politics in Denendeh and Nunuvut*. Winnipeg: University of Manitoba Press.

Lavoie, Judith. 2013. "Students Focus on Social Stigma at Idle No More Rally." *Victoria Times Colonist,* January 26. <timescolonist.com:news:local:students-focus-on-social-stigma-at-idle-no-more-rally-1.57427>.

Little Bear, Leroy. 2004. "Aboriginal Paradigms, Implications for Relationships to Land and Treaty-Making." In Kerry Wilkins (ed.), *Advancing Aboriginal Claims: Visions/Strategies/Directions*. Saskatoon, SK: Purich.

Lynes, David A. 2002. "Cultural Pain vs. Political Gain: Aboriginal Sovereignty in the Context of Decolonization." *Ethnic and Racial Studies* 25, 6.

Mack, Johnny. 2011. "Hoquotist: Reorienting through Storied Practice." In Hester Lessard, Rebecca Johnson, and Jeremy Webber (eds.), *Storied Communities: Narratives of Contact and Arrival in Constituting Political Community*. Vancouver: University of British Columbia Press.

Memmi, Albert. 1992. *The Colonizer and the Colonized*. Translated by Howard Greenfeld. Boston: Beacon Press.

Murphy, Rex. 2013. "A Rude Dismissal of Canada's Generosity." *National Post,* October 19. <fullcomment.nationalpost.com/2013/10/19/rex-murphy-a-rude-dismissal-of-canadas-generosity/>.

Palmater, Pamela. 2013. "Aboriginal Sovereignty Doesn't Need a 'Royal' Proclamation." *Rabble,* June 8. <rabble.ca/blogs/bloggers/pamela-palmater/2013/10/aboriginal-sovereignty-doesnt-need-royal-proclamation>.

Press, Jordan, and Michael Woods. 2013. "Idle No More Movement 'Different' from Anything the Government Had Ever Seen Before, Documents Reveal." *Postmedia News,* April 10. <canada.com/Idle+More+movement+different+from+anything...er+seen+before+documents+reveal/8218741/story.html — ixzz2QrV3lyWk>.

Sartre, Jean-Paul. 2001. "Colonialism Is a System." *Colonialism and Neocolonialism*. Translated by Azzedine Haddour, Steve Brewer, and Terry McWilliams. London: Routledge.

____. 1992. "Introduction." Translated by Howard Greenfeld. In Albert Memmi, *The Colonizer and the Colonized*. Boston: Beacon Press.

Schwartz, Daniel. 2013. "Idle No More Prepares for Day of Action, Activists Give Their Take on the Movement." *CBC News,* October 7. <cbc.ca/news/canada/idle-no-more-prepares-for-day-of-action-1.1913429>.

Sekyi-Otu, Ato. 1997. *Fanon's Dialectic of Experience*. Cambridge, MA: Harvard University Press.

Simpson, Audra. 2013. "The Chief's Two Bodies." Native American and Indigenous Studies Association Annual Meeting. Saskatoon, Saskatchewan (June 15).

____. 2007a. "On Ethnographic Refusal: Indigeneity, 'Voice' and Colonial Citizenship." *Junctures* 9.

____. 2007b. "On the Logic of Discernment." *American Quarterly* 59, 2.

Simpson, Leanne. 2013a. "I Am Not a Nation-State." *Indigenous Nationhood Movement.* November 6. <nationsrising.org/i-am-not-a-nation-state/>.

____. 2013b. "Fish Broth and Fasting." *Divided No More.* January 16. <dividednomore. ca/2013/01/16/fish-broth-fasting/>.

____. 2012. "Aambe! Maajaadaa! (What #IdleNoMore Means to Me)." *Decolonization: Indigeneity, Education and Society.* December 21. <decolonization.wordpress. com/2012/12/21/aambe-maajaadaa-what-idlenomore-means-to-me/>.

____. 2011. *Dancing on Our Turtle's Back: Stories of Nishnaabeg Re-creation, Resurgence, and a New Emergence.* Winnipeg, MB: Arbeiter Ring Publishing.

Sparke, Matthew. 2005. *In the Space of Theory: Postfoundational Geographies of the Nation-state.* Minneapolis: University of Minnesota Press.

Tobias, John L. 1991. "Protection, Civilization, Assimilation: An Outline History of Canada's Indian Policy." In J.R. Miller (ed.), *Sweet Promises: A Reader on Indian–White Relations in Canada.* Toronto: University of Toronto Press.

Tully, James. 2005. "Exclusion and Assimilation: Two Forms of Domination in Relation to Freedom." In Melissa Williams and Stephen Macedo Nomos (eds.), *Political Domination and Exclusion.* New York: New York University Press.

____. 2000. "The Struggles of Indigenous Peoples for and of Freedom." In Duncan Ivison, Paul Patton, and Will Sanders (eds.), *Political Theory and the Rights of Indigenous Peoples.* Cambridge: Cambridge University Press.

Waziyatawin (Angela Cavender Wilson). 2004. "Reclaiming Our Humanity: Decolonization and the Recovery of Indigenous Knowledge." In Devon Mihesuah and Angela Cavender Wilson (eds.), *Indigenizing the Academy, Transforming Scholarship and Empowering Communities.* Lincoln: University of Nebraska Press.

West, Douglas A. 1995. "Epistemological Dependency and Native Peoples: An Essay on the Future of Native/Non-Native Relations in Canada." *Canadian Journal of Native Studies* 15.

Wolfe, Patrick. 2006. "Settler Colonialism and the Elimination of the Native." *Journal of Genocide Research* 8, 4.

Chapter Nine

# A FOUR DIRECTIONS MODEL
## UNDERSTANDING THE RISE AND RESONANCE OF AN INDIGENOUS SELF-DETERMINATION MOVEMENT

*Jeff Denis*

On December 21, 2012, thousands of Indigenous peoples and their allies gathered in towns, cities and reserves across Canada to hold rallies, round dances and prayer circles to honour Indigenous self-determination and protect the earth, air and water. Simultaneously, Chief Theresa Spence of the Attawapiskat First Nation in Northern Ontario entered Day 10 of a hunger strike to raise awareness of her people's "Third World" living conditions and to call on Canada to fulfill its nation-to-nation treaty obligations. For months, such events, known together as the Idle No More (INM) movement, dominated Canadian news media and even gained international attention and support. How can we explain the rise and resonance of INM, one of the largest and potentially most transformative Indigenous movements in the history of Turtle Island?

The Medicine Wheel: A Four Directions Model
of Indigenous Self-Determination Movements
Non-Indigenous theories of social movements and protest activities are amply considered elsewhere (e.g., Goodwin and Jasper 2004; McAdam et al. 1996; Meyer 2004; Snow et al. 2007; Tarrow 2011; Tilly 2004). Here, I use an Indigenous teaching tool, the Medicine Wheel, to suggest a new model of Indigenous self-determination

movements that incorporates relevant Indigenous and non-Indigenous theories. Although I am a Canadian of European descent, several Anishinaabe Elders and Indigenous scholars have encouraged me to use and adapt the Medicine Wheel for research purposes. My aim is to help bring Indigenous theoretical concepts into a still-colonial academic setting. As the introduction to this book suggests, this is not without tensions because it includes the risk that my approach becomes a "White expert" misappropriation and misinterpretation. However, I hope my adaptation of the Medicine Wheel is useful as an orienting framework to help identify the conditions that gave rise to Idle No More, thereby offering not only theoretical understanding but also practical insights to support Indigenous resurgence.

In brief, the Medicine Wheel is a "centred and quartered circle" symbolizing many traditional teachings in many Indigenous cultures (Brant Castellano 2011: 43) (see Figure 1). The four quadrants may represent the four directions (north, east, south, west), four elements (earth, air, water, fire), four stages of life (infancy, adolescence, adulthood, old age), or the unity and diversity of the human race. Often, they depict a holistic understanding of health and well-being that includes analytically distinct but empirically interconnected physical, intellectual, emotional and spiritual elements.

**Figure 1 Medicine Wheel**

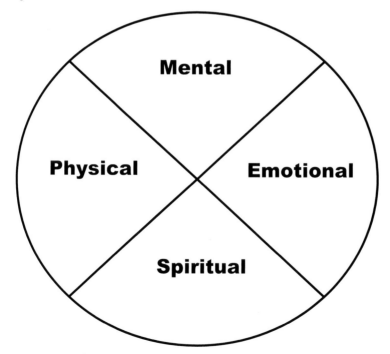

To be healthy and whole, these four aspects within the self and between the self, other humans and the natural environment must be in balance. As Onkwehonwe scholar Taiaiake Alfred (2012) asserts, "Indigenous resurgence ... is a linked movement that's cultural, spiritual, political and physical, everything all together." What does this mean in practice?

*Physical/Material Conditions*

In the physical or material realm, Indigenous self-determination requires Indigenous bodies on the land, on the water and in the streets. At a basic level, it attests to the reality that Indigenous peoples are here to stay despite centuries of genocidal and assimiliationist policies. Indeed, Indigenous peoples are the fastest growing of any racial, ethnic or national group in Canada, now comprising 1.4 million people or 4.3 percent of the total population, an increase of 20 percent over the last 5 years (Statistics Canada 2013). With a birth rate 1.5 times the Canadian average, they are a young population, with a median age of 27 (compared with 40 for non-Indigenous Canadians). Nearly 30 percent of Indigenous people are under the age of 15. In conventional social movement terms, this means that many are "structurally available" for mobilization (Snow et al. 1980).

More than half of the Indigenous peoples in Canada now live in cities. Urban Indigenous peoples face many challenges, including frequent encounters with racism, identity denial (questions about "authenticity"), and persistently poorer socioeconomic and health outcomes than their non-Indigenous counterparts. Nevertheless, they have created vibrant urban communities with friendship and community centres, healing lodges and other hubs in which Indigenous peoples from various nations gather, share experiences, and develop a sense of common interests and grievances (Environics Institute 2010; Urban Aboriginal Peoples Task Force 2007). Many urban Indigenous peoples retain strong connections to their traditional homelands, visiting back and forth; there is a high degree of mobility of both people and ideas between cities, towns and reserves (Hall 2013). Consequently, social ties within and increasingly between Indigenous nations are dense, especially among young people. Although tensions may arise between on- and off-reserve Indigenous populations (Lawrence 2004), these demographic developments potentially enhance organizational capacity and resemble those that, according to Nagel (1995), supported the rise of the 1970s American Indian Movement (AIM).

In INM, another important material or technological factor is social media. As in the Arab Spring (Brym et al. 2014), Facebook, Twitter, YouTube and other online tools were used, for instance, to create memes such as "Ottawapiskat" and "upsettlers." Participants, especially young people, used blogs, Twitter, and Indigenous print, radio and television media to help spread awareness and share information;

communicate when and where events would take place; express outrage; and expand activist networks, including internationally. Despite often crushing economic poverty, most First Nations, Métis and Inuit people in Canada, including remote northern communities, have broadband connections. At the movement's height in Winter 2013, participants shared pictures and videos from rallies, round dances and teach-ins around the world, including Indigenous nations from Australia to Greenland to Palestine, and supporters from Los Angeles to London. Local events were contextualized as part of an expanding global movement. Critically, Indigenous peoples decided what information and images to share, offering alternative frames to one another and (potential) allies, and making their presence felt across cyberspace.

This increased visibility online and in the media, especially Indigenous and alternative media, was matched by the reoccupation of physical space by Indigenous peoples and their allies in the form of round dances at major downtown intersections, marches on legislatures, and blockades of highways and rail lines. Chief Spence and Elders risked their lives with hunger strikes to draw attention to poverty and treaty violations. Indigenous youth, trekking thousands of kilometres from Northern Quebec, Saskatchewan and elsewhere to Parliament Hill in Ottawa, embodied and imprinted on the land a formidable message of Indigenous resurgence. As Anishinaabe academic, artist and activist Leanne Simpson puts it, such gestures join less-visible everyday acts of living on and from the land as a critical form of Indigenous self-determination: "Being on the land, living as an Nishnaabekwe and doing things that connect my children to the land is ... a deliberate act — a direct act of resurgence, a direct act of sovereignty" (2012).

*Intellectual/Cognitive Conditions*

Indigenous communities' long-standing but often thwarted efforts against dispossession and for social justice mean that Canada has experienced multiple "waves" of protest and resurgence (e.g., Coulthard 2012; Wilkes 2006). Some of them are well-known, even within mainstream society, evoked by names such as Elijah Harper and Donald Marshall, and places such as Oka and Ipperwash. But such waves of (de)colonization are being theorized in new ways within Indigenous communities.

Elementary and high schools, universities and colleges have all played critical roles in perpetuating colonialism as sites for the forcible assimilation of Indigenous peoples and the marginalization of Indigenous knowledges, practices and ways of being (e.g., Battiste 1986; Tuhiwai Smith 1999). In Chapter One of this book, James (Sa'ke'j) Youngblood Henderson describes how residential schools, in which thousands of Indigenous children were abused and died, brought Indigenous families "to the abyss" with lasting, often devastating, intergenerational consequences. Yet post-secondary institutions today are, to some extent, being Indigenized, even if

Indigenous faculty and students continue to be underrepresented and sometimes ghettoized in under-resourced Indigenous Studies programs. These decolonizing spaces, however incomplete, partial and fragmented, are now home to blossoming Indigenous theorizing and mentorship.

Despite persistent inequalities in the funding of on-reserve schools compared to off-reserve schools and persistently high Indigenous high school drop-out rates, more Indigenous students are graduating from high school and university than ever before. Currently, more than 22,000 Indigenous students attend university or college in Canada (Statistics Canada 2007). Between 2001 and 2006, the number of Aboriginal university graduates increased by one-third (Friesen 2013). Forty-one percent of Indigenous people aged 25 to 64 now have a university or college degree, compared with 56 percent of non-Indigenous Canadians. As Indigenous academic Winona Wheeler puts it:

> My generation was the first to get into postsecondary in any numbers and we raised a generation of kids in that environment … They've had more opportunities to see the options out there. They've been raised in an environment that gave them more critical thinking powers. (Quoted in Friesen 2013)

Some might challenge this view of universities as places of critical thinking, particularly for Indigenous students. For instance, remarking on the extent to which the university is an alienating place for Indigenous peoples, a student once said to Patricia Monture, "This is the same as the residential school, except that now we come here willingly" (2010: 26). Yet, insofar as Indigenous scholars in universities have certified "expertise" recognized outside of Indigenous communities, they may be more easily heard in mainstream society. At the height of INM, many Indigenous and allied academics were called on by Indigenous and other media to "make sense" of events, and many wrote powerful op-eds, organized teach-ins, and spoke out knowledgeably and passionately to support the movement (e.g., Kino-nda-niimi Collective 2014). Moreover, they know the Western education system from "the inside" and can both strategically use and sometimes challenge it.

Meanwhile, across Canada, there has been a return to traditional knowledge and cultures; and to learning and renewing the beliefs, principles and ways of Indigenous ancestors. Centuries-old efforts to maintain these knowledge systems and practices, against genocide and assimilation policies, are experiencing new impetus. Many Anishinaabe communities in Northern Ontario, for example, have recently developed language immersion camps, cultural workshops, and programs in which children are taken out on the land to learn from Elders. This is a huge shift from a generation ago, which directly experienced the abuse of residential schools.

*Emotional/Affective Conditions*

Increasing education and awareness in both traditional and mainstream-critical senses — in the context of ongoing colonialism — tends to create and reinforce the emotional conditions for collective action. Many Indigenous peoples seek well-paid jobs and opportunities in mainstream society (e.g., Environics 2010). At the same time, they seek to protect and revitalize traditional cultures and communities and to live as Indigenous peoples, on their lands, according to their laws and principles (see, for instance, Alfred and Corntassel 2005; Coulthard 2007; Simpson and Ladner 2010). Increasingly, they expect to be able to do both. Self-determination does not mean rejecting everything Western, but choosing whether and how to engage with or use traditional and mainstream knowledge and practices (e.g., Newhouse and Long 2011).

When governments apologize for historical mistreatment and promise to forge a "new relationship" based on "partnership" and "respect," in Prime Minister Stephen Harper's words (Government of Canada 2008), this further raises expectations. These expectations are repeatedly dashed when these same governments deny Canada's history of colonialism, cut Aboriginal health funding, refuse a public inquiry into the more than 1,100 missing and murdered Indigenous women across Canada, withhold residential school documents from the Truth and Reconciliation Commission (TRC), try to legally defend their chronic underfunding of First Nation schools and child welfare agencies, abandon land claim negotiations and eliminate environmental review processes. The widening gap between the official state rhetoric of reconciliation and respect and the realities of an ongoing, one-sided colonial relationship contribute to frustrated expectations for more just Indigenous-settler relations.

As Dene scholar Glen Coulthard argues, this frustration and anger has "critically transformative potential" (2012). Anger and resentment are necessary spurs to revolutionary, anticolonial action. Whether labelled "structural strain" (Smelser 1962), "relative deprivation" (Davies 1962), "moral shock" (Jasper 1998), or simply "grievances," these emotions arise not only from historical trauma but also from the ongoing appropriation and destruction of Indigenous lands, political impositions on Indigenous nations, socioeconomic and health disparities, and the social exclusion and marginalization of Indigenous peoples, despite rhetoric to the contrary. The necessary motivations for Indigenous uprisings have long existed.

Equally important, however, is critical hope. At a TRC event in Toronto in 2012, a group of Indigenous and settler youth brainstormed strategies to overcome colonialism and improve intergroup relations. Their optimism and passion for change was striking. According to a "Commitment of Reconciliation" that they drafted together and read aloud to 600 audience members:

> We, the youth from all nations at this gathering, came to listen and learn about the Indian residential school experience, which has hurt so many people across this land ... We respectfully acknowledge that solidarity ... means opening space in our hearts, in our minds, and in our schools for Indigenous well-being ... We commit every day to stamping out our colonial mindsets and replacing them with acceptance, support and appreciation of one another ... We commit to fostering relationships ... respectful dialogue ... and lobbying for change. We commit to be the change we want to see.

Although many youth may be alienated or overcome by self-destructive tendencies or apathy, there is also a growing sense of empowerment and pride in Indigenous identities and cultures, a desire to productively use anger against historical and ongoing injustices and a deep commitment to decolonization. Despite its shortcomings, the TRC creates opportunities to develop a shared critique of current Indigenous-settler relations and a sense that common action is necessary and possible.

*Spiritual Conditions*
The spiritual realm is largely neglected by social movements scholars within the mainstream non-Indigenous literature. Some sociological research does emphasize the role of Black churches in the Civil Rights movement (e.g., McAdam 1982). These churches were a source of social networks supporting mobilization and communication, and well-developed frames and metaphors that charismatic leaders such as Martin Luther King, Jr. could use to arouse supporters. To some extent, Indigenous spiritual traditions and networks were used in similar ways by INM activists and orators. Yet this alone fails to capture critical aspects of the spiritual dimensions of the movement.

Many Indigenous nations have a prophecy. The Anishinaabe call it the 8th Fire; other nations have other names for it. After seven generations of colonization and its devastating consequences, the people will begin to wake up and revive traditions. They will come to a fork in the road where they must choose between the current path of greed, competition and destruction; where some individuals get very wealthy at the expense of widespread poverty and polluted air, water and soil; or an alternative path of working together to find new ways of living that will restore balance to both social relations and the ecosystems on which we depend (e.g., Simpson 2008).

It has been about seven generations since Confederation, and leading up to INM, many signs suggested that the prophecy was being fulfilled: climate change, natural disasters, human-made disasters. Alternatives for future generations, centred on

Indigenous vitality, were becoming visible through a range of initiatives, including efforts to revitalize Indigenous languages and cultures, and protect the environment and even growing numbers of non-Indigenous people seeking guidance from Indigenous Elders. Thus, many wondered, "Is now the time? Is this the 8th Fire?"

The day before the first national INM Day of Action on December 10, 2012, sacred fires were lit. Ceremonies were held at numerous locations across Turtle Island. Organizers vowed to remain peaceful and positive. They creatively used spiritual practices — smudging, prayer circles, singing and drumming — in their tactical repertoires. Indigenous protest was thus at the same time an assertion of cultural identity and spiritual strength. The round dance quickly became an emblem for the movement, with strangers joining hands and dancing in circles in streets, shopping malls, public squares and university campuses — physically and often joyfully reclaiming space. Ceremonies guided decision-making. Symbols such as the Medicine Wheel and the Two-Row Wampum (or Guswenta), at once a spiritual and political concept, appeared in public discourse.

Thus far, I have written as if the four elements of the Medicine Wheel were distinct. They are not, of course. For instance, intellectual and cultural revitalization efforts inform the emotional realm in which shame is increasingly replaced by pride

**Figure 2 Four Directions Model of Indigenous Self-Determination Movements**

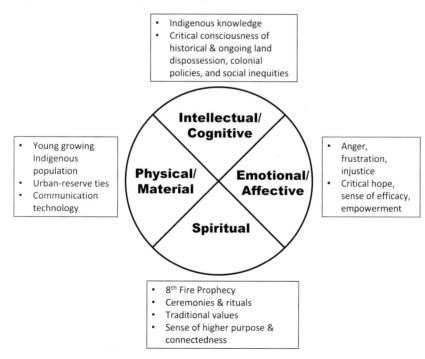

in Indigenous identities and a desire to learn and apply traditional knowledge and skills to the contemporary world. Indigenous knowledge is not simply cognitive but also physical, spiritual and emotional, embodied in holistic ways of being that involve intimate, sacred relationships with local ecological systems. Resurgence depends on well-connected Indigenous bodies on the land and water, engaged in reclaiming activities at once physical and spiritual. In short, all four interlinked elements are necessary for an Indigenous self-determination movement to emerge (see Figure 2).

*Triggers and Flashpoints: How the "2013 White Paper" Sparked a Movement*
Missing from this model, however, is a trigger to set the wheel in motion. When identifying triggers, mainstream scholarship speaks of openings in the political opportunity structure (McAdam 1982) or alternatively of threats or closing opportunities (Van Dyke and Soule 2002). Anishinaabe legal scholar John Borrows (2005) offers a more precise theory: what he calls "flashpoint" events in Indigenous communities depend on three precipitating factors: 1) the government violates an Indigenous or treaty right; 2) the government authorizes unwanted development on Indigenous lands or waters; and 3) negotiations fail (cf. Russell 2010). INM followed this pattern.

Under the Canadian Constitution (Canadian Constitution Act 1982), governments are legally obligated to "consult and accommodate" Aboriginal peoples about legislation that might infringe on their rights, lands or resources. In international law, the standard is higher: the United Nations Declaration on the Rights of Indigenous Peoples, reluctantly endorsed by Canada in 2010, guarantees Indigenous peoples rights to self-determination; to meaningful participation in decisions that impact them; and to free, prior and informed consent before states implement legislative or administrative measures that may affect them. Some Indigenous scholars (e.g., Corntassel and Holder 2008; Coulthard 2007; Hayden King in Chapter Seven of this book) argue that Indigenous rights to self-determination are inherent and do not depend on any colonial constitution nor on the United Nations. That said, the Canadian federal government clearly violated the UN Declaration and perhaps even its own Constitution when it drafted Bill C-45 in Autumn 2012. The omnibus budget bill was more than four hundred pages long and changed forty-four federal Acts, including everything from labour rights to criminal justice and environmental legislation. Changes to the Indian Act facilitated the "surrender" of reserve lands, including to non-Indigenous individuals or corporations, and gave the Minister of Aboriginal Affairs more control in that process. The Navigable Waters Protection Act was also overhauled, reducing the number of lakes and rivers subject to federal environmental assessment by 99 percent — from 32,000 lakes and 2.25 million rivers to only 97 lakes and 62 rivers. The Bill also removed many fish habitat protections. Why would the government do this?

These changes expedite natural resource extraction for oil, gas and minerals and the building of pipelines to transport tar sands along the Northern Gateway from Alberta to the Pacific Coast, along the Trans-Canada to the Atlantic Coast and along the Keystone XL, to Texas. In the context of a world capitalist system, struggling to recover from the worst financial crisis since the Great Depression and with unabated demand for fuel, Canada's "Economic Action Plan" depends on it. Yet many of these activities do or will take place on Indigenous territories. With an eye to short-term profit, and an apparent strategy of turning Canada into a "petro-state" (Nikiforuk 2012), the federal government and corporate oil lobbyists seek secure access to "Indian" lands, including limited environmental regulations.

Significantly, Indigenous peoples were not meaningfully "consulted" or "accommodated," much less approached for free, prior and informed consent. Moreover, the federal Conservatives used their "majority" of seats, but only 40 percent of the popular vote, to pass the Bill without substantial parliamentary or public discussion. At the same time, they have proposed or passed at least nine other pieces of legislation affecting First Nations education, drinking water, matrimonial rights and other domains. Under the First Nations Financial Transparency Act, which passed in March 2013, for example, the government requires public disclosure of financial information from First Nation governments and First Nation–owned businesses, creating an(other) unfair advantage for non-Indigenous businesses and increasing colonial state surveillance of Indigenous communities.

Mi'kmaq scholar Pamela Palmater has called this suite of legislation the "2013 White Paper" for its not-so-thinly-veiled assimilationist agenda. In her words:

> This legislative agenda ignores First Nation sovereignty and jurisdiction, violates First Nation laws, violates Treaty and Aboriginal rights, violates the United Nations Declaration on the Rights of Indigenous Peoples to have free, informed and prior consent, transfers jurisdiction from the feds to the provinces, transfers liability without funding and increases government control over First Nations … Canada's objective is assimilation … None of this legislation is dealing with the crisis happening right now in First Nations. (2013)

On December 4, 2012, when the federal government was set to pass Bill C-45, four First Nation chiefs split from an Assembly of First Nations meeting across the river in Gatineau, Quebec. With a handful of supporters, they arrived at the House of Commons, asserting that they had not been consulted and were there to discuss the Bill. Security guards physically blocked them from entering, and Bill C-45 was passed. In response, one Chief said:

> Wait and see what happens when they try to come to our lands … The

Prime Minister [is] sell[ing] our resources out to the world … He says there are going to be jobs for us [from natural resource development] … Sweeping the floor while some company … takes billions out of our territory is not the answer to poverty in our communities … Enough is enough. Our people … are fed up with this government that's passing legislation. They haven't consulted us. They don't have our consent. They're breaking their own laws, the United Nations Declaration, the Canadian Constitution … We've tried everything. We've met Members of Parliament, we've met the Senate, we've made petitions, we've written letters, [and] nobody is listening to us.

Warning that Indigenous peoples would take "direct action," another chief stated:

We're serving notice to the Canadian government that we will not be bullied anymore by their legislation and their laws. We don't recognize them. We are our own people, our own sovereign entity. We're asserting our sovereign right as a people to this land. (Quoted in Barrera and Jackson 2012)

## Indigenous Leadership: Taking a Stand

Four grassroots women in Saskatchewan, three Indigenous and one non-Indigenous, led the struggles against the government's colonial legislation. On Facebook, First Nations lawyer Sylvia McAdam said that in Canadian law, silence is interpreted as consent. Thus, if Bill C-45 or similar proposed legislative changes infringed on their rights or the health of Mother Earth, they must take a stand. Jessica Gordon replied "We're all being far too idle. We're going to be idle no more!" (Van Gelder 2013). After consulting Elders and conducting ceremonies, these four women began organizing teach-ins and rallies to raise awareness of the impending legislation. Soon, activists across the country followed suit under the banner "Idle No More." Eventually, a loose-knit group of activists organized a National Day of Solidarity and Resurgence on December 10, 2012. The immediate goal was to prevent the omnibus budget Bill C-45 from passing through the Senate, but the wider aim was to make a broad statement about Indigenous sovereignty and treaty rights, and our shared responsibility to protect the land, air and water for future generations.

The next day, another female Indigenous leader burst into the spotlight: Chief Theresa Spence announced that she would refuse to eat solid foods until the government took action to improve living conditions in her community, which had declared a state of emergency in 2011 due to an ongoing housing crisis.

She demanded that the prime minister and the governor-general, as Crown representative, meet with First Nation leaders across the country to discuss their nation-to-nation relationship and take concrete steps to honour the treaties and respect Indigenous rights. As Elders joined Chief Spence in her hunger strike, it galvanized media attention and spurred on the movement. The rallies and teach-ins grew; they began to be held across Canada daily and even spread to other countries: from Norway to Nicaragua to New Zealand. The flash mob round dance became a household name, alongside more conventional blockades of railways and highways and other direct actions. On January 11, 2013, INM events were held in at least 265 locations around the world, drawing tens of thousands of supporters <j11action.com>.

An Indigenous self-determination movement was born. There was no central organizing structure, but many loosely connected activists from different nations with different histories, languages, traditions and relationships with the Canadian and other states. All were united against colonialism, for self-determination, and for protection of Mother Earth.

## Possible Objections

Is this theory overdetermined, with too many variables to explain a single case? As many Indigenous scholars have argued, most events are multiply determined; the world "doesn't work in either-or-fashion," and the goal of social science should be to seek "complex understanding" in which "we begin to see a phenomenon from various perspectives" (Newhouse 2002, quoted in Brant Castellano 2010: 44). Moreover, the four directions model is not meant to explain INM alone, but the rise of Indigenous self-determination movements generally: The factors here may emerge and combine in different ways in different movements and waves of protest.

Others might argue that INM is nothing new; Indigenous peoples have resisted colonization ever since Europeans first set foot on Turtle Island (Coburn 2013; Coulthard 2012; Ritskes 2013). In the Canadian context, INM can be seen as an extension of the legacies of Poundmaker, Tecumseh, Louis Riel, Deskaheh, Harold Cardinal, Elijah Harper, the KI-6, Oka, Ipperwash, Gustafsen Lake, Caledonia, Grassy Narrows, the Lubicon Cree, Barriere Lake, Burnt Church, Anishinaabe Park, Goose Bay, Temagami and countless other cases. However, INM is, at the very least, a new phase in an ongoing decolonization movement. It is distinguished by how quickly and widely it spread, from small rallies in a dozen places on December tenth to a three thousand–strong convergence on Ottawa on December twenty-first, to hundreds of events attended by tens of thousands in dozens of countries on January eleventh.

The movement's distinctiveness is also suggested by the traction of the "Idle

No More" name. The name overlooks the many years of hard work and struggle among long-time activists and ordinary Indigenous peoples who have renewed their traditions and languages, despite colonial policies. But it resonated with those who had never been politically engaged. My recent research in Northwestern Ontario (Treaty 3 Territory) documents a "political avoidance norm" (Denis 2011) whereby, in daily interaction, many Indigenous people and settlers separate the interpersonal from the systemic and avoid open discussions of racism and colonialism. Particularly in the small towns in which these groups constantly interact, many choose keep their heads down and not rock the boat. As one Anishinaabe resident of Fort Frances, Ontario said, "The fundamental problem is that we've never ever talked about it [racism or colonialism]. And we don't want to ... We don't." According to another: "Our people are just so passive and orderly, it's like we don't want to hurt people's feelings."

It is difficult to fight back after centuries of land dispossession and coercive assimilation. Moreover, Indigenous peoples are vastly outnumbered by settlers with more money and weapons, including the official state force. Yet these statements were made a few years before INM. On December 21, 2012, more than three hundred Anishinaabe of all ages (and some non-Indigenous supporters) marched on the town of Fort Frances with banners reading "Anishinaabe Insurgence, Colonialism Disrupted!", "We are all treaty people" and "As long as the rivers flow, our rights will be honoured." The pent-up anger and frustration had finally burst, and many Anishinaabe felt empowered and hopeful for the first time. As one young man said:

> I am not afraid today to take a stand because this is not only about my future, but there will be a day when I have children, and I will sit down with them and look back ... I want [them] to say, "Daddy was there. Daddy fought for your rights." (Jeremy Jordan, quoted in Hicks 2012)

As a distinct phase in a broader and long-standing Indigenous self-determination movement, INM requires its own explanation. The four directions model begins to provide the necessary "complex understanding."

### Responses and Responsibilities of Settler Canadians to Idle No More

According to political process theory (McAdam 1982; Tarrow 2011), social movement outcomes depend on reciprocal interactions with the forces under contention, whether state or nonstate actors. Although international attention and support for INM was substantial, the responses of non-Indigenous Canadians were mixed.

Among many settlers, there was a strong backlash and evidence that some Canadians became more entrenched in racist views. In Edmonton and elsewhere, tempers flared and non-Indigenous individuals rammed into demonstrators with their trucks. In Northern Ontario, an Anishinaabe colleague received an email from a stranger saying "How 'bout you worry more about teaching your little future burdens on the social system to hold jobs not picket signs?" In Thunder Bay, an Indigenous woman was raped and left for dead; the White men who assaulted her reportedly said, "You Native people don't deserve your treaty rights" (CBC 2013).

Meanwhile, Conservative media questioned the veracity of Chief Spence's hunger strike, fundamentally misinterpreting her gesture, as Kelly Aguirre explains after Leanne Simpson (see Chapter Eight of this book). Sun News held a contest for the best description of Spence with published results including "fat, oink, garbage, chief two-chins, and stop sucking Lysol." The comments sections of online newspapers, as well as coffee shop conversations across Canada, were filled with the usual rancour: "Why are they protesting again? What do they want now? Those are my tax dollars! Get over it!" Supporting these stories with numbers, an Ipsos Reid (2013) poll of 1,023 Canadians in January 2013 found that although 38 percent of Canadians approved of Idle No More, 62 percent disapproved. Only 29 percent supported Chief Spence's hunger strike, with 71 percent disapproving. Despite the movement's peaceful tactics and inclusive messaging, a majority of settlers did not support it.

On more general questions, 60 percent of Canadians agreed that "Most of the problems of Native peoples are brought on by themselves," an increase from 35 percent in 1989, the year before Oka. A majority of Canadians, 64 percent, also agreed that "Aboriginal peoples receive too much support from Canadian taxpayers," and 81 percent said that no more funding should go to First Nations until "external auditors can be put in place to ensure financial accountability." These widespread opinions perpetuate stereotypes that have been discredited by studies showing that corruption and mismanagement levels in First Nation communities are no greater than in Canadian municipalities (Warry 2007).

Another recent survey (N=120) found that the percentage of non-Indigenous Canadians who believe that the 2008 residential school apology was sufficient to atone for historical mistreatment of Indigenous peoples and that no follow-up action is necessary has increased over time (Bombay and Denis 2014). This trend is especially prominent among Canadians whose national identity is highly "central" to their sense of self, who currently feel low pride in their Canadian identity and who score high on standard measures of racial prejudice. Together, these data point to pervasive "laissez-faire racism" — a tendency to blame Indigenous peoples for their problems and reject meaningful policies or practices to address them (Denis 2011, 2012a).

At the state level, the federal government initially tried to ignore INM, as did most provincial governments. But as Chief Spence's hunger strike continued and captured international headlines, the ruling Conservatives and their supporters attempted to blame Spence for her community's plight, accusing her of financial mismanagement. During the hunger strike, a damning audit report was released that showed a history of poor to questionable accounting practices at the Attawapiskat First Nation. What most media and right-wing politicians ignored, however, was that financial management had improved since Chief Spence's election, and that even if all federal funding had been spent as intended, it would not be nearly enough to relieve the long-standing housing, educational and healthcare needs in her community.

As public pressure mounted, Prime Minister Harper eventually agreed to meet with the Assembly of First Nations (AFN) executive, but without the governor-general, who represents the Crown partner of many First Nations–settler treaties. In response, Chief Spence and many other chiefs from Ontario, Manitoba and Saskatchewan boycotted the meeting. On January eleventh, they and thousands of grassroots INM supporters rallied outside the building in Ottawa in which the pivotal meeting was held. Inside, the AFN national chief presented a list of eight demands. Although the Harper government agreed to "high-level discussions" on treaty implementation, land claims and resource revenue sharing, it refused to repeal the relevant legislation and rejected all other demands, including calls for equitable school funding and for a public inquiry into missing and murdered Indigenous women.

Despite the rather cooperative and pragmatic approach of the AFN, its project funding was subsequently cut by 30 percent, or $1.7 million. Moreover, the federal government added new language to the annual contribution agreements of many First Nation communities whereby 2013–14 funding (for health and social services, education, housing, physical infrastructure and so on) would be contingent on support for Bill C-45 and other controversial legislation. When some First Nations refused to sign, citing blackmail, they were warned again that all funding would be discontinued. Meanwhile, in March 2013, the Journey of Nishiyuu — seven Cree youth and an Elder who walked nearly 1,600 kilometres from Northern Quebec, joined along the way by hundreds of Indigenous and non-Indigenous supporters — arrived in Ottawa. Their aim was to meet the prime minister and deliver a message about respect for Indigenous rights and the environment; the prime minister instead attended a photo-op with panda bears, newly arrived from China, at the Toronto Zoo. In short, the federal government's response was to ignore, blame, punish, coerce and refuse to act on INM concerns in any meaningful way.

From a sociological perspective, such backlash is unsurprising; it is consistent with group threat theory (Blumer 1958; Bobo 1999). In systems of racial domination and colonialism, when historically marginalized groups begin to fight back, the dominant group will feel threatened and do everything it can to maintain its power and privileges — starting perhaps with subtle forms of coercion, but turning increasingly to brute force if it does not get its way (Jackman 1994).

### Indigenous Resurgence and Our "Last Best Hope"

Nevertheless, many Indigenous participants said the support expressed by non-Indigenous Canadians for INM was the most they had ever witnessed from non-Indigenous Canadians. At every INM event I attended, a significant number of non-Indigenous allies actively participated in round dances and attended teach-ins and rallies for Indigenous and treaty rights and environmental protection. Some, especially younger Canadians, reported a growing awareness and deepening commitment to these issues. Even the police took a largely hands-off (and, in a few cases, an encouraging) approach. On Facebook, images of young Ontario Provincial Police officers drumming and singing alongside Indigenous protesters at Mishkeegogamang and Aamjiwanang First Nations circulated. At one rally in Toronto, when INM protesters shut down the busy downtown intersection of Yonge and Dundas and burst into a round dance, I overheard a White police officer tell an Indigenous onlooker, "It's good they are doing this. As long as it remains peaceful, people need to have their voices heard." In Ontario, this more conciliatory approach may stem in part from the new Framework for Police Preparedness for Aboriginal Critical Incidents (Ontario Provincial Police 1996), which developed after the shooting death of Anishinaabe protester Dudley George at Ipperwash Park in 1995. Progressive politicians, environmentalists, labour unions, church groups, immigrant organizations, artists, writers, academics and student groups all pledged public support for INM. Prominent Indigenous and allied musicians collaborated on a free downloadable album called "Idle No More: Songs for Life."

Against the expectations of group threat theory, a substantial minority of settler Canadians did not feel threatened and instead supported Indigenous self-determination. Arguably, these settlers understand their relationship with Indigenous peoples as a "treaty partnership." Indigenous peoples have unique identities, cultures and rights to political autonomy, and they must be respected; yet, according to the spirit of a treaty, Indigenous peoples and settler Canadians are also allies who have a shared responsibility to support one another in times of need and protect the environment for future generations. At least some of our ancestors understood the nation-to-nation relationship this way when they signed the original peace and friendship agreements in the seventeenth and eighteenth centuries; it is the premise of the Two-Row Wampum (1613), and it is the way many INM activists framed Indigenous-settler relations in public discourse.

The challenge for non-Indigenous allies is to educate fellow settlers and convince them that supporting INM and related movements is both a moral imperative and is in our long-term, collective interest. As I have argued:

> When corporate profit is privileged over the health of our lands and waters, we all suffer. When government stifles debate, democracy is

diminished. Bill C-45 is just the latest in a slew of legislation that under-mines [Indigenous rights but also] Canadians' rights. In standing against it, the First Nations are standing for us too.

Second, as Justice Linden of the Ipperwash Inquiry said, "we are all treaty people." When our governments unilaterally impose legislation on the First Nations, they dishonour the Crown, they dishonour us, and they dishonour our treaty relationship. We are responsible for ensuring that our governments fulfill their commitments. If our governments do not respect Indigenous and treaty rights, then the very legitimacy of the Canadian state — and thus of all our citizenship rights — is in doubt [because non-coerced treaties are the only ethical foundation for Canada itself]. That's what Idle No More is about. (Denis 2012b)

In addition to normative arguments about our responsibilities to one another and the earth, settlers may be reminded that it is economically beneficial to invest in Indigenous peoples. As Pamela Palmater explains, it takes

$100,000 to put one aboriginal man in prison for a year [but only] $60,000 to give him a four-year education … For every one dollar you put into a First Nations child, you save $7 down the road. There is no other invest-ment in this country that gives you that kind of payback. Canadians could be making money off us. But they would rather pay through the nose to keep us impoverished. (Quoted in Becking 2013)

Yet some Canadians apparently would "rather pay through the nose to keep [Indigenous peoples] impoverished" and under settler control; they are motivated by pride and a desire to protect their perceived status relative to Indigenous peoples (Blumer 1958; Bobo 1999; Denis 2011).

Others may simply be unaware of the stakes for Indigenous peoples and Canada, given the narrowness of the mainstream media and an educational system that ignores the colonial foundations of Canada. Many settlers live segregated enough lives to avoid daily confrontation with Indigenous realities. Such Canadians must be presented with historical and contemporary facts about Indigenous–colonial relationships and compelling stories to remind them that "we are all treaty people." We need to co-exist peacefully together and with the land. As Pamela Palmater says, supporting Indigenous and treaty rights may be "our last best hope" of protecting Mother Earth and all our rights. Idle No More may no longer be in the headlines. But it lives on in teach-ins, healing walks, blockades and eviction notices being issued to resource-extraction companies that fail to respect Indigenous rights. It lives on in the minds, bodies, hearts and souls of Indigenous peoples and their supporters, many of whom were politicized and empowered by this movement.

INM has been a critical part of struggles for Indigenous self-determination; these struggles are far from over.

## REFERENCES

Alfred, Taiaiake. 2012. "Idle No More." Edmonton: Acimowin CJSR 88.5 FM, December 20. <youtube.com/watch?v=JAwvAcGFn9Q>.

Alfred, Taiaiake, and Jeff Corntassel. 2005. "Being Indigenous: Resurgences against Contemporary Colonialism." *Government and Opposition* 40, 4.

Barrera, Jorge, and Kenneth Jackson. 2012. "Chiefs Take Fight to House of Commons' Doorstep." *Aboriginal Peoples Television Network*, December 4. <aptn.ca/pages/news/2012/12/04/chiefs-take-fight-to-house-of-commons-doorstep/>.

Battiste, Marie. 1986. "Micmac Literacy and Cognitive Assimilation." In Jean Barman, Yvonne Hébert, and Don McCaskill (eds.), *Indian Education in Canada: Volume 1: The Legacy.* Vancouver: University of British Columbia Press.

Becking, Marci. 2013. "Genocide, Genocide, Genocide." *Anishinabek News*, April 15. <anishinabeknews.ca/2013/04/15/genocide-genocide-genocide/>.

Blumer, Herbert. 1958. "Race Prejudice as a Sense of Group Position." *The Pacific Sociological Review* 1.

Bobo, Lawrence. 1999. "Prejudice as Group Position: Microfoundations of a Sociological Approach to Racism and Race Relations." *Journal of Social Issues* 55, 3.

Bombay, Amy, and Jeffrey S. Denis. 2014. "Modern Racism, Canadian Identity, and Responses to the Residential School Apology." Unpublished manuscript.

Borrows, John. 2005. "Crown and Aboriginal Occupations of Land: A History and Comparison." Report prepared for the Ipperwash Inquiry.

Brant Castellano, Marlene. 2011. "Elders' Teachings in the Twenty-First Century: A Personal Reflection." In David Long and Olive Patricia Dickason (eds.), *Visions of the Heart: Canadian Aboriginal Issues,* third edition. Don Mills, ON: Oxford University Press.

Brym, Robert, et al. 2014. "Social Media in the 2011 Egyptian Uprising." *British Journal of Sociology* 65.

Canadian Constitution Act. 1982. <laws-lois.justice.gc.ca/eng/const/page-15.html#h-38>.

CBC (Canadian Broadcasting Corporation). 2013. "Thunder Bay's Aboriginal Population Fears Racism and Violence." *CBC News*, February 20. <cbc.ca/news/canada/thunder-bay-s-aboriginal-population-fears-racism-and-violence-1.1391361>.

Coburn, Elaine. 2013. "'Idle No More' and Indigenous Resurgence." Congress 2013. Victoria, BC.

Corntassel, Jeff, and Cindy Holder. 2008. "Who's Sorry Now? Government Apologies, Truth Commissions, and Indigenous Self-Determination in Australia, Canada, Guatemala, and Peru." *Human Rights Review* 9, 4.

Coulthard, Glen S. 2012. "#IdleNoMore in Historical Context." *Decolonization: Indigeneity, Education and Society* (December 24).

____. 2007. "Subjects of Empire: Indigenous Peoples and the 'Politics of Recognition' in Canada." *Contemporary Political Theory* 6. <decolonization.wordpress.com/2012/12/24/idlenomore-in-historical-context/>.

Davies, James. 1962. "Toward a Theory of Revolution." *American Sociological Review* 27, 1.

Denis, Jeffrey S. 2012a. "Transforming Meanings and Group Positions: Anishinaabe-White Relations in Northwestern Ontario, Canada." *Ethnic and Racial Studies* 35, 3.

____. 2012b. "Why 'Idle No More' Is Gaining Strength, and Why All Canadians Should Care." *Toronto Star*, December 20. <thestar.com/opinion/editorials/2012/12/20/ why_idle_no_more_is_gaining_strength_and_why_all_canadians_should_care. html>.

____. 2011. "Canadian Apartheid: Boundaries and Bridges in Aboriginal-White Relations." PhD dissertation. Cambridge, MA: Department of Sociology, Harvard University.

Environics Institute. 2010. *Urban Aboriginal Peoples Study: Main Report.* Toronto: Environics. <uaps.ca>.

Friesen, Joe. 2013. "What's Behind the Explosion of Native Activism? Young People." *Globe and Mail*, January 18.

Goodwin, Jeff, and James M. Jasper (eds.). 2004. *Rethinking Social Movements: Structure, Meaning, and Emotion.* New York: Rowman and Littlefield.

Government of Canada. 2008. "Statement of Apology — to Former Students of Indian Residential Schools." June 11. <aadnc-aandc.gc.ca/eng/1100100015644/11001000 15649>.

Hall, Thomas D. 2013. "Indigenous Peoples, Frontiers and Self-Determination." Paper. New York: 108th American Sociological Association Conference.

Hicks, Duane. 2012. "'Idle No More' Takes Hold Here." *Fort Frances Times*, December 24. <fftimes.com/node/256642>.

Ipsos Reid. 2013. "Fast Fallout: Chief Spence and Idle No More Movement Galvanizes Canadians around Money Management and Accountability." January 15. <ipsos-na. com/news-polls/pressrelease.aspx?id=5961>.

Jackman, Mary. 1994. *The Velvet Glove: Paternalism and Conflict in Gender, Class, and Race Relations.* Los Angeles and Berkeley: University of California Press.

Jasper, James M. 1998. "The Emotions of Protest: Affective and Reactive Emotions in and Around Social Movements." *Sociological Forum* 13, 3.

Kino-nda-niimi Collective. 2014. *The Winter We Danced: Voices from the Past, the Future, and the Idle No More Movement.* Winnipeg, MB: Arbeiter Ring Publishing.

Lawrence, Bonita. 2004. *"Real" Indians and Others: Mixed-Blood Urban Native Peoples and Indigenous Nationhood.* Vancouver: University of British Columbia Press.

McAdam, Doug. 1982. *Political Process and the Development of Black Insurgency, 1930–1970.* Chicago: University of Chicago Press.

McAdam, Doug, John D. McCarthy, and Mayer N. Zald (eds.). 1996. *Comparative Perspectives on Social Movements: Political Opportunities, Mobilizing Structures, and Cultural Framings.* New York: Cambridge University Press.

Meyer, David S. 2004. "Protest and Political Opportunities." *Annual Review of Sociology* 30.

Monture, Patricia. 2010. "Race, Gender and the University: Strategies for Survival." In Sherene Razack, Malinda Smith, and Sunera Thobani (eds.), *States of Race: Critical Race Feminism for the 21st Century.* Toronto: Between the Lines.

Nagel, Joane. 1995. "American Indian Ethnic Renewal: Politics and the Resurgence of Identity." *American Sociological Review* 60, 6: 947–65.

Newhouse, David, and David Long. 2011. "Conclusion: Reconciliation and Moving Forward." In David Long and Olive Patricia Dickason (eds.), *Visions of the Heart:*

*Canadian Aboriginal Issues,* third edition. Don Mills, ON: Oxford University Press.

Nikiforuk, Andrew. 2012. "Canada's Hard Turn Right: A New Petrol State Has Emerged." *Adbusters,* June 26. <adbusters.org/magazine/102/canadas-hard-right-turn.html>.

Ontario Provincial Police. 1996. "A Framework for Police Preparedness for Aboriginal Critical Incidents." Field Support Bureau, Provincial Command, Field and Traffic Services. <attorneygeneral.jus.gov.on.ca/inquiries/ipperwash/policy_part/projects/pdf/OPP_Appendix_E_Framework_for_Police_Preparedness.pdf>.

Palmater, Pamela. 2013. "Idle No More: What Do We Want and Where Are We Headed?" *Rabble,* January 4.<rabble.ca/blogs/bloggers/pamela-palmater/2013/01/what-idle-no-more-movement-really>.

Ritskes, Eric. 2013. "The Sustainability of Indigenous Resistance." *Decolonization: Indigeneity, Education and Society.* January 22.

Russell, Peter. 2010. "Oka to Ipperwash: The Necessity of Flashpoint Events." In Leanne Simpson and Kiera L. Ladner (eds.), *This Is an Honour Song: Twenty Years Since the Blockades.* Winnipeg, MB: Arbeiter Ring Publishing.

Simpson, Leanne. 2012. "Aambe! Maajaadaa! (What #IdleNoMore Means to Me)." *Decolonization: Indigeneity, Education and Society,* December 21.

____. 2008. *Lighting the Eighth Fire: The Liberation, Resurgence, and Protection of Indigenous Nations.* Winnipeg, MB: Arbeiter Ring Publishing.

Simpson, Leanne, and Kiera L. Ladner (eds.). 2010. *This Is an Honour Song: Twenty Years Since the Blockades.* Winnipeg, MB: Arbeiter Ring Publishing.

Smelser, Neil J. 1962. *Theory of Collective Behavior.* Glencoe, IL: Free Press.

Snow, David A., Sarah A. Soule, and Hanspeter Kriesi (eds.). 2007. *The Blackwell Companion to Social Movements.* Oxford, UK: Blackwell Publishing.

Snow, David A., Lewis Zurcher Jr., and Sheldon Ekland-Olson. 1980. "Social Networks and Social Movements: A Microstructural Approach to Differential Recruitment." *American Sociological Review* 45.

Statistics Canada. 2013. "National Household Survey, 2011: Aboriginal Peoples in Canada: First Nations People, Métis and Inuit." Catalogue no. 99-011-X2011001. <12.statcan.gc.ca/nhs-enm/2011/as-sa/99-011-x/99-011-x2011001-eng.cfm>.

____. 2007. "Educational Portrait of Canada, 2006 Census: Aboriginal Population." Catalogue no. 97-560-XIE2006001. <12.statcan.ca/census-recensement/2006/as-sa/97-560/p15-eng.cfm>.

Tarrow, Sidney G. 2011. *Power in Movement: Social Movements and Contentious Politics,* third edition. New York: Cambridge University Press.

Tilly, Charles. 2004. *Social Movements, 1768–2004.* Boulder, CO: Paradigm.

Tuhiwai Smith, Linda. 1999. *Decolonizing Methodologies: Research and Indigenous Peoples.* London: Zed Books.

Urban Aboriginal Peoples Task Force. 2007. *Final Report.* Commissioned by the Ontario Federation of Indian Friendship Centres, the Ontario Métis Aboriginal Association, and the Ontario Native Women's Association.

Van Dyke, Nella, and Sarah A. Soule. 2002. "Structural Social Change and the Mobilizing Effect of Threat: Explaining Levels of Patriot and Militia Organizing in the United States." *Social Problems* 49, 4.

Van Gelder, Sarah. 2013. "Why Canada's Indigenous Uprising is About All of Us." *Yes! Magazine,*

February 7. <yesmagazine.org/issues/how-cooperatives-are-driving-the-new-economy/why-canada2019s-indigenous-uprising-is-about-all-of-us>.

Warry, Wayne. 2007. *Ending Denial: Understanding Aboriginal Issues.* Toronto: Broadview.

Wilkes, Rima. 2006. "The Protest Actions of Indigenous Peoples: A Canadian-U.S. Comparison of Social Movement Emergence." *American Behavioral Scientist* 50, 4.

Chapter Ten

# RHYTHMS OF CHANGE
## MOBILIZING DECOLONIAL CONSCIOUSNESS, INDIGENOUS RESURGENCE AND THE IDLE NO MORE MOVEMENT

*Jarrett Martineau*

On the evening of the 2012 winter solstice, I was up late editing a post written by Anishinaabe comedian and media producer Ryan McMahon for the Indigenous music platform Revolutions Per Minute. According to the Western world's dubious and anxious misreading of the Mayan calendar, it was the day before the world was supposed to end — the eve of the apocalypse. But the apocalypse was the furthest thing from my mind. The week prior, Chief Theresa Spence of the Attawapiskat First Nation began a hunger strike, demanding a meeting between Indigenous leaders, the Crown, and the Harper government "to meet with First Nation leaders and engage in meaningful dialogue on our rights" (ipsmo 2012) and to discuss the broken treaty relationship between Canada and Indigenous nations. Spence began her hunger strike "in protest of continuing governmental abuses against First Nations," contending that "Canada is violating the right of Indigenous peoples to be self-determining and continues to ignore our constitutionally protected Aboriginal and treaty rights in their lands, waters, and resources" (ipsmo 2012). Her calls went unanswered, however, and as her fast deepened into its first week, Grand Chief Derek Nepinak, head of the Assembly of Manitoba Chiefs, boldly declared that "The 'long silent war drums' of First Nations people will pound again if [Chief] Spence dies from her hunger strike" (aptn 2012: 1). But the drums had already started.

Idle No More was exploding all around us. Ryan's piece, appropriately titled "The Round Dance Revolution," tried to make sense of this spontaneous unfolding of Indigenous cultural and political action and the "mind-boggling confusion, anger, sadness and happiness" that it invoked (McMahon 2012: 1).

Ryan and I messaged back and forth as I was editing to compile a list of flash mob round dances being planned in the days ahead. More than two dozen events were being organized in urban centres and Indigenous communities across Turtle Island in that week alone. An update blinked across my timeline. The Indigenous DJ crew A Tribe Called Red had just released a new song on its SoundCloud. I clicked through to listen. It began with the drums. "The Road" is an introspective instrumental with a haunting lead melody, an insistent rhythm and a pow-wow–sampled vocal chorus that departs from the group's more overtly dance floor–oriented club tracks. It reverberated with a prescient sense of the movement's evolving form and affective potency: at once melancholic and triumphant, longing, hopeful and defiantly resistant. It captured in sound and carried in spirit the essence of the movement's resonant tension between force and restraint, outrage and introspection; it pushed and pulsed with a determined, rhythmic insistence and restless *motion* — an intangible, dynamic and energetic flow that, haunted by memory, resounded a renewed presence. It was moving. Inevitably, relentlessly forward. "The Road" was the calm before the storm, the anticipation of a *future anterior* world that will have already arrived. The world was not ending; it was beginning again.

We published Ryan's "Round Dance Revolution" piece late that evening, and I woke up the following morning to find the world still very much intact, albeit synchronously transformed. I woke up to the news that the Zapatistas had re-emerged. Masked-clad and silent, they mobilized 40,000 strong and marched through five towns in Chiapas, marking exactly 20 years to the day since the EZLN had first taken them over by military force. But this time there were no weapons. There was only the sound of their steps and the occasional cries of support from local villagers. Their message was clear: *To be heard, we march in silence*. Later in the day, the EZLN issued a brief communiqué that stated, simply:

> To whom it may concern:
> Did you hear it?
> It's the sound of your world crumbling.
> It's ours re-emerging.
> The day that was the day, was night.
> And night will be the day, that will be day
> —*Translation Collective 2012: 1*

This is a story of re-emergence.

## Idle No More

#IdleNoMore flashed onto screens and then exploded into public consciousness in the late fall of 2012. Its hashtag origin belied the fact that the movement marked the resurgent transformation of Indigenous activism on Turtle Island, forged in the mediatized spaces of the digital, that bloomed into a wave of resistant action shaped by a heady mix of spectacular protest, cultural assertion and spirited dissent. Idle No More not only gave renewed voice to the long continuum of Indigenous resistance struggles against colonialism and the ongoing, lived oppression of our peoples but also to our continued survival, presence and fugitive movement to "break *from* and *through* colonial enclosures to (re)discover ... open spaces of imagination and creativity" (Martineau and Ritskes 2014: X). Critically, it was a movement conceived and organized by the leadership of Indigenous women, operating outside of the mainstream Canadian political establishment and Indian Act governance structures and organizations. Idle No More grew rapidly: virally accelerating across media platforms and through flash mob round dances staged in shopping malls across Turtle Island and around the world. Striking simultaneously at the heart of capitalist consumerism at the height of the holiday shopping season and at the contemporary state of Indigenous absence in the public imaginary — in which Indigenous peoples have been disappeared, forcibly erased or rendered invisible — Idle No More signalled a collective rejection of colonial abjection and dispossession, a communal return to presence. The movement gave form and force to long-standing currents of Indigenous frustration against Settler society's biopolitical push to force us into the margins of bare-life survival (Agamben 1998: 65).

Idle No More promised an affirmative politics of presence in resistance to the imminent encroachment of death by neglect wrought by the destruction of our lands, waters and air through large-scale, transnational corporate development and resource extraction; and institutionalized forces of colonialism advanced by Settler governments through legislation and policy. Idle No More embodied the corporeal represencing of our peoples in a collective *becoming together* enacted through the Indigenous reoccupation and reclamation of public space. The movement drew inspiration, in tactical form if not in purpose, from recent contemporary global social movements that have also performed resistance through place-based actions discursively framed in the language of occupation. "Occupation," as W.J.T. Mitchell suggests, "is not only a visual and physical presence in a space but a discursive and rhetorical operation ... It is a demand in its own right, a demand for *presence*, an insistence on being heard" (2012: 10). Idle No More occupied multiple spaces and modalities of Indigenous resistance that were rooted in, and dynamic expressions of, Indigenous cultural, political, artistic and ceremonial praxis.

In this chapter, I argue that the Idle No More movement was mobilized in conflicted and contradictory sites of visibility and vulnerability in which its technologically coded communicative forms enabled, but also limited, its transformative political potential. I trace the movement's mediatization and concurrent attempts to forge resurgent languages of decolonial struggle constituted in flux and motion. "To create new forms of politics," which Saul Newman suggests "is the fundamental theoretical task today — requires new forms of subjectivity" (2012: 147). Idle No More sought to mobilize decolonial consciousness and grounded collective action, but its reliance on communicative technologies both precoded and limited its efficacy and potential. Although the movement initially created an affective transformation of public consciousness in Canada among both Indigenous and non-Indigenous populations, Idle No More's spontaneity produced an unsustainable aesthetics of immediacy, urgency and intensity. The movement thus reconfigured the temporality of Indigenous resistance according to the flow of code and the logic of the network, where circulation and movement are both generative and restrictive; powerfully immediate, yet deeply mediated. As Federico Campagna and Emanuele Campiglio note, "Politics of rebellion seem increasingly to incorporate the struggle between the voice and the limiting conditions in which it can be heard, between resistance and the annihilating counter-revolution of its spectacle" (Campagna and Campiglio 2012: 3). Idle No More occupied the dialectical space of this contested opening; where the ruptural performance that gives the struggle voice and spectacular visibility simultaneously marks its discursive limits and re-enclosure within the networked logics of colonial-capitalism.

## The Round Dance Revolution

The Round Dance Revolution was both a representational gesture of Indigenous resistance and performance, and a self-affirmation of Indigenous continuity, presence and struggle. It operated at both levels and frequencies simultaneously, making visible the disparity between Settler colonial realities and the lived experiences of Indigenous peoples, dispossessed from our homelands and territories. The round dances were an evocative interimage of indigeneity that reterritorialized Indigenous presence beyond the normative borders in which it is often inscribed (reservation and rural communities), or otherwise erased. The dual character of the round dance form was underscored by its repetition in public spaces: shopping malls, main intersections and government buildings.

The first Idle No More teach-in was organized by a group of Indigenous and non-Indigenous women in Saskatchewan in November 2012 to discuss the impending passage of omnibus Bill C-45 — which proposed unilateral changes to the Indian Act, the Fisheries Act, the Canadian Environmental Assessment Act, and

*Idle No More Round Dance, Victoria, B.C. 21 December 2012 (Photo credit: Keri Coles)*

the Navigable Water Act — all with serious implications for Indigenous nations, treaty rights and the radical reduction of environmental protection for lakes and rivers (Coulthard 2014: 160). Following the teach-in, the flash mob round dance was mobilized as a tactical form of resistant performance that self-authorized Indigenous presence in public spaces and brought Indigenous cultural and ceremonial practices into the view of Settler society. The round dance is a cultural form that originates among Indigenous nations of the prairies, but finds parallels and equivalence in the tea dances and drum dances of the north, and social and ceremonial dance forms among many Indigenous nations (Martin, 2013: 1). The form's inherent variability and transmutability, with its emphasis on social inclusion, participation and healing, encouraged broad-based participation; and the round dances spread rapidly and virally from urban centres to far-reaching and remote communities throughout Turtle Island. In one week in December 2012, for example, movement organizers in the greater Vancouver area mobilized more than one thousand people daily, in a wave of round dances held throughout the city.

The technique was simple: Create a Facebook event page, call local drummers and singers to perform, and invite community members and supporters to attend at a specific time and place. Gather, sing, disperse. In the early weeks of Idle No More, hundreds and then thousands of Indigenous bodies filled shopping malls across Turtle Island for temporary gatherings, where the sound of our hand drums and traditional songs echoed through the hallways of capitalist consumption, interrupting shoppers' attention, and bringing new acoustic resonance into the semipublic and Muzak–filled banal spaces of the everyday. The round dances brought spirit, energy and music *inside* the atriums of capitalism; and our songs and dances into auditory contact and visible dialogue with Settler society and government. And many did not know what to make of these simultaneously defiant and celebratory actions. Were they acts of resistance? Performance? Celebration? Or all the above?

The Idle No More round dances performed what Stephen D'Arcy calls a "disruptive convergence," in which "a crowd physically overruns a space, so that it can no longer be used in the way required by [a governing] institution or system" (2014: 91). The round dances ruptured both physical and symbolic spaces by transforming them through ceremony and bodies. This convergent technique of "disruptive outburst," as D'Arcy suggests, took "the form of insurgent street theatre performances in unauthorized spaces" (2014: 91) that disrupted the quotidian rhythms of the colonial-capitalist status quo by calling attention to asymmetries of power and the irrepressible spirit of Indigenous presence.

The heartbeat of Idle No More was, is and remains the drum. In the many territories in which round dances were held, the drum was the centre; the organizing principle and rhythmic force by which resistance was given voice in song. The songs performed at the round dances ranged from warrior songs and ceremonial chants to social and contemporary songs, thereby making visible not only the intergenerational survival and continuance of the songs themselves — and the song carriers who bring them forth in the present — but also their resilience and adaptability to new contexts and iterations. In this way, the round dances performed an apposite movement through remembrance and futurity, presence and return. As one CBC news report noted: "The Idle No More flash mobs are a part of … returning a beat, a song and a dance to the heart of the territories where they were born, and where they still thrive" (Martin 2013: 2).

The round dances' spirit of defiance against colonial erasure and self-affirmative celebration of Indigenous resistance called on Settler society to witness them as *performance*, join them in *celebration* of Indigenous resilience and survival, and to heed them as a *call to responsibility* — to account for historical injustice and to literally join hands with our people in building new relationships of solidarity and mutual understanding. For our own nations and peoples, this spectacularized performance brought Indigenous Peoples into mutual visibility for *each another*, thereby reaffirming and recognizing our shared presence and resistance.

Although the Idle No More movement was extensively documented and shared on social media, while its dynamic archive of evolving digital content was distributed across these channels, its techniques of circulation also called attention to the fleeting temporality of "disruptive outbursts," in which autonomous assertions of indigeneity (like the round dances) produced affective appeal, but not systemic change. Although the round dances were at once irruptive, eruptive and disruptive, their détourning of popular consciousness could only temporarily refigure the transit of indigeneity in the public mind. Indigenous struggles that had long remained marginalized or invisible were now brought into hypervisibility, thereby making them legible (and susceptible) to power, control and surveillance. In this conflicted push to give voice to our struggles and bring attention to our grievances, the movement was recast within an aestheticized regime of political performance, drawn into the machinic gaze of technology, and encoded according to the representational logic of spectacle.

## Networked Resistance

Idle No More embodied the dialectical nature of contemporary social movements that are bolstered by digital technologies of distribution and dissemination. They provide multiple actors with voice, influence and access to audience beyond established political channels and structures, yet such movements remain subject to the privatized strictures of code that dictate their spectacularized rise and fall in the public imagination. Although movements that are accessible to diverse publics and ostensibly to democratic or horizontal organizational forms are lauded for their inclusive and participatory forms, the metrics used to celebrate their success can also be used to denigrate their failure as they decline in public presence and pageviews. To this extent, mediatized movements remain vulnerable to shifting public sentiment and criticism by virtue of the form of their articulation and the techniques used in their creation and dissemination. Idle No More — as digitally encoded hashtag and social movement — was already subject to a latent potential for formal "collapse," even at the height of its online popularity.

But the movement moved within and beyond the limits of the digital to create an affective experience of potentiality among participants: the *sense* that change was imminent (despite this not being borne out by reality). Idle No More refused the confinement and enclosure of coloniality and cultivated decolonial consciousness: "the freedom to imagine and create an elsewhere in the here; a present future beyond the imaginative and territorial bounds of colonialism … a performance of other worlds, an embodied practice of flight" (Martineau and Ritskes 2014: IV). The movement was born out of the common experience of lived crisis that is coextensive with Indigenous survival under colonialism, but with the desire to transform it through performance and practice. Campagna and Campiglio describe this spontaneous re-visioning of the present as "the direct practice of *an affective necessity*" (2012: 4, emphasis added), in which the sense of emotional urgency and critical agentic capacity engendered by Idle No More compelled a young generation of digitally connected Indigenous youth and non-Indigenous allies to heed its calls to action. As we asserted our cultural practices, aired our grievances, proclaimed our desires and raised our voices in song, new political potentialities emerged in the discursive break that Idle No More had opened and claimed.

*Idle No More poster by Dwayne Bird (idlenomore.tumblr.com)*

*Idle No More poster by Andy Everson (idlenomore.tumblr.com)*

Like the Occupy Wall Street movement before it, Idle No More both welcomed and encouraged *multiplicity*, without conflating plurality and difference into the nebulous rhetoric of an inchoate multitude. The movement was Indigenous-centred, but neither exclusive nor exclusionary. Idle No More called on "all people," from every background and walk of life, "to join in a peaceful revolution, to honour Indigenous sovereignty, and to protect the land and water" (Idle No More 2013: 1). These broadly stated goals enabled organizers to interweave a vibrant evolving network of intergenerational, intercommunal and international participants. In a literal refusal of "idleness," Idle No More called for collective action against the stasis of the status quo; embodying a self-reflexive call to physical, symbolic, spiritual and cultural *movement* that mobilized supporters around the world.

The movement also sparked a wave of Indigenous cultural production. Art, music and media creation proliferated. Digital content went viral. Videos, visual art, posters, images, slogans and digital memes were continuously published, reproduced, and shared across social media. And the round dances brought our traditional songs into a newly emergent public lexicon. Idle No More took digital and Indigenous cultural forms and remixed them: détourning and repurposing photography, news stories and other artwork as the source material for shared social content and resistant truth-telling. But the movement's virality and memetic diffusion were possible only to the extent that Indigenous participation in digital and online media had reached a necessary critical mass.

Cultural production in contemporary social movements offers a recursive form of creativity that refigures individuated speech acts and communicative action within and through emergent networked collectivities. During Idle No More, Facebook and Twitter provided focal points for the amplification of movement messaging and the real-time coordination of public actions, but the movement enabled a dialogic interplay of forces and voices to be absorbed and reincorporated into its representational flows. These incorporative strategies are tactically effective because of their mobility and fluidity: their adaptive, formless and continuously reforming figuration of *movement* is expressed as constitutive of contemporary resistance. However, movement is also coded by the networks within which it circulates. Idle No More amplified Indigenous participation online, but this also contributed to a disjunction between the perception of the movement's digital reach and influence and its asynchronous impact within "offline" communities and place-based sites of struggle.

## Mediatized Subjects and Spectacular Dissent

In contemporary social movements, temporality and spatiality work both in concert and in conflict. Insofar as the contemporary injunction of social media is to *participate* (users are compelled to write, to represent, to speak), this injunction is primarily temporal: demanding one's *time* (within an economy of attention) rather than a specified *place* of participation. Hardt and Negri have observed that although in previous eras "political action was stifled primarily by the fact that people didn't have sufficient access to information or the means to communicate and express their own views[1] ... today's mediatized subjects suffer from the opposite problem, stifled by a surplus of information, communication, and expression" (2012: 9). This communicative surplus overwhelms us with limitless data and communicative possibilities, and the temporal occupation of our attention becomes spatialized through mediatization, the occupation of consciousness. Mediatization is an emblematic form of contemporary subjectivity in which we are "subsumed or absorbed in the web" (Hardt and Negri 2012: 10). In this view, the "mediatized subject" is not so much alienated, as perpetually *occupied*:

> The consciousness of the mediatized is not really split but fragmented or dispersed. The media, furthermore, don't really make you passive. In

fact, they constantly call on you to participate, to choose what you like, to contribute your opinions, to narrate your life. The media are constantly responsive to your likes and dislikes, and in return you are constantly attentive. The mediatized is thus a subjectivity that is paradoxically neither active nor passive but rather constantly absorbed in attention. (Hardt and Negri 2012: 9)

To effect social transformation without becoming fully "absorbed" by technologically mediated engagement, new subjectivities must be generated through collective action. "Facebook, Twitter, the Internet, and other kinds of communication are useful," Hardt and Negri suggest, "but nothing can replace the being together of bodies and corporeal communication that is the basis of collective political intelligence and action" (2012: 11). Although we would be wise to question the incontrovertibility of this claim, it is clear that one of the subsuming effects of mediatization is to displace other forms of collective action. A central challenge for the Idle No More movement was to navigate (and renegotiate) the tension between digital engagement and "offline" community-based organizing.

The movement first entered this representational regime on Twitter in late November 2012. Within weeks of its first mention, #IdleNoMore took hold of a massive public conversation online. The hashtag trended repeatedly on Twitter, reaching a precipitous height of 58,000 mentions in a single day on January 11, 2013 (Blevis 2014: 1). Until mainstream media reports began to amplify its signals, however, knowledge about the movement and its objectives and goals remained limited. But if access to influence can be redeployed to diffract the focus and intensity of a movement's demands, under mass media scrutiny and attention the movement's internal contradictions and limits can also be brought to light and exaggerated. Online debates routinely degenerate into futile flame wars between and among movement participants and dissenting voices. And the platforms used to coordinate movement planning and resistant actions can be, and are, continuously searched and surveilled by the State and its agencies.

The dual logic of the contemporary aesthetic regime of politics in the digital age is to order space and data as sites of visibility and access. The digital space of circulation is the grid of code, the matrix of big data. In Rancièreian terms, this involves the discursive partitioning of space, the distribution of the sensible; where the normative order is governed by the police, which "disavows ruptures, seams, sutures, gaps because the police is a horizon or landscape of continual continuity" (Gharavi 2011: 2). Social movements like Idle No More, which seek to disrupt this matrix of asymmetrical power must contend with the repressive force of the State (and, by extension, the regime of the police), who work to control circulation and surveil communication to prevent precisely those "ruptures, seams, sutures,

[and] gaps" that movement participants aspire to create. Representational practice within networked movements must be necessarily self-reflexive and attuned to this fraught relationality with power. "Rather than being spectators in a mediated struggle," the South London Solidarity Federation claims, "we must act for ourselves and represent ourselves" (SLSF 2012: 190). Yet self-representation is no guarantor of state-recognized self-determination. Like the Occupy Wall Street movement that preceded it, Idle No More's twinned tendencies toward self-affirmation and external recognition were deeply conflicted. Although Idle No More brought Canadian colonialism into stark focus and public view, it also engendered a significant public backlash.

As the movement circulated, the latent racism of Canadian society became plainly, painfully visible. Indigenous women were increasingly targeted by acts of gendered violence in many communities, including Thunder Bay, Ontario, in which Idle No More was perceived to have "inflame[ed] long-standing tensions between Aboriginal and non-Aboriginal communities" (CBC 2013b). In late December 2012, an Indigenous woman from the Nishnawbe-Aski Nation was brutally sexually and physically assaulted, an attack that was linked directly to Idle No More and investigated by local authorities as a racially motivated hate crime. Following the attack, the survivor, whose name has been protected, issued a public statement in which she urged Indigenous community members to be careful: "Right now with the First Nations trying to fight this Bill [C-45] everyone should be looking over their shoulder constantly because there are a lot of racists out there" (Kappo 2012: 1). Following the attack, and with rising racial tensions and violence in Thunder Bay, "more than a dozen [Indigenous] parents from remote communities chose not to send their children back to Thunder Bay for school [in the winter 2013] semester" (CBC 2013b).

For many movement organizers and participants, contending with increased threats of physical violence and responding to vicious debates in blog comment sections, racist editorial pieces in mainstream media, and a seemingly endless parade of anti-Indigenous "trolls" waging war on social media became a constant preoccupation. The terrain of struggle had been shifted, but an important transformation had also taken place: The movement had forced colonialism into view and, in so doing, into new spaces of discursive contention.

Idle No More made Indigenous resistance to colonialism a front-page story in every major newspaper and media outlet across the country by calling on the State, the Crown, and Settler society to account for ongoing injustices against our peoples and "the broken relationship" (CBC 2013b) between Indigenous Peoples and Canada. The movement successfully interrupted the State's narrative ordering of the colonial present by using embodied acts of performative resistance and communicative dissent to bring attention to the continuity of Indigenous presence amid the state's parallax push to consign colonialism to a "closed chapter" in its soon-to-be-reconciled mythic Settler history. These actions demonstrated that Indigenous Peoples were prepared to contest the State's (re)conciliatory object-ives and resist the assimilative passivity of the status quo. And it *represented* this resistant capacity as an "affective necessity" (Campagna and Campiglio 2012: 4). But despite its spontaneous flourishing, Idle No More could not translate its power into sustained transformations of the juridico-political regimes against which the movement had first been mobilized.

### After the Storm

Idle No More's explosive spectacle crested in the early winter of 2013, due in no small part to the increasing urgency of Attawapiskat First Nation Chief Theresa Spence's hunger strike. Her fast continued for six long weeks. Chief Spence stated that she would continue to fast until the Harper government and representatives of the Crown met with Indigenous leaders to discuss the repeated violation of treaty agreements and Indigenous inherent and treaty rights. She boldly declared that until a meeting was set, she would remain "ready to die for my people" (coo 2013: 1). Flaunting its disregard for her life and well-being, the Harper government refused to respond or agree to a meeting. Protests continued in the streets. Highways, railways and borders were shut down. Round dances were held around the world. Marchers and walkers began spiritual journeys to Ottawa. Others fasted in solidar-ity with Chief Spence. And the media storm began to swirl around Idle No More.

But after widespread debate and outcry over her prolonged fast and its unmet demands, Chief Spence decided to end her hunger strike on January 24, 2013. Following two months of massive public protests, and a disastrously inconsequen-tial January 11th meeting between Prime Minister Harper and First Nations Chiefs (many of whom boycotted the meeting), Spence signed a defanged declaration in partnership with opposition party leaders and Assembly of First Nations Chiefs that called for thirteen points of action. Intended to outline steps for Canada and Indigenous nations to work "towards fundamental change," the declaration was met, instead, with skepticism and disappointment. The movement's first wave of energetic force had been depleted. Idle No More had expected immediate action on its demands, but none had occurred. Although subsequent "days of action" were called for; and more demonstrations, rallies and marches were organized; the movement shifted from its intensifying crescendo of outrage and defiance to a decidedly more moderate (and modest) advocacy for incremental political reform.

The Spence declaration marked a passage from Idle No More's first phase, a cry of urgent protest emphasizing external representation toward a differential spatial configuration of protest actions recentred in place-based knowledge and community. The movement turned away from the overt spectacle of mass protest actions and toward self-affirmative, self-valorizing actions. But for witnesses to the communicative rise of Idle No More through its signifying practices and representational forms, its collapsing statistical metrics were quantified and equated with the movement's veritable "decline." Idle No More began as a spontaneous, horizontal and autonomous movement with organizers distributed across a wide geography of urban, rural, reservation and remote communities. There was no defined leadership, central hierarchy or organizing platform; actions were spontaneously organized through decentralized networks; and anyone could participate. As the movement progressed, there was much discussion of the so-called "grassroots" people, whom Idle No More claimed to represent. But as the movement continued from winter 2012 into spring 2013, Idle No More ignited a debate over the revolutionary subject of the movement's resistance and the question of its leadership. *Where* and *who* were the "grassroots" people? Who has the right and authority to *represent* Indigenous Peoples?

Mainstream media pundits used these questions as evidence of internal "divisions" within the movement. But as Anishinaabe scholar Hayden King wrote, "While we all may dance to a similar beat, our footwork can take us in different directions. And there is nothing wrong with that" (King 2013: 1). Nevertheless, perceived divisions and contestations over representational authority within the movement led some participants and organizers to disengage from and disidentify with Idle No More. Despite two months of unprecedented global mobilization on Indigenous issues that sought to reconfigure the very terms and form of our collective organizing, action and representation, what had been accomplished? The political unrest generated by the movement had intensified and continued, albeit unresolved. Chief Spence's demands remained unmet. Bill C-45 passed into law. And Idle No More kept moving, seeking new ways to sustain the momentum of the "Native Winter."

## "Reactivism" and Sustaining Momentum

For many Indigenous communities, the political status quo functions through a colonial modality of governance in response and reaction to crisis. Necessarily short-term and highly localized, this strategy demands that resources and action be mobilized in situations of immediacy, often with limited jurisdiction. Idle No More called attention to this crisis–based mode of governance by confronting multiple colonial temporalities and contexts simultaneously: the *immediate* (the imminent passage of Bill C-45), the *historical* (the abrogation of treaty and inherent rights) and the *present* (continuing forms of social suffering, colonial racism and violence). As such, it was a crisis-based response to crisis-based governance: a cross-temporal and multivalent expression of indignation that captured historical and contemporary Indigenous *ressentiment*, or "righteous resentment" (Coulthard 2014: 126), against evidence of our continued state of collective, colonial abjection. Dene scholar Glen Coulthard names this affective response to colonialism as necessary for overcoming colonial disempowerment; that is, "our bitter indignation and persistent anger at being treated unjustly by a colonial state both historically and in the present," is not only a valid response to colonial injustice but it is also "a sign of our critical consciousness" (2014: 126) and our love for our lands and people.

Although Idle No More mobilized this righteous form of resentment as a form of collective catharsis, it also operationalized a *reactive* mode of resistance that reinscribed indigeneity as the injurious site of "wounded subjectivity" and politicized identity (Brown 1995: 65). As an exclusively *oppositional* political practice, this mode of resistance risks reproducing the very "injury" it seeks to refuse. But "states of injury" cannot be the only basis from which to re/articulate Indigenous political claims. To be effective and transformative, decolonial struggle must move beyond a definitional frame determined exclusively by colonial interference and imposition. Resurgent forms of resistance that revalue and revitalize Indigenous governance systems, natural laws and self-valorizing political practices are equally necessary. Idle No More sought creative contention with the State and Settler society, but also posited alternate pathways of self-affirmative action that did not seek recourse to colonial authority for validation or recognition. As Coulthard notes, Indigenous resistance actions (such as blockades and, to a lesser extent, round dances) that disrupt the normative order (by blocking the flow of capital, access to infrastructure or the rote procession of consumerism) are also "affirmative gesture[s] of Indigenous resurgence insofar as they embody an enactment of Indigenous law and … uphold the relations of reciprocity that shape our engagement with the human and nonhuman world — the land" (2014: 170). Indigenous resistance, even in its most defiant, oppositional forms — *as the negation of domination* — always suggests the possibility of an affirmative counterpart hidden within.

By creating new networks of interconnected actors and rapidly increasing public consciousness *en masse* through social media, Idle No More effected a profound shift in the speed of *conscientization*. These networks created new spaces in which to coordinate collective action and strengthened existing connections between Indigenous communities and movement organizers. But the movement also captured the imagination and energy of a rising generation of Indigenous youth who were mobilized into action, many for the first time. Idle No More cut across territorial borders and nation state–based identifications: it was intergenerational, intercommunal and geographically distributed. On the #J11 Global Day of Action held on January 11, 2013, for example, 265 events were organized in more than 17 countries (J11Action 2013). But despite the movement's global expansion,

Idle No More needed to relocalize action and organizing at the community level by reprioritizing local struggles and longer–term political transformation. The movement refocused around three key areas. First, it shifted emphasis from direct contention with the State to the imminent ecological and political threats posed by large–scale resource development projects and extractive industries (pipelines, tar sands expansion, mining and hydraulic fracturing, and so on) to Indigenous homelands. Second, the movement turned to a self-reflexive analysis of challenges internal to Indigenous communities. Third, movement organizers began reorienting around shared commitments to the resurgence of Indigenous nationhood and governance. Idle No More has since directed much of its energy toward addressing these interrelated and contested sites of engagement.

Idle No More's "winter of discontent" expressed a collective surfacing of decolonial consciousness that shifted the terrain of struggle by refusing established modalities of resistance — lawful, expected and existent forms of "protest" — and creatively interjecting new forms of collective action into public discourse. The movement disrupted the expected terms of Indigenous engagement with Settler society, and brought Canada's colonial foundation into full view and contestation. In resistance, Indigenous Peoples affirmed our continuance and coherence as viable political communities that refused to be silenced. As journalist Stefan Christoff noted, "Canada's political landscape now faces an alarm on colonial questions commonly evaded in the halls of power" (2013: 1). But Idle No More could not transform this foundation; it could only call attention to it. Although it remained affectively powerful, the movement proved incapable of compelling the State to respond to its demands. And in the face of Idle No More's bold calls to action, the Harper government has remained intransigent.

## Communicative Capitalism and Possible Politics
Social media theorist Zeynep Tufekci argues that the disjunction between the spectacle of mass protests and their inability to produce substantive institutional and policy transformations is characteristic of contemporary social movements:

> Protests ... fueled by social media and erupting into spectacular mass events, look like powerful statements of opposition [and] ... pundits speculate that the days of a ruling party or government, or at least its unpopular policies, must be numbered. Yet often these huge mobilizations of citizens inexplicably wither away without the impact on policy you might expect from their scale. (2014: 1)

According to Tufekci, the seemingly contradictory and "muted effect" of the massive popular uprisings in Turkey, Egypt and the Ukraine — to which I would add the Idle No More movement — is not a result of their inherent inefficacy; it is a constitutive feature of their architecture. Social media–fuelled movements prioritize immediacy and networked communicative action over sustained and incremental infrastructural development:

> Digital tools make it much easier to build up movements quickly, and they greatly lower coordination costs. This seems like a good thing at first, but it often results in an unanticipated weakness: Before the Internet, the tedious work of organizing that was required to circumvent censorship or to organize a protest also helped build infrastructure for decision making and strategies for sustaining momentum. Now movements can rush past that step, often to their own detriment. (2014: 1)

Movements like Idle No More can collapse under the temporal "weight" of their speed-driven dissemination and metric "success," resulting in a vacuum of strategies for sustaining momentum after spectacular forms of public protest have exhausted their communicative currency. Tufekci argues that media is a powerful force for activism seeking to claim legitimacy in the public sphere, but she rightly points out that contemporary social movements and activists "who have made such effective use of technology to rally supporters, still need to figure out how to convert that energy into greater impact. The point isn't just to challenge power; it's to change it" (2014: 1).

To this end, it is critical to consider how communicative praxis circulates within global capitalist networks. Movements like Idle No More make use of available digital technologies to mobilize consciousness, action and resistance; however, these same technologies operate within tightly regulated circuits of power and control. Jodi Dean describes this technological entanglement, in which circulation usurps content, as *communicative capitalism:*

> Communicative capitalism designates that form of late capitalism in which values heralded as central to democracy take material form in networked communications technologies ... Ideals of access, inclusion, discussion and participation come to be realized in and through expansions, intensifications and interconnections of global telecommunications. But instead of leading to more equitable distributions of wealth and influence, instead of enabling the emergence of a richer variety in modes of living and practices of freedom, the deluge of screens and spectacles undermines political opportunity and efficacy for most of the world's peoples. (2005: 56)

The foreclosure of politics that Dean suggests inheres under communicative capitalism is the product of techniques wherein "communicative exchanges rather than being fundamental to democratic politics, are the basic elements of capitalist production" (2009: 56). The commodified circulation of information in and for itself displaces "on-the-ground" political struggle: content becomes secondary to the process of circulation that "is crucial to the ideological reproduction of capitalism" (2009: 59). This effects a depoliticization of networked communication "because the form of our involvement ultimately empowers those it is supposed to resist" (2009: 61).

Idle No More's ostensibly liberatory digital forms (tweetstorms, trending hashtags and Facebook petitions, and so on) did not compel power to respond and risked displacing forms of grounded place-based political struggle, that contended directly with oppressive institutions and policies, into "imaginary site[s] of action and belonging" (Dean 2005: 67). Further, this displacement tacitly supported the circulation of capital rather than its disruption. Movement organizers recognized the contradiction between making revolutionary calls for social change on social networks and being unable to realize such changes within the disciplinary spaces of privatization, commodification, surveillance and control instantiated by communicative technologies. This perception also risked reproducing the false binarism of "digital dualism," in which the online and offline worlds are understood as "separate" and "virtual," rather than enmeshed within lived reality under capitalism. As Nathan Jurgenson argues, "our reality is both technological and organic, both digital and physical, all at once. We are not crossing in and out of separate digital and physical realities … but instead live in one reality, one that is augmented by atoms and bits" (2011: 1). Rather than perceiving the digital as a discrete site of "virtual liberation," it is necessary to consider the ways in which networked action, communication and activism are inscribed within pre-existing social and power relations.

Indeed, as Astra Taylor suggests, the digital intersects with the analog in ways that can actually "magnify inequality" and exacerbate asymmetries of power:

> Despite proclamations to the contrary, the online and off-line worlds are not separate; the digital is not distinct from "real life," a realm where analog prejudices are abandoned. While the Internet offers marginalized groups powerful and potentially world-changing opportunities to meet and act together, new technologies also magnify inequality, reinforcing elements of the old order. Networks do not eradicate power: they distribute it in different ways. (2014: 108)

As Idle No More and other contemporary movements have effectively demonstrated, the network is a site of contradiction and contestation that marks the discursive battleground in a war over representation, influence and communicative control. For Idle No More, serious considerations began to arise over the long–term strategic utility and efficacy of mass mobilizations coordinated through social media: What alternative pathways could the movement pursue to break from this discursive trap of self-enclosure?

Idle No More's diverse tactics and open-ended goals were not coherently organized, and its multiform digital articulations subtended resistance actions oriented beyond the State. As the movement worked to address both the immediate states of crisis in our communities and ongoing forms of colonialism, there was a marked discursive turn among some organizers away from viral memes and mass mobilizations, and toward the strategic reaffirmation of Indigenous nationhood and the reclamation and reoccupation of our homelands and sacred sites. In late January 2013, Kanien'kehaka scholar Taiaiake Alfred observed that the movement had "plateaued," noting that "the kind of movement we have been conducting under the banner of Idle No More is not sufficient in itself to decolonize this country or even to make meaningful change in the lives of people" (2013: 1). Although Alfred recognized that the movement had drawn broad-based support from many Indigenous nations and Settler society, he argued that in order for the movement to revive its initial momentum for "fundamental change," Indigenous peoples

> need to focus our activism on the root of the problem facing our people collectively: our collective dispossession and misrepresentation as Indigenous peoples. Now is the time to put ourselves back on our lands spiritually and physically and to shift our support away from the Indian Act system and to start energizing the restoration of our own governments ... *Restoring our nationhood in this way is the fundamental struggle. Our focus should be on restoring our presence on the land and regenerating our true nationhood.* These go hand in hand and one cannot be achieved without the other. (2013: 1, emphasis added)

Alfred said that to break out of the echo chamber enclosure of social media's endless calls to action,

> we need to alter our strategies and tactics to present more of a serious challenge on the ground to force the federal government to engage our movement and to respond to us in a serious way ... we need to go beyond demonstrations and rallies in malls and legislatures and on public streets and start to reoccupy Indigenous sacred, ceremonial and cultural use sites to re-establish our presence on our land and in doing so to educate Canadians about our continuing connections to those places and how

important they are to our continuing existence as Indigenous peoples. (2013: 2)

Although Idle No More continued to organize public demonstrations, rallies and marches of precisely the kind Alfred criticized, the movement also began to reterritorialize. Idle No More's reterritorialization marked the movement's need to relocalize and reground its organizing and action *within* Indigenous communities and homelands. Although the strategic reorientation of the movement made sense among participants and organizers, mainstream Canadian media used the opportunity to declare the death of Idle No More. Other recent social movements have been subjected to a similar critique, however, as they effect strategic reterritorializations following a first wave of mass mobilization:

> Since the intention is to transform not just the occupied [square or shopping mall] but society as a whole, movements have gradually shifted into spheres more directly related to the lives of their participants, such as neighbourhoods and workplaces, where local needs can be addressed. Generally, this is when the media and many on the institutional left tend to declare the movements "dead," but … this is no reliable guide to the life of the movement." (Sitrin and Azzelinni 2014: 12)

To relate directly to the lives of its Indigenous participants, Idle No More sought out new forms of organizing that could be deployed at the local level in support of community struggles for nationhood and autonomy.

### The Indigenous Nationhood Movement and Reclaiming PKOLS

In May 2013, Indigenous community members, organizers, activists, academics and allies gathered at the University of Victoria to participate in an Indigenous Leadership Forum (ILF). Over the course of the week-long gathering, participants discussed the wave of resurgent action catalyzed by Idle No More and the possibility of building an Indigenous Nationhood Movement to carry the movement's momentum forward. ILF participants developed a collaborative framework and set of movement principles oriented toward long-term anticolonial social transformation and supporting Indigenous communities and community members in the restoration and reassertion of Indigenous laws, languages, governance and political autonomy.

The Indigenous Nationhood Movement (INM) was launched with a sacred act of reclamation and reoccupation on May 22, 2013. Under the guidance and leadership of hereditary chiefs and elders from the WSÁNEĆ nations, INM supported the reclamation and reinstatement of PKOLS: the original SENĆOŦEN place name of a sacred site at the summit of a promontory in Saanich, B.C. PKOLS, which can be translated as "White Head" or "White Rock," was formerly known by its colonial name, Mount Douglas, after Captain James Douglas (Reclaim PKOLS 2013). It is a sacred site for the WSÁNEĆ people and a historic meeting place for the Indigenous nations in the area; it is part of the WSÁNEĆ creation story and the site where the WSÁNEĆ first entered into treaty with Douglas in 1852 (Lavoie 2013: 1). Hereditary chief WEC'KINEM (Eric Pelkey) of STÁUTW̱ (Tsawout) First Nation led the reclamation with support from Indigenous and non-Indigenous volunteers, who worked with the local Indigenous nations to build public support for the campaign. The reinstatement of the original name fulfilled a long-standing request by local elders to "bring back the names we have always used to where they belong" (IC 2013: 1). I was fortunate to have been asked to participate and help with the reclamation. Following several months of planning, WEC'KINEM and the WSÁNEĆ nations led close to eight hundred supporters and community members to reclaim PKOLS.

On the evening of May twenty-second, marchers gathered at the base of the mountain and hiked to the summit, where they joined in a ceremony to reinstate the original name. The signing of the Douglas Treaty was re-enacted by a volunteer group of performers at the site where it was originally (and coercively) signed, but the inscribed colonial violence of dispossession was *inverted*: Instead of ceding land and territory to the invading colonial power, local Indigenous leaders presented and signed a new declaration honouring the restoration and reinstatement of PKOLS and committing to the future reclamation of other traditional place names throughout the WSÁNEĆ and neighbouring territories. The PKOLS declaration asserted WSÁNEĆ and LEKWUNGEN nationhood in terms consistent with their natural laws, traditions, inherent authority over their homelands, and rights as Indigenous Peoples and Nations (PKOLS Declaration 2013). Coast Salish master carver TEMOSEN (Charles Elliott) of W̱JOȽEȽP (Tsartlip) First Nation designed a large PKOLS sign from yellow cedar that was carried to the summit and installed at a high viewpoint — overlooking the surrounding mountains, ocean and the city of Victoria. Participants from the Indigenous Leadership Forum wore T-shirts identifying themselves as members of the INM and worked with local organizers to provide security; assist community members and elders; help carry and install the PKOLS sign; and liaise with civic authorities, media and law enforcement. During the reclamation ceremony, WSÁNEĆ community members recounted the story of PKOLS, first in SENĆOŦEN and then in English. After the declaration was signed, the event concluded with the sharing of food, songs and drumming by the local nations.

Having generated high-profile endorsements and support from intellectuals and organizations including Noam Chomsky, Naomi Klein, Tom Hayden, Greenpeace and the Sierra Club (PKOLS 2013), the reclamation gathered communicative momentum across social media channels; and photo, video and audio content shared online during the event provided witnesses who were unable to attend the event in person with a vicarious experience of immediacy and presence.

The reclamation of PKOLS was a potent assertion of Indigenous nationhood and autonomy that signalled new possibilities for Indigenous-Settler alliances, collective action and decolonizing praxis. The WSÁNEĆ did not seek permission from the State; they took action in alignment with their natural laws, customs, and inherent rights. In doing so, they were supported by a large community of local Indigenous nations, Indigenous visitors to their traditional territory and Settler allies. Against the strictly delimited forms of "permissible" Indigenous activism, the reclamation of PKOLS was empowering and emboldening, not only for the local nations but also for communities and supporters in solidarity across Turtle Island. The reclamation of PKOLS was simultaneously a symbolic, communicative and embodied enactment of autonomous movement within and against the colonial demarcations of "settled" territory and in refusal of Indigenous *displacement*. In literal terms, PKOLS refuted the dispossession of original place names by *re-placing*, or returning, the name to its rightful originary place.

In this way, PKOLS worked to overturn the binarism of Settler colonial relations by enacting a participatory process of renewal that inverted the colonial frame and proposed an "affirmative *enactment* of another modality of being, a different way of relating to and with the world" (Coulthard 2014: 169). This resurgent return to an originary form of place-based knowledge — rooted in the SENĆOŦEN language — presupposes the alterity of an *Indigenous* ontoepistemic foundation that comes from the land and is, quite literally, *of* that place. In reclaiming PKOLS, treaty-making was re-visioned as a processual form of collective action in the present. Demanding both an understanding of interdependent relationality and respect for WSÁNEĆ forms of life derived from millennia of embodied praxis in place, PKOLS marked multiple forms of embodied resurgence and return: It recuperated the spiritual force of Idle No More's round dance revolution and refigured resistance through ceremony. The return of original names to "where they belong" is, as Anishinaabe author Leanne Simpson suggests, not simply a symbolic action, but "a mechanism for reconnecting our peoples to the land, our histories and our cultures … Building a strong, connected Indigenous Nationhood Movement rests on reclaiming the lands and sacred sites we have been removed from" (2013: 1). Reconnection, reclamation and renaming are essential acts of decolonization.

PKOLS thus provided a resonant example of prefigurative decolonial politics in motion—a gesture of renewal that affirmed the critical potentialities inherent in affirmative forms of resistance that seek to make structural and historical injustice *visible* while self-valorizing Indigenous forms of life on our own terms and in our own languages. As one speaker declared during the reclamation: "We're Idle No More [and] acting outside the confines of Indian Affairs … *we are acting this time,*

*The Reclamation of* PKOLS, *May 22, 2013 (Photo credit: Amos Scott)*

*not reacting."* PKOLS pointed a pathway forward that drew from a long continuum of Indigenous resistances against colonialism, and reaffirmed the efficacy and power of an embodied praxis of presence made visible through *reclamation* and *reoccupation.* Although the reclamation of PKOLS was not a new form of resistance, it was a generative provocation that inspired other Indigenous people and communities to see the continuity and interconnections in our struggles to decolonize.

As Leanne Simpson observed:

> We all have within our territories our PKOLS, many PKOLS — sacred places waiting to be restored to their place within the fabric of Indigenous societies. Whether it is a mountain, burial ground, hot springs or spring water, buffalo rubbing stone, tipi ring, teaching rocks, a medicine picking spot, or a travel route or a city street, *the* PKOLS *reclamation provides us with impetus to not just feel inspired, but to act.* (2013: 2)

Against colonial legacies of dispossession and displacement, PKOLS embodied and compelled action: "to take up our responsibilities to our homelands ... to inhabit them, to maintain relationships with their features and to pass that presence down to our children and grandchildren" (Simpson 2013: 2). This dual movement of refusal and affirmation did not stop with the rejection of colonial naming; it renewed a place-based vision of Indigenous presence and continuity. And it is this "place-based imaginary," Coulthard argues, that "serves as the ethical foundation from which ... Indigenous peoples and communities continue to resist and critique the dual imperatives of state sovereignty and capitalist accumulation that constitute our colonial present" (2010: 82). PKOLS was not unique, but it was "an extraordinarily important act for the STÁUT<u>W</u>, Songhees and the WSÁNEĆ because it physically connects them to a powerful place, alive with story, and breathing with history" (Simpson 2013: 1). PKOLS reinstated a new history of the *Indigenous* present. "This action to reclaim #PKOLS is truly one of the most exciting I've seen in Canada," said one observer on Twitter. "This is the beginning of something" (Martineau 2013: 2).

## Conclusion: New Beginnings

Idle No More is about beginnings, not origins. It was a moment of rupture, a movement of return, a break in our collective consciousness that awakened new possibilities for creative resistance. The struggle to resurge and decolonize is continuous; and our survival compels our action. But resistance reaffirms our force and power; and resurgence reminds us why we are fighting. Idle No More marked both this continuation as well as the search for new languages and practices of struggle. By rejecting stasis and refuting fixity, the movement set in motion new rhythms of change. Idle No More was a movement of *movement* that mobilized decolonial consciousness among Indigenous people and newcomers alike, and it has enabled us as Indigenous Peoples to reorient our political practices toward rebuilding power and autonomy. Decolonization demands that we forge new political subjectivities through self-affirmative and transformative resurgent praxis. And as our lives and lands continue to be threatened by Settler colonial dispossession and capitalist exploitation, decolonization remains our critical imperative. The transformative becoming of resistant subjectivity is activated by affirming Indigenous ontological priorities and practices (Indigenous land-based knowledges, lifeways, natural laws, songs and ceremonies) and by navigating the shifting terrain of struggle. Our movement demands continual creative transformation.

Indigenous peoples must struggle *within and against* regimes of representation by mobilizing collective action on multiple fronts: through technology, art, music, culture and ceremony. Demands for accountability from the State and Settler society and to protect the land and water, to uphold treaty relationships, to renew balanced Indigenous-Settler relations, and, perhaps most importantly, for colonialism to end, have yet to realized. But Idle No More's *politics in motion* drew from the power of our collective ancestral and historical memory to bring a renewed sense of urgency to our ongoing struggle for decolonization. In so doing, new rhythms of resistance began to sound. New forms of transformative praxis began to be forged. And an emergent force of Indigenous resurgence was sparked that will resonate in the generations to come. Melancholic and triumphant, hopeful and defiant, with Idle No More we begin again. We continue. We move. We rise.

## Note

1. It is important to note that within Settler colonialism, Indigenous "political action" is consistently "stifled," silenced and delimited by State-sanctioned forms of violence and repression. For more on the effects of framing Indigenous political action as a threat to the state, see Craig Proulx (2014), "Colonizing Surveillance: Canada Constructs an Indigenous Terror Threat." *Anthropologica* 56, 1, 83–100.

## References

Agamben, Giorgio. 1998. *Homo Sacer: Sovereign Power and Bare Life*. Palo Alto, CA: Stanford University Press.

Alfred, Taiaiake. 2013. "Indigenous Nationhood: Beyond Idle No More." *Common Dreams*. January 1. <commondreams.org/view/2013/01/29-0>.

APTN (Aboriginal Peoples Television Network). 2012. "First Nations 'War Drums' Will 'Ring Loudly' if Attawapiskat Chief Spence Dies: Nepinak." December 16. <aptn.ca/news/2012/12/16/first-nations-war-drums-will-ring-loudly-if-spence-dies-nepinak/>.

Blevis, Mark. 2013. "Idle No More at Two Months: Traffic Analysis (part 1/6)." <markblevis.com/idle-no-more-at-two-months-traffic-analysis>.

Brown, Wendy. 1995. *States of Injury: Power and Freedom in Late Modernity*. Princeton, NJ: Princeton University Press.

Campagna, Frederico, and Emanuele Campiglio. 2012. "Introduction: What Are We Struggling For?" In Fredrico Campagna and Emanuele Campiglio (eds.), *What We Are Fighting For: A Radical Collective Manifesto*. London: Pluto Press.

CBC (Canadian Broadcasting Company). 2013a. "Chief Theresa Spence to End Hunger Strike Today." January 23. <cbc.ca/news/politics/chief-theresa-spence-to-end-hunger-strike-today-1.1341571>.

____. 2013b. "Idle No More and Tensions in Thunder Bay." *The Current*. January 25. <cbc.ca/thecurrent/episode/2013/01/25/idle-no-more-and-tensions-in-thunder-bay/>.

Christoff, Stefan. 2013. "'Idle No More' and Colonial Canada." *Al Jazeera*. January 30.

COO (Chiefs of Ontario). 2013. "Attawapiskat First Nation Chief Theresa Spence Hunger Strike." <chiefs-of-ontario.org/node/465>.

Coulthard, Glen. 2014. *Red Skin, White Masks*. Minneapolis: University of Minnesota Press.

____. 2010. "Place Against Empire: Understanding Indigenous Anti-Colonialism." *Affinities: A Journal of Radical Theory, Culture, and Action* 4, 2, 79–83. <affinitiesjournal.org/index.php/affinities/article/view/69/211>.

Darcy, Stephen. *Languages of the Unheard: Why Militant Protest Is Good for Democracy*. London: Zed Books.

Dean, Jodi. 2009. *Democracy and Other Neoliberal Fantasies*. Durham, NC: Duke University Press.

____. 2005. "Communicative Capitalism and the Foreclosure of Politics." *Cultural Politics* 1, 1.

Gharavi, Maryam Monalisa. 2011. "Becoming Fugitive: Carceral Space and Rancièreian Politics." *The Funambulist*. <thefunambulist.net/2011/08/25/guest-writers-essays-09-becoming-fugitive-carceral-space-and-rancierean-politics-by-maryam-monalisa-gharavi/>.

Hardt, Michael, and Antonio Negri. 2012. *Declaration*. Allen, TX: Argo-Navis.

Idle No More. 2013. "The Vision." <idlenomore.ca/vision>.

Intercontinental Cry. 2013. "First Nations Plan Day of Action to Reclaim Original Name of Mount Douglas: PKOLS." May 13. <intercontinentalcry.org/first-nations-plan-day-of-action-to-reclaim-original-name-of-mount-douglas-pkols/>.

IPSMO (Indigenous Peoples Solidarity Movement Ottawa). 2012. "Chief Spence Announces Hunger Strike in Ottawa." December 11. <ipsmo.wordpress.com/2012/12/11/chief-spence-announces-hunger-strike-in-ottawa/>.

J11Action. 2013. "#J11 Global Day of Action." <j11action.com>.

Jurgenson, Nathan. 2011. "Digital Dualism versus Augmented Reality." *The Society Pages.* February 24. <thesocietypages.org/cyborgology/2011/02/24/digital-dualism-versus-augmented-reality/>.

Kappo, Tanya. 2012. "First Nation Woman Brutally Attacked in Thunder Bay Urges Idle No More Protests to Remain Peaceful." *Media Knet.* December 30. <media.knet.ca/node/22231>.

King, Hayden. 2013. "We Natives Are Deeply Divided. There's Nothing Wrong with That." *Globe and Mail,* January 9.

Lavoie, Judith. 2013. "It's PKOLS, Not Mount Douglas, Marchers Proclaim." *Times Colonist,* May 22. <timescolonist.com/news/local/it-s-pkols-not-mount-douglas-marchers-proclaim-1.228920><rpm.fm/news/the-round-dance-revolution-idle-no-more>.

Martin, Melissa. 2013. "Round Dance: Why It's the Symbol of Idle No More." CBC. January 28. <cbc.ca/manitoba/scene/homepage-promo/2013/01/28/round-dance-revolution-drums-up-support-for-idle-no-more/>.

Martineau, Jarrett. 2013. "Hundreds Gather in Victoria to Reclaim PKOLS." *Storify.* <storify.com/culturite/hundreds-gather-in-victoria-to-reclaim-pkols>.

Martineau, Jarrett, and E. Ritskes. 2014. "Fugitive Indigeneity: Reclaiming the Terrain of Decolonial Struggle through Indigenous Art." *Decolonization: Indigeneity, Education & Society* 3, 1.

McMahon, Ryan. 2012. "The Round Dance Revolution: Idle No More." *Revolutions Per Minute* (RPM), December 20.

Mitchell, W.J.T. 2012. "Image, Space, Revolution: The Arts of Occupation." *Critical Inquiry* 39, 1.

Newman, Saul. 2012. "Why Do We Obey?" In Fredrico Campagna and Emanuele Campiglio (eds.), *What We Are Fighting For: A Radical Collective Manifesto.* London: Pluto Press.

PKOLS Declaration. 2013. <nationsrising.org/wp-content/uploads/2013/11/PKOLS-signed-declaration.pdf>.

Reclaim PKOLS. 2013. <web.uvic.ca/igov/uploads/pdf/PKOLS%20Pamphlet%203.pdf>.

Simpson, Leanne. 2013. "The PKOLS Reclamation: Saturating the Land with our Stories." <leannesimpson.ca/2013/05/22/the-pkols-reclamation-saturating-the-land-with-our-stories>.

Sitrin, M., and D. Azzellini. 2014. *They Can't Represent Us! Reinventing Democracy from Greece to Occupy.* New York: Verso.

SLSF (South London Solidarity Federation). 2012. "Direct Action and Unmediated Struggle." In Fredrico Campagna and Emanuele Campiglio (eds.), *What We Are Fighting For: A Radical Collective Manifesto.* London: Pluto Press.

Taylor, Astra. 2014. *The People's Platform: Taking Back Power and Culture in the Digital Age.*

Toronto: Random House.

Translation Collective. 2012. "Communiqué from the Indigenous Revolutionary Clandestine Committee." December. <translationcollective.files.wordpress. com/2013/12/happy-birthday-ezln.pdf>.

Tufekci, Zeynep. 2014. "After the Protests." *New York Times*, March 19. <nytimes. com/2014/03/20/opinion/after-the-protests.html?_r=1>.

Afterword

# A STEADILY BEATING HEART
## PERSISTENCE, RESISTANCE AND RESURGENCE

*Alex Wilson*

In First Nations communities, women provide leadership in the political continuum of persistence, resistance and resurgence. The steady leadership of women draws on values and practices of respect, relational responsibility and spiritual presence, and an accompanying commitment to love in action. They have maintained their leadership in spite of centuries-long colonial attacks on these values and practices. The attacks on First Nations women (and all women) are particularly vicious in the present-day neoliberal climate, in large part because they directly challenge the ideological framework (mind over body) and oppressive practices (self over others) that enable and animate neoliberalism. The leadership of women such as Chief Theresa Spence, the originators and organizers of Idle No More (INM), and the many women who take responsibility every day for the well-being of their families and communities shows us another path, where we nurture our own personal and political capacity to bring about justice.

### Relational Responsibility and Action that Effects Love
The democratic intellectual Cornel West has observed that "you can't lead the people if you don't love the people" (2008: 208). His statement offers some explanation of the astonishingly rapid growth of INM, which is many things — an affirmation of Indigenous sovereignty and protection of land and water; a reaction to old and new colonial forms of oppression; a series of nationally and locally organized teach-ins, rallies, protests, and round dances; and a call for peaceful revolution — but

always, at its core, it is a very contemporary political expression of old knowledge: that we, the land, the water, and all living creatures, are related and, as relatives, we are meant to love and care for each other. This commitment to relational responsibility and to action that effects love is the starting place of INM. The movement gained momentum from Prime Minister Harper's introduction of new legislation (now passed) that unilaterally rewrote the relationships between First Nations and the Canadian state by modifying the Indian Act and threatened water systems in unprecedented ways by removing their environmentally protected status. INM should not, however, be understood as simply a reaction to this legislation. Before the legislation was proposed, it began as (and has remained throughout) a positive affirmation of our responsibility to each other, the land and other living beings.

I am from the Opaskwayak Cree Nation, and my family clan name is *Wassenas*, which translates as "reflecting light from within."[1] Our name and the knowledge it contains came to me through my grandmother, passed to her through generations of women. My grandmother also passed on important lessons about leadership, most through her actions, but also with words. When, as a young woman, I asked what leadership meant to her, she replied, "Oh, I don't know much about that"; then, after a long pause, added, "My friend Martha was a leader. She was a spiritual woman. She lived the life of respect. She loved people." My grandmother identified three critical aspects of leadership in our communities: spirituality, respect and love. Collectively, these terms refer to principles and practices that focus on sustaining the continuity of life by caring for our relationships through the past, present and future.

As is true for many of my First Nation peers, I have always been surrounded by women who lead, most of them leading steadily, some quietly, a few raucously, but always with love in their actions. These women typically lead from outside the Chief and Council system imposed by the Indian Act or any of the other formal systems rooted in colonial governance. Rather, these women lead because they have maintained the principles and practices of spirituality, respect and love within the context of the ongoing challenges presented by the centuries-old, shape-shifting and steadfastly patriarchal colonial project. They possess what the Cree educator and activist Priscilla Settee (2011: iv) rightly identifies as *Âhkamêyimowak* — persistence:

> [*Âhkamêyimowak*] provides the strength for women to carry on in the face of extreme adversity. [It] embodies the strength that drives women to survive, flourish and work for change within [our] communities. Women are the unsung heroes of [our] communities, often using minimal resources to challenge oppressive structures.

I sing these women here.

INM comes from this history. It was started by and continues to be led by women. Women have set the beat and reached out to bring people into the circle. We invite people to step up into leadership by becoming political actors, raising their voices and joining the movement. As a revolutionary round dance, INM reclaims the sovereignty of Indigenous people's bodies and nations. The INM round dances bring Indigenous people and our allies together in malls, intersections, the grounds of government buildings and other public spaces. Our visible presence (not shopping, driving or legislating, but doing what we are not "supposed" to do — drumming, dancing and protesting) transforms these spaces into political spaces. They become sites of persistence (we are here today because we love and care for our people and our nations, and we will still be standing here tomorrow), resistance (we are here to put an end to the harm colonization inflicts on our people and our nations) and resurgence (we are here to repair that harm and reclaim the sovereignty of our bodies and our peoples).

## Undoing the Present Absence of Indigenous Peoples

The visible presence of INM exposes and undoes the "present absence" (Kathryn Shanley, cited in Smith 2006: 66) of Indigenous peoples in the Canadian colonial imagination — that is, wilfully not seeing Indigenous peoples or, as is our concern here, the contributions of Indigenous women. These acts of rendering Indigenous people invisible take place at multiple levels. They include (but are not limited to) the day-to-day failure, on the part of many Canadians, to recognize as Indigenous any individual who does not conform to their stereotypes about Indigenous people (Urban Aboriginal Peoples Study: Main Report 2010); Prime Minister Harper's statement at the 2009 G20 summit that Canada has "no history of colonialism" (Junggren 2009); the frequent failure of governments and corporations to consider the impacts of their policies and practices on Indigenous people and nations (Owen 2013); the steady bureaucratic erosion of First Nations identity effected by the Indian Act (Cornet 2007); and the ongoing gendered genocide and violence that has left 1,181 Aboriginal women missing or murdered in Canada (Royal Canadian Mounted Police 2014).

No longer "seeing" Indigenous peoples enables a self-justifying and entitling ideology and actions that dispossess us as Indigenous peoples from our traditional territories; abuse and destroy the lands and waters we have stewarded for millennia; and assault the well-being and integrity of our families, communities and nations. This has been especially true for Indigenous women. Anishinaabe activist and writer Leanne Simpson reminds us that Indigenous women have been actively "involved in resistance, dissent, mobilization and resurgence since the very beginnings of colonial occupation" and observes that

> The logics of colonialism, however, have consistently denied and obfus-
> cated these interventions, attacking the power of Indigenous women and
> Two-Spirit LGBTQI (Lesbian, Gay, Bisexual, Trans, Queer, Questioning,
> Intersex) people by framing these issues outside of the political sphere
> and placing them firmly in the place of perpetual victimhood. Too often,
> the "activism" of Indigenous women has been reduced in the academic
> literature to issues regarding identity, violence, and discrimination — in a
> context that removes these issues from their colonial roots and that under-
> mines and erases Indigenous nationhood. (Simpson et al. 2012: 1–2)

The marginalization of Indigenous women (including our gender and sexually
diverse community members) can be understood as an attempt to depoliticize
and deny our agency. The issues that Indigenous women raise often relate to their
identities or to their individual and collective experiences of discrimination and
violence, but in speaking out, they are not proclaiming themselves victims. When
the concerns of Indigenous women are collapsed into generic "women's issues,"
the real issues they are talking about (the ongoing violence of colonization and
the denial of Indigenous nationhood) are potentially silenced.

## Speaking Truth About Colonial Violence

The marginalization of women, and Indigenous women in particular, is an essential
component of Western cultures and one that serves the current neoliberal political
climate in Canada and the United States. The concerted effort to discredit and ridi-
cule Chief Spence and the fast she undertook to persuade Prime Minister Harper
to meet with First Nations leaders (which mobilized thousands of Indigenous
and non-Indigenous peoples to join INM actions) was a painful example of this.
Simpson refers to Chief Spence as

> not *Chief* Spence, but *Ogichidaakwe* Spence — a holy woman, a woman
> that would do anything for her family and community, the one that goes
> over and makes things happen, a warrior, a leader because *Ogichidaakwe*
> Spence isn't just on a hunger strike. She is fasting and this also has cultural
> meaning for Anishinaabeg. She is in ceremony. (2014: 155)

Simpson describes the abusive response she received to a message of support
for Chief Spence that she posted on Twitter: "Within minutes, trolls were commented on my feed with commentary on Chief Spence's body image, diet jokes,
calls for 'no more special treatment for Natives' and calls to end her hunger strike.
One person called her a 'cunt.'" Simpson continues:

I understand we need to be positive, I do. We also need to continue telling the truth. The racism, sexism and disrespect that have been heaped
on *Ogitchidaa* Spence have been done so in part because it is acceptable
to treat Indigenous women this way. These comments take place in a
context where we have nearly one thousand missing and murdered
Indigenous women. Where we have still have places named "squaw."
Where Indigenous women have been the deliberate target of gendered
colonial violence for four hundred years. Where the people who have
been seriously hurt and injured by the backlash against INM have been
women. Where *Ogichidaakw*e Spence's voice has not been heard.
(Simpson 2014: 156)

As Simpson's story points out, the bodies of Indigenous women are ridiculed,
reduced, targeted and under attack. Our women who lead, our *Ogichidaakwe*,
are still subject to a deep-rooted colonial culture of hate and violence, their bodies pushed to the foreground to block our view of their strong spirits — and yet
these women persist. Their hearts beat steadily, and our political resistance and
resurgence continues.

## Persisting as an Ethical Human Being

The relational psychologist and ethicist Carol Gilligan lays out the process through
which the voices and actions of women are marginalized in Western cultures,
throwing light on the mechanics of marginalization that strives to undermine
Indigenous women's value-driven leadership. Gilligan notes that in their earliest years, both boys and girls typically are guided by an ethical sensibility that is
rooted in relationality, a starting place that she describes as "very hopeful in terms
of ethics and transformational values" (2009). In Western cultures, boys are soon
pressured to surrender this sensibility and, in its place, elevate and embrace reason
and the autonomous self as their masculine identity. This process requires them
to simultaneously devalue and idealize emotions, relationship and the body as
feminine. As Gilligan reminds us:

[The culturally constructed process of gender-based initiation] under-
mines or puts at risk the very capacities that are fundamental to our ability
to function as ethical human beings in the world. If you separate reason
from emotion, if you separate voice from relationship, self from relationship, and mind from body, we lose our grounding in the human world
and then it's possible to act without knowing or even without register-
ing the consequence or the impact of our actions ... The very aspects of
our nature, our capacity to have a voice, to live in relationship, to resolve

conflict within a relationship are the grounds and the requisites both of love and of democratic citizenship ... If you're going to set up patriarchal structures, you are going to have to break those capacities. You are going to have to traumatize them ... What patriarchy precludes is love between equals. And therefore it precludes democracy founded on love and the freedom of voice that encourages. (2009)

This is a complex argument that begins with the recognition that our voice and our sense of self develop within relationship, and that knowing and being are both intellectual and embodied states. It reminds us that emotions matter to reason, and that our best decisions (whether as simple human beings or as political leaders) are driven by consideration of and care for the well-being of others. Put more simply, they are actions informed by love. But to live comfortably in the patriarchal colonial culture of mainstream Canada, it is easier to forget this — to place self above others, unhitch reason from emotions, mute the voices of those who speak with both heart and mind, and enable the violence of colonization to continue.

Ultimately, Gilligan points to political resistance as a way to return to our capacity as ethical beings and societies. Her understanding of why and how we *must* resist echoes what I hear in the amplified voices of Indigenous women who call for change. The Toronto-based curator and INM organizer Wanda Nanibush states that "I come to the ideas of resistance and resurgence from the place where intellectual engagement is not severed from the bodies' memories or the heart's commitments or my culture's knowledges and practices. Resistance is a daily practice and a community process with ever-changing meanings" (Simpson et al. 2012: 3). In the same essay, Leanne Simpson reminds us that "Indigenous women have always known that growing strong, resilient nations is based on diversity, generated consensus, authentic power rather than authoritarian power and the maintenance of good relationships rather than coercive ones" (Simpson et al. 2012: 2). Simpson is describing women who embody Gilligan's vision of democratic equality.

In Cree, the language of my family and community, the term *Sakihiwawin* declares our commitment to love in action. This is what has brought me to INM. *Sakihiwawin* calls us to move from apathy or passivity to passionate activism, to act in ways that express love and that consider the lasting implications of what we might choose to do or not do. It is based on Cree natural law, which recognizes that the nature of the cosmos is to be in balance, and when balance is disturbed, it must and will return. To disturb the balance has spiritual or energetic consequences (*pastah howin*) and physical or material consequences (*otcinawin*). I also learned at an early age the concepts of *kakinow ni wagomakanak* (we are all related), *akha ta neekanenni miso-an* (not to think of myself being ahead of or more important than others) and *akha ta aspahk kenimiso-an* (not to think that I am above anyone else). The development of my own sense of self and voice have been guided by these principles — principles that, again, reify Gilligan's vision of how we can become ethical beings and societies.

## The Language of Leadership

These words and my grandmother's words on spirituality, respect and love are the language of leadership. These words become our embodied knowledge. Before we gather sweetgrass from the land, we give something in return, laying down tobacco (*otcinawin*) and offering prayers (*pastah howin*), and we share the medicine we harvest with whomever needs it (*kakinow ni wagomakanak*). INM recognizes that all people may be leaders (*akha ta neekanenni miso-an* and *akha ta aspahk kenimiso-an*). Chief Spence fasts for our people, communities and Nations; and thousands of Indigenous people stand with her because we recognize and respond to her reminder that our commitment to love in action (*Sakihiwawin*) demands resistance.

Our family home is on a site called *pumuskatapan*, a term that refers to the place in a journey where you must get out and pull your canoe — a spot where, to reach your destination, you must find another way to move forward. *Pumaskatapan* also has another meaning: the place that is off to the side, away from the centre — that is, just the right location from which to take on patriarchy and hegemony. Gilligan suggests that the process of resisting patriarchy and hegemony must be traumatic, but the possibility of change can also be unearthed in traditional knowledge that reminds us that there is always more than one way to get to the place we want to be. We can sidestep violence and instead take a journey guided by spirituality, respect and love.

Gilligan offers a definition of feminism as "the movement to liberate democracy from patriarchy. The effects of patriarchy on men and women are fueling violence and blunting our capacity to know what we know" (2009). In my family and community, we were raised knowing that we have a deep relationship with and responsibility to each other, to the spirits, and to the land and the living things that sustain us. But, as Andrea Smith points out, the process of colonization works to undermine that sensibility: "In order to colonize peoples whose societies are not based on social hierarchy, colonizers must first naturalize hierarchy through instituting patriarchy" (2006: 72). I have witnessed how insidious and invasive this process can be. For example, many First Nation schools in the region in which I work have recognized that the revitalization of Indigenous languages can help strengthen the cultural identity and well-being of the students and communities they serve. One way in which this is articulated is to start the day with prayers in Cree — but too often the prayers are simply a Cree translation of The Lord's Prayer, in which our concept and term "the great mystery" (*kiche muntoo*) is replaced by the patriarchal

Christian concept and term "our father" (*Notawinan*). As both Smith and Gilligan (2009) might warn us, patriarchy can blunt our capacity to know.

Andrea Smith further observes that if our challenge to colonialism does not also substantially challenge patriarchy and heteronormativity, "[our] struggles will maintain colonialism based on a politics of secondary marginalization where the most elite class of [our] groups will further their aspirations on the backs of those most marginalized within the community" (2006: 72). We know this struggle. An analysis of the first six months of INM's presence online revealed that the vast majority of posts on social media were made by women and that those posts were overwhelmingly positive (Blevis 2013). The vast majority of negative posts had been made by men, providing small and sometimes mean-spirited examples of the extent to which patriarchy has misshaped our political culture. The Anishinaabe/Chicana scholar Dory Nason places us in the bigger picture:

> I would humbly ask all of us to think about what it means for men, on the one hand, to publicly profess an obligation to "protect our women" and, on the other, take leadership positions that uphold patriarchal forms of governance or otherwise ignore the contributions and sovereignty of the women, Indigenous and not. (2014: 187)

INM's commitment to leadership based on relational responsibility and to love in action is a direct challenge to the heteropatriarchal governance imposed on our communities by the Indian Act. As Andrea Smith reminds us:

> National liberation politics become less vulnerable to being coopted by the Right when we base them on a model of liberation that fundamentally challenges right-wing conceptions of the nation. We need a model based on community relationships and on mutual respect ... I see this as a starting point for women of color organizers that will allow us to re-envision a politics of solidarity that goes beyond multiculturalism, and develop more complicated strategies that can really transform the political and economic status quo. (2006: 73)

Over its relatively short history, INM has maintained focus on the affirmation of Indigenous sovereignty, a concept that extends far beyond nationhood. We recognize that individually and collectively our well-being relies on our ability to be responsible and respectful in our interactions with, to care for, and to protect from the violence of colonization the lands, water, and people, communities and nations to which we are connected.

## *Awuskahwinuk*: Shaking It Up! Waking It Up!

In Canada's current political context, INM's commitment to relational responsibility and an expanded understanding of sovereignty is a critical piece of Indigenous struggle. The Harper administration has steadily attacked First Nations sovereignty by moving rapidly away from a nation-to-nation relationship; failing to consult formal leadership on government Acts that affect our traditional lands, waterways and people; supporting the introduction of private property on reserve and gutting environmental laws to support resource development; rejecting United Nations resolutions calling for a national review to end violence against Aboriginal women; and strategically dividing First Nations leadership (Blanchfield 2013; Mas 2013). This is both a new attack and a familiar series of colonizers' moves against First Nations sovereignty.

Like a round dance, we are brought back to the notion of leadership. Leanne Simpson recognizes Chief Spence as *Ogichidaakwe* Spence: "the one that goes over and makes things happen" (2014: 155). A friend who was given a spirit name that includes *Ogichidaakw*e tells me that it came with a careful translation: "Leading. Not leader, but leading." I asked my father if we had a Cree word that expressed the same idea. "*Awuskahwinak*," he said, "Someone making something move that can't move without somebody moving it. Shaking it up or waking it up. An action. Someone activating something."

Provoking motion, shaking up, waking up, activating — INM continues to work to generate change through love in action. The movement's ongoing work still includes nonviolent direct action and, increasingly, outreach and education, undertaken with the recognition that strengthening the self-determination and sovereignty of Indigenous peoples is not just about governance and nationhood but also about nurturing the capacity of all people to become people who lead. Our commitment is to love in personal and political action and leadership: we offer radical education; we honour all our relations; and with them, we work for the persistence, resistance and resurgence of the individual and collective sovereignty of our individual bodies, our peoples, our nations and our lands.

### NOTE

1.  My family and community use the Swampy Cree or n-dialect. Currently, many people are suggesting that spelling of Cree dialects should use standardized Roman orthography (SRO). However, Mabel Bignell, Moses Bignell, Cornelius Constant and Stan Wilson, who are Elders and Cree language teachers in my home community of Opaskwayak Cree Nation, have requested that we use phonetic spellings in our written work that preserve the nuances of our local dialect.

## REFERENCES

Blanchfield, Mike. 2013. "Canada Rejects UN Call for Review of Violence Against Aboriginal Women." *Globe and Mail*, September 19.

Blevis, Mark. 2013. *Idle No More at Six Months: Analysis of the First Six Months of the Idle No More Movement*. Ottawa: Full Duplex.

Cornet, Wendy. 2007. "Indian Status, Band Membership, First Nation Citizenship, Kinship, Gender, and Race: Reconsidering the Role of Federal Law." In Jerry Patrick White et al. (eds.), *Aboriginal Policy Research: Moving Forward, Making a Difference*, Volume 5. Toronto: Thompson Educational Publishing.

Gilligan, Carol. 2009. "Learning to See in the Dark: The Roots of Ethical Resistance." Lecture. April 24. The Dalai Lama Center for Ethics and Transformative Values. MIT Simmons Hall, Cambridge, MA.

Junggren, David L. 2009. "Every G20 Nation Wants to Be Canada." *Reuters,* September 25.

MacCharles, Tonda. 2013. "Conservative MP and Senator Belittle Chief Theresa Spence, Idle No More Movement." *The Star,* January 30.

Mas, Susana. 2013. "Harper Government on Collision Course with First Nations?" CBC, September 21.

Nason, Dory. 2014. "We Hold Our Hands Up: On Indigenous Women's Love and Resistance." In the Kino-nda-nimi Collective (ed.), *The Winter We Danced: Voices from the Past, the Future, and the Idle No More Movement*. Winnipeg, MB: Arbeiter Ring Publishing.

Owen, Bruce. 2013. "Delay Keeyask Hearings for Full Review: First Nations." *Winnipeg Free Press*, September 12.

Royal Canadian Mounted Police. 2014. "Missing and Murdered Aboriginal Women: A National Operational Overview." Ottawa: Royal Canadian Mounted Police. *Winnipeg Free Press*, September 12.

Settee, Priscilla. 2011. *The Strength of Women: Âhkamêyimowak*. Regina, SK: Coteau Books.

Simpson, Leanne. 2014. "Fish Broth & Fasting." In The Kino-nda-nimi Collective (ed.), *The Winter We Danced*. Winnipeg, MB: Arbeiter Ring Publishing.

Simpson, Leanne, Wanda Nanibush, and Carol Williams. 2012. "Introduction: The Resurgence of Indigenous Women's Knowledge and Resistance in Relation to Land and Territoriality: Transnational and Interdisciplinary Perspectives." *InTensions Journal* 6 (Fall/Winter).

Smith, Andrea. 2006. "Heteropatriarchy and the Three Pillars of White Supremacy: Rethinking Women of Color Organizing." In INCITE! Women of Color Against Violence (ed.), *Color of Violence: The INCITE! Anthology*. Cambridge. MA: South End Press.

Urban Aboriginal Peoples Study: *Main Report*. 2010. Toronto: Environics Institute.

West, Cornel. 2008. *Hope on a Tightrope: Words and Wisdom*. New York: Hay House.